W9-ADG-872

Educating the Gifted

A SOURCEBOOK

Educating theGifted

A SOURCEBOOK

M. Jean Greenlaw

Margaret E. McIntosh

AMERICAN LIBRARY ASSOCIATION

Chicago and London 1988

Designed by Charles Bozett

Composed by Precision Typographers
in Palatino on a Quadex/Compugraphic
8400 typesetting system

Printed on 50-pound Glatfelter, a pH-
neutral stock, and bound in Holliston
Roxite 3 cloth by Bookcrafters
∞

Library of Congress Cataloging-in-Publication Data

Greenlaw, M. Jean.
  Educating the gifted.

  Bibliography: p.
  Includes index.
  1. Gifted children—Education—United States—Handbooks,
manuals, etc.   I. McIntosh, Margaret E.   II. Title.
LC3993.9.G74   1988   371.95   87-26915
ISBN 0-8389-0483-1

Copyright © 1988 by the American Library Association.
All rights reserved except those which may be granted by
Sections 107 and 108 of the Copyright Revision Act of 1976.
Printed in the United States of America.

LC
3993.9
.G74
1988

Contents

Preface

PURPOSE AND AUDIENCE

Interest in the gifted individual is once again on the upswing, and this recent upsurge seems to be the most long lasting in the last hundred years. Perhaps, because the public recognizes that our society faces many difficulties, it also realizes the need for trained, talented individuals to find solutions to these problems. Perhaps media attention to gifted individuals and to programs for them has lessened opposition to the programs and mobilized their proponents. In any case, school districts, universities, local and state governments, parents, and others are realizing the need for special education to meet the needs of gifted children. And in response, publications and support groups have multiplied during the last several years.

The purpose of the book is to serve as a concise, clear reference tool for persons interested in the gifted individual. The text offers an overview of the major aspects of gifted education, combining theoretical and practical information of use and interest to a wide audience: parents, educators, administrators, counselors, and students in preservice and inservice situations. The annotated portion of the book is intended for those readers who wish additional information on a particular topic.

ACKNOWLEDGMENTS

Our interest in the gifted is of long duration and has been magnified by the opportunity to work with gifted students. One deserves special recognition. Debbie Chung has worked as a research assistant for us for two years, and we would never have met our deadline without her. This very talented high school student has been of invaluable aid in our library research, and we expect great things of her in the future.

CHAPTER 1

A Historical Look at
Gifted Education

Any movement's past has shaped its present and affects its future. The gifted education movement is no different. It is helpful, therefore, to know "from whence we came" as we look at where we are—and the direction we might be going. This chapter will briefly explore the history of gifted education in the United States since the late 1800s.

DEFINITIONS

Definitions of who is considered talented and gifted change as a society's needs change. Social needs and values specify who and how many are deemed gifted and talented. A primitive tribe that depends on hunting wild game defines talent as the ability to hunt well. A warring tribe values the fiercest warrior. But,

> Even nations which produced men whose brilliant insights and ideas are still recognized today had a limited view of man's talents. The Greeks honored the orator and the artist—but failed to appreciate the inventor. Rome cherished the Roman soldier and the administrator—but failed to recognize the many other potential talents of either its citizens or its slaves. (Flanahan et al. in Gallagher 1975, 10)

Over the years, numerous conceptions and countless definitions of giftedness have been proclaimed. Most can be analyzed on a continuum that ranges from "conservative" to "liberal," depending on the degree of restrictiveness used to determine eligibility for special privileges and programs (Renzulli 1978). A restrictive definition may limit the number of performance areas (e.g., academic only, excluding mu-

1

sic, leadership, social service, creative writing, etc.), or it may restrict by setting a high level of excellence as a criterion.

The definitions of giftedness in the late 1800s and early 1900s were conservative. They dealt only with intelligence, especially as measured by IQ (intelligence quotient) tests. Terman's 1921 definition of giftedness defined it as "the top 1% level in general intellectual ability . . . measured by the Stanford-Binet Intelligence Scale or a comparable instrument" (in Renzulli 1978). Before World War II, only the top 1–2 percent were considered gifted, but after 1940, the definition of gifted was expanded to include the top 10–15 percent (DeHaan & Havighurst 1961). Some educational researchers who felt that society would benefit from the developed talents of this larger group advocated using a broader definition of gifted that would include 10–20 percent (still measured in terms of IQ) (reported by Havighurst et al. 1958). By the late 1950s, the terms *gifted* and *high IQ* had become synonymous. But, according to Getzels and Jackson (1958), despite its longevity, the IQ score need not inevitably have been the definer of giftedness. They say that use of the IQ score was historical happenstance, since early inquiries used the classroom as their context and so developed an attendant concern with academic progress.

Soon after the beginning of Terman's studies, some people began to call for broader definitions of giftedness than those limited to IQ scores (Witty 1971). Witty expanded his definition in the 1930s to include "any child whose performance in a worthwhile type of endeavor is consistently or repeatedly remarkable" (1971, 2). He proposed this expanded definition because he felt that the intelligence tests did not successfully identify those students with a high potential for creative expression. He believed that it was evident that intelligence tests did not elicit any kind of imaginative, original, or unique response. Witty, along with many others, believed that ignoring the creative students would be an injustice to them and to society.

Nevertheless, consideration of a person's IQ score has remained in nearly every definition of giftedness since it was first conceived in the early 1920s up through the mid 1980s. Although an exact score demarcation may not always be referred to, it sometimes is alluded to, as in Hollingworth's definition: "Gifted children are those identified by mental tests as very superior to the average" (1926, 31).

Experts continued to fight for expanded definitions. For example, DeHaan and Havighurst said any child would be considered gifted "who is superior in some ability that can make him an outstanding contributor to the welfare of, and quality of living in, society" (1961, 15). This seems to have been the first time that making some sort of contribution to society was included in a definition for determining giftedness. Hollingworth though, already believed that gifted youngsters would grow up to be gifted adults and would make great contributions. She said "Individuals of surpassing intelligence create national wealth, determine the state of industry, advance science, and make general culture possible" (1926, 297). She appeared to think that identifying and providing for gifted students were social obligations.

Fliegler and Bish (1959) reviewed the literature on the gifted from 1953 to 1959. Their definition of the term *gifted* encompassed children who possess superior intellectual potential as well as a functional ability to perform in the top 15–20 percent, talents in such specific areas as science and mathematics, or unusual creative ability. This definition was the first to mention potential. All previous definitions used some outward sign of "remarkableness" or a measurable trait to prove that a person was gifted. The idea of including potential in the definitions has continued, especially as educators realize that a significant number of persons capable of making contributions to the nation are excluded by other definitions. Fliegler & Bish's definition was also significant in that it listed specific "special areas of talent," at the time—just after the launching of the first spacecraft, *Sputnik,* by the U.S.S.R.—when the United States was realizing that it had fallen behind Russia in certain areas of technology.

Two definitions, both from the early 1960s, seem to focus on "thinking" abilities—in a creative, abstract, problem-solving mode. Since definitions do indeed reflect the times, it is apparent that these came out of a period when the nation was realizing its needs for thinkers and problem solvers. Sumption and Luecking defined the gifted as possessing the "potential to perform tasks requiring a comparatively high degree of intellectual abstraction or creative imagination or both" (1960, 6). Lucito said:

> The gifted are those students whose potential intellectual powers are at such a high ideational level in both productive and evaluative thinking that it can be reasonably assumed they could be the future problem solvers, innovators, and evaluators of the culture if adequate educational experiences are provided. (Lucito 1963, in Alexander & Muia 1982, 11)

One of the major reasons for the aroused interest in providing for the gifted at this time was the growing awareness of society's needs during these troubled times.

Although interest shifted somewhat during the 1960s, it began to revive in the 1970s, and Congress commissioned a report on the status of education for the able in the United States. In the report of U.S. Commissioner of Education Sydney P. Marland to Congress (1972), the following definition was established:

> Gifted and talented children are those identified by professionally qualified persons who by virtue of outstanding abilities, are capable of high performance. These are children who require differentiated educational programs and/or services beyond those normally provided by the regular school program in order to realize their contribution to self and society.
>
> Children capable of high performance include those with demonstrated achievement and/or potential ability in any of the following areas, singly or in combination:
>
> 1) general intellectual ability
> 2) specific academic aptitude
> 3) creative or productive thinking
> 4) leadership ability
> 5) visual and performing arts
> 6) psychomotor ability

Marland's definition included many aspects of its forerunners: achievement, potential, and talent in specific areas. It was the first time, however, that "professionally qualified persons" were mentioned and the first time that psychomotor ability was mentioned. However, motivating people to provide "differentiated education" for those gifted in psychomotor ability has not been a problem either before or after the Marland definition appeared.

One of the most recent definitions, and one that has gained favor in a number of areas, was developed by Renzulli, creator of the Enrichment Triad Model. He says that

> Giftedness consists of an interaction among three basic clusters of human traits—these clusters being above-average general abilities, high levels of task commitment, and high levels of creativity. Gifted and talented children are those possessing or capable of developing this composite set of traits and applying them to any potentially valuable area of human performance. Children who manifest or are capable of developing an interaction among the three clusters require a wide variety of educational opportunities and services that are not ordinarily provided through regular instructional services (1978, 184).

Renzulli's definition is broader in one sense than some previous ones, but narrower in another sense. It is broader in that it includes many general performance areas and an endless number of specific performance areas. Its narrowness comes from the requirement that the gifted possess all three of the traits that Renzulli says characterize a gifted person. As a result, the nonachieving gifted student would be excluded. Creativity alone does not make a gifted person, says Renzulli; above-average ability alone does not make a gifted person; task commitment alone does not make a gifted person; neither do any two of the above in combination. All three must interact.

In 1980, Title IX, Part A, of Public Law 95-561 said that gifted and talented children were

> children, and where applicable, youth, who are identified at the preschool, elementary, or secondary level as possessing demonstrated or potential abilities that give evidence of high performance capability in areas such as intellectual, creative, specific academic, or leadership, or in the performing and visual arts, and who by reason thereof require services or activities not ordinarily provided by the school (in Sellin & Birch 1980, 22).

This definition was a throwback to some previous ones, and it is more general than other recent definitions. Its most significant contribution is its mention of identification at the preschool, elementary, and/or secondary level. Only recently have educators begun to see the value in early identification of exceptional children at both ends of the spectrum (i.e., gifted and mentally handicapped); so this inclusion was a significant marker of the time.

Thus the century's progression of definitions has gone from a strictly numerically one based on IQ score and including only the top 1 percent, to including the top 20 percent in IQ, to including those who exhibit some consistently remarkable trait, to those who are "more human" (Drews 1980) and can make some sort of contribution to society—not just in terms of an intellectual feat but also in terms of helping solve society's woes. There lately appears to be a desire to include anyone who might need the differentiated services required by the "talented and gifted" and to come up with some kind of definition that will serve in every arena—psychological, political, and educational.

A review of the literature reflects the continuous change in definitions. No one definition has gained acceptance, but there are commonalities in those that are presented—for example, "Gifted children generally refers to those possessing exceptional potential for academic success and productive intellectual pursuits" (Whitmore 1980, 61). No entirely satisfactory measure can be derived. The unavailability of an objective or even a commonly agreed-upon definition is revealing, for it allows us to consider as a criterion the openness of gifted programs to all students. As the variables of ability often occur in different combinations, one might justly argue for bringing many children into some aspect of the gifted program. Possibilities suggested by the chapter on programming should be considered with this criterion in mind.

HISTORY

The quest for the ideal definition has gone on for several decades and reflects the fact that any definition of talent has a social reference. By looking back over the events and attitudes of the past hundred or so years, one can see what has been valued and what has therefore been judged as high-level talent.

Modern interest in the gifted child seems to have sprung from the publication of Sir Francis Galton's book *Hereditary Genius* in 1869. Galton considered heredity the prime determinant of intellectual ability.

Before 1870, St. Louis established a program which allowed able students to complete eight grades in less than eight years—a sort of flexible promotion (DeHaan & Havighurst 1961). The man responsible for the first comprehensive plan to introduce flexibility in the graded program for able students was W. T. Harris, superintendent of the St. Louis Public Schools. He believed that it would hold "bright pupils up to the work of which they are capable and keep them from acquiring habits of carelessness and listlessness" (Henry 1920, 12).

In 1886, Elizabeth, New Jersey, initiated an accelerated, multiple-track system for the gifted (Abraham 1976). The Cambridge (Massachusetts) Double Track Plan, begun in 1891, allowed bright students to complete six grades in four years (third grade through ninth grade) (Abraham 1976). According to Henry (1920), the plan employed special "coach" teachers to help those students who appeared capable of doing the allotted amount of work in less than the allotted amount of time.

Another early flexible-promotion plan was the Woburn, Massachusetts, "Double Tillage Plan" which was started in 1884. This plan provided for covering the year's work for each grade during the first half of the year and then going over it again in greater detail during the second half of the year. Bright pupils could then be promoted mid-year so that they could cover two years' work in one (Henry 1920).

Except for the aforementioned, and similar, attempts to provide for able students, relatively little was done before 1900 either to investigate the needs of the gifted or to provide for them educationally. Witty (1958) says this paucity was due to superstitious beliefs about the nature of the "Great Man," that could not be explained by the laws of nature, and to the belief that intellectual precocity was pathological. In addition, the growth of democratic sentiment worked against providing for individual differences, as did the lack of knowledge of genetics, psychology, and educational precepts.

Many of the misconceptions that hindered positive attention toward the gifted stemmed from the work of two men: Lombroso and Nisbet. Their respective books, *The Man of Genius* and *The Insanity of Genius*, both published in 1895, told of their attempts to prove that insanity and genius were closely related (Barbe & Renzulli 1971). Even in the 1980s, the term *genius* is still avoided by some because it is "historically shrouded in mystery and charged with negative emotional connotations" (Tannenbaum 1958, 26). Much of this negative feeling is due to the myths propounded by Nisbet and Lombroso.

In addition, the notion that it is somehow undemocratic to value and encourage giftedness is still a hindrance to gifted education. Goddard recognized this sentiment and tried to defuse it:

> When Thomas Jefferson wrote "We hold these truths to be self-evident, that all men are created equal, that they are endowed by their creator with certain inalienable rights, that among these are life, liberty, and the pursuit of happiness," it was perfectly well understood that he was talking of human rights, not individual capacities, of social relations, not biological. The utterance no more implies that men were created equal in ability and in intelligence than it does that they were created of equal stature. (1933, 54)

Terman and Oden (1954, 230) expressed the same idea when they scoffed at the argument that all children should have the same kind of schooling. They said that idea is "no less absurd than to argue that all children should have the same kind of medical treatment." Sadly, this notion still persists today.

Although intensive study about the gifted was not undertaken before the early 1900s, there were those interested in measuring intelligence and differentiating between individuals of high intelligence and those of low intelligence. In France at the beginning of the twentieth century, A. Binet and T. Simon developed a scale to measure "judgment." The resultant score was called "mental age," and it "was intended to discriminate between children who were educable and those who were not capable of academic learning" (Whitmore 1980, 12). In the United States, Terman worked on refining this scale and, after several years, had adapted it in such a way that he purported to measure both subnormal and supernormal intelligence (as well as "normal").

As described above, some attempts were made to provide for gifted students in the late 1800s, and such efforts continued in the early 1900s. In 1900, New York City began its "rapid-progress classes" which made it possible for students to complete three years of junior high in two years (DeHaan & Havighurst 1961). All prior provisions for abler students had been within regular schools, with able students being served by special classes, but in 1901, the first special school for gifted students was established in Worcester, Massachusetts. It was called a "preparatory school" and was for grades seven through nine (McDonald 1915 in Henry 1920).

Even though the school in Worcester was established early in the century, it was many years before other schools offering full programs were initiated. From 1900 to 1920 the main alternative for the brighter students was acceleration (skipping grades). (Tannenbaum 1958).

One new approach was offered by Los Angeles in 1915. Its attempt to provide for its gifted students was through enrichment in "opportunity classes," which were comprised of the top 5 percent or so of the school population. The students in the opportunity classes were "given individualized instruction and allowed to make the rapid progress for which their native endowment fits them" (Washburne 1918, 39).

During this same period, the intelligence test was becoming more widely used. Largely because of Army Alpha, a group intelligence test given to thousands of soldiers enlisting to fight in World War I, the term IQ become familiar to many citizens. Soon after the war, most "up-to-date" school systems used intelligence testing in some form and to some degree (Gowan 1977).

With the advent of widespread intelligence testing, children who differed from the norm did receive some attention, but most of the extra resources went to those at the lower end of the scale. In 1899, one hundred large cities had special education classes for the mentally deficient, and by the early 1920s, two-thirds of all large cities had special education classes (albeit in basements and dark halls) (Abraham 1976). Hollingworth posited that the reason for the

> preoccupation with the incompetent resulted from the natural tendency of human beings to notice whatever is giving them pain or annoyance, taking for granted that which proceeds in an orderly and agreeable manner. (1929, vii)

A few people were concerned about the paucity of provisions for the bright students. The Women's City Club of Cleveland asked the Cleveland school board what the schools were doing for their gifted children—and out of the answer to that question came the Cleveland Major Works Classes in 1922 (Norris 1958), but "almost nobody seemed to notice" (Abraham 1976, 5). A few other special classes were formed in California, Ohio, New York, and Pennsylvania, but the practice did not really spread because many communities had inadequate numbers of gifted students (by then-current definitions) and

> because of the prevailing attitude which led to a fear of the creation of an intellectually elite group through special attention to the gifted. Moreover, many administrators believed that the gifted pupil could take care of himself. (Witty 1971, 110)

However more attention was paid to the gifted during the 1920s than at any previous time in American education. This was partly due to the economic expansion of that decade. If one were to create a time line that charted interest in the gifted along with events in American history, it would become obvious, as Adler (1967, 476) posited that

> interest in the gifted appears to follow a pattern similar to the economic situation of the Nation. During periods of economic boom and growth, interest in the gifted appears high. Conversely, during times of depression and economic stagnation, the gifted tend to be neglected or even discriminated against.

The 1920s were also a milestone decade because Lewis M. Terman began his monumental longitudinal study during the 1921–22 school year. The original funding for the study (a total of $34,000) was provided by a grant from the Commonwealth Fund of New York City (Terman 1924 and 1981). He collected a group of 1,528 children with IQs over 140 from the California schools. Others continued his research after his death in the early 1970s. Many of his findings dispelled earlier beliefs about gifted persons. For example:

1. Intellectually gifted children, either because of better endowment or better physical care, or both, are as a group slightly superior to the generality of children in health and physique and tend to remain so.
2. Children above 140 IQ are not as a group characterized by intellectual one-sidedness, emotional instability, lack of sociality or of social adaptability, or other types of maladjusted personality.
3. Indeed, in practically every personality trait and character trait such children average better than the general school population.

4. In social-intelligence ratings, social interests, and play activities, gifted children as a group are either normal or superior. (Hollingworth et al. 1940, 67)

In 1930, a survey of cities over 10,000 people revealed that only 30 out of 762 school districts had special classes for the gifted (Tannenbaum 1958). The 1920s provisions for the gifted were characterized by homogeneous grouping of the top third of the students to form accelerated classes (Tannenbaum 1958). After 1930, this practice declined and enrichment, both in the regular classes and in special classes, became more popular (DeHaan & Havighurst 1961; Tannenbaum 1958).

As we know, the 1930s were "characterized by unemployment, business failures, and general economic depression" (Adler 1967, 477). Concurrently, public interest in the gifted diminished and, in many cases, reversed itself into negativism. Special provisions for the gifted student became equated with the building of an elite and were seen as undemocratic. Bright people were looked upon with suspicion and once again, genius and mental illness were linked. In the 1930s genetic genius was attributed by some to bastardization and racial mixture (Whitmore 1980).

This attitude prevailed until World War II started. The war caused two things to happen:

1. The need for highly trained personnel increased.
2. The economy improved. (Adler 1967)

Two notable organizations were formed after World War II. The American Association for Gifted Children was established in 1946 to foster interest in the education of the gifted (Witty 1971). Then, in 1949, the National Scholarship Service and Fund for Negro students was started. Its purpose was to encourage able black students and to increase their opportunities in interracial colleges and universities (DeHaan & Havighurst 1961).

Financial aid for able students continued in the 1950s. In 1956, the National Merit Scholarship Corporation screened students for the first time, with the objective of awarding 556 scholarships to bright students (Witty 1967).

One of eight trends in gifted education articulated by Fliegler and Bish (1959) was increased funding for research into gifted education. Three major experiments were sponsored in 1953 and 1954 by the Fund for the Advancement of Education:

1. The Study of General Education in School and College, which documented the waste and duplication that occur

when strong schools offer challenging programs for abler students and when these efforts are not articulated with the work of the first two years of college (i.e., good high schools may be ahead of some colleges).

2. The second study dealt with the early admission to college and showed that, given the right circumstances, able students could enter college a year or two early and successfully undertake the academic work. Early admission, however, misjudged the mood of high schools. It failed to recognize that the schools were not willing to admit their inability to deal with able students, because they depended on them to set the pace for the rest of the students. This position of the high schools was reinforced by the finding from the early admission study which revealed that academic talent and emotional maturity do not always develop at an even rate. There were good grounds to believe that the place for the able student of high school age was in school, with other students of his own age.

3. The School and College Study of Admission with Advanced Standing and its successor, the Advanced Placement Program, rest on the belief that schools could, if they would, offer work of college caliber; that able students could handle such work in the twelfth grade and, occasionally, earlier; and that schools and colleges together could devise the mechanisms to get the job done in the schools and get it recognized in the colleges. (Pearson, in Foreword to Copley 1961)

Thus, advanced placement courses were born. The event was significant because it recognized that the needs of able, college-bound students were not being met under the current system.

Many people think that it was not until *Sputnik* that educators and others recognized the hiatus between bright students' abilities and American schools' provisions for them. This was not the case, as evidenced by the various advanced placement programs and by a statement made in 1950 by the National Education Association's Educational Policies Commission. The commission "decried the schools' neglect of mentally superior children" (Tannenbaum 1979, 7). In 1954, Dael Wolfle, director of the U.S. Commission on Human Resources and Advanced Training, called for better preparation of bright young people. He encouraged them to go into the natural sciences, the health fields, teaching, and engineering. He lamented the fact that only six out of ten students in the top 5 percent of their high school class and only half the top 25 percent of high school graduates went on to earn their college diplomas (Tannenbaum 1979).

The explosion of interest in the gifted student in the late 1950s was

> partly the result of a demand for greater numbers of people with highly developed economic skills to meet the needs of postwar economic expansion superimposed in the increased complexity of modern society. (Havighurst et al. 1958, 3)

But the development was largely due to the Russians' launching of *Sputnik*. After *Sputnik*, there were many "crash" programs and courses, but most did not last long (Tannenbaum 1958).

During the 1950s, there had been talk of a wasted talent, but Havighurst et al. (1958) contend it could more accurately be called a "shortage of trained talent." To meet this shortage, there was what Tannenbaum (1958, 25) called a "period of total talent mobilization." This period stimulated eight trends:

1. Curriculum development.
2. Expansion of the definition of giftedness.
3. Acceleration.
4. Expansion of college and university programs for teacher training.
5. Increase in research and funding for research.
6. A closer look at blacks, women, and low-socioeconomic-status gifted students.
7. Increased funding at state and national levels.
8. An increase in the number of local programs (Fliegler & Bish 1959, 408).

Until 1958, only Pennsylvania had special licensing for teachers of the gifted (Tannenbaum 1958). Hebeler (in Fliegler & Bish 1959) reported that Delaware and Indiana established requirements for special certification of teachers of the gifted in 1958.

The trends noted by Fliegler and Bish continued into the 1960s. Research concerning, and encouragement of, gifted students expanded. In 1960, Project Talent (financed by the U.S. Office of Education) began to collect data representative of students nationwide in grades nine through twelve to determine the quality and potential of American youth. Later that same year, the Superior and Talented Student Project of the North Central Association began. It had two goals:

> 1. To find, develop, and implement procedures and programs in secondary schools to identify, guide, and motivate the maximum number of superior and talented students in all areas of school achievement.

2. To help those students plan for and acquire a thorough college education. (DeHaan & Havighurst 1961, 68)

DeHaan and Havighurst went on to explain the criteria used to identify those students:

1. An IQ of 110 or above.
2. Achievement test scores at the seventy-fifth percentile or above.
3. Grades of B or above.
4. Teacher recommendations.
5. Standardized reading score at the fiftieth percentile or above.

A program to encourage outstanding black students was begun in 1964: the National Achievement Scholarship Program (Witty 1967). This program did not weigh the IQ as heavily as many programs because some felt that the IQ tests were unfair to minorities, because of cultural bias. Although the assumption that the IQ was a valid measure of intelligence was vigorously challenged in the 1960s, it continued to influence decision making. However, Anderson said that an IQ test score was "a symptom of a child's learning potential, but is neither a complete nor an entirely reliable measure of the child's true potential" (1961, 12). Whitmore added that many in the 1960s felt that use of the IQ test as the primary criterion for determining giftedness perpetuated and intensified "the old fear of undemocratic elitism and an intellectual aristocracy" (1980, 15).

A book that satirized this fear of elitism was *The Child Buyer* by John Hersey (1960). In it, a man from United Lymphomilloid Corporation is trying to buy all the brightest children so that his company can use their intelligence to solve the company's "extremely difficult problem, a project, a long-range government contract, fifty years, highly specialized and top secret." The book is written in the form of testimony given before a committee of senators. The following excerpt is from Miss Henley, the State Supervisor for Exceptional Children:

> Miss Henley: "Well, yes, I'd just like to say that where you run into trouble with these children is in singling them out. The kind of thing Dr. Gozar has done in the lab work with this boy. I came right out and said this in my lecture. We talk about the defense of democracy—how undemocratic can you get? Why shouldn't the next child get the extra help—the slow learner? The extremely gifted child should not be removed from the common-learning situation. He's the last one who needs extra attention. . . . I may specialize in deviates, but I don't forget the norm. The norm is the bedrock of our society. You can't neglect the median child in favor of the exceptions.

> You remember F.D.R.s' great declaration: 'This is the era of
> the common man.' That's democracy, gentlemen! Not a soci-
> ety where you have an elite telling the rest of us how to live.''
> (p.123)

Some educators and politicians, though, felt that it was imperative
to develop the talent of American youth. Opened in 1962, the Governor's School in Winston-Salem, North Carolina, was designed to provide a comprehensive program for gifted high school students (Witty
1967). President Kennedy pledged to have a man on the moon by 1970,
and he surrounded himself with scholars referred to as the ''Whiz
Kids'' (Tannenbaum 1979). Vernon et al. (1977, 11) thought it probable
that ''the 1960s provided the most favourable climate of the twentieth
century for special education of gifted American children.''

By the end of the 1960s, there were calls for some type of federal legislation regarding gifted education. In 1970, a congressional mandate
added Section 806c to Public Law 91-230 (the Elementary and Secondary Education Amendments of 1969). Section 806c, ''Provisions Related to Gifted and Talented Children,''

> required the Commissioner of Education to determine the ex-
> tent to which special educational assistance programs were
> necessary or useful to meet the needs of gifted and talented
> children, to evaluate how existing Federal educational assis-
> tance programs can be more effectively used to meet these
> needs, and to recommend new programs, if any, needed to
> meet these needs. (Khatena 1977, 380)

The resulting commissioner's report stimulated interest in gifted education (Marland 1972). A further increase in interest, in the mid 1970s,
came as citizens became cognizant of the need for solutions to problems such as:

> overpopulation; diminishing natural resources; hunger, irre-
> versible inflation, and unstable economies; corruption and
> crime; possible nuclear warfare and continuing wars; problems
> of gerontology, diseases, and handicapping conditions; a need
> for alternative sources of energy; possible space travel and de-
> velopment of communities in space; and many more. (Whit-
> more 1980, 7)

During early 1970 , for the first time, there were calls for programs
providing early education for the gifted (Witty 1971). Attention,
though, was not just on early education for the gifted but also for early
treatment and education of the learning disabled and mentally defi-

cient. As usual, much more attention was paid to the other exceptional children rather than to the gifted.

One cannot tell what will finally characterize the 1980s in terms of their position on gifted education. But Passow and Tannenbaum said that momentum for gifted education

> will make sense only if it has the long-term effect of setting the able child's need for a personally self-fulfilling life on a par with society's need for a rich talent bank. (1976, 4)

One hopes that gifted students who have grown up to be gifted adults will help the nation focus on individual gifted children's needs for satisfying lives so that the cycle of interest does not wane again in the near future.

RESEARCH

Research regarding the gifted has been conducted in the United States for over sixty years, since the 1920s when Terman initiated his longitudinal study. During the 1920s and 1930s, studies of genius, distinction, and eminence were predominant. Research dropped off during the 1940s and early 1950s, but during the post-*Sputnik* era there was much research into the characteristics and education of gifted children. Hildreth (1966) reported that twenty times as much material was published between 1950 and 1960 on the subject of giftedness than in any previous ten-year period. French (1964) stated that 1957, 1958, and 1959 saw more articles published on gifted education than in the previous thirty years.

As with any discipline, a review of the research of the past sixty years reveals a great variety in quality. Long-term studies, such as those conducted by Terman, are few and need to be emulated. Most studies consider only a small question, and there are few systematic research efforts. It is possible that this lack is related to the uncertainty surrounding the definition and scope of gifted programs.

Research seems to be expanding as some psychologists, educators, and psychometricians begin to work together in the area. One dimension where the combined efforts could produce information regards society's need for the gifted (Newland 1976). Positive results of such research could cut down on the dramatic swings in the public's opinion of gifted education.

WHY ATTITUDES TOWARD THE GIFTED FLUCTUATE

Tannenbaum says that no other group in education "has been alternately embraced and repelled with so much vigor by educators and laymen alike" as have the gifted (1979, 20). What are the reasons behind this push-pull affair with the gifted? Four factors seem important: availability of money; a sudden, intense need for a particular kind of "brain power"; current popular belief about education; and a struggle between elitism and egalitarianism.

During the periods of economic hardship, over the past eighty to one hundred years, gifted programs were among the first cut. If the money was not there, neither was the commitment. Whitmore says

> Just as one may learn about the values of an individual by examining the person's calendar of time commitments and the checkbook, which reveals monetary investments, one may learn clearly about the prioritized values of a government and its schools by examining its appropriation of funds and the allocation of time to various needs. (1980, 20)

Although gifted children are the least costly of all exceptional children to provide for (Trezise 1978), convincing taxpayers of this fact is next to impossible. They object to spending money on the gifted because it is believed that "they will get along anyway," but they are willing to finance education for the handicapped because "their life will be so difficult" (DeHaan & Havighurst 1961; Vernon et al. 1977).

The tendency to associate gifted programs and aristocracy may stem from the time when public schools were first established. Many families with bright children did not send them to public school but continued with private schools, tutoring, or study with a mentor (Whitmore 1980). Vernon et al. (1977) support this idea with their discussion of schools in the nineteenth and early twentieth centuries. Until well into the nineteenth century, the few children who were educated came from wealthy families. The schools they attended had small classes and were ability grouped. Then public schools were established; they were seen as a unifying force for Americanizing the children of immigrants from many lands. At first, the "dull and disinterested" could and did drop out. The above average were usually academically motivated and could progress rapidly to the higher grades. But as more and more children stayed in school, and especially as school attendance became mandatory, the differences between the top and bottom students became marked, and parents and educators began calling for special education.

Others though were calling for egalitarian education. American society favors community control of education, with the consequent dominance of ostensibly egalitarian values. In the allocation of funds by local school boards, rigorous thinking is overlooked. Teachers will not fail to recognize ability, but the constructs of the educational program handicap adequate provisions for it.

American society has tended to be suspicious of differences among children. It seems to prefer children who are "well-rounded" in their social and emotional adjustment rather than children who distinguish themselves academically or artistically. Even in the 1970s, *gifted* was "associated with geniuses or young prodigies, and genius is traditionally, though unjustifiably, associated with neurosis, or even insanity" (Vernon et al. 1977, 9). Thus many parents have not wanted to have a talented and gifted child (Barbe & Renzulli 1971). In *The Child Buyer*, previously mentioned, Miss Cloud, the librarian, is being questioned by the district attorney:

> Mr. Broadbent: "Would you say that your, ahem, misfortune, madam, has made the boy Barry Rudd feel specially close to you, with his, ahem, exaggerated mentality?"
> Miss Cloud: "Why don't you come out from behind those euphemisms, Mr. District Attorney, or whatever you are? 'Misfortune?' You mean my hunch back? You mean that Barry's brilliant mind is like a crooked back, and that's why we're pals? Deformity is our bond? More like it that you have a twisted mind, sir." (p. 125)

Although this attitude has abated somewhat, it can still be found in America today.

So too does the idea continue that gifted education is elitist. Switzer and Nourse comment:

> It is an interesting phenomenon that in an age such as ours, when so much attention in education is directed toward excluded minorities, so little attention is given to the education of the gifted. (1979, 323)

They go on to say that gifted students are the most neglected minority—probably because it is thought elitist to attend to gifted students' needs. What seems to be difficult for many people to resolve is the idea that democracy is indeed served by educating the gifted. Bagford said that educators understand that democracy in teaching means providing opportunities so that all pupils have an *equal* opportunity to achieve according to their full potential. Being democratic to gifted children means that they, too, must receive their fair measure of special attention. To do otherwise wastes the nation's human resources. (1981, 1)

Those people who do not want to waste human resources know that "a good society cultivates its members, and by their fruits the society is made better" (Havighurst et al. 1958, 9). The concern for exceptional human beings is an outgrowth of a concern for all human beings. This concern arose from the humanistic psychology movement exemplified by William James. According to Gowan, humanistic psychology

finds intrinsic value in the individual who is considered as an end and not as a behavioristic means. He/she has potential for good, for development and for process that is much more important and much more germane than merely dealing with his quirks and ills. (1977, 7)

Humanists—and others who are concerned about people and whether or not they are receiving an education that cultivates excellence—do not always influence policy as much as they would like. However, espousing a goal more obviously in the public interest may get results. Whitmore (1980) said that often public interest in the gifted is tied to society's need for leaders—political, scientific, and others. As Passow (1958, 219) pointed out, war often accentuates the need for highly trained personnel in specialized areas—and may thus promote education of the gifted to fill the talent reservoir.

It seems reasonable to say that when societies have recognized and responded to the needs of the gifted, it has not been out of respect for the rights and value of these persons, but rather because society needs their talents. In other words, gifted persons have been used—or ignored!

Can a change be expected? Or will the gifted only be wanted when a crisis evinces the fact that they are needed? If history is a reliable indicator, the gifted are soon due for a rejection.

SELECTED BIBLIOGRAPHY

Abraham, Willard. "The Early Years: Prologue to Tomorrow." *Exceptional Children* 42: 330–35 (March 1976).
    Willard presents a brief history of the Council for Exceptional Chil-

dren and a look "into the crystal ball" to project the future for exceptional children.

Abrams, Kathleen Serley. "Gifted Students: The Public Schools' Neglected Minority." *Curriculum Review* 20: 110–13 (April 1981).

Abrams, who says the gifted have been neglected for too long, provides suggestions for how to change their status.

Adler, Manfred. "Cycles of Interest in the Gifted Student." *Clearing House* 41: 476–78 (April 1967).

Adler takes a look at the dynamics in operation each time there is an upsurge in interest in gifted education. He sees a relationship between economic cycles and interest in the gifted.

Alexander, Patricia A., and Muia, Joseph A. *Gifted Education: A Comprehensive Roadmap*. Rockville, Md.: Aspen, 1982. 323 pp.

Chapter one is entitled "Gifted: Historical Perspective and Definition." One of its key features is a "schematic representation of historical developments related to the gifted movement." It includes a time line featuring notable individuals, intellectual measures, definitions of intelligence, and the theoretical basis for these definitions.

Alvino, James. "Existential Foundations of Gifted Education." *Roeper Review* 5: 2–4 (April/May 1983).

Experts in gifted education need to "practice what we preach"— i.e., "Education for the gifted and talented as a professional field of scholarship should exemplify the principles it espouses for gifted children"; we need to work at integrating other disciplines into our understanding of gifted education.

Anderson, K. E., ed. *Research on the Academically Gifted*. Washington, D.C.: National Education Association Project on the Academically Talented Student, 1961. 102 pp.

Anderson has included the pertinent research from the late 1950s in his booklet, which is part of the NEA's significant series on the education of the gifted/talented.

Bagford, J. *Talented and Gifted: Forgotten Children*. Paper presented at the annual meeting of the Plains Regional Conference of the International Reading Association, October 1981. (ERIC Document Reproduction Service No. ED 210 668).

This paper deals primarily with the reading needs of gifted students.

Barbe, Walter B., and Renzulli, Joseph. "Innovative Programs for the Gifted and Creative." In *Reading for the Gifted and Creative Student*, edited by Paul A. Witty, pp. 19–32. Newark, Del.: International Reading Association, 1971.

The authors discuss specific reading programs for gifted students in the primary grades, the middle grades, junior high, and high school.

"A Better Break in Schools for Gifted Children." *U.S. News and World Report* 80: 56–57 (April 12, 1976).

This article from the 1970s briefly describes that era's renewed interest in identifying and serving the gifted. Several programs are discussed.

Birch, Jack W., and Reynolds, Maynard C. "The Gifted." *Review of Educational Research* 33: 83–98 (February 1963).

The authors reviewed major research regarding the gifted in the following areas: economics of talent; intellectual characteristics, personal and social characteristics, creativity, achievement, underachievement and achievement motivation, curriculum development and adaptations, community and parental attitudes toward special education for the gifted, ability grouping, acceleration, curriculum studies, major books, and needed research.

Bruch, Catherine B. "Schooling for the Gifted: Where Do We Go from Here?" *Gifted Child Quarterly* 28: 12–16 (Winter 1984).

A Nation at Risk and four other reports are summarized. Issues that relate to the gifted are synopsized.

Callow, Ralph. "Recognizing the Gifted Child." In *Educating the Gifted Child*, edited by R. M. Povey, pp. 109–19. London: Harper & Row, 1980.

Provides a little different slant on identifying gifted students; the author and editor are British.

Colangelo, Nicholas. "A Perspective on the Future of Gifted Education." *Roeper Review* 7: 30–32 (September 1984).

Discusses issues that have hindered the field (e.g., narrow conceptions of giftedness); issues which reflect problems in the field today (e.g., overemphasis on creativity, vagueness in definition); and perspectives on the future (e.g., attention to cultural diversity, reconceptualization of giftedness).

Copley, Frank O. *The American High School and the Talented Student*. Ann Arbor: Univ. of Michigan Pr., 1961.

Copley spent a year studying talented students and how they were faring in American high schools. He discusses the issues and problems and then presents some alternatives.

DeHaan, Robert F., and Havighurst, Robert J. *Educating Gifted Children*. Chicago: Univ. of Chicago Pr., 1961. 362pp.

A comprehensive handbook on gifted education which reflects the knowledge and attitudes of the late 1950s and early 1960s.

Deiulio, Anthony M., and Deiulio, Judith Moore. "And Now (At Last)

We Turn to the Gifted/Talented. *Kappa Delta Pi Record* 17: 25–27 (October 1980).

The authors make a case for commitment to education for the gifted and talented.

Drews, Elizabeth Monroe. "The Gifted Student: A Researcher's View." In *Readings in Foundations of Gifted Education*, edited by David M. Jackson, pp. 32–39. Guilford, Conn.: Special Learning Corporation, 1980.

Drews suggests that there are at least three ways to explore the broad array of gifted students' abilities: by inquiring into their interests, by judging their performance, and by administering tests.

"Education for the Gifted." *Teachers College Record* 42: 375–460 (February 1941).

In honor of Leta S. Hollingworth, a conference on education for the gifted was held under the auspices of Teachers College, Columbia University, where Hollingworth had taught prior to her death. The entire issue is devoted to papers presented there. The reader obtains a good feel for the period and its attitudes toward gifted education.

Feldhusen, John J., and Hoover, Steven M. "The Gifted at Risk in a Place Called School." *Gifted Child Quarterly* 28: 9–11 (Winter 1984).

The authors compare the outlook presented in John Goodlad's *A Place Called School* and the National Commission on Excellence in Education's *A Nation at Risk*. Using the two books as springboards, the authors give numerous suggestions to improve education for the gifted.

Feldman, David Henry. "A Follow-Up of Subjects Scoring Above 180 IQ in Terman's 'Genetic Studies of Genius.'" *Exceptional Children* 50: 518–23 (April 1984).

Using the Terman files, twenty-six individuals with IQ's of 180+ were compared with twenty-six randomly selected from the original 1,500 subjects. The author concluded that there were few significant differences and that "on the whole, one is left with the feeling that the above 180 IQ subjects were not as remarkable as might have been expected."

Fliegler, Louis A., and Bish, Charles E. "Summary of Research on the Academically Talented Student." *Review of Educational Research* 29: 408–50 (December 1959).

This review covers the six years since Newland's review in 1953. The bibliography provides 251 references.

French, Joseph L., ed. *Educating the Gifted: A Book of Readings.* New York: Holt, Rinehart, and Winston, 1964. 555 pp.

SAINT PETER'S COLLEGE LIBRARY
JERSEY CITY. NEW JERSEY 07306

French's book of readings contains articles by many of the experts in gifted education from the late 1950s and early 1960s.

Frierson, Edward C. "Education of Gifted Youth in Secondary School and College." *Education* 88: 25–29 (September/October 1967).

The author describes the significant changes in education for gifted secondary and college age youth during the preceding twenty years. He sees gifted education as no longer unpopular and in fact demanded as a necessary response to the world's social, political, and technical revolution. Also, new instructional methods pioneered during this period are described.

Gallagher, J. J., and Rogge, W., "The Gifted." *Review of Educational Research* 36: 37–55 (1966).

The authors have reviewed major research regarding the gifted in the following areas: identification and definitions; characteristics: learning, attitude, and personality; sex differences; grouping; acceleration; independent study and honors; teacher training; grading and prediction; counseling and careers curriculum; perception of gifted by others; underachievement; and the talented and the culturally disadvantaged.

Gallagher, James J. *Teaching the Gifted Child*, 2d ed. Boston: Allyn & Bacon, 1975. 431pp.

Gallagher's book is divided into five sections: The Gifted Child and His School; Content Modifications for the Gifted; Stimulation of Productive Thinking; Administration and Training for the Gifted; Special Problem Areas. It offers a clear discussion of many of the issues about which educators must be concerned as they strive to educate the gifted.

Getzels, J. W., and Jackson, P. W. "The Meaning of 'Giftedness'—An Examination of an Expanding Concept." *Phi Delta Kappan* 40: 75–77 (November 1958).

The authors discuss their research on students of high IQ and students of high intelligence.

Getzels, J. W., and Dillon, J. T. "The Nature of Giftedness and the Education of the Gifted." In *Second Handbook of Research on Teaching*, edited by Robert M. W. Travers, pp. 689–731. Chicago: Rand McNally, 1973.

This excellent chapter reviews and organizes research regarding the nature, recognition, and education of the gifted. The authors examine definitions of giftedness in a historical context and discuss the three major categories of giftedness (superior intellectual ability, superior creative ability, and superior talent in any of a multitude of human endeavors). Over 250 entries are included in the bibliography. For those interested in the historical perspective, a table of selected bibliographies and reviews on giftedness is included.

Goddard, Henry H. "The Gifted Child." *Journal of Educational Sociology* 6: 354–61 (February 1933).

Goddard believes that gifted children need special consideration and special treatment in the interest of the children themselves, in the interest of the schools, and in the interest of the community.

Gowan, J. C. "Background and History of the Gifted-Child Movement." In *The Gifted and the Creative: A Fifty-Year Perspective,* edited by J. C. Stanley, W. C. George, and C. H. Solano, pp. 5–27. Baltimore: Johns Hopkins Univ. Pr., 1977.

Gowan sets the gifted child movement within the overall humanistic psychology movement. He discusses leaders and "godfathers" of humanistic psychology and then covers the work of Terman, Montessori, Hollingworth, and others who have been contributors to the growth in knowledge and interest in the gifted.

Greenberg, Benjamin B. "The Education of the Intellectually Gifted." *Journal of Exceptional Children* 5: 101–9, 124–25 (February 1939).

Greenberg provides a rationale for educating the ablest which is as apropos now as it was fifty years ago. He also describes the Speyer School, which had a special program for fifty gifted pupils.

Havighurst, Robert J., Hersey, John, Meister, Morris, Cornog, William H., and Terman, Lewis. "The Importance of Education for the Gifted." In *Education for the Gifted, The Fifty-Seventh Yearbook of the National Society for the Study of Education, Part 2,* edited by Nelson B. Henry. Chicago: Univ. of Chicago Pr., 1958.

This chapter is a collection of five essays by the authors. The individual essays are entitled: "Wanted: A Larger Frame of Reference"; "Why Should Educators Pay Special Attention to Gifted Youth?" "We Have Neglected Talent"; "The Meaning of Opportunity for Gifted Youth," "What Education for the Gifted Should Accomplish."

Henry, Theodore S. "Classroom Problems in the Education of Gifted Children," In *Nineteenth Yearbook of the National Society for the Study of Education,* edited by Guy Montrose Whipple, p. 7–10. Bloomington, Ill.: Public School Publishing Co., 1920.

This yearbook covers instruction and programming for gifted children—both specifically and generally.

Hildreth, Gertrude H. *Introduction to the Gifted.* New York: McGraw-Hill, 1966. 572pp.

Hildreth, who gained interest in giftedness through her work with testing and measuring intelligence, provides a general overview of the field of knowledge pertaining to the gifted.

Hollingworth, Leta S. *Gifted Children: Their Nature and Nurture.* New York: Macmillan, 1926. 374 pp.

This book is a classic and should be read by those interested in the history of education and gifted education. The author provides an in-depth look at highly gifted children which is drawn from her extensive work in this area.

_____. "The Development of Personality in Highly Intelligent Children," *The Intellectually Gifted: An Overview,* edited by W. Dennis and M. W. Dennis. New York: Grune & Stratton, 1976.

This selection is from Hollingworth's *Children above 180 IQ* (1942). She succinctly discusses characteristics of extremely gifted children.

Hollingworth, Leta S., Terman, Lewis M., and Oden, Melita. "The Significance of Deviates." In *Intelligence: Its Nature and Nurture.* Part I of *Thirty-Ninth Yearbook of the National Society for the Study of Education.* Bloomington, Ill.: Public School Publishing Co., 1940.

The authors review the research concerning intellectual deviates (at both ends of the spectrum) which has been conducted since 1927 as well as looking specifically at the research dealing with children and adults with IQs above 140.

Hylton, Yvonne V. "Gifted Education in a Conservative Environment." *Delta Kappa Gamma Bulletin* 48: 28–30 (Winter 1982).

Hylton bemoans the fact that the current conservative attitude of the country is hurting gifted education.

Khatena, Joe. "Educating the Gifted Child: Challenge and Response in the U.S.A." *Gifted Child Quarterly* 20: 76–90 (Spring 1976).

Khatena considers some of the major contributions made by U.S. educators in the areas of identification, providing special educational opportunity, recognition of special problems, legislation, and other private and public supportive efforts for the advancement of gifted/talented education.

_____. "The Gifted Child in the United States and Abroad," *Gifted Child Quarterly* 21:372–86 (Fall 1977).

Summarizes the extent of educational opportunities for the gifted in the U.S. and abroad and assesses the contributions that national associations for gifted/talented students and national governments make in that education. He also draws implications for future directions.

_____. "Some Advances in Thought on the Gifted." *Gifted Child Quarterly* 22: 55–61 (Spring 1978).

Khatena holds that, although Terman's monumental study provided significant and salient base data for the development of thought on gifted education in the United States, it had significant design problems. He reviews these and discusses an expanded notion of giftedness that includes creativity.

Klein, Ronald D., and Lyon, Harold C., Jr. "Education of the Gifted and Talented: A Context of Excellence for the Transformation of American Education." *Elementary School Journal* 82: 285–91 (January 1982).

   The authors posit that "history could show the 1980s to be the turning point for renewed excellence for all students," if the current crisis in American public education provides the impetus for radical change and improvement. They report on several practices proven to increase cognitive and affective growth: empathetic teachers, early identification, and diverse programming.

Kreuter, G. "Vanishing Genius: Lewis Terman and the Stanford Study." *Historical Education Quarterly* 2: 6–18 (March 1962).

   Kreuter gives a brief history of Terman and his genetic studies of genius.

LeBlanc, Robert M., and Verner, Zenobia B. "Elite Is Not a Four-Letter Word: A Democratic Society Needs Gifted Leaders." *Clearing House* 55: 12–13 (September 1981).

   The authors point out the urgent need to educate the intellectually elite.

Lyon, Harold C., Jr. "Talent down the Drain." *American Education* 8: 12–16 (October 1972).

   Lyon bemoans the fact that so many gifted students are going "down the drain." He also relates some of the ways that the U.S. Office for Gifted and Talented is working to improve education for the gifted.

_____. "Gifted and Talented: A New Federal Priority." *Today's Education* 65: 33–35 (January/February 1976).

   Lyon reports on efforts of the federal government to stimulate appropriate educational provisions for the gifted and talented.

Magary, James F., and Freehill, Maurice F. "Critical Questions and Answers Relating to School and Society in the Education of the Gifted." *Gifted Child Quarterly* 16: 185–94 (1972).

   The authors ask and answer fourteen questions regarding societal and school-related issues in gifted education (e.g., Which goals of education for the gifted are not supported by society? What should the gifted person contribute to society? Does the gifted person's ability bring about special responsibilities? Where should individuality and creativity be placed among educational goals?)

Maker, C. June, and Schiever, Shirley W. "Excellence for the Future." *Gifted Child Quarterly* 28: 6–8 (Winter 1984).

   The authors point out that our nation was not founded to be "as good as" another country; it has always been our intention to be the best. They say that rather than lowering our standards, we must change them. Suggestions are given for changing education to better educate the gifted.

Marland, Sydney P. *Education of the Gifted and Talented.* Report to the Congress of the United States by the U.S. Commissioner of Education. Washington, D.C.: U.S. Government Printing Office, 1972.

Marland's report brought national attention to the state of gifted education in the U.S. Few documents have had such far-reaching effects for gifted education.

Mead, Margaret. "The Gifted Child in the American Culture of Today." *Journal of Teacher Education* 5: 211–14 (September 1954).

Mead describes the context in which gifted students find themselves. The present (1950s) culture frowns upon anything seemingly obtained for nothing (e.g., above-average ability); thus, gifted education has gotten short shrift.

Mitchell, Bruce M. "An Update on Gifted/Talented Education in the U.S." *Roeper Review* 6: 161–63 (February 1984).

The fifty states were surveyed to obtain a picture of the status of gifted education in the United States. The information is presented in two tables, State Funding for 1982–1983 School Year and Gifted/Talented Data from State Departments of Education.

Mitchell, Patricia Bruce, and Erickson, Donald K. "The Education of Gifted and Talented Children: A Status Report." *Exceptional Children* 45: 12–16 (September 1978).

The Council for Exceptional Children was awarded an information contract to assess the progress made in education for the gifted and talented since the 1972 Marland report. Major findings are reported in five areas: gifted and talented children (identification and services); state policy; state personnel; federal and state funding; preparation of personnel.

Newland, T. Ernest. *The Gifted in Socioeducational Perspective.* Englewood Cliffs, N.J.: Prentice-Hall, 1976. 406 pp.

In the preface, Maurice Freehill says, "The distinctive theme of this work is [that] . . . not in a special section but persistently, Dr. Newland places society at the center of support and nonsupport of high potential." This book provides essentially the same information as other books about the gifted written in the 1970s, but sets it in a whole different context. The book is worth reading.

Norris, Dorothy E. "Programs in the Elementary Schools." In *Education for the Gifted,* Part 2 of *Fifty-Seventh Yearbook of the National Society for the Study of Education,* edited by Nelson B. Henry, Chicago: Univ. of Chicago Pr., 1958.

Norris describes various programs for educating the gifted that were in place at the time of writing (e.g., Cleveland Major Works Classes, Hunter College Elementary School, University City Enrichment Program, the Colfax Plan).

Passow, A. Harry. "Enrichment of Education for the Gifted: The Meaning of Enrichment." In *Education for the Gifted,* Part 2 of *Fifty-Seventh Yearbook of the National Society for the Study of Education,* edited by Nelson B. Henry. Chicago: Univ. of Chicago Pr., 1958.

Passow discusses goals for the gifted and how these goals should affect the type of education developed for able students. He presents the current (1958) thinking on enrichment.

Passow, A. Harry, and Tannenbaum, Abraham J. "Some Perspectives for the Mid-70s: Education of the Gifted and Talented." *National Association of Secondary School Principals Bulletin* 60: 3–12 (March 1976).

The authors note the swings in attention toward the gifted. They are encouraged by the recent interest and call for an increase in legislation and funding.

Pleasants, Samuel A. "Spotlight on the Superior Student." *Clearing House* 33: 342–44 (February 1959).

The author summarizes three reports published in 1958: the Rockefeller Commission study of the American school system; the Litchfield report on education in the Soviet Union; and the Columbia University Forum Report.

Powell, Phillip M. "Educational and Occupational Attainments in Two Intellectually Gifted Samples." *Gifted Child Quarterly* 27: 73–76 (Spring 1983).

Powell compared Terman's gifted sample at about age forty-five with another large sample of gifted adults (members of Mensa). Although he found that the Mensans were far ahead of the Termites educationally and occupationally, he acknowledges that the difference could be due to historical era, social milieu, and cultural setting.

Renzulli, Joseph S. "What Makes Giftedness? Reexamining a Definition." *Phi Delta Kappan* 60: 180–84, 261 (November 1978).

Renzulli explains and supports his concept of giftedness which includes three clusters of traits: above-average general ability, task commitment, and creativity. This is must reading.

————. "Will the Gifted Child Movement Be Alive and Well in 1990?" *Gifted Child Quarterly* 24: 3–9 (Winter 1980).

Renzulli posits that in order for gifted education to maintain and increase its current status, several areas must become more defensible: identification, curriculum, teachers of the gifted, and evaluation. The conclusions are interesting and thought provoking.

Sears, Pauline Snedden. "The Terman Genetic Studies of Genius,

1922–1972." In *The Gifted and the Talented: Their Education and Development*, Part 1 of *Seventy-Eighth Yearbook of the National Society for the Study of Education*, edited by A. Harry Passow. Chicago: Univ. of Chicago Pr., 1979.

Sears presents the data that resulted from the 1972 mailing to the subjects of the 1922 genetic study of genius.

"Selected References on Gifted Education." *Understanding the Child* 17: 56–64 (April 1948).

The references are selected from 1942–46 U.S. Office of Education pamphlets that deal with gifted children.

Sellin, D. F., and Birch, J. W. *Educating Gifted and Talented Learners.* Rockville, Md.: Aspen Publications, 1980.

The authors present a great deal of information in a well-organized, interesting format. This would be a good textbook for beginning courses in teaching the gifted.

Stanley, Julian C. "Introduction." In *The Gifted and the Creative: A Fifty-Year Perspective*, edited by J. C. Stanley, W. C. George, and C. H. Solano. Baltimore: Johns Hopkins Univ. Pr., 1977.

Stanley introduces the book, which is divided into four sections: The Gifted-Child Movement; Two Longitudinal Studies at the Johns Hopkins University—The Study of Mathematically Precocious Youth and the Intellectually Gifted Child Study Group; Creativity; Discussion of the Symposium (from which these papers came).

Sumption, M. R., and Luecking, E. M. *Education of the Gifted.* New York: Ronald Press, 1960. 499 pp.

This book provides a good picture of the status of gifted education just following *Sputnik*.

Switzer, C., and Nourse, M. L. "Reading Instruction for the Gifted Child in First Grade." *Gifted Child Quarterly* 23: 323–31 (1979).

The authors draw the following conclusions based on their research: (1) gifted readers have been neglected in the educational system; (2) gifted readers' needs can only be met through special instructional practices; (3) only limited information is available to help teachers plan and implement this differential instruction.

Tannenbaum, Abraham J. "History of Interest in the Gifted." In *Education for the Gifted*, Part 2 of *Fifty-Seventh Yearbook of the National Society for the Study of Education*, edited by Nelson B. Henry. Chicago: Univ. of Chicago Pr., 1958.

Tannenbaum presents a succinct but comprehensive overview of the history of gifted education.

————. "A Backward and Forward Glance at the Gifted." *National Elementary Principal* 51: 14–23 (February 1972).

Tannenbaum discusses the cyclical nature of interest in the

gifted—how it is considered icing on the curriculum cake but never part of the cake. He says education of the gifted should deal with values, since bright children are concerned with humanitarian issues and need to learn how to do something to further their beliefs.

_____. "Pre-Sputnik to Post-Watergate Concern about the Gifted." In *The Gifted and the Talented: Their Education and Development,* Part 1 of *Seventy-Eighth Yearbook of the National Society for the Study of Education,* edited by A. Harry Passow. Chicago: Univ. of Chicago Pr., 1979.

Tannenbaum discusses the cyclical nature of concern for gifted students. He hypothesizes about some of the reasons for the push-pull attention paid to this minority.

Terman, Lewis M. "The Physical and Mental Traits of Gifted Children." In *The Education of Gifted Children,* Part 1 of *Twenty-Third Yearbook of the National Society for the Study of Education,* edited by Guy M. Whipple. Bloomington, Ill.: Public School Publishing Co., 1924.

Terman summarizes information regarding the physical and mental traits of the group of 643 gifted children that he and his team located during 1921–22. The following chapter summarizes the educational achievements of these same children.

_____. "The Discovery and Encouragement of Exceptional Talent." In *Psychology and Education of the Gifted,* edited by Walter B. Barbe and Joseph S. Renzulli. New York: Irvington Publishers, 1981.

This is the speech the author gave for the American Psychological Association's Walter V. Bingham Lectureship series. In it, he reviews how he became interested in giftedness and began his Genetic Studies of Genius. Some of the results he obtained are also presented.

Terman, Lewis M., and Oden, Melita H. "Major Issues in Education of Gifted Children." *Journal of Teacher Education* 5: 230–32 (September 1954).

The authors briefly discuss five unresolved issues in gifted education: democracy and the IQ; the educational lockstep; early identification of the gifted; educational opportunities that are feasible; needed guidance and counseling.

_____. "The Terman Study of Intellectually Gifted Children." In *The Intellectually Gifted: An Overview,* edited by W. Dennis and M. W. Dennis. New York: Grune and Stratton, 1976.

This selection is taken from *The Genetic Studies of Genius,* vol.5, *The Gifted Group at Mid-Life: Thirty-Five Years' Followup of the Superior Child.* It provides an overview of the study and its results up to 1959.

Torrance, E. Paul. "Emerging Concepts of Giftedness." In *Psychology and Education of the Gifted,* edited by Walter B. Barbe and Joseph S. Renzulli. New York: Irvington Publishers, 1981.

This chapter is an excerpt from Torrance's book *Gifted Child in the Classroom.* He recommends that a new concept of giftedness be established, one that recognizes creative, productive thinking.

_____, ed. *Talent and Education: Present Status and Future Directions.* Minneapolis: University of Minnesota Press, 1960. 210 pp.

The book contains papers presented at the 1958 Institute on Exceptional Children. It is divided into six sections: Introduction; Talented Individuals; Life Experiences as Talent Evokers; Schools as Talent Evoking Situations; Brief Reports of Exploratory Studies; Research on Identification, Development, and Utilization of Talent.

Treffinger, Donald J. "Dymythologizing Gifted Education: An Editorial Essay." *Gifted Child Quarterly* 26: 3–8 (Winter 1982).

Treffinger's essay introduces a whole issue of *Gifted Child Quarterly* dedicated to "demything" gifted education. He provides cogent thoughts concerning definitions of the gifted and identification and delivery of services to them. He also provides some cautions and hunches concerning the future of gifted education.

Trezise, R. L. "What about a Reading Program for the Gifted." *The Reading Teacher* 31: 742–47 (1978).

Interest in the gifted is resurging, says Trezise, and programs for the gifted need not be expensive. He outlines ideas for differentiated reading programs that are economical but still offer sound instruction.

Tyler, Ralph W. "Meeting the Challenge of the Gifted," *Elementary School Journal* 58: 75–82 (November 1957).

Tyler discusses the reasons for renewed interest in gifted education and makes recommendations for meeting the challenge.

Vernon, Philip E., Adamson, Georgina, and Vernon, Dorothy F. *The Psychology and Education of Gifted Children.* Boulder, Colo.: Westview Press, 1977. 216 pp.

Although written from a British point of view, the book also refers to North America, and the authors appear sensitive to the gifted-child movement in the United States.

Ward, Frederick C. "Gifted Children's Educational Assistance Act." *Journal of General Education* 25: 247–52 (January 1974).

Here is a transcription of Ward's statement in hearings of the Committee on Labor and Public Welfare of the U.S. Senate concerning Senate Bill 874—The Gifted and Talented Children's Educational Assistance Act (June 28, 1973). At that time, Ward was chairman of the White House Task Force on the Education of Gifted Persons.

Washburne, Carleton W. "Breaking the Lockstep in Our Schools." *School and Society* 8: 391–402 (October 5, 1918).

Washburne says it is imperative that individual instruction replace the lockstep of class instruction. He provides a rationale that would have worked in 1918—and would work in 1988.

Whitmore, Joanne Rand. *Giftedness, Conflict, and Underachievement.* Boston: Allyn and Bacon, 1980. 462 pp.

Whitmore's first section provides an excellent historical perspective on gifted education and an overview of research concerning gifted children and youth.

Wilson, Frank T. "A Survey of Educational Provisions for Young Gifted Children in the U.S. and of Studies and Problems Related Thereto." *Pedagogical Seminary and Journal of Genetic Psychology* 75: 3–19 (September 1949).

The author reports on a survey sent to a wide sampling of colleges and universities providing teacher training, to all state departments of education, and to more than 100 large-city school districts. The conclusions: (1) There is a strongly felt need for curricular materials and procedures, trained teachers who understand the nature and needs of the gifted, and more information regarding the nature of gifted children; (2) research findings concerning gifted children and youth are not reaching school people; (3) teacher-training institutions do not recognize the needs listed above.

Witty, Paul A. "Exploitation of the Child of High Intelligence Quotient." *Educational Method* 15: 298–304 (March 1936).

Witty strongly questions the propriety of publicizing "geniuses" with extraordinarily high IQs. Says society is ignoring gifted and precocious children's education and is only treating them as an oddity.

————. "Thirty Years of Research upon Gifted Children." *Understanding the Child* 17: 35–40 (April 1948).

Witty reviews some of the major studies conducted since 1920.

————. "Who Are the Gifted?" In *Educational for the Gifted,* Part 2 of *Fifty-Seventh Yearbook of the National Society for the Study of Education,* edited by Nelson B. Henry. Chicago: Univ. of Chicago Pr., 1958.

Witty discusses ways to identify the gifted—both general and specific characteristics.

————. "Recent Publications Concerning the Gifted and the Creative Student." *Phi Delta Kappan* 46: 221–24 (January 1965).

An excellent summary of 1960–65 publications about the gifted.

————. "Twenty Years in Education of the Gifted." *Education* 88: 4–10 (September/October 1967).

The author reviews the progress made since the American Association for Gifted Children was founded in 1946. He says there is much left to be done, especially in seeking out the gifted among the disadvantaged.

_____. "The Education of the Gifted and the Creative in the U.S.A." *Gifted Child Quarterly* 15: 109–16 (Summer 1971).

Witty provides a brief historical perspective and discusses the new trend of recognizing creativity as worthy of encouragement.

_____, ed. *The Gifted Child.* Boston: D. C. Heath, 1951. 338 pp.

This classic reference chronicles interest and advances in gifted education up to the 1950s.

_____, ed. *Reading for the Gifted and the Creative Student.* Newark, Del.: International Reading Association, 1971. 63 pp.

This small book, written by experts in the field of gifted education, contains chapters on characteristics of gifted students and their needs for reading experience, innovative reading programs for the gifted, the role of parents and teachers in the reading education of gifted students, and a look at the future of gifted education.

Zettel, Jeffrey J., and Ballard, Joseph. "A Need for Increased Federal Effort for the Gifted and Talented." *Exceptional Children* 44: 261–67 (January 1978).

The authors discuss the recommendations made by the Council for Exceptional Children to focus needed attention on gifted and talented students. A strong rationale is provided.

CHAPTER 2

Who Are the Gifted?

To be able to answer the question Who are the gifted? one must first decide what is meant by the term *gifted*. Of course this book is being written in the United States during the twentieth century. The definition of giftedness would have been different had it been written in another time or place. Any attempt to define giftedness is bound both culturally and socially. Recognizing this phenomenon, and knowing that the present American culture values high intellectual ability that can be used creatively to better the society, we define giftedness as including intelligence, creativity, and social concern.

> The gifted child possesses cognitive ability that is noticeably superior to that of age-mates. This cognitive superiority is coupled with a propensity for creative action in any of a multitude of areas.

The term *gifted* will not be used interchangeably with the term *talented*. The latter refers to those students who are indistinguishable from average individuals of the same chronological age except for a single outstanding ability, such as sculpting or miming. Talent, unlike intelligence, is expressive rather than analytic. This is not to imply that talented students cannot also possess high intelligence, for studies done at the New York City School of Performing Arts showed that "generally, the most talented students in music, drama, and the dance also rated high on general intelligence" (Strang 1958, 66). However, while *talented* will not be used, the terms *superior, bright, able,* and *capable* will be used in order to relieve the monotony of the single term *gifted*.

33

CREATIVITY AND GIFTEDNESS

Before examining specific characteristics of bright children, a brief discussion regarding creativity as it relates to giftedness is appropriate. For many, *creativity* suggests the ability to produce a great painting, an intricate piece of pottery, or a Pulitzer Prize–winning novel. While all of these products are the result of creativity, the term also has a broader connotation. It involves production versus reproduction; divergent versus convergent thinking. The creative person is able to produce original ideas with fluency, flexibility, association, and elaboration. Such ideas are not limited to any particular field (such as art). Creativity may be manifested in science, the dance, urban planning, song writing, leadership, photography, architecture, world hunger relief, and so on. No apparent limit exists for the places where creativity is needed or the ways in which it may be revealed.

It is difficult to be specific in a definition of creativity. According to Treffinger, "given the complexity of the construct of creativity and the variety of its manifestations in daily life, it seems unlikely that there will be a . . . general theory" (1986, 15). Taylor (1984), who has studied scientists and what constitutes a significant scientific contribution, attempts to be specific about the construct of creativity.

> The first and crucial quality could be called Creative Quality. It is an uncommon, uncustomary, unconventional quality due to its breaking away from established patterns and standards and from currently accepted ideas. In a broad sense, it does not emphasize uncommonness by merely being different, per se, but it is a creative or original or imaginative type of quality. We have sometimes described this creative quality in a contribution as being not sterile, but full of excitement which causes a tickling of the imagination and a tingling up the spine of the recipient. If the contribution were sterile, it would be something with nothing new in it. Instead, any contribution possessing the creative quality contains the potential seeds of new blossomings, of new things unforeseen, of new visions of exciting, surprising things yet to come. (Taylor 1984, 106)

Although creativity is not restricted to the gifted, they are the ones in whom it is most likely to be developed and the ones in whom it is most expedient that it be cultivated. "Creativity can and should continue to be involved in giftedness in any area" (Treffinger 1986, 18). Both creativity and intelligence are necessary ingredients for productive problem solving. Simply producing massive quantities of ideas is not sufficient. An intelligent "sorting" must also occur; the problem solver must possess the judgment necessary to reject those ideas that are banal, irrelevant, or faulty, and to accept and express those that are fresh, germane, and potentially beneficial.

Getzels and Jackson (1962) and Wallach and Kogan (1967) have conducted research that separated students into four groups: High Intelligence– High Creativity, High Intelligence–Low Creativity, Low Intelligence–High Creativity, Low Intelligence–Low Creativity. They posit that a distinction does seem to exist between creativity and intelligence, but Sanderlin contends that although creativity and intelligence are not synonymous, creativity "is a function, and one of a very high order indeed, of the mind" (1979, 24–25). Torrance says that people who try to make clear distinctions between creativity and intelligence are involved in a futile task. He believes the two are "interacting variables and that trying to force clear distinctions would create false distinctions which do not exist in real life" (1979, 362).

Since the early 1960s, a great deal of attention has been paid to creativity as it relates to giftedness. The days of considering only a high IQ score when determining giftedness are almost over—especially as the citizenry looks to the gifted to contribute to, and solve the problems of, society. An obviously forward-thinking educator, Carroll realized that a high IQ alone would not suffice. He said that, although the intelligence test measured a child's ability to learn, it did not give a complete picture of all the mental qualities of a gifted child. Furthermore, he believed that

> A child may rate high on an intelligence test and yet fall short of being a genius because though he possesses a large body of information, he has relatively little ability to make that information function creatively. It may never be possible to measure creative imagination objectively, yet certainly this is an aspect of genius that must not be overlooked. (1940, 214)

This aspect of genius must not be overlooked because it is the creative aspect that solves problems, makes inroads, creates beauty, challenges inertia, sees possibilities, and constructs bridges—across races, across time, across space, across disciplines.

> Creation is a disturbing force in society because it is a constructive one. It upsets the old order in the act of building a new one. This activity is salutory for society. It is, indeed, essential for the maintenance of society's health, for one thing that is certain about human affairs is that they are perpetually on the move, and the work of creative spirits is what gives society a chance of directing its inevitable movement along constructive instead of destructive lines. (Taylor 1984, 107)

When one comes to understand the necessity of creativity, one also comes to understand why some societies are opposed to its development.

To summarize, modern definitions of giftedness include creativity, which is different from, but integrally related to, intelligence. A gifted person has a superior intellect with at least a measure of creativity, which can be further developed. For those interested in further reading on the subject of creativity, a section is included in the annotated bibliography at the end of this chapter.

It is important for the reader to realize, as the characteristics of gifted children are discussed, that no one particular gifted child was singled out, studied, and used as the basis for conclusions derived about all gifted children. These characteristics are drawn from a compendium of more than sixty years of observation and research on gifted children by hundreds of researchers, parents, teachers, and writers. Every gifted child is an individual and should not be expected to exhibit all or even most of the characteristics attributed to the gifted. For every trait ascribed to the very able, there exists a wide range of variability. General statements will be made, but one should expect many exceptions.

INTELLECTUAL CHARACTERISTICS

The intellectual characteristics of the gifted are those traits that highly able students exhibit as they use their intellect—that is, their power for knowing and their capacity for rational or intelligent thought. The acquisition and application of knowledge is an ability that is markedly superior in gifted children.

Gifted students are distinguished in acquiring and applying knowledge because of their intellectual advancement and their supernormal capacity for knowledge. Their ability to learn is enhanced by an extraordinary memory and quickness to see relationships. The combination of these traits along with varied intellectual interests, almost insatiable curiosity, and a penchant for independent learning presents a marvelous challenge for parents, teachers, librarians—and all who come in contact with gifted children.

Gallagher and Lucito (1961) used various Wechsler subtests to study and compare the patterns of intellectual strengths and weaknesses in seven samples (three gifted, three retarded, one average). They concluded that different intellectual levels have specific intellectual patterns and that the most familiar property of the pattern for the gifted is intellectual advancement. It seems reasonable to conclude that the intellectually superior child could be termed the intellectually advanced child. Baker (1949) said that the gifted have a "surplus" of mental age beyond their chronological age; by age six, gifted children have a mental age of at least one year beyond their chronological age.

One of the most conspicuous indicators of intellectual advancement is gifted children's early and accurate use of a large vocabulary. Goodenough (1956) suggests that some young gifted children play with words the way average children play with toys. Thus, many gifted students are intrigued by word games and books that deal with words. Much more than average children, the gifted read atlases, encyclopedias, and dictionaries. Observation of gifted students reveals that they are more interested in reference books in their early youth than most people ever are.

Another early indication of exceptional intelligence is the proficient use of linguistic structure. They often speak in phrases and whole sentences earlier than average children, and they are also able to reproduce stories at an early age (Witty 1958). The gifted subjects in a study done by Guilford et al. (1981, 162) "demonstrated advanced receptive language operations of auditory memory and memory for linguistic information."

Gifted students are not endowed with a totally different intellect, but they seem able to use it in a different way. For example, able and average children pass through the same sequence of Piagetian stages, but it appears that gifted students may enter the stages earlier and progress through them more rapidly than do average children (Carter & Ormrod 1982). Webb compared gifted children's intelligence with skilled use of tools. He said:

> The development of the tools themselves (operations) may be a human species-specific trait relatively stable across a range of environments, constrained by maturational factors. How well the tools will be used, on the other hand, is a function of a number of things, including experience and intelligence. Bright children use the tools characteristic of their developmental stage very well compared to their peers. If bright children develop new tools any sooner, however, the precocity is not striking. (1974, 294)

This analogy extends to bright children's use of language. Guilford et al. (1981) conjectured that their gifted subjects did not have a better selection of linguistic rules than their average subjects, but they appeared able to use them more effectively in comprehending and reproducing verbal syntax.

Although not possessing different tools, the gifted may (figuratively) have a larger toolshed: a superior intellectual capacity. Because of their extraordinary ability to assimilate (to take into their mind and thoroughly comprehend), the gifted are able to absorb large amounts of material in a fraction of the time required by average students. Then, making use of their accurate memory, the highly able develop a broad knowledge in many different areas. Gifted students' range of learning is wider and deeper than average students', and it is often apparent that the gifted know about things of which other children are unaware. For example, a bright eight-year-old may be able to discuss numerous battles of the Civil War, or a gifted twelve-year-old may spend a great deal of time at a museum arguing with the curator about particular naturalistic tendencies shown by an artist whom most consider to be an impressionistic painter.

This depth and breadth of knowledge are the result of, and are fed by, highly capable children's superior assimilation, greater capacity, keen observation, marked retention, and varied intellectual interests. Whereas an average child may be interested in motorcycles, tetherball, and dogs, a gifted counterpart may be interested in those three areas in addition to the saxophone, photography, political scandals of the 1940s, and designing and solving intricate logic problems.

Gifted children's wide range of interests stem from their great desire for learning, and, in their quest for knowledge, a continuous discovery of new areas to explore. Their curiosity sometimes seems insatiable, but the questions it spawns are asked neither ostentatiously nor to annoy (as is sometimes believed) but rather as a means of finding out. When gifted children ask questions, their primary purpose is to obtain answers—about the reasons behind an occurrence, the motivation behind an action, or the purposes for completing a task. Their questions may at times seem like defiance because of a perceived challenge to the status quo or the authority figure present (e.g., "Why are we doing this assignment?") but in fact, the queries represent independent thinking and a need for explanations. Sometimes the gifted seem to have a striving for knowledge (learning) that is almost subconscious. In a book by gifted teenagers describing their emotions and needs, one teenager exclaims "'Gifted and talented' is not something you can take up lightly on free weekends. It's something that's going to affect everything about your life, twenty-four hours a day, 365¼ days a year" (Krueger 1978, 141).

Besides satisfying their intellectual curiosity by asking questions, gifted children read and observe a great deal. Many, but by no means all, gifted children read early. They read more history, biography, science, informational books, poetry, drama, and folktales than their average age-mates. This wide reading allows them to begin to satisfy their craving for information.

Often, bright children will choose to study some subject that is difficult for them, both for the knowledge it will afford and for the challenge. Academically motivated, able children find the challenge and accomplishment of a difficult task rewarding in itself—much more so than many little tasks. For example, a highly gifted nine-year-old, enrolled in a gifted program and with many other outside enrichments, taught herself Hebrew "because she thought she ought to know it." Taking this type of initiative to learning is one personality characteristic of the gifted.

Gifted students do well and often like to pursue topics independently. Such initiative is indicative of the distinctive thinking they will do later within their chosen vocations. They will feel compelled to say or do things distinctively. Since they may have interests that go beyond what any available person (teacher, parent, neighbor) can directly help them with, they often work alone. Some sort of guidance at the beginning stages of learning is preferable but not always possible. Baker and Bender recommend providing a "framework for thinking" for the intellectually gifted, "not as a restraint, but as a secure mooring from which they can venture forth on their own" (1981, 274).

The gifted can work alone for long periods without frequent checks by others. Their sustained attention span is a by-product of their mental endurance, and during these periods, they are able to accomplish greater units of work than would an average person within the same constraints. The gifted child has a superior ability to focus on a task and a tenacity of purpose rarely seen in the average child.

In speaking of the young gifted child, Hildreth declared, "His mental energy is comparable with an electric filament that glows continuously without exhausting itself. He hungers for problems, asks for more or invents new problems when the supply gives out" (1938, 301). This hunger does not come in spurts but is rather a continuous, gnawing hunger that cannot really have the edge taken off it. There is a flow, a relatedness in the efforts and attention of the superior mind. "Relatedness" and "relationship" are key words in characterizing the mind of the gifted child. Strang wrote that many of the characteristics of the gifted "stem directly from their powers to organize and relate their experiences" (1958, 77). Gifted children are less likely to see things as discrete and isolated, but rather are quick to see relationships and to observe and associate similarities. This ability helps able children to readily absorb abstract concepts and then organize them and apply them efficiently.

Such rapid absorption and efficient organization of concepts allows gifted students to generalize readily. They look for and easily grasp the principles that underlie their learning and are quick to see the applications of these principles (as in mathematics), thus preferring to delve into the *why* behind a concept rather than the *what*.

Intelligence tends to build on itself. Strang said,

> Intelligence is not something given at birth; it constantly creates itself through life experiences that it selects, relates, and organizes. In this sense, intelligence is learned. The gifted child becomes increasingly able to use his environment to good advantage. (1954, 215)

This observation should not be taken to mean that the gifted should be left to their own devices—far from it. But by providing the appropriate environment and the correct guidance, one can help gifted students use their supernormal abilities to great advantage.

Because of the way gifted children learn, they do better in some subjects than in others. They tend to do very well in reading, mathematics, language, science, and the arts. Their written and oral communication skills are quite effective. Their ability to utilize rather complex associative methods often gives them a flair for science and math. They do less well in history and spelling because, as usually taught, the latter two depend more on rote memory than on understanding principles and concepts. Often, a gifted student's poorest grade will come in handwriting because of the repetition involved, which the gifted child finds less than stimulating. Overall, though, gifted students have above-average grades and perform significantly better than their average age-mates in the various subject areas.

To summarize the intellectual characteristics of the gifted child, Wallach and Kogan's definition of intelligence makes a good baseline:

> The psychological concept of intelligence defines a network of strongly related abilities concerning the retention, transformation, and utilization of verbal and numerical symbols; at issue are a person's memory capacities, his skill in solving problems, his dexterity in manipulating and dealing with concepts. The person high in one of these skills will tend to be high in all; the individual who is low in one will tend to be low in all. (1967, 38)

The key word in this definition is *tend*. Most likely, the student with a 138 IQ will have a superior memory, show facility with verbal expression, employ strong associative capabilities when dealing with new material, and be able to spend long periods deeply absorbed in one project. But another student with a similar IQ may possess an extraordinary ability to see relationships and have fluent verbal skills but make poor grades because of a short attention span. There is no one mold into which the highly intelligent youngster fits, especially if that youngster is also highly creative. As Hallahan and Kauffman note, "gifted children as a group have specific characteristics that show about as much variation around the mean as the variation shown by any other group around its mean" (1982, 389). The gifted child must indeed be seen as an individual with concomitant strengths and weaknesses.

PERSONALITY CHARACTERISTICS

Webster's *New Collegiate Dictionary* defines *personality* as "the complex of characteristics that distinguishes an individual; the totality of an individual's behavior and emotional tendencies." Describing the personality characteristics of a group of individuals seems like a tall order, because every individual has a very distinct personality. However, it is possible to attribute *certain* characteristics to the gifted as a group; the characteristics that *many* of them share give them a degree of commonality.

Self-Concept

An adult's self-concept is derived from many factors, including home, peers, work, and hobbies. A child also develops a self-concept based on several factors, but family and school dominate the list. The family's influence on the gifted child's self-concept will be discussed thoroughly in the chapter "Parenting Gifted Children"; the emphasis here is on the school's influence.

Children's self-concepts are not based on a single perception but rather on a compendium of perceptions, which concern their ability to succeed in academic subjects in addition to other areas. In general, gifted students' self-concepts are closely tied with their academic learning. Since they usually do well academically, it follows that most gifted students have positive self-concepts. It is important to watch for the exceptions, though, and these should be conspicuous.

Students who are gifted but have not had their giftedness recognized—or have had it consistently denied—will probably not have a good self-concept. Likewise, students who are very capable in most areas but fall short in a few may have less than a positive self-image. Those students who are both gifted and handicapped often fall into this latter group, particularly if they are learning disabled. They are intelligent and sensitive enough to realize that their gifts are being fettered by their learning disabilities. They may experience extreme frustration, whether they work in a "regular" classroom, performing at an average level because their giftedness allows them to compensate for their learning disabilities, or in a learning-disability resource room, where many of the activities are remedial and/or repetitive.

Terman, in his effort to dispel the myth that gifted students are scrawny, one-sided social misfits, unwittingly created another myth—that gifted students excel in all areas. Gifted children do tend to be above average in most dimensions, and superior in some, but their development is not necessarily even in all areas. People who work with the gifted must be aware that being gifted does not ensure perfection. If gifted youth feel that they "should" be superior in every area, but in fact they are not, then they may believe themselves failures. In a book written and compiled by gifted students, they wrote

> We tend to be more sensitive than other people. Multiple meanings, innuendos, and self-consciousness plague us. Intensive self-analysis, self-criticism, and the inability to recognize that we have limits make us despondent. In fact, most times our self-searching leaves us more discombobbled than we were at the outset. (Krueger 1978, 9)

Gifted students are competent in their self-criticism; they recognize what they do and do not know. Awareness of a lack of knowledge of information can lead to new insights, so this trait should be encouraged. However, one should also assure gifted students that not knowing something is all right. Far from encouraging laziness, such reassurance may promote their self-concept and their later original contributions.

In fact, a common misconception about the gifted is that, since their work is good and their self-concept is fairly high, they do not need any encouragement. They do! Werblo and Torrance (1966) found that even high-achieving, gifted students tend to underestimate themselves. They not only need encouragement to "keep up the good work" (affirming their present successes) but also motivation to do more, to strive beyond what they have already accomplished. If bright students can get by with less than their best, they may develop careless and indifferent attitudes. In heterogeneous classes, highly able students tend to shine in comparison with the rest. But their better-than-average work may also be far less than they are capable of accomplishing. If the gifted are permitted to perform at such a level, they may acquire habits that will be very difficult to break.

So, for two reasons, parents, teachers, and mentors must help their gifted students make a realistic estimate of their abilities: (1) they need to realize the heights to which they can rise; (2) they must also realize that they cannot do everything perfectly.

An interesting phenomenon occurs when gifted students are segregated. Because of a tendency to compare oneself with others in whom there is a perceived similarity, gifted students compare themselves with the other superior students in their homogeneous classroom rather than with their average age-mates. Thus, their self-concept may decline when they are first placed in a homogeneous grouping, but it will reascend when their primary reference group is comprised of a heterogeneous mixture (Coleman & Fults 1982). Teachers and parents should anticipate this problem when gifted children are segregated.

EMOTIONAL CHARACTERISTICS

A common misconception is that persons of superior intellect are often on the borderline of mental instability. But in fact, giftedness is neither a shield from nor a lodestone to emotional problems. Numerous researchers have found the gifted to be emotionally stable, both as children and as adults (Gallagher 1975; Hollingworth & Rust 1937; Monks & Ferguson 1983; Strang 1958).

The idea that the gifted are emotionally unstable may stem from observations of the "pseudogifted"—children of average intelligence whose parents have pushed them so that they are trying to achieve beyond their capability (Strang 1958). In fact, the percentage of maladjusted gifted children is less than the percentage of maladjusted children in the total child population. Adjustment problems among the gifted tend to result from "adult misunderstanding, underachievement, unfulfilled social, personal, and status drives, and poor self-concept" (Love 1972, 42). If gifted children are better adjusted than the average, it is not because they have fewer adjustments to make—in fact they may face more due to their variance from the norm. However, they generally make such adjustments successfully, observe Barbe and Renzulli (1975). In fact, the gifted are "a group of individuals who are especially advantaged in confronting and mastering the challenges of life in every sphere" (Suran & Rizzo 1979, 286). Perhaps their superior minds enable them to recognize and analyze their problems of adjustment and then find the best ways of coping with them. In any case, the emotional profile of gifted children is stable, not neurotic. They possess many characteristics of the self-actualized person.

In fact, gifted children tend to be more cheerful and happy than the norm for their age group. They also display a sense of humor that is both quick and sophisticated. They are especially adept at punning and other word plays. This characteristic alone may be a clue that a child is gifted, even if grades and performance indicate otherwise.

The highly intelligent child's remarkable sense of humor is rarely used at the expense of someone else. Their sensitivity promotes heightened empathy for their fellows.

> The characteristic most readily identifiable in gifted children, varying both in kind and degree, is sensitivity. Whether the sensitivity is to one or more particular areas of learning, sensitivity to discovering or solving problems, or sensitivity to the feelings of one's fellow man, it is so much a characteristic of giftedness that it can almost be said that the two terms are synonymous. (Barbe 1967, 13)

This sensitivity may be the governor behind the higher level of physical and emotional self-control exhibited by the gifted. When compared to their age-mates, the gifted are more likely to control aggression and are less likely to display anger or tease others, especially those younger than themselves. It seems that the gifted engage in fewer anti-social behaviors than the norm.

The behavior of highly capable children is usually more dependable, responsible, and conscientious than that of average children. As a group, they are more trustworthy and more likely to resist the temptation to cheat than a group of nongifted children.

The gifted have less need for approval from authority figures. They have a stronger sense of who they are and are more self-sufficient than the average. Autonomy and independence are nearly always attributed to the gifted. In parents' ratings of children's independence, gifted scored higher than average children. Researchers got the same results from tests designed to measure autonomy (Monks & Ferguson 1983). In another study bright and dull sixth graders were compared; the bright were more independent and less conforming than the dull (Lucito 1964).

To be less conforming requires the superior ego strength possessed by the gifted. But the highly able child is determined and persistent, possessing strong willpower. As a result, gifted students are often characterized as individualists. Nichols and Davis's (1964) study showed that National Merit scholars described themselves as either politically liberal or politically conservative—few characterized themselves as politically neutral. In one study, forty-two intellectually gifted adolescents were compared with forty-two adolescents of average intelligence. These youths were matched on the variables of age, sex, religion, social class, and nationality. The gifted were different in one major area of personal and social adjustment—their tendency to display more dominant, forceful, independent, and competitive behaviors (Smith 1962).

The gifted often have intense responses to others: David Wechsler (in Drews 1972, 59) called the gifted "more of" people. When one observes a group of gifted youngsters, their "more of" intelligence is easily recognized, but so is their "more of" personality; the gifted are not dull. Their heightened awareness, sensitivity, forcefulness, humor, responsiveness, and self-respect all interact to form a "more of" group of students. Thus, it is not surprising that gifted children are often social leaders, or that they possess dormant leadership ability that, once awakened, can be both powerful and charismatic.

SOCIABILITY CHARACTERISTICS

Picture a heterogeneous classroom. Look around the room to find the gifted child. Is it the child who is obviously an isolate, almost totally ignored by the others? Or is it the child being teased and taunted by other children? Almost without exception, for the moderately gifted child (IQ 130–160), the answer to both questions is no. An extra endowment of intelligence does not mean a lack in all other areas. Sociability is no exception to that rule.

This section is not about average children who are, incidentally, socially adept. It is about intellectually gifted children, who as a group, possess particular social characteristics just as they possess particular intellectual characteristics. For the person who has not associated a great deal with gifted children or young adults, this section may come as the biggest surprise, because the myth of the gifted social isolate has been propounded for so long that many accept it as fact.

Of course, conditions affect outcomes and certain distinctions can be made between the gifted and the highly gifted. However, on the whole the gifted tend to be very sociable. In a study of 294 elementary school children, the gifted children were not social isolates. They generally ranged from moderately to most popular in their classrooms; very few were rated as least popular (Grace & Booth 1958). In a study of 54 children with an IQ of 150 or more, 52 percent were in the top quarter of the class in terms of social choice. Only 11 percent were in the lowest quarter (Gallagher 1958). In a later book (1975), Gallagher speculated that even though average children see a difference between themselves and the gifted, they choose them as friends because they serve as "ego ideals." Researchers have found that bright children are popular with all intellectual groups, not just other gifted children. And a study of 350 fifth graders showed that bright students (IQ 130 or more) are not more cliquish or snobbish than their less-bright classmates (Silverstein 1962).

Who are gifted children's friends? This depends on, among other things, the degree of a child's giftedness. When gifted students are segregated, they tend to choose each other for friends, whether the segregation is complete or just for part of the day. Otherwise, gifted students tend to prefer (and choose) playmates older than themselves, for obvious reasons. If a gifted child has an MA (mental age) of ten and a CA (chronological age) of six, then playing with other six-year-olds may not be much fun. A younger gifted child may thus have a problem finding playmates; for example, most ten-year-olds are not going to want to play with a six-year-old of *any* MA!

Another problem for young gifted children is the way they want to play, as opposed to the way average children want to play. The gifted often know more games of intellectual skill (e.g., bridge, chess) for which they have trouble finding opponents, and they have less of an affinity for seemingly aimless sensorimotor games. For the abundantly gifted (IQ 160 or more), finding playmates may be quite difficult. Their MA is so advanced that they try to organize the play situation into a complicated pattern that has a remote, but definite climax as its goal (Hollingworth 1931). For children of similar CA, or for average children of similar MA, this type of play is not appealing. And, trying to force a very gifted five-year-old into a game of "ring-around-the-rosy" is not going to serve anyone. Gifted children should not be forced to "make friends" with children of the same CA but lower IQ than themselves.

These extremely bright children, who have difficulty finding playmates, are the exception to the gifted group. The San Diego Pupil Study Center looks at gifted students who score at or above the third standard deviation above the mean on the Revised Stanford-Binet. Their results reveal that the farther from the mean a student scores on the test, the more apt the child is to have problems. As with other characteristics particular to the tiny proportion of students at the upper end of the intelligence scale, "characterizing the gifted by describing only those with IQ's of 180 or higher is roughly analogous to characterizing the retarded by describing those with IQ's of 20 or less" (Swassing 1980, 456).

The social status of the gifted does seem to fluctuate, depending on certain age and environmental factors. Researchers have reported that at the secondary level, the social status of gifted children seems to show a relative decrease (Austin & Draper 1981; Gallagher 1975; Martyn 1957). This comes at a time when the need for peer acceptance is at its peak, but peer-group conformity is sometimes a problem for the gifted youth. (Here, *peer group* refers to age-mates in a heterogeneous high school.)

Freeman (1979) reported that gifted children are not bothered by their relative lack of friends and especially of friends the same age. One cannot say that having fewer friends does not bother the gifted person at all, but it is possible to conjecture that the gifted person can accept and deal with that fact. Barbe (1967) says the gifted have "adjustment superiority"; they learn early how to cope with themselves and their problems and they avoid situations in which they know they cannot cope.

Gifted children seem to develop early an understanding of the social setting in which they live and the way in which they fit in. In other words, their social cognition is precocious. Gifted children seem able intuitively to recognize the dynamics of group behavior, often quite early. They identify the social status of others and themselves better than average students do. Their ability to pick up and interpret nonverbal cues is superior (Boston 1979). They quickly discern when something is wrong. They are capable of great empathy and insight into a situation. Superior children, as a group, tend to develop and "cultivate comparatively unselfish and social points of view," usually at a very early age (Baker 1949). Superior social cognition helps gifted children cope with their differences, which are often the result of nonconformity. For one thing, gifted children's "tendency to be perceptually more sensitive to the problems of right and wrong may make it difficult for them to conform in situations which cause them to compromise their views" (Brode 1980). So, in work with the gifted, making the distinction between nonconformity and poor adjustment is essential. Often, gifted students' search for answers to perceived problems may necessitate behaviors that differ sharply from the others'. They often make judgments regardless of group pressures and may act against the norm, depending on their perception of the situation.

Thus, persons who are concerned about the very bright cloistering themselves and developing a master plan for ridding the world of all but themselves are mistaken. The gifted not only enjoy others and are enjoyed in return, but their perceptive sensitivity moves them to do the kinds of things necessary to improve society.

Much of the fear of elitism is based on the assumption that if individuals discover that they are more able than others, they will develop aristocratic values, caring little for the plight of others. Research indicates that exactly the opposite is true; gift-edness is often accompanied by a strong sense of obligation, re-sponsibility and empathy. (Silverman 1982, 171)

The gifted's sense of obligation, responsibility, and empathy, teamed with a heightened ability to reason out moral questions, offers fertile ground for sowing the seeds of, and cultivating, ethical leadership qualities.

MORAL AND ETHICAL CHARACTERISTICS

One argument often used to convince others that the gifted need dif-ferentiated education is that these bright youngsters are the future leaders and problem solvers of the world. In the late 1950s, the recog-nized deficit in the United States was technological. Today, people probably worry more about the way the United States deals with social problems. If the gifted are to help solve these problems, it is valid to assess their moral and ethical reasoning characteristics. Unethical, im-moral, or amoral persons do not meet the requirements for the job of solving social problems and providing social leadership at the end of this century and the beginning of the next. Can the gifted be consid-ered any more adept at handling these problems than anyone else?

On the whole, gifted children tend to be advanced for their ages in ethical and moral sensitivity. In fact, a gifted child of nine may have the moral development of a fourteen-year-old (Santayana 1947). More than average persons, they tend to be keenly aware of the sad state of the world and feel compelled to do something about it (Drews 1972). They are also concerned with religion and issues of right and wrong, good and evil, justice and injustice much earlier than other youth (Diessner 1983; Krause 1962).

Very bright young children may ask parents or teachers to answer questions that have been puzzling philosophers for thousands of years. When unable to get an acceptable answer, these gifted children may ponder the issue deeply and continue to seek an answer from vari-ous sources (books, religious figures, grandparents). Frequently the answers that these children eventually find are original and unconven-tional. They are, however, the result of systematic logic that is reflec-tive of high moral reasoning.

Why are the gifted capable of precocious and sophisticated moral and ethical reasoning? Perhaps because "intellectual functioning which allows them to have superior memories, capacities for learning, and powers of assimilation . . . also allows them a superior moral reasoning capability" (Sisk 1982, 221). It is true that a child whose moral reasoning is high is likely to score well on an IQ test as well (Maccoby 1980). High IQ does not guarantee a high level of moral reasoning, but both developmentalists and social learning theorists agree that certain levels of intelligence are necessary for high moral reasoning (Diessner 1983).

Although the gifted are provided with both the seeds and the fertile ground for becoming the ethical leaders and problem solvers of the future, proper cultivation is necessary. Parents and teachers should strive to connect intellectual experiences with the consciences of gifted children. Diessner (1983) believes that since the gifted are looked to for their future service to society, it is "particularly sane" to educate them ethically and morally. As Santayana said, "nature needs nurture to round out its human possibilities" (1947,260).

FAMILY CHARACTERISTICS

Is there a particular family configuration, a particular ethnic group or socioeconomic class that predisposes a youngster to be gifted? No. So, why talk about the family characteristics of a gifted person? Many, many studies of gifted persons' backgrounds have been conducted. These studies have involved questionnaires, interviews, surveys, observations, and evaluations of biographies. Researchers have looked at the backgrounds of young gifted children, of highly able seventh and eighth graders participating in the Talent Search for Mathematically Precocious Youth, of National Merit scholarship finalists, and of eminent men and women. These research studies have produced so much information that it is possible to paint a picture of a "typical" gifted child's family. However, more than any other generalization concerning the gifted child, the family picture depicts only favorable conditions or tendencies. Absence of such conditions does not preclude the possibility of a gifted child, and their presence does not guarantee a gifted child—nor should the composite be used in any way to identify gifted children.

Until fairly recently, the typical identified gifted child was from a white family in an above-average income bracket. The family was intact (i.e., mother and father were still married to one another), and the father and mother both had education above the national average. The father most likely held a white-collar or professional position. If the mother worked outside the home, she most likely also had a job that ranked above the blue-collar level. Also, the gifted child would be the first born or the only child in the family.

What are some possible explanations for this configuration? Regarding the notion that most gifted children are white, there are several—none of which is racial superiority. The first is that there are proportionately more whites than any other racial group in the United States. Second, segregated school districts, which provided separate, but not equal, education for whites and blacks, may have provided for bright white youngsters but not for bright black children. Thus, researchers who looked at the school district's records or asked to use the gifted group for research purposes found that the predominant ethnicity was white. Third, as will be discussed in the chapter "Identification," many if not all IQ tests have been accused of cultural bias, especially against minorities and the poor. Consequently, schools using such IQ tests as the main criterion for determining giftedness fail to identify many bright youngsters who are black, Hispanic, and/or poor. Fourth, as Roedell et al. (1980) suggest, low-income or minority families are less likely to choose to participate in research, resulting in an underrepresentation of their ranks in studies of the gifted. Such reluctance may be culture bound, or it may involve time and attitude.

Time and attitude may also be one reason why the "typical" family of the gifted child seems to be above average financially. Generally speaking, who has more time and inclination to spend with their child in a nurturing kind of way—parents whose bills are paid and who know a paycheck will come again next month, or parents who either have no job or have a menial one that barely covers expenses? According to Maslow's hierarchy of needs, if one is worrying about food, clothing, and shelter, one can devote little attention to emotional and intellectual needs—of oneself or one's family (Maslow 1954). Gifted children are born into poor families, not just well-to-do ones, but too often the poor families cannot provide much encouragement and nurture along the way.

> Although gifted and talented students can be found in all walks of life and in all racial and ethnic groups, they are more likely to be found in some groups than others. The groups with high incidence of the gifted place a great emphasis on intellectual values and have more extensive opportunities to develop talents and skills already present in the child. (Gallagher 1975, 52)

Also, especially until recently, programs for gifted children were much more numerous where the families were more affluent. In education, as in other institutions, the squeaky wheel gets the grease.

Families of above-average income often also have above-average education. Children in such families are raised in an atmosphere that values education and encourages academic achievement. So, a gifted child's interest in archaeology is more likely to be encouraged by educated parents than by parents with a grade-school education.

What about the likelihood that a gifted child is the firstborn or only child? A few studies have refuted the idea that birth order makes a difference (e.g., Benbow & Stanley 1980; Cicirelli 1967). But many others support it (e.g., Cox 1977; Pulvino & Lupton 1978). Barbe (1956) reported that of his 456 gifted subjects, 52.5 percent were firstborn. Goddard (1928) reported that half his 253 subjects were firstborn and three-fourths were born either first or second. Cobb and Hollingworth (in Barbe 1956) found that half their subjects were the firstborn in their families. In a study of 1,184 National Merit scholarship finalists, semifinalists, and winners, these students not only had a significant tendency to be the older children in their families, but the differences were large enough to suggest a strong relationship between birth order and exceptional ability (Nichols & Davis 1964).

So far, no one seems to have pinpointed a genetic or otherwise inherent reason for this phenomenon, but Zajonc (1976) has an interesting theory called the confluence model, which posits that within a family, the amount and rate of intellectual growth of each member is dependent on that of all the other members and the family configurations; different configurations constitute different intellectual environments. The oldest child has the greatest opportunity for developing within the intellectual environment of a family. As each successive child joins the family, the "space" within the intellectual environment becomes smaller. This confluence model does not, however, account for the many exceptions to be found within our society.

Despite the evidence that indicates tendencies otherwise, a gifted child can be the fifth child born into a Hispanic home, raised by one parent who works to barely eke out a living. Data from thousands of gifted and thousands of retarded students show that the positive relationships between socioeconomic status and mental ability hold primarily for group averages. "Knowledge of the parent's occupation or the socioeconomic condition of the home of the child is a very precarious index of the child's intelligence" (McGehee & Lewis 1942, 380). This was true forty-five years ago, and it is true today.

Being born gifted is not indigenous to the wealthy, the bright, or the white. It is an occurrence that crosses educational, economic, and racial lines.

PHYSICAL CHARACTERISTICS

(a) The intellectually superior child tends to be physically weak.
TRUE _____   FALSE _____

(b) The intellectually superior child tends to be physically strong.
TRUE _____   FALSE _____

The first statement is a myth that has existed for many years, probably growing out of the idea that "nature is just" (Hollingworth & Taylor 1924)—that is, it evens the score by giving those of superior intelligence inferior physical stature (maybe even a handicap for the extraordinarily bright!). The second statement is also a myth, unwittingly created by Terman's Genetic Studies of Genius and numerous studies that followed. Terman and others weighed and measured their gifted subjects, tested their strength, monitored their health, and so determined that gifted students are physically superior to average students. In that these conclusions were contrary to the previous notion of the puny, physically inept gifted child, they had a positive effect. But unfortunately, they went too far, until another, equally inaccurate stereotype was formed. The gifted, as a group, were reported to be taller, heavier, stronger, healthier, and generally superior in their physical attributes. Terman also found that gifted children maintained this superiority into middle age. Barbe (1955) noted that even though the gifted tended to be superior in their physical development, the superiority was not so marked as was their mental superiority.

However, soon after the reports claiming physical superiority of the gifted began coming out, some questioned their validity, wondering whether the groups measured were representative of the population as a whole. Usually, the answer was no. As discussed in the last section, the upper socioeconomic groups were overrepresented (or lower socioeconomic groups were underrepresented). This led many to speculate that the results were skewed because the children studied had superior nutrition, medical attention, and other care. However, researchers who tried to support this speculation found it difficult to match gifted and nongifted children on sex, age, socioeconomic status, and general background. Laycock and Caylor (1964) measured eighty-one gifted students and their eighty-one significantly less bright siblings (thus matching the groups on general background). They concluded that the gifted are not physically larger or heavier than their average and below-average counterparts. Studies replicating Laycock and Caylor's—as well as common sense—would seem to indicate that bright children do not turn out to be significantly larger or smaller than average students when one takes their home backgrounds into consideration. In a group controlled for socioeconomic status, using physical size and strength to identify the gifted would be impossible.

However, choosing gifted students from a group would not be impossible using the criterion of physical energy. Terman called the abundant energy that the gifted seem to have their "ZQ" or "zip quotient." When very young, the gifted child with a high "ZQ" may appear hyperactive—a result of the lack of availability of meaningful tasks and challenges. The gifted often have a less than average need for sleep and exhibit an intense physical and psychological drive. This drive can become almost an obsession when they are particularly involved in a task; they may work until physical exhaustion prevails.

Therefore, it would seem that the most legitimate distinguishing physical characteristic of the gifted is their intense drive and perseverance. In terms of "packaging," gifted children come in all sizes, shapes, and colors.

SUMMARY

To provide a conspectus of the characteristics of the gifted is a difficult task. "Gifted people are not 'superhumans,' rather they are human beings with extraordinary gifts in particular areas" (Hallahan & Kauffman 1982, 375). Probably no gifted person exhibits or possesses all the characteristics discussed in this chapter.

It would behoove a person interested in the gifted to become familiar with the traits most often exhibited by very bright youngsters and to be watchful for them. At the same time, keep an open mind so as not to miss the exceptions among the gifted population—those who are just as gifted and just as needy and worthy of the differentiated attention that will allow them to blossom and become all they possibly can.

SELECTED BIBLIOGRAPHY

The bibliographic categories are sequential in relation to the information discussed in the body of the text. Generally the headings are the same as those used within the text. If a source is cited in more than one category, it will be annotated in the first entry, and all subsequent entries will indicate the category under which it is annotated.

Introduction

Barbe, Walter B. "Characteristics of Gifted Children." *Educational Administration and Supervision* 41:207–17 (April 1955).

Barbe summarizes research regarding the characteristics of gifted children.

_____. "Identification of Gifted Children." *Education* 88:11–14 (September/October 1967).

Barbe groups the primary traits of gifted students in three categories: genetic endowment, adjustment, and performance superiority. He alleges that the highly gifted child is somewhat different and says that sensitivity is almost synonymous with giftedness.

Barbe, Walter B., and Renzulli, Joseph S. *Psychology and Education of the Gifted.* 2d ed. New York: Halstead Pr., 1975. 481 pp.

This collection of journal articles about gifted children includes work by many of the experts in the field—Gallagher, Torrance, Renzulli, Tannenbaum, etc. For the person needing a good general compendium regarding the gifted, this would serve the purpose.

Bish, Charles E. "The Academically Talented." *NEA Journal* 50:33–37, (February 1961).

Bish describes general characteristics of the academically talented, answers arguments about creating an elite by educating the able student, and discusses ways to provide an effective program for the gifted.

Boston, H. *Characteristics of the Gifted and Talented.* Washington, D.C.: Office of the Gifted and Talented, U.S. Department of Health, Education, and Welfare, 1979. 74 pp.

Boston provides information on the gifted child's characteristics in several categories. The book would be useful to the general reader.

Carroll, Herbert A. "Intellectually Gifted Children—Their Characteristics and Problems." *Teachers College Record* 42:212–27 (December 1940).

Carroll's discussion of gifted children (defined as the top 1 percent) is excellent; everything he says is backed up by well-explained research. Categories explored include identification, constancy of mental status, capacity versus achievement, heredity and environment, social adjustments, and educational problems.

Cox, R. L. "Background Characteristics of 456 Gifted Students." *Gifted Child Quarterly* 21:261–67 (Summer 1977).

Children selected to attend a summer program for the gifted were studied, and the findings supported the major studies. Significant numbers were firstborn and some walked and talked early. The children had many and varied interests and high participation in many free-time activities—the favorite of which was reading.

Davidson, Janet E., and Sternberg, Robert J. "The Role of Insight in Intellectual Giftedness." *Gifted Child Quarterly* 28:58–64 (Spring 1984).

The authors propose that a distinctive characteristic of the intellectually gifted is their exceptional insight. They present a subtheory of intellectual giftedness based upon the centrality of insight skills in giftedness. Instruments that can be used to assess this ability are described, along with means of enhancing insight.

Davis, Helen. "Personal and Social Characteristics of Gifted Children." In *Report of the Society's Committee on the Education of Gifted Children*, Part 1 of *Twenty-Third Yearbook of the National Society for the Study of Education*, edited by Guy M. Whipple. Bloomington, Ill.: Public School Publishing Co., 1924.

Numerous mental, social, and physical characteristics of gifted students are described, based on others' research and on a questionnaire used by the author. Much of what she reported is still supported by research today.

Duncan, James A., and Dreger, Ralph Mason. "Behavioral Analysis and Identification of Gifted Children." *Journal of Genetic Psychology* 133:43–57 (September 1978).

Duncan and Dreger report on their study of sixty children age eleven to thirteen, including thirty gifted and thirty average youngsters. One parent of each child completed the Children's Behavioral Classification Instrument. Certain behavioral characteristics of the gifted were manifested in the behavioral analysis—for example, greater than average ability to control aggressiveness and fewer temper tantrums.

Durr, William K. "Characteristics of Gifted Children: Ten Years of Research." *Gifted Child Quarterly* 4:75–80 (1960).

Durr reviews the research done during the 1950s.

Gallagher, James J. *Teaching the Gifted Child.* 2d ed. Boston: Allyn Bacon, 1975. 431 pp.

Chapter 2, "Characteristics of Gifted Students," reviews research concerning characteristics of gifted students. Someone trying to get a broad overview will find this reference complete and easy to understand.

Getzels, J. W., and Jackson, P. W. "Distinctive Characteristics of Able Learners." In *Promoting Maximal Reading Growth among Able Learners*, edited by William S. Gray. Chicago: Univ. of Chicago Pr., 1954.

The personal, social, and creative characteristics of the able learner are discussed, and research is cited to support statements.

Goddard, Henry H. *School Training of Gifted Children.* Yonkers-on-Hudson, N.Y.: World, 1928. 132 pp.

The author served as an advisor to the Cleveland Major Works Program in the 1920s. For five years, he observed two days per month in these schools, which were at the forefront of gifted education. This book is a product of his observations and rates as a classic for those interested in the beginnings of gifted schooling in the United States.

Goodenough, Florence L. *Exceptional Children.* New York: Appleton-Century-Croft, 1956. 428 pp.

This book is considered one of the classic writings on exceptional children. Part 2 (chapters 6–11) concerns the superior student.

Hewett, Frank M., and Forness, Steven R. *Education of Exceptional Learners.* Boston: Allyn & Bacon, 1974. 564 pp.

Chapter 15, "The Gifted Learner," is a good general discussion of the gifted. It includes a table, "Characteristics of the Gifted and Concomitant Problems," and a brief case study that illustrates the authors' points.

Hildreth, Gertrude H. "Characteristics of Young Gifted Children." *Pedagogical Seminary and Journal of Genetic Psychology* 53:287–311 (December 1938).

Fifty gifted children (age three to nine) were matched with fifty control children, and Hildreth reports on intellectual, personality, and behavioral traits of both groups. Several verbatim excerpts from test reports sketch typical students in the gifted group.

Kitano, Margie K. "Ethnography of a Preschool for the Gifted: What Gifted Young Children Actually Do." *Gifted Child Quarterly* 29:67–71 (Spring 1985).

The author used naturalistic (participant observer) methods to collect observational data that would describe the behaviors of gifted preschool children. The categories of behavior discussed in the article are cognitive and achievement-related behavior; social, affective, and motivational characteristics; individual differences. Information gathered on the parents is also presented. Kitano concludes that first and foremost, gifted children are children—displaying characteristics similar to those of other children. Second, they are gifted, displaying evidence of cognitive advancement and maturity.

Krause, Irl Brown. "Some Attributes, Aptitudes, and Interests of the Gifted." *Gifted Child Quarterly* 6:139–140+ (1962).

This brief article reviews some of the results of an eight-year study of college programs for superior students. It found, for example, that gifted college students enrolled in honors classes in English more than in any other area; foreign language came next.

Lewis, W. Drayton. "Some Characteristics of Very Superior Children." *Pedagogical Seminary and Journal of Genetic Psychology* 62:301–9 (June 1943).

In a study of 45,000 children in grades four to eight, students with an IQ of 145 or more were compared with those with scores between 125 and 144. Definite differences were found, and the author concluded that it was much more desirable to be in the "lower" group.

Nichols, Robert C., and Davis, James A. "Characteristics of Students of High Academic Aptitude." *Personnel and Guidance Journal* 42:794–800 (April 1964).

A group of 1,184 college seniors who had been National Merit scholarship semifinalists was compared with 3,397 college seniors representative of all graduating seniors in the United States. The author concluded, "Not a single item in the entire questionnaire failed to show a significant difference between the Merit and average groups."

Piechowski, Michael M., and Colangelo, Nicholas. "Developmental Potential of the Gifted." *Gifted Child Quarterly* 28:80–88 (Spring 1984).

The authors present a model that defines five parallel dimensions or modes of mental functioning. The strength of these five dimensions is taken to be a measure of a person's developmental potential and, therefore, giftedness. The five dimensions are: psychomotor overexcitability, sensual overexcitability, intellectual overexcitability, imaginational overexcitability, emotional overexcitability. The authors describe a study that compared the overexcitability profiles of gifted adolescents with those of gifted and nongifted adults. The article presents a fascinating concept!

Renzulli, Joseph S., and Hartman, Robert K. "Scale for Rating Behavioral Characteristics of Superior Students." *Exceptional Children* 38:243–48 (November 1971).

The article presents a full copy of the rating scale, which appears to cover everything regarding four behavioral characteristics: learning, motivation, creativity, and leadership. References for each item on the scale are cited next to the item. This is an excellent resource.

Roedell, Wendy Conklin; Jackson, Nancy Ewald; and Robinson, Halbert B. *Gifted Young Children.* New York: Teachers College Press, 1980. 107 pp.

Chapter 2 deals quite extensively with the characteristics of *young* gifted children. The whole book is recommended reading for parents of young children who may be gifted and for teachers of very young children.

Russell, Donald W. "The Gifted and the Terminology Dilemma." *Gifted Child Quarterly* 3:56–57+ (1959).

Russell makes a plea for use of consistent terminology in reference to the gifted. After a rather tongue-in-cheek consideration of other terms (superior, able learner, genius), he discards them, believing that "gifted" will suffice.

Sanderlin, Owenita. *Gifted Children: How to Identify and Teach Them.* Cranbury, N.J.: A. S. Barnes, 1979. 180 pp.

Written in a chatty style, the book is a basic introduction to the identification and teaching of gifted children. Some of the statements are somewhat sexist. Each chapter opens with a relevant quote, which is a good means of introduction to the topic.

Santayana, S. George. "The Intellectually Gifted Child: His Nature and His Needs." *Clearing House* 21:259–67 (January 1947).

After providing some historical background of attention to the gifted, Santayana quite thoroughly discusses their various characteristics. Proper schooling is seen as expedient.

Schiever, Shirley W. "Creative Personality Characteristics and Dimensions of Mental Functioning in Gifted Adolescents." *Roeper Review* 7:223–26 (April 1985).

Using the theory of emotional development, the author identifies five psychic overexcitabilities (psychomotor, sensual, imaginational, intellectual, and emotional) as the basis for her study. Her purpose was to gather and examine OE (overexcitability) profiles of gifted students and to compare these with a creativity measure. She found that imaginational, emotional, and intellectual OE's seem to be related to the creative personality in the population she studied.

Shields, James B. *The Gifted Child.* New York: Humanities Press, 1968. 96pp.

This short book contains quite a bit of information. Chapters include "Problem of Definition," "A High I.Q.," "Creativity," "Logical Thinking," and "Educating the Gifted Child."

Silverman, Linda Kreger. "The Gifted and Talented." In *Exceptional Children and Youth,* edited by Edward L. Meyen. Denver: Love Publishing, 1982.

Silverman's book has a good introductory chapter, a checklist of characteristics, and explanations of various intervention methods for teaching the gifted.

Sisk, Dorothy. "Unusual Gifts and Talents." In *Children with Exceptional Needs,* edited by M. Stephen Lilly. New York: Holt, Rinehart, and Winston, 1979.

This is an excellent general introductory chapter by one of the experts in the field of gifted education. Topics include characteristics of the gifted, strategies for working with them, and intervention options.

Strang, Ruth. "The Psychology of Gifted Children." *Journal of Teacher Education* 5:215–17 (September 1954).

This article comprises a brief discussion about gifted students and their needs as youngsters—for love, stimulation, different teaching techniques, etc. Some of their learning and emotional characteristics are also discussed.

————. "The Nature of Giftedness." In *Education for the Gifted*, Part 2 of *Fifty-Seventh Yearbook of the National Society for the Study of Education*, edited by Nelson B. Henry. Chicago: Univ. of Chicago Pr., 1958.

Strang provides an excellent compendium of characteristics of the gifted, with good explanations for each.

Suran, Bernard G., and Rizzo, Joseph V. *Special Children: An Integrative Approach*. Glenview, Ill.: Scott, Foresman, 1979. 532 pp.

Chapter 10, "Gifted Children" provides a good introduction to the topic.

Swassing, Raymond H. "Gifted and Talented Children." In *Exceptional Children: An Introductory Survey to Special Education*, edited by William L. Heward and Michael D. Orlansky. Columbus, Ohio: Charles E. Merrill, 1980.

Chapter 10 is a well-written introduction to the gifted.

Taylor, Calvin W. "Developing Creative Excellence in Students: The Neglected History-Making Ingredient Which Would Keep Our Nation from Being at Risk." *Gifted Child Quarterly* 28:106–9 (Summer 1984).

Taylor makes a strong case for fostering creativity in every field of endeavor. He draws heavily on the writing of Toynbee and Machado—but to good effect.

Treffinger, Donald J. "Research on Creativity." *Gifted Child Quarterly* 30:15–19 (Winter 1986).

Treffinger concludes that, although creativity has been of interest to researchers for thirty years—and progress has been made in our understanding of the nature, assessment, and nurture of creativity—it is still a field that offers many and varied opportunities for research and development. His discussion of the significant research is clear and cohesive.

Wall, W. D. "Highly Intelligent Children: The Psychology of the Gifted, Part 1." *Educational Research* 2: 101–10 (1960).

This article provides a good summary of many characteristics of gifted students, especially those "discovered" by Terman. Wall describes ways in which the culture a child grows up in influences development.

_____. "Highly Intelligent Children: The Psychology of the Gifted, Part 2." *Educational Research* 2: 207–17 (1960).

Wall discusses the dire need to train and guide the talents of highly intelligent children. Also, the need for creativity is discussed. The latter part relates different methods used to provide for the gifted—acceleration, enrichment, selective schools, etc.

Witty, Paul. "Who Are the Gifted?" In *Education for The Gifted*, Part 2 of *Fifty-Seventh Yearbook of the National Society for the Study of Education*, edited by Nelson B. Henry. Chicago: Univ. of Chicago Pr., 1958.

Witty describes the characteristics of the young child who is gifted in science, writing, or leadership.

Creativity and Giftedness

Carroll 1940. *See* Introduction

Carroll, James L., and Laming, Lester R. "Giftedness and Creativity: Recent Attempts at Definition: A Literature Review." *Gifted Child Quarterly* 18: 85–96 (Summer 1974).

This article focuses on research done between 1962 and 1971 in the United States. It includes two easy-to-use tables that summarize the research: "Criteria Used to Measure Giftedness" and "Characteristics Ascribed to Gifted Children."

Damm, Vernon J. "Creativity and Intelligence: Research Implications for Equal Emphasis in High School." *Exceptional Child* 36:565–69 (April 1970).

The author studied 208 high school students to determine the possible relationship between creativity, intelligence, and self-actualization. He found that students who obtained high scores on both intelligence and creativity were superior in self-actualization compared to those who were high on only one or the other. Damm suggests that the curriculum should develop creative and intellectual abilities.

Drews, Elizabeth Monroe. *Learning Together: How to Foster Creativity, Self-Fulfillment, and Social Awareness in Today's Students and Teachers.* Englewood Cliffs, N.J.: Prentice-Hall, 1972. 324 pp.

Chapter 4, "The Creative Intellectuals," provides an excellent characterization of those persons high in intellectual ability and also high in creative ability.

Frierson, Edward C. "The Gifted." In *Exceptional Children Research Review*, edited by G. Orville Johnson and Harriett D. Blank. Washington, D.C.: Council for Exceptional Children, 1968.

The chapter provides lengthy annotations on some of the significant research pertaining to the gifted conducted in the sixties. The
bulk of the chapter is devoted to creativity research.

Getzels, Jacob W., and Jackson, Philip W. "The Meaning of Giftedness: An Examination of an Expanding Concept." *Phi Delta Kappan*
40:75–78 (November 1958).

Getzels and Jackson write this article at the beginning of their famous study that resulted in the book *Creativity and Intelligence*. They
report some of their early findings comparing high IQ and high-
creativity children.

————. *Creativity and Intelligence*. New York: Wiley, 1962. 293 pp.

Getzels and Jackson describe their research regarding the relationship between creativity and intelligence. All the instruments developed for the research are included in the book.

Gowan, John C. "The Relationship between Creativity and Giftedness." *Gifted Child Quarterly* 15:239–43 (Winter 1971).

The author says the definition of giftedness should include the
phrase "has the potential to develop creativity." He also suggests
that the IQ cutoff score for giftedness should be dropped to 120,
since that seems to be the point below which there is high correlation
between intelligence and creativity, and above which not much correlation exists.

Karowe, Harris E. "Giftedness and Creativity." *Gifted Child Quarterly*
7:165–75 (Winter 1963).

Karowe analyzes and discusses current writings on giftedness and
creativity, concluding that there is a relationship between the two.
He believes that most educational systems stifle growth in creativity.
Especially deadly is the step-by-step progress required of students.

Mednick, Martha T., and Andrews, Frank M. "Creative Thinking and
Level of Intelligence." *Journal of Creative Behavior* 1:428–31 (Fall
1967).

The findings of this study did not support the idea that creativity
and intelligence are relatively independent processes among the
very bright but more closely related at lower levels of intelligence.

Milgam, Roberta M. "Creativity in Gifted Adolescents: A Review."
Journal for the Education of the Gifted 8:25–42 (Fall 1984).

This review focuses on the interplay between cognitive growth
and creative behavior during adolescence. Three issues are discussed: (1) evolution of creativity in adolescence; (2) important personality traits of gifted and creative youth; (3) creative behavior of
gifted youth.

Nichols, Robert C. "Parental Attitudes of Mothers of Intelligent Adolescents." *Child Development* 35:1041–1049 (December 1964).

The author reports on a study of mothers of National Merit scholarship finalists. He found that authoritarian child-rearing attitudes correlated positively with better grades and more favorable ratings by teachers and correlated negatively with originality and creativity in the students. Authors said "observed relations were quite small and reached significance only by virtue of the large sample" (1,200+).

Rekdal, C. K. "Hemispheric Lateralization, Cerebral Dominance, Conjugate Saccadic Behavior, and Their Use in Identifying the Creatively Gifted." *Gifted Child Quarterly* 23:101–8 (Spring 1979).

The author searched the literature regarding hemispheric lateralization, cerebral dominance, and conjugate saccadic behavior to find research that would help in identifying creatively gifted students. According to Rekdal, there is a plethora of information, but none of it can yet be used productively.

Sanderlin 1979. *See* Introduction

Taylor 1984. *See* Introduction

Torrance, E. Paul. "Problems of Highly Creative Children." *Gifted Child Quarterly* 5:31–34 (1961).

Problems that Torrance saw for the highly creative child were: sanctions against divergence, pressure from the less creative to conform, discouragement of independent learning and attempting difficult tasks, and fears that the student may not be well-rounded.

_____. "Unique Needs of the Creative Child and Adult." *The Gifted and Talented: Their Education and Development*, Part 1 of *Seventy-Eighth Yearbook of the National Society for the Study of Education*, edited by A. Harry Passow. Chicago: Univ. of Chicago Pr., 1979.

This article provides a persuasive case for identification of, and provision for, creative individuals.

_____. "Growing Up Creatively Gifted: A 22-Year Longitudinal Study." *Creative Child and Adult Quarterly* 5:148–58, 170 (Fall 1980).

The article includes several quite interesting case studies of students involved in Torrance's study. Torrance believes "that it is possible to predict, to a significant degree, adult creativity from the performances of children during the elementary school years." Mentors, teachers who value creativity, and having a future career image all make a significant difference in whether adult achievement is commensurate with creative ability.

Treffinger 1986. *See* Introduction

Wallach, Michael A., and Kogan, Nathan. "Creativity and Intelligence in Children's Thinking." *Trans-Action* 4:38–43 (January/February 1967).

This article is based on the research reported in the authors' book

Modes of Thinking in Young Children: A Study of the Creativity-Intelligence Distinction (1965). They contend that creativity and intelligence cannot be distinguished from each other.

Weisberg, Paul S., and Springer, Kyla J. "Environmental Factors in Creative Functions: A Study of Gifted Children." *Archives of Genetic Psychiatry* 5:554–64 (1961).

In their study of thirty-two gifted children and their families, the authors determined that certain family characteristics correlated with creative performance in children: expressiveness without domination; acceptance of regression; and parents who do not depend on each other, the marriage, or the family to reinforce their own individual status.

Witty, Paul, Conant, James B., and Strang, Ruth. *Creativity of Gifted and Talented Children.* New York: Teachers College Press, 1959. 51 pp.

This book comprises the texts of four speeches given at an American Educational Research Association meeting. Speech titles: "Identifying and Educating Gifted and Talented Children," "The Highly Creative Three Percent of the Population," "Developing Creative Powers of Gifted Children," and "Qualities in Teachers Which Appeal to Gifted Children."

Intellectual Characteristics

Alvino, James. "Do Gifted and Nongifted Children Learn Differently?" *Principal* 60:38–40 (May 1981).

Alvino encourages principals to integrate learning-style-preference information into their curricula for gifted and talented students.

Baker, Harry J. "Characteristics of Superior Learners and the Relative Merits of Programs of Enrichment and Acceleration for Them." In *Conference on Reading.* Vol. 9, *Classroom Techniques in Improving Reading.* Chicago: Univ. of Chicago Pr., 1949.

Baker says two groups of characteristics differentiate superior learners: quantitative differences in intelligence, and qualitative differences in intelligence (including learning by associative methods, generalization abilities, ability to do independent work, ability to excel physically if motivated, and unselfish, social viewpoint).

Baker, Philip D., and Bender, David R. *Library Media Programs and the Special Learner.* Hamden, Conn.: Library Professional Publications, 1981. 384 pp.

Chapter 4, "The Gifted and Talented," lists and discusses characteristics of the gifted that would concern a librarian. Since the library is often the place where the gifted student is sent, the authors urge librarians to recognize and seize the opportunity they have for teaching these students.

Benbow, Camilla P., and Stanley, Julian C. "Intellectually Talented Boys and Girls: Educational Profiles." *Gifted Child Quarterly* 26:82–88 (Spring 1982).

This article reports on questionnaires filled out by the 1976 cohort (873 students) in the Study of Mathematically Precocious Youth. Participants exhibited a strong liking for school and viewed their status in math as above average. However, only 11 percent of the boys and 6 percent of the girls had participated in any kind of special program related to their superior abilities. No important difference was found among students attending private, parochial, or public schools.

Boultinghouse, Ann. "What Is Your Style? A Learning Styles Inventory for Lower Elementary Students." *Roeper Review* 6:208–10 (April 1984).

Boultinghouse explains her instrument, "What Is Your Style?" which is intended for use with students in grades one through three. Students respond on a continuum of "like" to "dislike." Research support is discussed.

Carter, Kyle R., and Ormrod, Jeanne E. "Acquisition of Formal Operations by Intellectually Gifted Children." *Gifted Child Quarterly* 26:110–15 (Summer 1982).

Carter and Ormrod investigated the differences between gifted and normal children during the transition to and progress through the formal operations stage. Subjects were age ten through fifteen. In 125, IQ was 130 or more; in 98, IQ was 98 to 115. As measured by the Social Sciences Piagetian Inventory, the gifted group acquired formal operations by age thirteen, while the normal group had not acquired that stage by age fifteen.

Gallagher, J. J., and Lucito, L. J. "Intellectual Patterns of Gifted Compared with Average and Retarded." *Exceptional Children* 27:479–82, (1961).

The authors compared three groups of gifted students with three groups of retarded students and one average group. They determined that the gifted group and the retarded group had very different intellectual patterns: they were almost mirror images of each other. Even the "weaknesses" of the gifted were substantially above the strengths of the other two groups.

Goodenough 1956. *See* Introduction

Griggs, Shirley A., and Dunn, Rita S. "Selected Case Studies of the Learning Style Preferences of Gifted Students." *Gifted Child Quarterly* 28:115–19 (Summer 1984).

This article summarizes the research on learning styles of gifted and talented students and discusses selected case studies that illustrate these characteristics. The authors stress the need to assess and accept various learning styles.

Guilford, Arthur M., Scheuerle, Jane, and Shonburn, Susan. "Aspects of Language Development in the Gifted." *Gifted Child Quarterly* 25:159–63 (Fall 1981).

The authors tested eleven gifted preschoolers (age 4.1–4.11, IQ 140–160+) using four different language tests. They determined that, as a group, the gifted students did not know a better selection of rules for deep structure and transformation of language but that, in the comprehension and verbal production of language, they used such rules better than average children did.

Hallahan, Daniel P., and Kauffman, James M. *Exceptional Children: Introduction to Special Education.* Englewood Cliffs, N.J.: Prentice-Hall, 1982. 473 pp.

Chapter 9, "Giftedness," provides a good introduction to the field. Topics include misconceptions about the gifted, changes in definitions of giftedness, and a whole range of characteristics of the gifted—emotional, educational, occupational, social, etc.

Harty, Harold, and Beall, Dwight. "Reactive Curiosity of Gifted and Nongifted Elementary School Youngsters." *Roeper Review* 7:214–17 (April 1985).

This article reports on a study that looked for differences in reactive curiosity between gifted and nongifted and between genders in elementary school children. The authors did not find a significant difference between gifted and nongifted but thought that unidentified gifted students in the nongifted group might account for the unexpected result.

Hildreth 1938. *See* Introduction

Krueger, Mark L., ed. (Project director, National Student Symposium on the Education of the Gifted and Talented) *On Being Gifted.* New York: Walker and Co., 1978. 150 pp.

This book, written by twenty talented and gifted teenagers, provides a "life in the trenches" look at being gifted. Parents and bright students should read this book.

Powell, Philip M., and Haden, Tony. "The Intellectual and Psychosocial Nature of Extreme Giftedness." *Roeper Review* 6:131–33 (February 1984).

The authors compare the intellectual performance of the highly gifted with that of the moderately gifted and the average person in order to clarify the nature of extreme giftedness. A helpful chart that depicts this comparison is also presented.

Ricca, Judith. "Learning Styles and Preferred Instructional Strategies of Gifted Students." *Gifted Child Quarterly* 28:121–26 (Summer 1984).

Ricca examined the relationship between observed differences which are found with the Dunn, Dunn, and Price Learning Style Inventory and the Renzulli-Smith Learning Style Inventory. Both instruments reveal significant differences on several dimensions between gifted students' learning-style preferences and those of the general population.

Scruggs, Thomas E., and Cohn, Sanford J. "Learning Characteristics of Verbally Gifted Students." *Gifted Child Quarterly* 27:169–72 (Fall 1983).

This study uncovered no evidence that verbally gifted students learn in a manner qualitatively different from that of more typical students. The authors suggest that the strategies that facilitate verbal learning in the gifted also work for typical older subjects.

Strang 1954. *See* Introduction

Strang 1958. *See* Introduction

Terman, Lewis M., and DeVoss, James C. "The Educational Achievements of Gifted Children." In *Report of the Society's Committee on the Education of Gifted Children,* Part 1 of *Twenty-Third Yearbook of the National Society for the Study of Education,* edited by Guy M. Whipple. Bloomington, Ill.: Public School Publishing Co., 1924.

In this article the students in the Genetic Studies of Genius were evaluated in terms of the knowledge they possessed. Many were accelerated in school but their advancement was nowhere near their actual capability.

Wallach and Kogan 1967. *See* Creativity and Giftedness

Webb, Roger A. "Concrete and Formal Operations in Very Bright 6–11 Year Olds." *Human Development* 17:292–300 (1974).

This study found that there was an association between the acquisition of formal operations and IQ, but there did not seem to be any precocity associated with high IQs below age eleven.

Willerman, Lee, and Fiedler, Miriam Forster. "Infant Performance and Intellectual Precocity." *Child Development* 45:483–86 (1974).

The authors did a retrospective analysis of 100 white children (age four) whose IQ's were 140 or more. All were members of a group that had been administered the research version of the Bayley Scales of Mental and Motor Development at eight months. Results of analysis were that those children who were gifted could not be differentiated from the general population at eight months.

Witty 1958. *See* Introduction

Personality Characteristics

Bloom, Benjamin S. "Affective Outcomes of School Learning." *Phi Delta Kappan* 59:193–98 (November 1977).

Bloom discusses the "manifest" curriculum and the "latent" curriculum. The latter, being based on the interactions of persons within the school, is taught uniquely to each child and thus learned differently in each case. The article explores the effect of the two curricula on the child's self-concept.

Cashdan, Sheldon and Welsh, G. S. "Personality Correlates of Creative Potential in Talented High School Students." *Journal of Personality* 34:445–55 (September 1966).

The authors studied 311 adolescents who participated in the North Carolina's Governor's School for talented juniors and seniors. They found that bright students who were also highly creative were independent, nonconforming, sought change, and had open and active interpersonal relationships. Bright students with low creativity were somewhat compulsive with a strong desire to achieve.

Coleman, J. Michael, and Fults, Betty Ann. "Self-Concept and the Gifted Classroom: The Role of Social Comparisons." *Gifted Child Quarterly* 26:116–20 (Summer 1982).

The Piers-Harris Children's Self-Concept Scale was administered to 180 subjects three times in eighteen months. Ninety had been selected for participation in a gifted program, and ninety had been nominated but not selected; all had an IQ of 126 or more and were in grades four to six. Gifted students who participated one day a week in a program for the gifted used that class as their reference group. As a result, their self-concept went down, and it remained lower than in students not selected to participate. But when segregated sixth graders became seventh graders, they were "mainstreamed," and their self-concepts went back up.

Franks, Beth, and Dolan, Lawrence. "Affective Characteristics of Gifted Children: Educational Implications." *Gifted Child Quarterly* 26:172–78 (Fall 1982).

The authors discuss three affective characteristics as they relate to gifted children: persistence, independence, and self-concept. They see a need for investigation into at least two questions: (1) Do some children conform to the image of the gifted child and thus become labeled *gifted*? (2) Does being labeled *gifted* affect a child's behavior? Giftedness must be viewed as "a process of becoming rather than an exercise in being."

Jacobs, Jon C. "Rorschach Studies Reveal Possible Misinterpretations of Personality Traits of the Gifted." *Gifted Child Quarterly* 15:195–200 (Fall 1971).

This study suggests that gifted students are generally advanced in personality development. For example, they show greater productive capacity, greater motivation and interest, and greater self-reliance. Some of these personality characteristics may elicit negative reactions from others. For example, some adults disapprove of children who do not rely on adults for approval or who see shades of gray rather than absolute badness or goodness.

Karamessinis, Nicholas P. "Personality and Perceptions of the Gifted." *G/C/T* 13:11–13 (May–June 1980).

Karamessinis reviews twenty-eight studies and articles that examine the personality and perceptions of the gifted. He concluded that there is a need for a consistent definition of *gifted, creative,* and *talented;* that the gifted have better personality adjustment, greater emotional security, higher self-esteem, and more popularity with peers; and that these qualities persist as the gifted grow older.

Killion, Janice. "Personality Characteristics of Intellectually Gifted Secondary Students." *Roeper Review* 5:39–42 (February 1983).

Killion compared sixty-three intellectually gifted students with sixty students selected at random. The study showed no significant effect on personality characteristics from either SES or giftedness. She did find sex-related differences. Teachers are urged to help girls overcome their difficulty in making decisions based on their own needs, and especially to intervene so that the gifted girls can reach their potential.

Krueger 1978. *See* Intellectual Characteristics

Lightfoot, Georgia. *Personality Characteristics of Bright and Dull Children,* Contributions to Education Bulletin no. 969. New York: Columbia University Teachers College, 1951. 136 pp.

The author conducted a study at the Speyer School for the gifted to determine whether there are personality differences between bright and dull students. The results from all six techniques used to measure personality showed that the gifted rated more favorably in these six categories: achievement (overcoming obstacles), affiliation (friendship), autonomy, cognizance, creativity, and dominance. Five of the tests favored the gifted in appearance, protectiveness (empathy), and recognition (seeking distinction).

Lundy, James R. "The Psychological Needs of the Gifted." *Roeper Review* 1:5–8 (December 1978).

Lundy says that the psychological needs of the gifted must be recognized and satisfactorily managed if they are to achieve self-actualization. He uses Maslow's hierarchy of needs to describe the five psychological needs of the gifted: to adaptably manage the anger response, to adaptably manage the helplessness response, to adaptably manage the xenophobic response, to achieve and sustain high self-esteem, and to effectively play.

Porter, Rutherford B. "A Comparative Investigation of the Personality of Sixth-Grade Gifted Children and a Norm Group of Children." *Journal of Educational Research* 58:132–34 (November 1964).

The author studied sixty-six gifted children who had just completed sixth grade and found, for example, that the gifted are warm, sociable, intelligent, conscientious, and self-sufficient.

Tidwell, Romeria. "A Psycho-Educational Profile of 1,593 Gifted High School Students." *Gifted Child Quarterly* 24:63–68 (Spring 1980).

Tidwell describes her research involving nearly 1,600 tenth-grade students with a mean IQ of 137. Six instruments were used to gather the information necessary to profile the mentally gifted student. The students were found to have a positive self-concept, high locus of control, fairly high goals, and a balance of activities (school, work, etc.), but they viewed themselves as less than popular with peers.

Werblo, Dorothy, and Torrance, E. Paul. "Experiences in Historical Research and Changes in Self-Evaluations of Gifted Children." *Exceptional Children* 33:137–41 (November 1966).

The authors discuss a study done to determine whether high-achieving gifted students who underestimate their abilities in such areas as reading, vocabulary, and curiosity will make a more realistic judgment after being instructed in systematic research (histography). Results were positive.

Emotional Characteristics

Alexander, Patricia A. "Gifted and Nongifted Students' Perceptions of Intelligence." *Gifted Child Quarterly* 29:137–43 (Summer 1985).

Written reports from 127 gifted and 116 nongifted students (ages twelve to seventeen) were gathered. The questionnaire had nineteen questions designed to elicit students' concepts of intelligence. (What is it? What behavioral signs are there?) The results are summarized in six categories: definitions, visible signs, self-assessment, qualities of intelligence, heredity and environment, constancy and malleability.

Barbe 1967. *See* Introduction

Barbe and Renzulli 1975. *See* Introduction

Bloom 1977. *See* Personality Characteristics

Cashdan and Welsh 1966. *See* Personality Characteristics

Colangelo, Nick, and Pfleger, Lawrence R. "Academic Self-Concept of Gifted High School Students," *Roeper Review* 1:10–11 (October 1978).

This article summarizes a study by the authors in which students who succeeded academically indicated a positive self-concept about their academic abilities. The authors conclude that recognition and reward of school performance plays a role in building self-concept in high-ability students.

Coleman and Fults 1982. *See* Personality Characteristics

Culbertson, Susan. "How Does It Feel to Be Gifted?" *G/C/T* 33:47–49 (May/June 1984).

Culbertson shares the responses of her sophomore gifted students who were asked: (1) to define giftedness; (2) how the gifted should be educated; and (3) how it feels to be gifted.

Davis, Hilarie B., and Connell, James P. "The Effect of Aptitude and Achievement Status on the Self-System." *Gifted Child Quarterly* 29:131–36 (Summer 1985).

The purpose of the study reported herein was to compare four groups (gifted achievers and underachievers and average achievers and underachievers) to investigate the independent and joint effects of aptitude and achievement on domain-specific assessments of self-esteem processes in upper elementary school children. Results indicate that "higher aptitude is associated with realistically higher proportions of competence, greater understanding of what controls success and failure in school, less anxiety concerning school performance, and a more intrinsic motivational orientation in the classroom."

Dean, Raymond S. "Effects of Self-Concept on Learning with Gifted Children." *Journal of Educational Research* 70:315–18 (July/August 1977).

A study of forty-eight gifted seventh and eighth graders indicated that self-concept in the gifted is related to learning across tasks. Also, gifted students with high self-concepts employed different learning strategies for the tasks than did students with low self-concepts.

Drews 1972. *See* Creativity and Giftedness

Exum, Herbert A., and Colangelo, Nick. "Enhancing Self-Concept with Gifted Black Students." *Roeper Review* 1:5–6 (March 1979).

Gifted black students have self-concept needs that differ from those of other blacks and other gifted students; the article gives seven reasons why. The authors also provide a sample cognitive curriculum for gifted adolescents that addresses black students' self-concept needs.

Feldhusen, John F., and Klausmeier, Herbert J. "Anxiety, Intelligence and Achievement in Children of Low, Average and High Intelligence." *Child Development* 33:403–9 (1962).

The authors studied anxiety levels of 120 fifth-grade students—40 of low ability, 40 average students, and 40 gifted students (IQ 120 or more). Scores on an anxiety scale showed a higher anxiety level for the lower and average students than for the gifted. The authors suggested, "Superior mental ability may make it possible for a child to assess more adequately the real and present danger in any current threatening object, situation, or person. Thus, his fears may be specific and ascertainable and unrelated to variations in an already high mental ability."

Feldhusen, John F., and Kolloff, Margaret Britton. "Me: A Self-Concept Scale for Gifted Students." *Perceptual and Motor Skills* 53:319–23 (August 1981).

The article describes research conducted to construct a short self-concept scale for gifted students. A copy of the scale is included. Preliminary research indicates promising reliability and possibly good validity.

Franks and Dolan 1982. *See* Personality Characteristics

Gallagher 1975. *See* Introduction

Harty, Harold, Adkins, Darlene M., and Hungate, Eugene W. "Exploring Self-Concept and Locus of Control of Students in Two Recognized Approaches to Elementary School Gifted Education." *Roeper Review* 7:88–91 (November 1984).

The authors' purpose in designing their study was to describe the status of students' self-concept and locus of control, dependent upon the type of program in which they were served and as compared to nongifted youth. In terms of self-concept, no significant differences were found. Students in self-contained gifted classes were found to have significantly greater internal locus of control than students in the other two groups.

Hollingworth, Leta S., and Rust, Metta M. "Application of the Bernreuter Inventory of Personality to Highly Intelligent Adolescents." *Journal of Psychology* 4:287–93 (October 1937).

The study discussed here used the Bernreuter Inventory of Personality in adolescents who as young children had tested at 135–190. Results were compared to those for college students in general. The gifted were much less neurotic, much more self-sufficient, and much less submissive.

Jacobs 1971. *See* Personality Characteristics

Janos, Paul M., Fung, Helen C., and Robinson, Nancy M. "Self-Concept, Self-Esteem, and Peer Relations among Gifted Children Who Feel 'Different.'" *Gifted Child Quarterly* 29:78–82 (Spring 1985).

The authors asked high-IQ elementary-age children, "Do you feel different from other children?" and "If so, why?" Forty percent of the children answered in the affirmative, and half of these children stated that they were superior in some way to their age-mates. Self-esteem scores for the group who saw themselves as different were significantly lower than those of the other children.

Kaiser, Charles F., and Berndt, David J. "Predictors of Loneliness in the Gifted Adolescent." *Gifted Child Quarterly* 29:74–77 (Spring 1985).

The authors investigated the loneliness of gifted adolescents who attended the Governor's School in South Carolina. They were particularly interested in determining which facets of depression were most related to loneliness and in the relationship between increased stress, depression, anger, and loneliness in gifted adolescents. Their results correlate loneliness with depression and suggest that loneliness is characterized by frustrated dependency and recognition needs, alienation, and cognition of insufficient love, understanding, and social support. The findings have implications for counselors and teachers of the gifted.

Karamessinis 1980. *See* Personality Characteristics

Kelly, Kevin R., and Colangelo, Nicholas. "Academic and Social Self-Concepts of Gifted, General, and Special Students." *Exceptional Children* 50:551–54 (April 1984).

This study indicates that gifted students hold significantly higher academic and social self-concepts than their nongifted age-mates. The authors note overall "health" in both academic and social self-concept among their gifted subjects.

Ketcham, Bunty, and Snyder, Robert T. "Self-Attitudes of the Intellectually and Socially Advantaged Student: A Normative Study of the Piers-Harris Children's Self-Concept Scale." *Psychological Report* 40:111–16 (February 1977).

The authors administered the Piers-Harris Self-Concept Scale to 148 children in grades two to four. The children of superior intelligence and strong socioeconomic status scored higher on the self-concept scale than students from the normative population. Of the bright students, even those having academic problems generally showed good to excellent self-concepts. Their school was found to be very supportive of students and seemed to build and sustain strong self-concepts.

Killion 1983. *See* Personality Characteristics

Krueger 1978. *See* Intellectual Characteristics

Lightfoot, Georgia. 1951. *See* Personality Characteristics

Love, Harold D. *Educating Exceptional Children in Regular Classrooms.* Springfield, Ill.: Charles C. Thomas, 1972. 235 pp.

Chapter 3, "The Gifted Child in the Regular Classroom," an excellent essay, provides several fascinating case studies, describes general characteristics of the gifted, and lists the national trends, issues, and influences affecting them.

Lucito, Leonard J. "Independent-Conformity Behavior as a Function of Intellect: Bright and Dull Children." *Exceptional Children* 31:5–13 (September 1964).

This study compared fifty-five bright students (mean IQ 126) with fifty-one dull students (mean IQ 77). As a group, the bright students were significantly less conforming in their decisions than the dull children.

Lundy 1978. *See* Personality Characteristics

Maddux, Cleborne D. "Self-Concept and Social Distance in Gifted Children." *Gifted Child Quarterly* 26:77–81 (Spring 1982).

Maddux reports on a study of fifth- and sixth-grade gifted students, comparing those who had been identified and placed in a gifted program with those not identified and placed. Overall results indicated no real difference in self-concept and peer acceptance, whether gifted pupils were segregated or integrated.

Monks, Franz J., and Ferguson, Tamera J. "Gifted Adolescents: An Analysis of Their Psychological Development." *Journal of Youth and Adolescence* 12:1–18 (1983).

The authors provide a model for viewing giftedness in adolescence. It considers changes in biological, cognitive, and social states, and the interaction between these states and six behavior patterns: attachment, friendship, sexuality, achievement, autonomy, identity. The authors review the literature regarding gifted adolescents as they proceed through this framework. They conclude that gifted adolescents compare favorably with their age-mates—but one must also remember that giftedness is embedded in a number of personal and situational factors.

Nichols and Davis 1964. *See* Introduction

Porter, Rutherford B. "A Comparative Investigation of the Personality of Sixth-Grade Gifted Children and a Norm Group of Children." *Journal of Educational Research* 58:132–34 (November 1964).

The author studied sixty-six gifted children who had just completed sixth grade and found, for example, that the gifted were warm, sociable, intelligent, conscientious, self-sufficient.

Ritchie, Allan C., Bernard, Janine, and Shertzer, Bruce E. "A Comparison of Academically Talented Children and Academically Average Children on Interpersonal Sensitivity." *Gifted Child Quarterly* 26:105–9 (Summer 1982).

The authors compared seventeen academically talented ten-year-olds (Iowa Test of Basic Skills ninetieth to ninety-ninth percentile), fifteen academically average ten-year-olds, and twenty academically average twelve-year-olds (fortieth to sixtieth percentile). The children were shown videotaped vignettes of interactions between two adults or two children or an adult and a child. A five-item forced-choice questionnaire was administered after each vignette to measure subjects' interpersonal sensitivity. The study did not find the gifted to be any more sensitive than the average.

Ross, Allen, and Parker, Marolyn. "Academic and Social Self Concepts of the Academically Gifted." *Exceptional Children* 47:6–10 (September 1980).

A study of 147 fifth- through eighth-grade gifted students indicated that gifted students have significantly lower social than academic self-concept.

Schetky, Diane H. "The Emotional and Social Development of the Gifted Child." *G/C/T* 18:2–4 (May/June 1981).

The author, a child psychiatrist, addressed her comments to parents, encouraging them to know the assets and liabilities of their gifted child and the possible concomitant social problems. She then discussed several of these and reminded parents that, first and foremost, the gifted child is a child.

Scholwinski, Ed, and Reynolds, Cecil R. "Dimensions of Anxiety among High IQ Children." *Gifted Child Quarterly* 29:125–30 (Summer 1985).

The purpose of the study reported herein was to delineate the underlying factors and patterns of responses for high IQ children on the Revised Children's Manifest Anxiety Scale (using factor analysis) and to determine the comparability of the test across groups of gifted and nongifted children. Five factors emerged. The authors conclude that the results indicate that high IQ children demonstrate lower levels of anxiety than peers with lower IQ.

Sisk, Dorothy A. "Relationship between Self-Concept and Creativity: Theory into Practice." *Gifted Child Quarterly* 16:229–34 (Fall 1972).

Forty-five students with IQ's between 132 and 148, identified as low creative by their teachers and examiners, were involved in a ten-week program of classes (three hours each Saturday) engineered for success. A conscious effort was made to praise children, to listen to them, and to "lift the tops from their cages," thus allowing their creativity to flourish. Results indicated that the children became more aware of their strengths and self-worth through small groups emphasizing the individual.

Smith, D. C. *Personal and Social Adjustment of Gifted Adolescents.* Washington, D.C.: Council for Exceptional Children Research Monograph no. 4, 1962. 65 pp.

Smith describes his study, the purpose of which was to evaluate the relative personal and social adjustment of adolescents of superior and average intelligence. The only remarkable distinction between the gifted group and the average group was the prevalence of Independent-Dominant interpersonal traits among the gifted: they were more dominant, forceful, independent, and competitive.

Sonntag, Joyce. "Sensitivity Training with Gifted Children." *Gifted Child Quarterly* 13:51–57 (Spring 1969).

A forty-eight-hour sensitivity training session was done with nine- and ten-year-olds at a summer workshop for the gifted. Even in the short time provided, the participants became involved, discussed experiences at a feeling level, and appeared to grow in the ability to respond directly and honestly to each other.

Strang 1958. *See* Introduction

Suran and Rizzo 1979. *See* Introduction

Tidwell 1980. *See* Personality Characteristics

_____. "A Psycho-educational Profile of Gifted Minority Group Students Identified without Reliance on Aptitude Tests." *Journal of Non-White Concerns in Personnel and Guidance* 9: 77–86 (January 1981).

Tidwell describes her study which had as its purpose to provide psycho-educational information about four racial groups of youth identified for the Mentally Gifted Minor Program in California. Information relating to students' self-concepts, locus of control, and attitudes toward school is presented.

Torrance, E. Paul. "Identity: The Gifted Child's Major Problem." *Gifted Child Quarterly* 15:147–55 (Fall 1971).

Torrance says the most precious truth for which the gifted child searches is a personal identity—and teachers must recognize this need. The article gives case studies of six gifted persons who were in search of self.

Werblo and Torrance 1966. *See* Personality Characteristics

Witteck, M. J. "Reflections of the Gifted by the Gifted on the Gifted." *Gifted Child Quarterly* 17:250–53 (Winter 1973).

Twenty open-ended statements were given to three classes of fifth-, sixth-, and seventh-grade gifted children. Responses to some of the statements are summarized. Overall, Witteck concluded that the children in this sample were highly motivated, recognized and were proud of their special status in school, competed for school honors, and were quite sensitive to parental pressure. He also notes low self-concept.

Sociability Characteristics

Abroms, Kippy, and Collins, Emily. "Precocious Social Development: A Theoretical Approach." *Southern Journal of Educational Research* 11:91–94 (Spring 1977).

The article contends that there is a need for research in the area of social giftedness. It also attempts to validate the developmental evolution of social behavior and to suggest that when very young children are advanced in this area, social precocity is indicated.

Austin, Ann Berghout, and Draper, Dianne C. "Peer Relationships of the Academically Gifted: A Review." *Gifted Child Quarterly* 25:129–33 (Summer 1981).

The authors reviewed twenty-one sources regarding the peer relationships of the academically gifted and concluded that gifted preschoolers develop cognitive facility with social knowledge earlier than average. Elementary school gifted children tend to be more popular than average children. Adolescent gifted students usually lose status socially.

Baker 1949. *See* Intellectual Characteristics

Barbe 1967. *See* Introduction

Barnett, Lynn A., and Fiscella, Joan. "A Child by Any Other Name . . . A Comparison of the Playfulness of Gifted and Nongifted Children." *Gifted Child Quarterly* 29:61–66 (Spring 1985).

The authors investigated the differences in play of children of above average intelligence and those of average intelligence, focusing on the individual child's internal playful disposition. The authors observed a variety of play activities and interactions in order to note social, cognitive, and physical play styles. The prototype of the gifted child that emerged was a physically active, socially advanced one. Play interactions with other children were actively solicited and play was more creative, unusual, and imaginative than that of other children.

Boston 1979. *See* Introduction

Brode, Diane S. "Group Dynamics with Gifted Adolescents." *G/C/T* 15:60–62 (November/December 1980).

Brode suggests that the way to help gifted youth deal effectively with the special problems of adolescence is to involve them in group-dynamics training in middle school. The training should involve experiences in setting goals, communication, decision making, coping with conflicts, developing effective interpersonal relationships.

Freeman, Joan. *Gifted Children: Their Identification and Development in a Social Context*. Baltimore: University Park Pr., 1979. 294 pp.

The author was the director of the Gulbenkian Research Project on Gifted Children. Her book describes gifted children in their social context. Their characteristics are discussed along with a description of the project and other research regarding gifted children in society.

Gallagher, J. J. "Social Status of Children Related to Intelligence, Propinquity, and Social Perception." *Elementary School Journal* 58:225–31 (1958).

Gallagher did a study of 355 children in grades two to five to determine whether intelligence, propinquity, and social perception were related to social choice (popularity). He found that bright children were more popular with children of all intellectual levels, that "best" friends often lived close together, and that bright children do not choose only other bright children as their friends.

Gallagher 1975. *See* Introduction

Grace, H. A., and Booth, Nancy L. "Is the Gifted Child a Social Isolate?" *Peabody Journal of Education* 35:195–96 (1958).

The authors tested 294 children in grades one through six. The subjects were the five most gifted and the five least gifted in each class. The most gifted were found to be among the best liked.

Hollingworth, Leta S. "Playmates for the Gifted Child." *Child Study* 8:103–4 (December 1930).

Hollingworth briefly discusses the problems that highly gifted students may have in their search for playmates.

_____. "The Child of Very Superior Intelligence as a Special Problem in Social Adjustment." *Mental Hygiene* 15:3–16 (January 1931).

This wonderful article deals with highly gifted children's social adjustment problems. Hollingworth believes that the problems are not really the child's but are society's problem in understanding and responding to the gifted child.

Lehman, Elyse Brauch, and Erdwins, Carol J. "The Social and Emotional Adjustment of Young, Intellectually Gifted Children." *Gifted Child Quarterly* 25:134–37 (Summer 1981).

This article describes a study that compared a group of gifted third grade students (IQ 141–165) with two groups of average children (third grade and sixth grade). The gifted children were judged to be quite well adjusted: they scored higher than their chronological age-mates on adjustment scales and even higher than their mental age-mates on some of the social adjustment subtests. Overall, a positive picture emerged. The authors concluded that the gifted differed more from their chronological age-mates than from their mental age-mates.

Ludwig, Gretchen, and Cullinan, Douglas. "Behavior Problems of Gifted and Nongifted Elementary School Girls and Boys." *Gifted Child Quarterly* 28:37–39 (Winter 1984).

This article reports on a study that compared the personal and social adjustment of gifted elementary students and that of their non-gifted peers. Their adjustment was measured with the Behavior Problem Checklist (a teacher rating scale). Results indicate that gifted elementary students show fewer behavior problems than their nongifted classmates.

Miller, Maurice, Richey, D. Dean, and Lammers, Carla A. "Analysis of Gifted Students' Attitudes toward the Handicapped." *Journal for Special Education* 19:14-21 (Spring 1983).

The authors obtained some strikingly consistent results for the gifted (across grade levels and sexes). The conclusions drawn are very telling and have implications for using gifted students in mainstreaming situations. They say, "Generally, gifted students have not been afforded opportunities to apply their particular strengths—social skills, problem-solving, creativity, and goal-oriented behavior—to the task of integrating handicapped students into regular classrooms."

O'Shea, Harriet E. "Friendship and the Intellectually Gifted Child." *Exceptional Child* 26:327-35 (February 1960).

O'Shea makes a case for not forcing gifted children to make friends with children of the same chronological age—calls that a bankrupt concept.

Roedell, Wendy C. "Vulnerabilities of Highly Gifted Children." *Roeper Review* 6:127-30 (February 1984).

Roedell says that children with unusually advanced intellectual development are uniquely vulnerable. She discusses their vulnerabilities in terms of the possible uneven development, perfectionism, adult expectations, intense sensitivity, self-definition, alienation, inappropriate environments, and role conflict. She says that awareness of these vulnerabilities is not enough; committed support systems must be developed.

Roedell et al. 1980. *See* Introduction

Sheldon, Paul M. "Isolation as a Characteristic of Highly Gifted Children." *Journal of Educational Sociology* 32:215-21 (January 1959).

Sheldon reports on a study of twenty-eight highly intelligent children (IQ 170 or more). The researchers wanted to determine the degrees of self-perceived isolation and outsider-perceived isolation. They concluded that high intelligence does not cause or lead to isolation. The earlier perceived isolation may stem from family or role dynamics.

Silverman 1982. *See* Introduction

Silverstein, Samuel. "How Snobbish Are the Gifted in Regular Classes?" *Exceptional Child* 28:323-24 (February 1962).

This article is based on the author's dissertation study, which investigated the social acceptance and friendship ratings of 350 fifth graders. The gifted were found to be no more snobbish than other children in the heterogeneously grouped classes.

Swassing 1980. *See* Introduction

Moral and Ethical Characteristics

Boehm, Leonore. "The Development of Conscience: A Comparison of American Children of Different Mental and Socioeconomic Levels." *Child Development* 33:575–90 (September 1962).

Using a story-interview technique and protocol analysis, researchers tested 237 average and above-average six- to nine-year-olds for their moral judgment and conscience development. The author concluded that gifted children mature earlier in moral judgment and that the upper-class children mature earlier than the working-class. There was a greater difference between the responses of the gifted and average children of the upper class than between gifted and average of the working class.

Colangelo, Nicholas, and Parker, Marolyn. "Value Differences among Gifted Adolescents." *Counseling and Values* 26:35–41 (October 1981).

This article reports on a study of fifty-eight ninth through twelfth graders in the GIFTS program (Guidance Institute for Talented Students) at the University of Wisconsin–Madison. All filled out a values survey. Results showed that gifted boys and girls hold similar value patterns—for example, boys don't value ambition or logic more than girls. Results hold implications for guidance counselors and teachers serving the gifted.

Diessner, Rhett. "The Relationship between Cognitive Abilities and Moral Development in Intellectual Gifted Children." *G/C/T* Number 28:15–17 (May/June 1983).

Diessner discusses Kohlberg's stages of moral development and their relationship to the intellectual levels of gifted youth. He concludes that high intelligence does not guarantee high moral development, but it is a prerequisite for mature moral reasoning.

Drews 1972. *See* Creativity and Giftedness

Krause 1962. *See* Introduction

Maccoby, Eleanor E. *Social Development: Psychological Growth and the Parent-Child Relationship.* New York: Harcourt Brace Jovanovich, 1980. 436 pp.

This clearly written book is intended for use by college students and parents. It deals with the family's contribution to the socialization process whereby children acquire the habits, values, goals, and knowledge that will enable them to function satisfactorily as members of society. Chapters 8 and 9 deal with the moral development of students.

Roedell et al. 1980. *See* Introduction

Santayana 1947. *See* Introduction

Schab, Fred. "Deceit among the Gifted." *Journal for the Education of the Gifted* 3:129–32 (1980).

The author found that many more bright students (A grade average) in 1979 were pessimistic regarding others' moral behavior and the honesty of both professionals and semiprofessionals than were those bright students surveyed in 1969.

Sisk, Dorothy A. "Caring and Sharing: Moral Development of Gifted Students." *Elementary School Journal* 82:221–29 (January 1982).

Sisk defines moral reasoning as a function of the intellect and discusses the level of moral development gifted children tend to possess. She encourages group interactions to help the gifted clarify their values and attitudes and to firm up their moral development.

Tan-Willman, C., and Gutteridge, D. "Creative Thinking and Moral Reasoning of Academically Gifted Secondary School Adolescents." *Gifted Child Quarterly* 25:149–53 (Fall 1981).

The authors studied 115 students enrolled in an academically gifted high school program. The subjects' creative-thinking and moral-reasoning abilities were tested. Their creativity was highly developed, drawing on their superior academic competencies, creative thinking abilities, and high socioeconomic background. Their moral reasoning could be considered underdeveloped, although it was higher than in the general population. This finding suggests that moral reasoning is an area that needs immediate attention and encouragement.

Family Characteristics

Barbe, Walter B. "A Study of the Family Background of the Gifted." *Journal of Educational Psychology* 47:302–9 (May 1956).

This article reports on a study of 456 gifted subjects (IQ 120 or more) who were graduates of the Cleveland Major Works Program. It found that subjects tended to be upper middle class, firstborn or only children, and reared by their own parents, over 50 percent of whom were foreign-born.

Benbow, Camilla P., and Stanley, Julian C. "Intellectually Talented Students: Family Profiles." *Gifted Child Quarterly* 24:119–22 (Summer 1980).

Using the questionnaire filled out by the 1976 cohort (873 students) of the Study of Mathematically Precocious Youth, the authors constructed a family profile of these gifted youth. They came from larger-than-average families (1.7+ children); their parents were living; their fathers had an average educational attainment almost at the college graduate level; their mothers had some college education; their fathers had high occupational status.

Cicirelli, Victor G. "Sibling Constellation, Creativity, I.Q. and Academic Achievement." *Child Development* 38:481–90 (June 1967).

The author did a study of 641 sixth-grade students in a suburban school. Results were: (1) there was no relation between family size and the ability and achievement of the students; (2) birth order was not related to ability or achievement; (3) there was some relationship between sibling constellation factors and ability and achievement.

Cox 1977. *See* Introduction

Frierson, Edward C. "Upper and Lower Status Gifted Children: A Study of Differences." *Exceptional Children* 32:83–89 (October 1965).

Frierson reports on comparisons made between gifted and average students of upper and lower socioeconomic background. Measures were taken of personality, interests, activities, creativity, height, and weight. The data clearly indicated that several of the differences between the groups of gifted children were associated with differences in their socioeconomic status (e.g., size). It was also clear that some of the differences between the gifted and average existed regardless of the socioeconomic background (e.g., personality).

Gallagher 1975. *See* Introduction

Goddard 1928. *See* Introduction

Maslow, Abraham. *Motivation and Personality*, 2d ed. New York: Harper & Row, 1954. 369 pp.

One of the classic reference books in the field of personality.

McGehee, William, and Lewis, W. Drayton. "The Socio-Economic Status of the Homes of Mentally Superior and Retarded Children and the Occupational Rank of their Parents." *Pedagogical Seminary and Journal of Genetic Psychology* 60:375–80 (June 1942).

This study indicated that knowledge of parents' occupation and/or socioeconomic status is a "very precarious index of the child's intellect."

Nichols and Davis 1964. *See* Introduction

Pulvino, Charles J., and Lupton, Paul E. "Superior Students: Family Size, Birth Order and Intellectual Ability." *Gifted Child Quarterly* 22:212–16 (Summer 1978).

A study of 380 gifted and talented high school students led to the conclusion that, although it is so far impossible to specify exactly what is happening, it seems for intellectual skill development, it is an advantage to be firstborn in a small family.

Roedell et al. 1980. *See* Introduction

Shade, Barbara J. "Social-Psychological Characteristics of Achieving Black Children." *Negro Educational Review* 29:80–86 (April 1978).

The author reviews research and concludes that "the most significant variance between black achievers and nonachievers is the behavior of the parents or guardians."

Zajonc, R. B. "Family Configuration and Intelligence." *Science* 192:227–36 (1976).

Zajonc explains his confluence model of intelligence—that each family member's intellectual environment is determined by the number of other family members and their respective intelligence. He illustrates this model and supports it with research, concluding that intellectual performance increases with decreasing family size and other factors.

Physical Characteristics

Barbe 1955. *See* Introduction

Hollingworth, Leta S., and Taylor, Grace A. "Size and Strength of Children Who Test above 135 I.Q." In *Report of the Society's Committee on the Education of Gifted Children,* Part 1 of *Twenty-Third Yearbook of the National Society for the Study of Education,* edited by Guy M. Whipple. Bloomington, Ill.: Public School Publishing Co., 1924.

These authors compare their own findings with others' tests of average and feeble-minded children. The gifted tend to be superior physically.

Laycock, F., and Caylor, J. S. "Physiques of Gifted Children and Their Less Gifted Siblings." *Child Development* 35:63–74 (1964).

The authors wanted to test Goodenough's proposal that possibly the reason gifted students tended to be larger and heavier than average was because they came from superior homes. Their results (from a comparison of eighty-one gifted students with their less intelligent siblings) did not show that gifted students' physiques were significantly bigger.

Summary

Hallahan and Kauffman 1982. *See* Intellectual Characteristics

CHAPTER *3*

Identification of the Gifted

Sue J.: IQ = 130

Mark W.: ''My son talked when he was ten months old, walked at eight months, and began reading at thirty-seven months. He belongs in a gifted program.''

Cedrick T.: Achievement test composite score = eightieth percentile

Cory T.: ''Cory has been an outstanding student all year. She is always helpful, gets her work in on time, and keeps her desk extremely neat and tidy.''

Sandra S.: IQ = 115

Are these students gifted? Based on the limited amount of information given, there is no way of knowing for sure. However, depending on the school district, any or all of these students may be considered gifted. And students who have been identified as gifted in one district may move to a neighboring district that uses different criteria for identification—and may no longer be classified as gifted. Does this mean that the student is no longer gifted after the move? Or does it mean that the district has lost its opportunity to help an able student to reach full potential? The latter seems more plausible.

At this juncture, probably no subject within gifted education is as controversial or as likely to spark debate as the question of identification. It is ironic that identification is the crux of gifted education but is still nebulous.

What makes the question of identification of the gifted so sensitive? Carter and Kontos explain that while

> many in the field of gifted education treat the concept of gifted-ness as something tangible, a trait that is easily observed, on the contrary, giftedness is a highly abstract concept, or con-struct, created by scholars to summarize the common charac-teristics of a select group of people. Unfortunately, there is wide disagreement over the set of characteristics that define the construct of giftedness. Yet individuals use the same term to refer to a different set of characteristics. This practice has led to much confusion about the nature and identification of gifted-ness.(1982,17)

As we begin to look at the sensitive issue of the identification of the gifted, three tenets must be recognized:

1. The definition of gifted varies with the dominant culture (High & Udall 1983; Kirschenbaum 1983; Renzulli 1978).
2. One's definition of giftedness determines the criteria one uses to identify gifted students.
3. The identification process must "be intricately tied to the pro-gram and curriculum model to be implemented" (Kirschenbaum 1983, 6).

As the first principle states, definitions of giftedness have always had a social referent. Those abilities that are valued by the society are the ones identified and developed (High & Udall 1983). For example, American society values the ability to communicate verbally; so stu-dents who are verbally adept are often identified as gifted, and their skills in writing and oral communication are nurtured by the schools. And since the dominant culture in the United States is middle class, the definitions of giftedness that prevail in the schools are based on middle-class values.

Not only will cultural values drive the criteria used to identify gifted students (Kontos, Carter, Ormrod, & Cooney 1983), but

> the way one "views" giftedness . . . gives direction to the types of instruments and procedures used for selecting stu-dents for supplemental services . . . . (Renzulli & Smith 1980, 4)

For example, if the definition for giftedness used by a school district is "having an IQ of 130 or more," then that district will use the scores from tests that have been administered to groups or individually and will provide services for those students scoring 130 or higher. As an alternative, if a school district uses Witty's (1958, 62) definition of a gifted person as "one who shows consistently remarkable performance in any worthwhile line of endeavor," then the district will determine for itself those areas it considers worthwhile and will then look at manifestations of remarkability—for example, excellent art work, achievement in mathematics, or demonstrated leadership.

Once the students have been identified, the third principle comes into play: the identification process is closely linked with the program. The question that arises, however, is what Cox and Daniel (1983) call the "chicken or the egg" syndrome: Should students be identified who will best fit into the currently established program—or should students be identified because of their remarkable promise and then have a program tailored to their needs? To most effectively utilize scarce resources such as expertise and money, school districts may tend to identify those able students who will fit into an established program. However, school districts also have a responsibility to educate students to their potential. Therefore, it seems that the most desirable tack is to identify students who require special programming in order to reach their exceptional potential—and then make the necessary arrangements so that they get the appropriate programming. To reverse this configuration would be just as absurd as setting up a program for learning disabled students that only provides instruction through the auditory mode and then either serving only those learning-disabled students who can learn auditorially or forcing all the identified learning-disabled students to be in an auditory program.

The ultimate goal of special education programs for gifted students should be to enable these students to perform at their capacity. In order to attain this goal, programs must be tailored to the students being served.

To adequately identify those students with the greatest potential for future high level intellectual and creative contributions, a four-part procedure is recommended: nomination, screening, selection, and validation. Such a process is necessary in order to be relatively sure that those able students in need of special instruction will be identified to receive it.

While we do adhere to the tenet that every child is unique and deserves an appropriate education, we do not espouse the notion that every child is gifted and needs to be served in a differentiated gifted program. We do believe that many gifted and talented youngsters are excluded from the education they need and deserve because of narrow identification measures (e.g., exclusive use of IQ tests). Our recommended identification procedure is designed to reduce the possibility of excluding the children and youth who are cognitively and creatively gifted.

Westcott and Woodward (1981) say that many gifted students are not identified because of the inability or unwillingness of school districts to ask the right question: How might we identify every gifted student in our district? This approach is much more inclusive than to ask, Which children comprise the top 3 to 5 percent of our school-age population? An inclusive identification process is more time consuming, costly, and involved than simply administering a group IQ test and calling those who score above a certain cutoff "gifted."

The analogy we will use for identification is that the process should be like a sifter, which is shaped thus: the nomination portion of the process gets students into the sifter; the screening portion moves students down to the filter of the sifter; the selection portion involves getting through the screen; and the validation portion is looking at the products made by the gifted students who got through the sifter.

NOMINATION

Tittle (1979) recommends "casting a wide net" in identification and programming so that as many able students get "caught" and as few able students escape as possible. Inherent in casting this wide net is a community mind set that allows for the nomination of any student. Every student served by a school district can be considered eligible for the gifted program—regardless of ethnicity, age, socioeconomic status, physical (dis)ability, learning (dis)ability, or any other limiting factor. To get as many potentially gifted students into the "sifter" as possible, nominations must be sought from both traditional and nontraditional sources.

For example, traditionally, teachers are asked to nominate those students whom they see as potentially gifted. Unfortunately, without training specifically designed to aid teachers in identifying gifted students, their nominations often miss the mark completely (Gear 1976). In fact, with and without training, parents are more effective at identifying their children as gifted than are teachers (Hanson 1984; Jacobs 1971). "Teacher pleasers" tend to get nominated, while highly creative students and underachieving students are rarely nominated (Hall 1983). However, with training, teachers can become effective "talent scouts" (DeHaan 1959; Gear 1978).

Training can be provided in a myriad of ways, but the goal should always be to give teachers both knowledge and experience in identifying potentially gifted children and youth. Therefore, training will necessarily involve two components: (1) information regarding characteristics and behaviors exhibited by the able (see chapter 2) and (2) practice using that information.

The information component is necessary to help eliminate stereotypes that often impede correct identification (House 1979; Whitmore 1982) and to deliver information that will serve as validation for the hunches teachers often have concerning latent talent. Whitmore says that

> Recognizing something for what it is requires accurate knowledge of the characteristics distinguishing that particular object. (1982, 275)

So, if teachers are to be called upon, as they should be, to nominate students as gifted and talented, they must be given the knowledge to recognize that talent. When teachers are given proper information, they are much more accurate in their identification. Borland (1978) reports that although many studies have shown teachers to be poor judges of giftedness, these studies shared a common problem: the teachers were asked to make global judgments of student potential rather than being asked to rate children on specific behavioral traits.

Once teachers know the characteristics of able students, their training should allow them the opportunity to put that knowledge to work. Classroom visits, videotapes, slides, verbal descriptions—all can be opportunities to practice identifying the able. It is essential that those responsible for the practicum present opportunities to identify gifted students other than upper-middle-class whites. One of the biggest hurdles for teachers and others who serve as "talent scouts" is the idea that gifted students can be found among minority, learning-disabled, and physically handicapped populations (Sarnecky & Michaud 1979; Stefanich & Schnur 1979; Whiting 1980).

In order to elicit nominations from less traditional sources, training programs should also be offered members of the community other than teachers. People who come in regular contact with children and youth—parents, day-care operators, summer-camp counselors, youth directors—should also serve as "eyes" for the school district in nominating potentially able youngsters. The training programs could be made available for PTA meetings, service clubs (Lions, Rotary, Elks, etc.), professional organizations (League of Women Voters, Association of Business and Professional Women, American Bar Association, etc.), parks and recreation programs—the list is long. People who attend such gatherings are involved and knowledgeable enough to have a vested interest in developing talent among the youth of today.

A presentation about recognizing able youth should provide the sponsoring school district's address, phone number, and the name of a contact person. In addition, forms requesting information may be distributed (see Fig. 3.1; see also Nasca 1979).

Such forms should also be readily available in all schools and school administration offices. The attitude of the educational system must be that locating all the gifted and talented students in a school district requires a team of "spotters"—all working together.

Nominations can also be generated in ways other than referrals. Because most school districts have student data computerized, it should be fairly easy to assemble the names of students who score above a certain score on achievement or aptitude tests or who have earned at or above a particular grade point. In addition, students who receive awards or hold office should go into the sifter (e.g., an Eagle Scout, the president of the sixth grade). Two other sources of talent recognition involve students. Both peer nominations and self-nominations should be solicited. Young people are amazingly cognizant regarding their own abilities and the abilities of their peers—and their insights are more likely to be free of some of the stereotypes held by adults.

Students who have been nominated have *something* going for them—or they would not have been recognized as different. Therefore, they should be allowed the opportunity to be carefully considered for determination of giftedness.

SCREENING

Once a large group of students has been nominated as potentially gifted or talented, the next step is to compile data for use in determining which would benefit most from services. This step is the most involved of the four steps of the identification process. It requires the most time and effort, but if it is done correctly, then those students who must have differentiated instruction to reach their extraordinary potential will be identified and will be eligible to receive that instruction.

Giftedness must be probed for in as many ways as it is manifested. *An IQ test is a limited probe* (Sternberg 1985; Thorndike in White 1977; Washburn 1977). Walter Lippman expressed his concern thus:

> Because the results are expressed in numbers, it is easy to make the mistake of thinking that the intelligence test is a measure

Name of student _____

Address of student (if known) _____

_____

School (if known) _____

Capacity in which you know this student _____

_____

Reasons why you believe this student could benefit from special
programming to develop his or her potential (please be as specific as
possible)

_____

_____

_____

_____

Your name _____

Address _____

Phone _____

Fig. 3.1. Nomination of Potentially Gifted Person

like a foot rule or a pair of scales. . . . But "intelligence" is not
an abstraction like length and weight; it is an exceedingly complicated notion which nobody has as yet succeeded in defining. . . . If the impression takes root that these tests really measure intelligence, that they constitute a sort of last judgment on
the child's capacity, then it would be a thousand times better if
all the intelligence testers and their questionnaires were sunk
without warning in the Sargasso Sea. (1920 in Houts 1977)

Houts (1977, 15) posits that "a careful look at the existing (IQ) tests
should assure most everyone that such instruments cannot possibly
measure anything so wonderfully variegated as human ability." Both

educators and the lay public must divorce themselves from the notion that giftedness and measured high IQ are two completely intersecting sets. People with high measured IQs are gifted—but many people without high measured IQ are also gifted.

A number of reasons can be given for poor performance on an IQ test. Nasca (1979, 39) believes that many gifted students fail to demonstrate their unusual intellectual ability on group-administered IQ tests for one of the following three reasons:

1. They have a greater store of information than the population on which the test was normed and can often justify more than one correct answer. As a result, they may become quite frustrated with multiple-choice formats.
2. Intellectually gifted students are often more interested in processes and causes than with "fill-in-the-blank" type questions and see little significance in low-level cognitive questions, so they treat these tests with indifference.
3. Intellectually gifted students may be bored with traditional knowledge-oriented courses of study and may fail to accumulate the standard set of knowledge sampled on popular group-administered tests.

Padilla and Garza posit that IQ tests do not measure intelligence—actual mental capability—at all, but rather measure a number of extraneous variables:

1. The skill of the test administrator.
2. The child's ability to perform under pressure.
3. The child's motivation to identify success or failure in the testing situation.
4. The values underlying many of the test items, which are outside the life experiences of some children. (1977, 129–130)

Two other groups of students also may not perform well on group-administered IQ tests: the culturally different and the learning or physically handicapped. Students who come from a culture or ethnic group other than that of the mainstream tend to score lower on traditional tests—not because of lower intellectual capacity but because of the testing instruments, which many have found to be culturally biased (Adler 1967; Witty 1978). For example, the Mexican-American Education Study Project of the U.S. Commission on Civil Rights found that Mexican-American children were twice as likely to be in classes for slow learners in Texas and two-and-a-half times as likely in California, primarily due to low scores on IQ tests (Padilla & Garza 1977). The possibility of cultural bias must be taken into consideration wherever students' scores are assessed during the screening process. Likewise, students who are learning disabled or have a physical disability are less likely to have their intellectual ability accurately assessed by group-administered IQ tests (Elkind 1973).

The point of this discussion is not that different standards be established for students who do not fall into the mainstream—either culturally, ethnically, or physically. The point is that alternative means may have to be used in order to ensure that able students are not excluded from gifted programming just because of poor performance on an instrument that may provide a less-than-valid indicator of their ability. Group-administered IQ tests yield scores that are but one possible indicator of giftedness. A student who obtains a WISC-R score of 145 should "sift through" to selection for a gifted program. But a student who obtains an IQ score of 110 should not immediately be eliminated from consideration. "Intelligence is among the most elusive of concepts" (Sternberg 1985, 3) and must therefore be sought with diligence and creativity. Multiple criteria should be used in screening the students who have been nominated (Alvino & Wieler 1979). Every effort must be made to find outstanding ability—and sometimes it is dormant, thereby requiring some patience to find. Delisle and Renzulli warn that

> as surely as a sophisticated metal detector will locate metallic debris with greater accuracy than a magnet on a stick, both will, in their turn, bypass some shards of tin or copper. Likewise, despite the greatest variety of objective and nominative measures, some children who have high abilities will elude detection. (1982, 89)

It may be helpful to think about the screening process as a series of opportunities given to a student to demonstrate giftedness. This is much more productive than viewing it as a series of hurdles that a student must scale. Bernal (1983, in Cox & Daniel 1983) cautions against allowing multiple criteria to become multiple hurdles. Cox and Daniel go on to say,

> Care must be taken . . . lest the use of multiple measures become progressive screening and so exclude children who don't score in the superior range on several tests. (1983, 55)

What multiple criteria should be used—that is, in what ways should gifted students be given the opportunity to manifest their abilities? Ten criteria may be used.

1. *Intelligence tests.* IQ tests are one source of information regarding ability. However, individually administered tests are much more accurate than those administered to groups (Hunter & Lowe 1978), especially for young children (Hanson 1984). Because many factors besides intelligence affect test scores, *no absolute cutoff score should be set,* regardless of whether the test is group or individually administered.

   Sternberg, one of the nation's foremost experts on intelligence, states that

   > There is much more to intellectual giftedness than high IQ. Conventional intelligence tests measure some of the structures and processes underlying intelligence as an "internal trait," but their measurement is incomplete and, in some instances, misleading. (1986, 147)

   He also expressed dissatisfaction with current IQ tests, stating that "intelligence exists in a world that is much broader and more complex than are the testing situations and tasks of most psychologists" (1985, 30).

2. *Achievement tests.* According to the *Dictionary of Reading and Related Terms,* an achievement test measures "knowledge of or proficiency in something learned or taught." Students who are quite proficient in one or more particular areas *may* have that ability reflected in their score on an achievement test.

3. *Aptitude tests.* The *Dictionary of Reading and Related Terms* defines an aptitude test as one "used to predict future performance in a given activity." Major educational efforts, such as the Johns Hopkins University Study of Mathematically Precocious Youth, use aptitude tests as their primary screening instruments. They have found aptitude tests to be valid predictors of success in their accelerated programs. It may be especially useful to use off-level tests, because highly able students may reach the ceiling of on-level tests, and a lineup of scores at the ninety-ninth percentile does not give a true picture of a student's abilities or gaps (Feldhusen, Baska, & Womble 1981).

4. *Tests of creative abilities.* E. Paul Torrance and others have designed a number of tests that purport to measure students' creative abilities. Since many highly creative students are missed by more conventional instruments (Kirschenbaum 1983), the Torrance Tests of Creative Thinking and portions of the Structure of Intellect instru-

ment should be administered to students who have been nominated and who may not have performed well on other measures.

5. *Behavioral checklists.* The most well-known and well-constructed behavioral checklist comprises the Scales for Rating Behavioral Characteristics of Superior Students (Renzulli 1983; Renzulli, Hartman, & Callahan 1971). Teachers and other observers can learn to use the checklist very effectively with a moderate amount of in-service training. Extensive use of this instrument is recommended (see also Delisle & Renzulli 1982).

6. *Anecdotal records.* Teachers and other observers (principals, counselors, parents) can be trained to keep anecdotal records. Although some would argue that such a measure is too subjective, we agree with Renzulli, who says,

> The issue boils down to a simple and yet very important question: How much of a trade-off are we willing to make on the objective/subjective continuum in order to allow recognition of a broader spectrum of human abilities? If some degree of subjectivity cannot be tolerated, then our definition of giftedness and the resulting programs will logically be limited to abilities that can only be measured by objective tests. (1978, 181)

Renzulli & Smith (1977) also recommend a case study approach to identifying able students.

7. *Interviews.* Another subjective means to use in determining a student's giftedness is a personal interview. Important information about the student's background, abilities, and commitment to learning can be gleaned by a skilled interviewer. The information may be unobtainable through any other channel, or it may support other indications of potential.

8. *Products and performance.* Student products and performance may be defined as any tangible or visible evidence that the student has unusual ability—for example, sculpture, painting, drawing, musical performance, or written compositions. Such products should whenever possible be judged by an expert in their field.

9. *Leadership.* Some children are natural leaders. Their leadership ability is evident from the time they begin to organize children in the neighborhood. Such students can benefit from a program that will develop this ability even further.

10. *Grades:* Grades may be indicative of above-average ability but should be viewed with a heavy emphasis on *may*, since there are many ways to obtain good grades without having unusual ability.

Obviously, no student will be screened in all ten ways, but neither should a student be eliminated because of average or poor performance on only one or two. Every student in the nominated group was mentioned for some reason—someone or some criteria indicated their uniqueness. Each student should therefore be given the chance to justify provision of differentiated education.

It is imperative that school district personnel keep flexibility in mind during the screening process. Since giftedness and talent can be manifested in different ways, a rigid, inflexible testing program is inappropriate. The psychological testing department or the special education department of a school should have a battery of instruments available for use. Although Brown is referring to testing of sensorially or physically impaired students, his statement can be generalized:

> It is better to select the best instrument for the assessment of a specific child rather than utilizing an instrument because of convenience or some other invalid reason. (1984, 22)

SELECTION

During the screening step, nominated students are observed, tested, interviewed, and otherwise assessed. The selection step determines which students belong in a program for the gifted and which do not. These decisions should be made by a team at the school-building level, comprising the building principal and/or assistant principal for instruction, the classroom teacher of the gifted, the school counselor, a parent whose child has been in the gifted program but is no longer attending the school, and at least one regular classroom teacher.

The committee members must be clear on the school's definition of giftedness and possible options, and they must reach agreement on exactly what their task is: (1) Are they to select students for a one-day-per-week pullout program? (2) Are they to select students to attend special schools for the highly able? (3) Are they to select students who will receive attention from specially trained teachers within the regular classroom? (4) Are they to select students to be part of a special talent pool? (Renzulli & Smith 1980). Because the purpose affects the selection process, it must be articulated clearly. Members of the committee must also have a *vision* of what gifted education is, what it can be, and what difference it can and must make in the lives of highly able children and youth.

All group members should have copies of the information gathered during the screening stage. Prior to evaluating any of the student profiles, the group members should spend time iterating the criteria that each believes should warrant "certifying" a student for the gifted program. Settling differences ahead of time will prevent some later haggling. It might even behoove the group to go through several mock profiles before starting on the actual ones.

Next, the actual student profiles should be assessed. Groups may decide that they want to rank nominees, or sort them into "yes," "no," and "maybe" piles, or use one of the matrix systems currently in use. Realistically, there will be little or no question as to the placement of some students. When this is the case, no time should be spent in discussion. On the other hand, other students will have uneven profiles or meet criteria thought important by some committee members but not by others. When this happens, time should be spent weighing the student's potential and need for a special program. Lynn Fox, who has been involved with the Johns Hopkins Study of Mathematically Precocious Youth and has therefore had a great deal of experience in locating talent, recognizes problems inherent in making judgments about students:

> Any problem of classification or selection requires that a value judgement be made about the problems of false positives and false negatives. In the case of the academically talented, it might be wise to risk identifying students as gifted when they are not and give them the opportunities for special or individualized programs rather than to err by overlooking many talented students who are bored, frustrated, and unchallenged in their classes. (1981, 1109)

Even if a mistake is made, selection is not set in stone, and improper placement can be remedied.

VALIDATION

The term *validate* implies proving and confirming. The validation step of identification involves proving the validity of or confirming the decision to provide a student with differentiated education. As we said at the beginning of this chapter, validation is looking for proof in the product.

Who is involved in the validation step of identification? The gifted program teacher, classroom teachers, parents, and building administrators should all have a part. What part each will play depends on the size of the building, the size of the program, the type of program, and its level (elementary, middle, or secondary). A system should be established to invite written comments, products, test scores, and other evidence that students are—or are not—benefitting from their instruction and experiences in a gifted program. If the school has established an atmosphere of collegiality and team spirit coupled with the desire to provide the best education for every student, teachers and administrators will be watchful for evidence.

Students who are selected do not have their place in a special program guaranteed for life. If an error is made in selection, or if funding for special educational services is cut, reassessment can be planned. All four steps in the identification process are ongoing; the school calendar should *not* read: August 20–September 20, NOMINATION; September 20–October 10, SCREENING; October 11–20, SELECTION; May 1–30 VALIDATION. The entire process is dynamic—new names should appear and be solicited for nomination year-round; screening should be continuous, as students are nominated; selection committees may establish regular monthly meetings to keep selections current; and the validation process should be ongoing as the program and students are constantly evaluated.

Serving the gifted begins with identification. It is a process that requires personnel, financial resources, and time. However, the investment is vital in order to reap the greatest benefit from our investment in the future through our youth.

SELECTED BIBLIOGRAPHY

Achey-Cutts, Patricia, and Garvin, Karen. "Identifying the Gifted: A Step-By-Step Procedure." *G/C/T* 27:16–17 (March/April 1983).
    The authors briefly explain the three basic steps of identification: nomination, screening, and selection.
Adler, Manfred. "A Study of the Effects of Ethnic Origin on Giftedness." *Gifted Child Quarterly* 7:98–101 (Autumn 1963).
    The author found that children of Jewish descent were overrepresented among the gifted in the Cleveland Major Works Program. He posits that the Jewish culture places a high value on giftedness, education, and achievement.
_____. "Reported Incidence of Giftedness among Ethnic Groups." *Exceptional Children* 34:101–5 (October 1967).
    Adler reviewed some of the major studies of giftedness and intelligence testing among ethnic groups. He drew several conclusions and summed up his research by saying, "There has been little evidence that one ethnic or racial group is superior to another with respect to superior intellectual potential. In light of this, the answer to

the uneven distribution of giftedness will have to be sought else-where. Some of the factors behind these differences may be the na-ture of our current intelligence tests, language facility, differences in cultural value systems and background, socioeconomic class, physi-cal and psychological environment, schooling, and perhaps others still not identified.''

Alvino, James, McDonnel, Rebecca C., and Richert, Susanne. ''Na-tional Survey of Identification Practices in Gifted and Talented Edu-cation.'' *Exceptional Children* 48:124–32 (October 1981).

Results of the authors' national survey are presented. They con-clude that ''the state of the art of identification of gifted/talented youth is in some disarray'' (for example, tests and instruments are used incorrectly).

Alvino, James, Renzulli, Joseph, and Smith, Linda. ''The Devil's Ad-vocate: The Ins and Outs of Revolving Door.'' *Journal for the Educa-tion of the Gifted* 4:8–14, 67–73 (Fall 1980).

Alvino interviewed Renzulli and Smith concerning their Revolv-ing Door Identification and Programming Model. Their comments provide clarification on numerous points brought up in their other articles. This article should be read after one is familiar with at least two or three other pieces on the Revolving Door Model.

Alvino, James, and Wieler, Jerome. ''How Standardized Testing Fails to Identify the Gifted and What Teachers Can Do About It.'' *Phi Delta Kappan* 61:106–9 (October 1979).

The authors say that, while abolishing standardized testing is not necessarily desirable, one should be ''certain that significant steps be taken to safeguard the gifted from the discrimination they suffer when testing methodologies and instruments are not useful in iden-tifying their talents.''

Baum, Susan, and Kirschenbaum, Robert. ''Recognizing Special Tal-ents in Learning Disabled Students.'' *Teaching Exceptional Children* 16:92–98 (Winter 1984).

The authors ask and answer the question, How can a child learn and not learn at the same time? They present examples of students who are both learning disabled and extraordinarily talented in one or more areas.

Bernal, Ernest M., Jr. ''Gifted Mexican American Children: An Ethnoscientific Perspective.'' *California Journal of Educational Research* 25:261–73 (November 1974).

The author studied giftedness as perceived by Mexican-Americans. He found that they see intelligence plus ''verve'' or ''style'' as necessary for giftedness, along with extraordinary aware-ness, sensitivity, maturity, and independence. This research is an important first step toward appropriately identifying gifted Mexican-American children.

Birch, Jack W. "Is Any Identification Procedure Necessary?" *Gifted Child Quarterly* 28:157–61 (Fall 1984).

Birch recommends replacing the traditional "identification to placement" paradigm with the "assess to educate" model. He provides a strong rationale.

Borland, James. "Teacher Identification of the Gifted: A New Look." *Journal for the Education of the Gifted* 2:22–32 (September 1978).

The author describes his investigation of whether teachers can identify gifted children through the use of a behavioral rating scale. He obtained significant, moderate, positive correlations between teacher ratings and IQ, and the ratings were both stable and efficient.

Brown, Scott W. "The Use of WISC-R Subtest Scatter in the Identification of Intellectually Handicapped Children: An Inappropriate Task?" *Roeper Review* 7:20–23 (September 1984).

Brown says the WISC-R should not be used to determine giftedness among the handicapped population. He supports his contentions.

Bruch, Catherine B. "Modification of Procedures for Identification of the Disadvantaged Gifted." *Gifted Child Quarterly* 15:267–72 (Winter 1973).

Bruch describes characteristics that can be used to recognize disadvantaged black students as gifted, based on a modified interpretation of the Stanford-Binet, using the SOI (Structure of Intellect) method.

Callahan, Carolyn M. "Myth: There Must Be "Winners" and "Losers" in Identification and Programming." *Gifted Child Quarterly* 26:17–19 (Winter 1982).

This interesting article raises several pertinent points. Callahan says, "the key issue is not whether a child is gifted or not gifted. Those labels are useful to us only in the sense that they *a*) create an awareness that there exists a population of students whose exceptional abilities differentiate them from the rest of the student population and *b*) suggest some characteristics which we should attend to in planning educational programs for those children."

Carter, Kyle R., and Kontos, Susan. "An Application of Cognitive-Development Theory to the Identification of Gifted Children." *Roeper Review* 5:17–20 (November 1982).

The authors have conducted research based on the relationship between Piaget's theory of cognitive development and gifted children's cognitive development. They believe that when children reach the end of the concrete operational stage (at age eight to ten), it is possible to distinguish between gifted and nongifted.

Chambers, Jack A., Barron, Frank, and Sprecher, Jerry W. "Identifying Gifted Mexican-American Students." *Gifted Child Quarterly* 24:123–28 (Summer 1980).

The authors report on their study which examined a method for identifying gifted Mexican-American children and tried to determine its advantages over the method currently in use across the country. A teacher ranking form was used in combination with product evaluation. Students were also tested using several "culturally fair" instruments.

Chen, Jocelyn, and Goon, Suzanne W. "Recognition of the Gifted from among Disadvantaged Asian Children." *Gifted Child Quarterly* 20:157–64 (Summer 1976).

The authors report on their study, which focused on determining the number of gifted and potentially gifted low-socioeconomic-status Asian children, describing their characteristics, describing certain classroom activities, and analyzing factors important in identifying gifted children from disadvantaged Asian backgrounds.

Clarizio, Harvey F., and Mehrens, William A. "Psychometric Limitations of Guilford's Structure-of-Intellect Model for Identification and Programming of the Gifted." *Gifted Child Quarterly* 29:113–20 (Summer 1985).

In a clear and thorough discussion, the authors raise some questions regarding the SOI (Structure of Intellect) concept, and the tests based on this model. A response to this article follows on p. 121.

Coleman, Laurence J. "An Unsolved Mystery: Interpreting Grade Scores or How Come My Seven Year Old Scored at the Sixth Grade Level and She Can't Do Fourth Grade Work?" *G/C/T* 28:24–27 (May/ June 1983).

The author states that his purpose in writing the article is to explain what grade equivalent scores mean and do not mean. He does so in very clear, understandable language.

Cox, Joseph A. "Suggested Instruments for the Identification of the Preschool and Kindergarten Disadvantaged Gifted." *Southern Journal of Educational Research* 8:198–208 (Winter 1974).

Cox lists instruments that can be successfully used for identifying gifted preschool and kindergarten children. The instruments are grouped into four categories: spatial relations, memory, convergent production, and classification.

Cox, June, and Daniel, Neil. "Identification." *G/C/T* 30:54–61 (November/December 1983).

The authors focus on identification of youngsters with special problems and from special populations. They provide anecdotes and examples to illustrate the need for appropriate identification and programming.

Cunningham, Claude H., Thompson, Bruce, Alston, Herbert L., and Wakefield, James A., Jr. "Use of S.O.I. Abilities for Prediction." *Gifted Child Quarterly* 22:506–12 (Winter 1978).

The authors conducted a study that provides some preliminary results concerning the value of the SOI (Structure of Intellect) test— for identifying gifted children and for predicting teacher perception of the gifted. The study indicates that the SOI Learning Abilities Test can be useful for predicting certain teacher perceptions and, to the extent that the teachers' perceptions of identification effectiveness are assumed valid, the study also tentatively indicates that Meeker's test provides useful identification information.

Davis, Betty W. "Identifying the Gifted Child in the Average Classroom." *Peabody Journal of Education* 41:28–32 (July 1963).

Davis cites a number of research studies regarding characteristics of the gifted. She stresses that gifted children need to be identified and served.

DeHaan, Robert T. "Identifying Gifted Children." *School Review* 65:41–48 (March 1957).

DeHaan outlines a program for the identification of gifted children.

————. "Identification of the Gifted." *Education* 80:135–38 (November 1959).

Although somewhat dated, DeHaan's article provides encouragement for the teacher as "talent scout."

DeLeon, Josie. "Cognitive Style Difference and the Underrepresentation of Mexican-Americans in Programs for the Gifted." *Journal for the Education of the Gifted* 6:167–77 (Spring 1983).

The author provides information concerning cognitive styles and the effect they may have on being identified as gifted. The majority of the article deals with field-dependence and field-independence, especially in terms of the tendency of Mexican-American children to be field-independent.

Delisle, James R., Reis, Sally M., and Gubbins, E. Jean. "The Revolving Door Identification and Programming Model." *Exceptional Children* 48:152–56 (October 1981).

The Revolving Door Identification and Programming Model is based on the "conception of giftedness as a clustering of above average abilities, creativity, and task commitment brought to bear upon specific topic areas." This article describes the model's use as it was implemented in Torrington, Connecticut.

Delisle, James R., and Renzulli, Joseph S. "The Revolving Door Identification and Programming Model: Correlates of Creative Production." *Gifted Child Quarterly* 26:89–95 (Spring 1982).

The authors report on their study employing the Revolving Door
Identification and Programming Model in ten school districts
(grades 1–8, total N = 1,121). The implications they see are: (1) A
high rank in class, while an effective predictor of resource-room involvement, "misses" a substantial proportion of students who function effectively on an independent basis, despite their less-than-
superior academic achievement. (2) Class rank, while discriminating
among students who "revolve in" to a resource room, does not differentiate between pupils who complete attempted products and
those who fail to complete products. (3) Academic self-concept appears to play an important role in a child's decision to pursue a topic
of interest, and also in the child's likelihood to complete attempted
projects. (4) Bright children tend to "take credit" for their academic
successes while delegating to others, fate, or "bad luck" a substantial portion of school failure.

Dorhout, Albert. "Identifying Musically Gifted Children." *Journal for
the Education of the Gifted* 5:56–66 (Winter 1982).

Dorhout says that a delay in maturation can mask a child's true
musical talents because a lack of psychomotor coordination may preclude the ability to demonstrate a high degree of sensitivity to sound
and mature insights into the meanings of that sound. It is therefore
necessary to use a multifaceted approach in identifying musically
gifted children. Dorhout makes specific suggestions concerning instruments to use.

Elkind, Joel. "The Gifted Child with Learning Disabilities." *Gifted
Child Quarterly* 17:96–97, 115 (Summer 1973).

This is a good introductory article on the subject.

Elman, Linda, Blixt, Sonya, and Sawicki, Robert. "The Development
of Cutoff Scores on a WISC-R in the Multidimensional Assessment
of Gifted Children." *Psychology in the Schools* 18:426–28 (October
1981).

The authors found that the Vocabulary-Block Design dyad of the
WISC-R could be useful (within limits) for predicting the full-scale
IQ of some children. This finding may be especially useful since administering an entire individual intelligence test takes thirty to
ninety minutes.

Engin, Ann W. "An Analysis of Supplementary Subtests and Their Influence on Total WISC Scores of High Achieving Students." *Journal
of Psychology* 88:121–25 (September 1974).

The author found that for high-achieving students, certain subtests actually depress overall IQ scores. These findings have implications for psychometricians administering the WISC, for admissions personnel at private schools, and for persons making selections for gifted programs based on WISC scores.

Feldhusen, John F., Asher, J. William, and Hoover, Steven M. "Problems in the Identification of Giftedness, Talent, or Ability." *Gifted Child Quarterly* 28:149–51 (Fall 1984).

The authors state that a sound identification process includes five major steps: (1) defining program goals and types of gifted youth to be served; (2) nomination procedures; (3) assessment procedures; (4) individual differentiation; (5) validation of the identification process. The authors go through each of these steps and discuss problems that may be encountered.

Feldhusen, John F., Baska, Leland K., and Womble, Stephen. "Using Standard Scores to Synthesize Data in Identifying the Gifted." *Journal for the Education of the Gifted* 4:177–86 (Spring 1981).

The authors' purpose in the article is to demonstrate a statistical system for determining student selection for gifted programs. They explain the weaknesses in several of the current methods and then clearly defend their system and demonstrate how to use standard scores.

Ford, Barbara. "Student Attitudes toward Special Programming and Identification." *Gifted Child Quarterly* 22:489–97 (Winter 1978).

Ford reports on a survey she conducted of 500 middle-grade children who had been identified and placed in special programs for the gifted. From her analysis, she concluded that: (1) most gifted or talented youth are aware of their identification as such and know why they are placed in special programs; (2) most appreciate being in special programs as long as placement does not lead to conflict with regular teachers or their friends (neither of which happens very often); (3) most have noted indifferent attitudes on the part of family, friends, and teachers regarding their work in special programs.

Fox, Lynn H. "Identification of the Academically Able." *American Psychologist* 36:1103–1111 (October 1981).

Fox makes a strong case for use of aptitude tests in the identification and placement of academically gifted students.

Gagne, Francoys. "Giftedness and Talent: Reexamining a Reexamination of the Definitions." *Gifted Child Quarterly* 29:103–12 (Summer 1985).

The author attempts to demonstrate that the concepts of giftedness and talent are not synonymous and, indeed, encompass completely separate ideas. She reviews relevant literature and examines Renzulli's and Cohn's models and definitions. According to Gagne, "giftedness corresponds to competence which is distinctly above average in one or more domains of ability" and "talent refers to performance which is distinctly above average in one or more fields of human performance." A fascinating model is presented.

Garrett, John E., and Brazil, Nettye. "Categories Used for Identification and Education of Exceptional Children." *Exceptional Children* 45:291–92 (January 1979).

Surveys were sent to each of the fifty states and the District of Columbia to determine if there is any movement away from the traditional categories used for the estimation, identification, and education of exceptional children. The results are presented in tabular form, and it is clear that gifted/talented is one of the least-used categories.

Gay, Joyce E. "A Proposed Plan for Identifying Black Gifted Children." *Gifted Child Quarterly* 22:353–60 (Fall 1978).

Gay presents a plan for identifying gifted black children. A very useful table is included which compares behavioral characteristics from the literature on giftedness with the manifestations of these characteristics in black children.

Gear, Gayle Haywood. "Accuracy of Teacher Judgment in Identifying Intellectually Gifted Children: A Review of the Literature." *Gifted Child Quarterly* 20:478–89 (Winter 1976).

Gear reviews the literature dealing with teachers' accuracy in the identification of gifted children. Her review indicates that teachers are relatively poor at this task.

————. "Effects of Training on Teachers' Accuracy in the Identification of Gifted Children." *Gifted Child Quarterly* 22:90–97 (Spring 1978).

The author's study indicated that teachers who were appropriately instructed in referral of gifted children performed this task significantly more effectively and equally efficiently as teachers in the control group, who were given no instruction.

Gourley, Theodore J. "Do We Identify or Reject the Gifted Students?" *Gifted Child Quarterly* 28:188–90 (Fall 1984).

Gourley asks, "Are gifted children identified or do they meet selection criteria?" He describes four "self-selection" or "tryout" procedures: magnet schools that allow self-enrollment, the convocation model, Olympics of the Mind, ROGATE: SAT testing of seventh graders.

Gowan, John C. "Issues in the Education of Disadvantaged Gifted Students." *Gifted Child Quarterly* 12:115–19 (Summer 1968).

Gowan answers questions concerning the disadvantaged gifted: (1) How do we tell if these children are really gifted? (2) How do they differ from other gifted children? (3) When should intervention most efficaciously take place? (4) What can intervention do?

Granzin, Kent L., and Granzin, Wilma J. "Peer Group Choice as a Device for Screening Intellectually Gifted Children." *Gifted Child Quarterly* 13:189–94 (Fall 1969).

The authors conducted a study in which fourth graders first had to distinguish between fifteen traits that pertained to children in general and fifteen that pertained primarily to gifted children. Next, they had to list peers whom they considered gifted. It was found that gifted and nongifted children were able to distinguish traits of giftedness and were both able to recognize gifted students in agreement with teacher ratings.

Gregory, Estelle H. "Search for Exceptional Academic Achievement at California State University—Los Angeles." *Gifted Child Quarterly* 28:21–24 (Winter 1984).

Gregory describes a program designed to differentiate among very bright junior high school students. The Washington Pre-College Test was the standardized instrument used. Sixty-eight students met the criteria for early college entrance.

Guilford, J. P. "The Structure of Intellect." *Psychological Bulletin* 53:267–93 (July 1956).

In Guilford's classic article, he reports on his theory that intelligence involves various components.

Hall, Eleanor G. "Knowing Who Is Gifted." *G/C/T* 11:14–15, 50–51 (January/February 1980).

Hall points out that although lists of characteristics of the gifted are available, they are not well understood. She advocates using slides and specific examples to help train teachers to identify the gifted. This article would be helpful to a university instructor or gifted coordinator who was developing training materials.

_____. "Recognizing Gifted Underachievers." *Roeper Review* 5:23–25 (May 1983).

The author designed a characteristics checklist that incorporated characteristics of nonconforming gifted students and provided teachers with awareness training regarding the traits common to the four different types of gifted students. The results of Hall's survey using the checklist indicate that few teachers are willing to nominate students as gifted if they exhibit the characteristics of underachievement. She recommends that teachers be trained to recognize (and accept) the notion of gifted underachievement.

Hanson, Irene. "A Comparison between Parent Identification of Young Bright Children and Subsequent Testing." *Roeper Review* 7:44–45 (September 1984).

The author, director of a special summer program for gifted youngsters, reports that testing on four-, five-, and six-year-old participants confirmed parents' accuracy in identifying their children as gifted.

Higbee, Walter R. "Lost Balls, Paperback Books, and Blueberry Muffins." *G/C/T* 38:34–35 (May/June 1985).

The author relates marvelous anecdotes regarding some of his experiences administering the WISC-R to bright students. The anecdotes could be used in training psychometricians who will be testing creative children.

High, Mari Helen, and Udall, Anne J. "Teacher Ratings of Students in Relation to Ethnicity of Students and School Ethnic Balances." *Journal for the Education of the Gifted* 6:154–66 (Spring 1983).

The authors conducted a fascinating study that attempted to answer the following question: Does the social and cultural milieu of a school influence teachers' ratings of culturally different children on the Scale for Rating Behavioral Characteristics of Superior Students? They compared three categories of schools and got mixed results. Overall, though, Hispanic children were less apt than Anglo children to be identified as gifted.

Hirsch, Fern J., and Hirsch, Steven J. "The Quick Test as a Screening Device for Gifted Students." *Psychology in the Schools* 17:37–38 (1980).

The authors report that, based on the data collected, the Quick test underestimated the cognitive abilities of the gifted students in the sample by from two to thirty-four points. Thus, it seems that the QT was unable to identify 60 percent of the gifted students in the sample and is therefore not useful as a screening device.

House, Peggy A. "Through the Eyes of Their Teachers: Stereotypes of Gifted Pupils." *Journal for the Education of the Gifted* 2:220–24 (Summer 1979).

House reports on research she conducted to determine attitudinal changes in teachers enrolled in a master's program in gifted education. Some change occurred as their knowledge increased.

Houts, Paul L. "Introduction: Standardized Testing in America." In *The Myth of Measurability,* edited by P. L. Houts. New York: Hart Publishing Co., 1977.

Houts clearly presents justification for the book *The Myth of Measurability.*

Hunter, John A., Jr., and Lowe, James D., Jr. "The Use of the WISC-R, Otis, Iowa, and SRBCSS in Identifying Gifted Elementary Students." *Southern Journal of Educational Research* 12:59–64 (Winter 1978).

The purpose of the authors' study was to obtain an estimate of adequacy of several screening instruments for identifying gifted children and to determine the most accurate prediction scheme available from a combination of these group measures for predicting the Full Scale WISC-R IQ. They found that none of the group measures is an effective predictor of the WISC-R FSIQ. They suggest individually administering short forms of the WISC-R.

Isaacs, Ann Fabe. "The Isaacs Three-Way Gifted-Talented-Creative Development Growth Check List." *Creative Child and Adult Quarterly* 3:191-202 (Fall 1978).

This checklist can be used in many different ways to determine one's own gifted-talented-creative development and/or growth. Space is provided on the checklist for two other persons to rate the subject. An explanation of the form is given.

Jacobs, J. C. "Effectiveness of Teacher and Parent Identification of Gifted Children as a Function of School Level." *Psychology in the Schools* 8:140-42 (1971).

The author found that in the early school years, parents do better than teachers in the identification of their children as gifted. Parents nominated fewer total children and were more accurate in their nominations.

Jenkins-Friedman, Reva. "Myth: Cosmetic Use of Multiple Selection Criteria." *Gifted Child Quarterly* 26:24-26 (Winter 1982).

Jenkins-Friedman says there is a major flaw in applying multiple-selection criteria to a pool comprised only of students who have already demonstrated high intellectual or academic ability.

Johnson, Lynn G. "Giftedness in Preschool: A Better Time for Development than Identification." *Roeper Review* 5:13-15 (May 1983).

Johnson recommends "an enriched, child-responsive preschool environment that affords opportunities for all children to demonstrate and develop gifts specific to them (which) would meet the educational and affective needs of children who normally would have been identified as gifted, as well as the children who would have been overlooked."

Kammer, Phyllis Post. "Conceptual Level of Development as It Relates to Student Participation in Gifted Programs." *Gifted Child Quarterly* 28:89-91 (Spring 1984).

The author conducted a study to determine how students identified as gifted compared to nongifted students on a measure of conceptual level. She found gifted students to be significantly higher and recommended that the measure be used as a tool in identification and in the selection of specific learning activities for these students.

Kaufmann, Alan S. "K-ABC and Giftedness." *Roeper Review* 7:83–88 (November 1984).

The Kaufman Assessment Battery for Children is an individually administered measure of intelligence and achievement in 2½- to 12½-year-old children. The author presents a strong rationale for his test, research results on the instrument, and practical implications of using the K-ABC for identifying gifted students. School directors of testing and gifted coordinators should investigate this instrument.

Kavett, Hyman, and Smith, William E. "Identification of Gifted and Talented Students in the Performing Arts." *G/C/T* 14:18–20 (September/October 1980).

The authors give numerous suggestions for ways to identify students who would benefit from placement in special programs for artistically gifted and talented. In summary: (1) eliminate multiple test instruments (IQ and achievement tests) as the situation warrants; (2) consider biographical data; (3) strongly consider the opinions of competent professionals; (4) use peer evaluations; (5) consider (with care) teacher recommendations; (6) temper judgments made by a teacher committee in light of the school and community situation.

Khatena, Joseph. "Something about Myself: A Brief Screening Device for Identifying Creatively Gifted Children and Adults." *Gifted Child Quarterly* 15:262–66 (Winter 1971).

Khatena presents data on the construction, administration, and scoring procedures for Something About Me in addition to preliminary reliability, validity, and normative data on the instrument.

Killan, Janice B., and Hughes, Larry C. "A Comparison of Short Forms of the Intelligence Scale for Children—Revised in the Screening of Gifted Referrals." *Gifted Child Quarterly* 22:111–15 (Spring 1978).

Results of the authors' comparison suggest that the Verbal and Block Design dyad of the WISC-R may be a useful screening device for superior students.

Kirschenbaum, Robert J. "Let's Cut Out the Cut-Off Score in the Identification of the Gifted." *Roeper Review* 5:6–10 (May 1983).

The author makes a case against using a rigid IQ score cutoff as the criterion for identification as gifted. He also provides an excellent bibliography.

Kontos, Susan, Carter, Kyle R., Ormrod, Jeanne E., and Cooney, John B. "Reversing the Revolving Door: A Strict Interpretation of Renzulli's Definition of Giftedness." *Roeper Review* 6:35–39 (September 1983).

The results of the authors' study indicate that a strict application of Renzulli's definition of giftedness results in a small number of students being identified—and this is incongruent with his program-

ming model. They also found that different individuals were identified depending on the configuration of instruments administered.
Verbally oriented tests for intelligence and/or creativity identify different children than do analogous tests that are nonverbal. Renzulli's response follows (see Renzulli & Owen 1983).

_____. "Another Look at the Revolving Door: A Reply to Renzulli."
Roeper Review 6:41–42 (September 1983).

This article is a response to Renzulli and Owen 1983.

Long, Julie, and Clemmons, Myra. "Creating Classroom Situations to
Encourage the Display of Gifted Behaviors: An Aid to Identification." *G/C/T* 25:38–40 (November/December 1982).

The authors have put forth examples of situations that teachers can
set up in their classrooms so that the gifted children will have opportunities to exhibit their abilities. This would be an excellent stimulus
for an in-service training program.

Male, Robert A., and Perrone, Philip. "Identifying Talent and Giftedness." Parts 1,2,3. *Roeper Review* 2:5–7 (September, December 1979,
February/March 1980: 5–7, 5–8, 9–11).

The first two articles focus on the GIFTS screening instrument and
the rationale for its development. The instrument is included. The
third article presents pertinent data and implications for the use of
the GIFTS Screening and the GIFTS Identification Instruments as
part of a program designed to meet the needs of gifted and talented
youth.

McCallum, R. Steve, Karnes, Frances A., and Bracken, Bruce A.
"Comparison of the PPVT, PPVT-R, and the WISC-R with Gifted
Students." *Journal for the Education of the Gifted* 54:274–81 (1983).

This study indicates the PPVT-R is a viable test for screening gifted
children.

McFarland, Suzanne L. "Guidelines for the Identification of Young
Gifted and Talented Children." *Roeper Review* 3:5–7 (November/De-
cember 1980).

The author lists six criteria for selecting identification procedures
and seven steps toward identification. She also includes a table that
lists identification instruments and each instrument's advantages
and disadvantages.

Meeker, Mary N. "Identifying Potential Giftedness." *National Association of Secondary School Principals Bulletin* 55:92–95 (December 1971).

Meeker says the schools have three tasks: (1) to change the definition of giftedness so that it includes giftedness in motor, figural,
leadership, and creative skills; (2) to find tools for identifying giftedness in each of these dimensions; and (3) to recognize that their function includes enhancing these gifts through the curriculum.

_____. "The Prophecy of Giftedness." *Gifted Child Quarterly* 20:100–104+ (Spring 1976).

Meeker offers a paradigm for the education of the gifted that divides a child's unique functioning into three areas: academic, social-emotional-environmental, and psychomotor.

Miller, Pamela, and Ford, Barbara Gay. "A New Way to Identify G/C/T Children: The Anecdotal Approach." *G/C/T* 14:14–16, 27 (September/October 1980).

The authors constructed a log that they used in training teachers in the identification of gifted and talented children. The log makes it quite clear that gifted students exhibit particular behaviors that should be taken into account as part of an overall identification plan.

Murphy, Douglas, Jenkins-Friedman, Reva, and Tollefson, Nona. "A New Criterion for the 'Ideal' Child?" *Gifted Child Quarterly* 28:31–36 (Winter 1984).

Torrance's (1963) Ideal Child Checklist is discussed and its continued relevance is questioned. The results from the authors' study suggest two major shifts since 1963 concerning conceptualization of the ideal child among teachers and experts in gifted child education: (1) the image of ideal child and (2) the nature of agreement between teachers and experts.

Nasca, Don. "Teacher Nomination of Intellectually Gifted Students." *G/C/T* 7:38–41 (March/April 1979).

Nasca discusses the reasons why approximately 50 percent of the gifted are not identified by traditional IQ or achievement tests. He has designed a nomination form to help teachers identify students missed by the other measures. An efficient teacher nomination form must: (1) focus on the characteristics of underachievers; (2) be brief; (3) avoid duplication of characteristics normally assessed by group-administered standardized tests; (4) provide sufficient information to ensure teacher attention to relevant student characteristics. The form and its rationale are included.

Navarre, Jane. "How the Teacher of the Gifted Can Use the S.O.I." *G/C/T* 26:16–17 (January/February 1983).

Navarre supports the use of the SOI by teachers of the gifted. (We concur but the author makes its administration and scoring sound too simple.)

Otey, John W. "Identification of Gifted Students." *Psychology in the Schools* 15:16–21 (January 1978).

Using the PL 91-230 definition of giftedness, the author discusses various ways for schools to identify their gifted.

O'Tuel, Frances S., Ward, Marjory, and Rawl, Ruth K. "The S.O.I. as an Identification Tool for the Gifted: Windfall or Washout?" *Gifted Child Quarterly* 27:126–34 (Summer 1983).

The authors investigated the relationship between the SOI-LA and variables of grades, achievement, IQ and aptitude scores, and performance in the gifted program for fourth, seventh, and tenth graders. Their results did not indicate the efficacy of including the SOI in the identification battery. A useful student evaluation checklist is included.

Padilla, Amado M., and Garza, Blas M. "IQ Tests: A Case of Cultural Myopia." In *The Myth of Measurability*, edited by P. L. Houts. New York: Hart Publishing Co., 1977.

The authors state that "no test of intelligence can be divorced from the cultural frame in which the examinee is expected to perform." They go on to present support for that statement.

Pearce, Norma. "A Comparison of the WISC-R, Raven's Standard Progressive Matrices, and Meeker's SOI-Screening Form for Gifted." *Gifted Child Quarterly* 27:13–19 (Winter 1983).

The results of Pearce's study indicate that the Standard Progressive Matrices test is a significant predictor of intelligence. A lower correlation between SOI abilities and intelligence was found. She states that cautious use of the SPM and SOI for screening gifted students is warranted, but that the real value may be in their use to advance curriculum.

Pedriana, Anthony J., and Bracken, Bruce A. "Performance of Gifted Children on the PPVT and PPVT-R." *Psychology in the Schools* 19:183–85 (April 1982).

The authors found that the correlation between standard scores on the PPVT and PPVT-R is .83. The PPVT-R yields lower scores, is much more current, is better normed, and is therefore the most appropriate one to use for screening receptive vocabulary.

Reis, Sally M., and Renzulli, Joseph S. "A Case for a Broadened Conception of Giftedness." *Phi Delta Kappan* 63:619–20 (May 1982).

The authors report on their research on the Revolving Door Model. They were able to draw several conclusions from this research: Services to the gifted are increased even as more gifted children are served. High-ability children are served, which helps minimize elitism concerns. More of the "right" students are served using this model. The model allows for more flexible and appropriate identification of the gifted.

Rekdall, C. K. "In Search of the Wild Duck: Personality Inventories as Tests of Creative Potential and Their Use as Measurements in Programs for the Gifted." *Gifted Child Quarterly* 21:501–16 (Winter 1977).

The author supports the idea that creativity cannot be overlooked in determining giftedness. He cites numerous sources to reinforce his view. He also reviews four representative studies that have used personality inventories as screening devices for gifted programs.

Renzulli, Joseph S. "What Makes Giftedness? Reexamining a Definition." *Phi Delta Kappan* 60:180–84, 261 (November 1978).

Renzulli explains and supports his concept of giftedness, which includes three clusters of traits: above-average general ability, task commitment, and creativity. This article is must reading.

————. "Rating the Behavioral Characteristics of Superior Students." *G/C/T* 29:30–35 (September/October 1983).

An updated version of the Scales for Rating Behavioral Characteristics of Superior Students is included, along with specific suggestions for helping teachers learn to use the instrument. The article would be an excellent basis for in-service training.

————. "The Triad/Revolving Door System: A Research-Based Approach to Identification and Programming for the Gifted and Talented." *Gifted Child Quarterly* 28:163–71 (Fall 1984).

Renzulli provides an overview of the Revolving Door Identification Model and the ways in which it is used in conjunction with the Enrichment Triad Programming Model. The rationale and underlying principles of the models are presented along with a description of how to implement them.

Renzulli, Joseph S., Hartman, Robert K., and Callahan, Carolyn M. "Teacher Identification of Superior Students." *Exceptional Children* 38:211–14 (November 1971).

The authors explain how the Scale for Rating Behavioral Characteristics of Superior Students was developed. They also present data on its use. The scale is included in the same journal issue (see Renzulli 1983).

Renzulli, Joseph S., and Owen, Steven V. "The Revolving Door Identification Model: If It Ain't Busted, Don't Fix It; If You Don't Understand It, Don't Nix It." *Roeper Review* 6:39–41 (September 1983).

The authors respond to Kontos, Carter, Ormrod, & Cooney 1983 (same issue). They point out flaws they see in the study by Kontos et al. and defend the Revolving Door Identification Model.

Renzulli, Joseph S., Reis, Sally M., and Smith, Linda H. "The Revolving Door Model: A New Way of Identifying the Gifted." *Phi Delta Kappan* 62:648–49 (May 1981).

The authors explain the Revolving Door Identification Model, which allows students to move into and out of special programs for the gifted as the need arises.

Renzulli, Joseph S., and Smith, Linda H. "Two Approaches to Identification of Gifted Students." *Exceptional Children* 43:512–18 (May 1977).

The authors report on their study, which compared two general approaches to identification using an alternative criterion measure to judge efficiency and effectiveness. They also looked at costs and usefulness of information provided. Their recommendations include the use of the case study approach along with intelligence testing.

————. "An Alternative Approach to Identifying and Programming for Gifted and Talented Students." *G/C/T* 15:3–11 (November/December 1980).

The authors make a clear case for implementing the Revolving Door Identification and Programming Model. They explain its strengths and suggest ways of avoiding its pitfalls.

Rimm, Sylvia. "Identifying Creativity." Part 1. *G/C/T* 27:34–37 (March/April 1983).

Rimm draws a marvelous analogy between identifying students who are talented in basketball and identifying students who are creative. This article would provide a good framework for opening an in-service session on identification of creative individuals.

————. "The Characteristics Approach: Identification and Beyond." *Gifted Child Quarterly* 28:181–87 (Fall 1984).

Rimm provides a rationale for using a characteristics approach in identification of able youth. She also discusses several instruments that she and Gary A. Davis have developed (GIFT, GIFFI, and PRIDE), all of which reflect the characteristics approach.

Rimm, Sylvia, and Davis, Gary A. "Identifying Creativity." Part 2. *G/C/T* 29:19–23 (September/October 1983).

The authors summarize four instruments that can be used to help identify the gifted—GIFT: Group Inventory for Finding Creative Talent; GIFFI I and GIFFI II: Group Inventory for Finding Interests; PRIDE: Preschool Interest Descriptor. New validation research is presented for each. They conclude that the "characteristics approach as measured by self-report and parent-report inventories appears to be an efficient and effective method of selecting creative students for gifted programs when combined with at least one other method."

Rosenberg, Leon A. "Identifying the Gifted Child in the Culturally Deprived Population: The Need for Culturally Fair Instruments." *American Journal of Orthopsychiatry* 37:342–43 (March 1967).

Briefly describes an instrument developed by the author for use in identifying preschool gifted children. The author has found the instrument to be culturally fair.

Rubenzer, Ron. "Identification and Evaluation Procedures for Gifted and Talented Programs." *Gifted Child Quarterly* 23:304–16 (Summer 1979).

The author briefly touches on some of the ways to identify gifted students, and goes into detail with others (e.g., Gowan's Reservoir Model). Included is an extensive appendix that lists representative tests for each of the USOE talent areas.

Rubin, Larry. "Tapping the Iceberg: A Search for the Unchosen Gifted and Talented." *G/C/T* 19:36–37 (September/October 1981).

Rubin calls for a renewed effort to nurture and identify those students who are being missed by traditional methods of identification.

Sarnecky, Ellen, and Michaud, Ted. "Local Programs for Gifted and Talented Hearing Impaired Students." *Language, Speech, and Hearing Services in the Schools* 10:191–94 (July 1979).

The authors discuss reasons why hearing-impaired children are almost always excluded from gifted programs. They give the results of a questionnaire sent to school districts regarding provisions for their aurally handicapped students. Not much is done.

Sawyer, Robert N., and Daggett, Lynn M. "Duke University's Talent Identification Program." *G/C/T* 22:10–14 (March/April 1982).

The authors describe the Duke University Talent Identification Program, which is modeled after the Johns Hopkins University Study of Mathematically Precocious Youth. Over 8,000 students participated during the first year of Duke's program, and plans for expansion are under way.

Schwartz, Lita Linzer, and Fischman, Ronald. "Integrating the Potentially Able/The Exceptionally Able." *Gifted Child Quarterly* 28:130–34 (Summer 1984).

This article describes the Potentially Academically Talented Students (PATS) project implemented in Pennsylvania. The project sought to locate "unidentified" gifted students and expose them to an enrichment program with identified gifted students. Several painful lessons learned by the staff are shared.

Sheverbush, Robert L., Jr. "An Analysis of Subtests Performance of Gifted Students in the Stanford-Binet Intelligence Scale (1960 Form L-M)." *Gifted Child Quarterly* 18:97–107, 115 (Summer 1974).

The author reports on a study that had as its purpose to go beyond the simple general intelligence score (IQ) to an analysis of responses on each subtest in order to try to gain a more detailed understanding and additional information regarding the characteristics of the gifted.

Silverstein, A. B. "WISC and WPPSI IQ's for the Gifted." *Psychological Report* 22:1168 (June 1968).

Tables in this article extrapolate WISC IQ scores and WPPSI IQ scores up to the maximum possible sum of scaled scores so that psychologists can determine the IQ of gifted subjects with these instruments.

Stanley, Julian C. "The Predictive Value of the SAT for Brilliant Seventh- and Eighth-Graders." *College Board Review* 106:30–37 (Winter 1977/1978).

Stanley shares cases indicating that use of the SAT to locate exceptional talent is quite valid. He also makes a case for acceleration of such able students.

_____. "Use of General and Specific Aptitude Measures in Identification: Some Principles and Certain Cautions." *Gifted Child Quarterly* 28:177–80 (Fall 1984).

Stanley discusses several measures used to identify gifted youth. He concludes that the SAT is the optimum screening instrument. He offers nine precautions—for example, be sure the test is difficult enough for the child being tested, recognize degrees of intellectual talent, prescribe instruction only after diagnostic testing.

Stanley, Julian C., and Benbow, Camilla P. "Using the SAT to Find Intellectually Talented Seventh Graders." *College Board Review* 122:2–7, 26–27 (Winter 1981).

The authors strongly support the use of the SAT for locating exceptionally talented youth. They share some of their successes at Johns Hopkins University.

Stefanich, Greg, and Schnur, James O. "Identifying the Handicapped-Gifted Child." *Science and Children:* 17:18–19 (November/December 1979).

The authors say that the four major criteria used for identification of the gifted (teacher nomination, group achievement-test scores, group intelligence-test scores, and previously demonstrated accomplishments) generally discriminate against children who are gifted and handicapped. They suggest: (1) having lower acceptance levels for initial screening; (2) having the second screening conducted by either similarly handicapped persons or persons who are thoroughly familiar with the instrument and the child's particular handicap; and (3) using instruments that assess broader ability ranges.

Stern, Jane. "A New Strategy to Dissolve a Current Problem: How to Identify Giftedness." *G/C/T* 27:47–51 (March/April 1983).

The author has developed an identification grid to be used with Renzulli's three-ring definition of giftedness. Marvin Gold (editor of *G/C/T*) responds to Stern's idea, and Renzulli responds to Gold and Stern.

Sternberg, Robert J. "Nonentrenchment in the Assessment of Intellectual Giftedness." *Gifted Child Quarterly* 26:63–67 (Spring 1982).

Sternberg very clearly presents the concept of "entrenched" and "nonentrenched" ideas and the notion that intelligence and creativity test results are confounded by entrenchment and nonentrenchment. He makes suggestions for rethinking intelligence tests. This is a good article.

———. *Beyond Intelligence.* New York: Cambridge University Press, 1985. 405 pp.

This complex yet amazingly readable book presents Sternberg's Triarchic Theory of Human Intelligence. Sternberg states that this theory precludes his previous ones. His work is on the cutting edge of theories of intelligence.

Sternberg, Robert J. "Identifying the Gifted through IQ: Why a Little Bit of Knowledge Is a Dangerous Thing. *Roeper Review* 8:142–47 (February 1986).

Sternberg states succinctly his triarchic theory of intellectual giftedness and illustrates it with profiles of three graduate students. He makes a case against using IQ scores as a measure of intelligence.

Swassing, Ray. "The Multiple Component Alternative for Gifted Education." *G/C/T* 33:10–11 (May/June 1984).

Swassing explains his Multiple Component Model (MCM) which is built on the following premises: (1) A complete program for gifted/talented children is at least the sum of its component parts. (2) Multiple selection criteria should reflect the character of the component for which selection is being made. (3) Selection and development of components must be systematic, with evaluation and feedback as integral parts of the cycle. (4) Selection and development needs to be based on both ongoing activities that can be effectively utilized with the gifted and on components not currently available.

Taylor, Calvin W. "Developing Creative Excellence in Students: The Neglected History-Making Ingredient Which Would Keep Our Nation from Being at Risk." *Gifted Child Quarterly* 28:106–9 (Summer 1984).

Taylor makes a strong case for fostering creativity in every field of endeavor. He draws heavily on the writing of Toynbee and Machado—but to good effect.

Taylor, Calvin W., and Ellison, Robert L. "Searching for Student Talent Resources Relevant to Our USDE Types of Giftedness." *Gifted Child Quarterly* 27:99–106 (Summer 1983).

The authors discuss the Form U Biographical Inventory, which is a 150-item multiple-choice instrument that yields four scores: academic performance, creativity, leadership, and artistic potential.

They also present information regarding other biographical inventories.

Thompson, Bruce, Alston, Herbert L., Cunningham, Claude H., and Wakefield, James A. "The Relationship of a Measure of Structure of Intellect Abilities and Academic Achievement." *Educational and Psychological Measurement* 38: 1207–10 (Winter 1978).

The authors found a moderate correlation between nine SOI ability scores (hypothesized to be related to reading achievement) with the reading achievement portion of the ITBS.

Thompson, Jack M., and Finley, Carmen J. "Abbreviated WISC for Use with Gifted Elementary School Children." *California Journal of Educational Research* 14:167–77 (September 1963).

The authors describe how they developed an abbreviated scale of the WISC for use with the gifted. They determined that this form was a valid predictor of full-scale IQ with gifted students.

Tittle, Bess. "Searching for Hidden Treasure: Seeking the Culturally Different Gifted Child." *Journal for the Education of the Gifted* 2:80–93 (Winter 1979).

Tittle has worked extensively with culturally different gifted children—especially at the preschool level. She presents her concept of how best to identify these children.

Torrance, E. Paul. "Finding Hidden Talents among Disadvantaged Children." *Gifted Child Quarterly* 12:131–37 (1968).

Torrance discusses a creativity workshop format to use in discovering talents among disadvantaged students. One of his graduate students said, "One thing I noticed about all of these activities is that we were concerned about how much we could bring out of these children—not how much we could cram into them."

_____. "What Gifted Disadvantaged Children Can Teach Their Teachers." *Gifted Child Quarterly* 17:243–49 (Winter 1973).

Torrance proposes not only that teachers encourage gifted students to teach those things they know well, but also that teachers deliberately become aware of and acknowledge their gifted students' expertise.

_____. "The Role of Creativity in Identification of the Gifted and Talented." *Gifted Child Quarterly* 28:153–56 (Fall 1984).

Torrance traces his trek through the last forty years as he has fought to get creativity considered as a criterion for identifying gifted and talented students.

Treffinger, Donald J. "The Progress and Peril of Identifying Creative Talent among Gifted and Talented Students." *Journal of Creative Behavior* 14:20–34 (1980).

Treffinger provides a rationale for a multidimensional definition of talent: (1) human abilities and talents are of complex natures, and (2) multiple screening procedures are much more fair.

_____. "Research on Creativity." *Gifted Child Quarterly* 30:15–19 (Winter 1986).

Treffinger concludes that, although creativity has been of interest to researchers for thirty years—and progress has been made in our understanding of the nature, assessment, and nurture of creativity—it is still a field that offers many and varied opportunities for research and development. His discussion of the significant research is clear and cohesive.

VanTassel-Baska, Joyce. "Profiles of Precocity: The 1982 Midwest Talent Search Finalists." *Gifted Child Quarterly* 27:139–44 (Summer 1983).

VanTassel-Baska reports on data grouped in the following categories: personal, familial, behavioral, and educational. The report is based on information obtained from 64 percent of the 270 students identified in the Midwest Talent Search.

_____. "The Talent Search as an Identification Model." *Gifted Child Quarterly* 28:172–76 (Fall 1984).

The author discusses the Talent Search Identification Model and how it addresses three issues in gifted education: (1) establishing a talent pool, (2) combatting the ceiling effect on testing, and (3) providing effective data for program planning at the school district, university, and state levels.

Vermilyea, John. "Common Sense in the Identification of Gifted and Talented Students Who Need Alternative Programming." *G/C/T* 16:11–14 (January/February 1981).

The author describes an identification system based on the experiences of various school districts as they developed their gifted/talented programs. Samples of the forms used are included.

Washburn, S. L. "Evolution and Learning: A Context for Evaluation." In *The Myth of Measurability*, edited by P. L. Houts. New York: Hart Publishing Co., 1977.

Washburn compares the schooling of children and youth today with the learning situations of previous cultures. He finds that we are going about teaching and learning in an inefficient way.

Weber, Patricia, and Battaglia, Catherine. "Reaching beyond Identification through the "Identi-Form" System." *Gifted Child Quarterly* 29:35–47 (Winter 1985).

The authors present the "Identi-Form" approach to gifted programming. Extensive explanations and support are offered. This article should be reviewed by directors of programs for the gifted.

Wechsler, David. "Intelligence Defined and Undefined: A Relativistic Appraisal." *American Psychologist* 30:135–39 (February 1975).

In this classic article, Wechsler first refutes what he calls "common but unwarranted assumptions" about intelligence. His final point is that what is measured with intelligence tests is not what intelligence tests measure—i.e., not information, not spatial perception, not reasoning ability. "These are only a means to an end. What intelligence tests measure . . . [is] the capacity of an individual to understand the world about him and his resourcefulness to cope with its challenges."

Westcott Gary L., and Woodward, Jewell. "Locating the Not So Obvious Gifted." *G/C/T* 20:10–11 (November/December 1981).

The authors describe the Spokane, Washington, two-part identification process that involves screening and validation.

Wheaton, Peter J., and others. "Comparability of the WISC and WISC-R with Bright Elementary School Students." *Journal of School Psychology* 18:271–75 (Fall 1980).

Fifty intellectually gifted subjects in grades three to five were given the WISC and WISC-R in counterbalanced order (test-retest). The authors found that higher mean IQ scores were obtained by the total group on the WISC. However, results showed that when the WISC-R was administered first, subsequent student WISC performance was significantly higher on all scales. It appears that the WISC-R has a facilitative effect on the WISC.

White, Sheldon H. "Social Implications of IQ." In *The Myth of Measurability*, edited by P. L. Houts. New York: Hart Publishing Co., 1977.

White contends that, amidst the social arrangements and social changes of the early 1900s, American psychology was born—and that IQ testing was born out of these same social changes. He also believes that the concept of IQ has continued to affect and be affected by society.

Whiting, Sally Anita, Anderson, Lonna, and Ward, Janet. "Identification of the Mentally Gifted Minor Deaf Child in the Public School System." *American Annals of the Deaf* 125:27–34 (February 1980).

This good article explains the screening used by the Covina-Valley United School District to identify and provide for aurally handicapped mentally gifted minors. Descriptions of identified students are included.

Whitmore, Joanne R. "Gifted Children with Handicapping Conditions: A New Frontier." *Exceptional Children* 48:106–14 (October 1981).

Whitmore says the "gifted/handicapped child is one who requires special educational programming (*a*) to accommodate one or more handicapping conditions and (*b*) to fully develop his or her potential for exceptional achievement in one or more areas in which he or she may be gifted or talented." She discusses methods of identification of such children and the challenge of providing for them.

————. "Recognizing and Developing Hidden Giftedness." *Elementary School Journal* 82:274–83 (January 1982).

Whitmore focuses on the "characteristics and educational needs of children with unrecognized giftedness, and the specific role of curriculum and instructional methodology in the identification and development of these students' potential for exceptional intellectual achievement." This is an excellent resource.

Witty, Elaine P. "Equal Educational Opportunity for Gifted Minority Group Children: Promise or Possibility." *Gifted Child Quarterly* 22:344–52 (Fall 1978).

Witty states that equal educational opportunity for minority-group children who are gifted means: (1) early identification with attention to special needs; (2) careful programming in light of their strengths, characteristics, and learning and living styles; (3) intelligent and caring teaching free of limiting expectations; (4) wide-range "releasing" counseling programs; and (5) parental and community support services interacting freely with the schools.

Witty, Paul. "Who Are the Gifted?" In *Education for the Gifted*, Part 2 of *Fifty-Seventh Yearbook of the National Society for the Study of Education*, edited by Nelson B. Henry. Chicago: Univ. of Chicago Pr., 1958.

Witty describes the characteristics of the young child who is gifted in science, writing, or leadership.

Yarborough, Betty H., and Johnson, Roger A. "Identifying the Gifted: A Theory-Practice Gap." *Gifted Child Quarterly* 27:135–38 (Summer 1983).

The authors conducted a nationwide survey of outstanding programs for the gifted to determine prevailing trends in identification as actually used in the schools. Seventy percent of the programs surveyed used combinations—for example, IQ tests and achievement tests along with behavioral procedures.

Zimmerman, Irla L., and Woo-Sam, James. "The Utility of the Wechsler Preschool and Primary Scale of Intelligence in the Public School." *Journal of Clinical Psychology* 26:472 (October 1970).

Zimmerman found that WPPSI IQ scores are lower than those of the Stanford-Binet at the upper end (maximum possible WPPSI = 155, compared to maximum possible Stanford-Binet = 170).

CHAPTER 4

Counseling the Gifted and Those around Them

Classroom teachers—whether teaching preschool, elementary, secondary, or postsecondary students—wear many different hats, not the least frequent being that of counselor. Teachers see their students for extended periods each day, and they see them month in and month out. Thus, teachers have an opportunity to witness subtle or drastic changes in students' lives. The extended time frame also allows some students to develop trust in their teacher as a confidant and counselor.

Likewise, counselors must often wear the hat of teacher. They may be called upon to teach study-skills courses for students, in-service workshops for classroom teachers, or seminars for parents or administrators. Most school counselors were classroom teachers at one time and continue to consider themselves teachers.

Although teachers and counselors have distinct roles in schools and in the lives of students, it is difficult to completely separate the roles. However, teachers are charged with the task of instructing students, while counselors are charged with tending to the students' emotional and psychological needs, among other tasks. It is neither expected nor desirable for teachers or counselors to assume the others' job, but it is advantageous for them to strive for both formal and informal cooperation as they serve the students in their care. This chapter will refer to *counselors* and to *teachers*, and while it is intended that teachers and others who work in a guidance role with gifted youth will read themselves into the counselor's role wherever appropriate, it is also expected that readers will recognize the distinctive role that counselors can play in the school community.

Gifted students are different from other members of the student population of a school community. The gifted tend to be able to learn more and learn faster than other students. They have a proclivity toward creativity and possess a sensitivity more pronounced than that of nongifted students. Gifted students often know quite a bit about a wide variety of subjects and usually know a great deal about one or two subjects that are of special interest to them. These and other characteristics (which are discussed in greater detail in chapter 2) differentiate gifted from nongifted students. Because gifted students are different from other students both academically and socially, their counseling needs are also different. Belief in this tenet is essential if a counselor is to be successful in working with gifted students and their families (Lester & Anderson 1981). It is also true that each individual gifted student is just that—individual; Sanborn (1979) says the most important principle to consider when counseling the gifted is that they differ from each other in more ways than they resemble each other.

Counseling the gifted places special demands on the practitioner. Counselors of the gifted should be open, caring, warm, intelligent, nonauthoritarian, not biased toward one field of study, not prejudiced, experienced, and able to communicate effectively with students, teachers, and parents. They should be good role models for gifted students, and aware that they may play a significant role in whether a gifted student achieves or does not achieve. James B. Conant, in the Foreword to *Guidance of American Youth* (Rothney & Roens, 1950), said

> It would not be too much to say that on the success or failure of our guidance program hangs, in all probability, the success or failure of our system of public education . . . . Guidance could be the catalytic agent that not only reduces the loss but stimulates the whole educational process so that greater gains can be achieved.

Since the greatest potential lies in the gifted youth, guidance for them is expedient.

Three main groups of individuals with whom counselors will need to deal in the course of guiding academically able students are (1) individual gifted students, (2) teachers and administrators, and (3) gifted students' parents. Each group of individuals will make specific demands on the counselors, for which they should be prepared.

CHARACTERISTIC PROBLEMS OF GIFTED STUDENTS

Many people erroneously assume that the only students who need counseling are those who are "in trouble"—skipping classes, vandalizing school property, making extremely low marks, or suffering through an overt family tragedy, such as death or divorce. The view that a student needs a counselor only in such situations is "crisis-centered counseling" or "why fix it before it's broken" counseling. This is not the most efficacious for students. According to Safter and Bruch,

> Most school counseling begins and ends with a problem, is crisis-oriented, and is ad hoc in applications. However, students traditionally identified as gifted usually do not display behaviors that bring them to the attention of school counselors. (1981, 167)

This being the case, many gifted students will never avail themselves of counseling.

While a certain proportion of gifted students do need crisis counseling, most do not. This does not mean that they are devoid of the need for guidance-counseling services. These students have unique imperatives that relate to their longing for intellectual challenges and that sometimes put them at odds with their peers. Not only do the gifted need "preventive" counseling in order to remain mentally healthy and productive, but they need counseling just as a matter of course, to ensure that the paths their lives take are both satisfactory and fulfilling for themselves and society.

Beginning in elementary school, the gifted student needs the services of a counselor. Zaffrann and Colangelo (1979) summarized several studies and concluded that gifted children need more than the usually expected amount of guidance in order to be mentally healthy enough to be creative. One of the studies they summarized showed that a class of twenty-five gifted students could consume the full-time services of one counselor.

Such riches in personnel are rare, but nonetheless, gifted elementary students need the services of a guidance counselor just as gifted middle school and high school students do. At each level, the students' needs are different.

In the elementary school, gifted children are having their first exposure to school and its inherent challenges. It may be the first time they have had their learning structured; it may be the first time that they have been put in a situation that not only did not challenge their intellect but stifled it; it may be the first time that they have been around other children. There are many firsts which come with elementary school and, depending on the child, some of them may cause problems or set the stage for later problems to develop (e.g., being in an unchallenging situation may set up future underachievement).

In the middle school, peer pressure is at its height. Gifted students may feel pressure to conform—in ways that are socially unacceptable or in ways that are self-defeating, in terms of their intellectual and creative potential. The middle school years are also the time when gifted girls begin to fall behind gifted boys, and therefore preventive counseling is necessary. Early adolescence is a difficult time for all students, but because the gifted tend to be highly introspective and sensitive, this passage can be especially traumatic for them.

While high school and middle school students have some of the same problems, gifted students in high school have additional counseling needs. *Guidance* is the key word: guidance concerning courses that should be taken, possible internships or mentorships that would benefit the student, colleges or universities to consider, ways to seek and secure scholarships and other financial aid.

Gowan and Bruch (1971, 2) posit that "the gifted profit from guidance, and even with minimal guidance make greater strides towards solving their problems than do average youngsters with equal guidance time." At all levels, because of the gifted students' extraordinary intelligence and creativity—which pose both problems and opportunities—and because of other characteristics of able learners, the expertise of a counselor is required. The primary focus of the counselors' expertise should be the gifted students themselves.

From the time gifted children first associate with other children, they may begin to realize that they are different. Depending on the level and type of a child's giftedness, and depending on the children with whom the gifted child is associating, the difference may be blatant, or it may be less noticeable and therefore take longer to realize. But at some point, highly able children recognize that they are different from those around them. Merrill (1979) says that gifted children need to be helped to accept their differentness, not deny it.

Sometimes upon entering school, children perceive that "sameness" and conformity are rewarded but differentness is not. A counselor should work with gifted children (and their parents and teachers) to help them understand their differentness as both acceptable and valuable. Knowing *how* they are unique is much more helpful for extraordinary young persons than just knowing that they are gifted.

Group counseling for gifted students is often recommended (Allan & Fox 1979; Harris & Trolta 1962; Merrill 1979; Walker 1982; Zaffrann & Colangelo 1979) for a number of reasons, including the "different-ness" issue. When gifted children and young adults meet in a group, they are able to see others like themselves—that is, alike in their differentness. In group counseling, one of the goals of the counselor should be to build a safe, trusting, accepting environment to allow the students to establish interpersonal communications and build interpersonal relationships. This will help relieve some of the emotional isolation gifted students tend to feel at times. This group support is invaluable, especially as the youth mature and need encouragement and backing from peers. Group counseling is effective with able youth, not because of common personality traits, but because of a common collection of problems, some of which will be discussed below.

Unequal Levels of Intellectual, Physical, and Emotional Development

One of the problems gifted children and youth need help coping with is the discrepancy that often exists between their intellectual capacity and their physical and/or emotional capacity. Very young children concoct games that they are physically unable to play due to lack of coordination. The same sort of frustration presents itself when a younger gifted child, in the search for mentally equivalent playmates, plays with older children. Physical immaturity may prevent the gifted child from participating in some of the activities that the older playmates do. The ensuing frustration may cause the intellectually able child to withdraw from physical activities (sports) because of the feeling of inadequacy. A person in a guidance role can watch for this sort of avoidance behavior and help the child realize that the comparison is with children who are physically older and thus more mature in their coordination. The younger child should be helped to find a physical activity in which to participate.

The discrepancy between a gifted child's intellect and emotions can result in misunderstanding by the child, parents, and teachers. Especially during the teenage years, when hormone changes are causing a physical and emotional metamorphosis, gifted adolescents need help to understand this phenomenon. They are able to intellectualize certain situations, but because adolescence is wreaking havoc with their body and emotions, a mental struggle ensues. Although counseling cannot change what nature does, it can provide information that leads to understanding.

Parents and other adults often forget that gifted children and youth, although intellectually advanced, and sometimes emotionally advanced to a degree, are still children or teenagers with emotions more closely commensurate with their chronological age than with their mental age. For example, a highly gifted seven-year-old girl may be able to discuss theories of what causes sunspots with her father one minute, and be bounding off to her room to play with her dolls and dollhouse the next. And a gifted teenage boy may have just received word that he has been named a National Merit scholar, but because his girlfriend has just informed him that she wants to date other people, he could not care less about the National Merit scholarship award. In summary, people who work with the gifted should keep in mind that in areas in which degree of intelligence is not a factor, the gifted are very much like their age-mates.

Peer Relationships

It should be iterated that many gifted students are among the most popular in their classes and enjoy a wide range of friends. More gifted students than not are leaders in their schools and neighborhoods and have formed friendships with peers at different levels and in different contexts. But on the other hand, some superior students, especially the highly gifted and/or the highly creative, have difficulties in peer relationships.

These difficulties arise when some able children are unable to find anyone with whom they can relate intellectually. The highly gifted student thinks in a different way and on a different level than the majority of the children in the neighborhood or students at the school. As a result, the student may be ostracized or may choose to withdraw. In either instance, a counselor needs to intervene—by helping the parents find other able children for their child to play with, by working in a classroom to build up better relations among all the students, by working with the individual student, alone or in a group, on "how to make friends." Although it seems amazing, some children have no social skills, and so their limited attempts to make friends or to be a part of the group are doomed to failure.

One such example is Ben. From the time he first entered school, it was apparent that he was far above average intellectually. In kindergarten, he frequently threw tantrums when he did not get his way, a behavior that continued in high school. Although placed in gifted programs early in his school career, Ben was never able to develop any friendships, or if he did, they never lasted longer than a few weeks. His typical behavior in a classroom was to continuously "throw his knowledge around." He seemed to see himself as omniscient, although his giftedness was well within the normal range of giftedness. From early elementary school on, he was the object of classmates' taunting and teachers' ire. Because so many times when others were talking and laughing, they were talking and laughing at his expense, Ben became somewhat paranoid, so that even when students were not talking about him, he assumed that they were and either complained loudly to the teacher or told the suspected "taunters," "Quit talking about me!" His fine mind and the resiliency he displayed after being put down were heartening, but there was no doubt that without counseling he would continue to be hurt by his ineptness in social relationships.

For young people such as Ben, whether in elementary or secondary school, the ineptness is evident whether the other people involved are intellectual peers or not. These young people need direct teaching of the social graces. The alternative is to allow them to go painfully alone through their lives until, through either observation or trial and error, they discover a way to be social persons. Unfortunately, this is exactly what happens, to the detriment of these young people and those around them.

Counselors and teachers, through observation and/or the use of sociograms, can determine social isolates. When one or more are discovered in a class, immediate steps to remedy the situation should be set in motion. If the first plan does not work, another one should be found. Sometimes solving the problem is a challenge, and if the teacher runs out of ideas for a solution, then the counselor should be asked for help.

In some special schools for the gifted, such as magnet schools or private schools, more than one culture, either ethnic or socioeconomic, may come together for the first time in the students' experience. Preventive counseling, prior to the onset of problems, is infinitely better than crisis-centered counseling, which would wait until severe "culture shock" problems had occurred before doing anything. Counselors should plan activities (e.g., using media developed for the purpose, simulation games, or role playing) to enable the students to sensitize themselves to the situation and to each other. Although young people have less bias and prejudice than adults, many of them are carrying their parents' views with them and need a chance to develop their own unbiased values.

Ambivalence over Upward Social Mobility

Another dilemma faced by some gifted adolescents concerns upward social mobility (Gowan 1960). Many gifted students are capable of achieving far more than their parents did. Some of them have difficulty resolving the resultant conflict: they worry about "showing their parents up," about implying that the way they were brought up was not good enough, and about leaving family and friends behind as they pursue their own dreams. This problem goes beyond normal adolescent rebellion because it also threatens the relationship with the peer group. So, as counselors encourage gifted youth to strive and stretch, they should be aware that growth may generate inner conflict, which the students may need help to resolve.

Academic Choices

One ability normally expected of school counselors at the high school level is knowing about colleges. With gifted students, college advising becomes even more challenging than with average students. Academically able students are currently being actively recruited by colleges, in the same way that physically able students have been for many years. These students need someone knowledgeable about scholarships and programs available to help them navigate this maze. Gowan and Demos (1965) perceive that one role of the counselor is "scout or coach for the academic varsity." Part of this job is to match students and universities so that both are satisfied. The concept of a match between student and university is an important one to consider. Often the reputation of the university is influential, rather than the quality of its specific program that interests the student. Some gifted students have a fairly clear idea of their interests and will benefit from an elaborate program of particular offerings. Others do not, and they will benefit from an education in a school with a range of good academic departments.

Counselors for gifted students need to have wide experience in working with college and university admission and scholarship programs. They should know, or be able quickly to find out, which schools are considered the leaders in various fields, which have early admissions programs, what the entrance requirements are, and what financial aid is available for highly able students.

Able students have a much broader educational horizon than their average counterparts. Some students choose a college or university at a very young age. Others take the initiative to write for information from various schools and are involved in actively searching for the best schools for their particular interests and needs. Others, though, have never thought beyond high school, or if they have, they have only considered the local community college. For this latter group, in particular, counselors need to concentrate on enlarging students' scope to include the vast array of options available to them.

Faulty Self-Image

One reason many gifted students never think beyond high school is that they hold an unrealistically low self-image. Some very able youth have no concept of how bright they really are. For example, a fourteen-year-old Mexican-American girl with an IQ of 140+, identified as gifted in elementary school, complained to her teacher that she was not too happy about the idea of being cooped up in an office all her life. When questioned about what she meant, Carla replied that a secretary is stuck in an office all day, and that really did not sound too appealing to her. Her mother, an uneducated mother of sixteen children, had always encouraged her daughter to stay in school so she could get a good job as a secretary when she finished high school. The teacher suggested that Carla had many more options open to her, some of which would not keep her "cooped up in an office all day." Carla was astonished that she was considered capable of being something besides a secretary.

Students like Carla need the opportunity to compete with other able students. To participate, though, they must be *willing* to compete. Many—especially girls—need encouragement to join the competition. They may not realize that they are championship quality because they have never been given the opportunity to compete with champions and come out at or near the top. This can be a problem in particularly small or rural communities where the school population is limited. It is up to the counselor to help such students see how bright they are. The counselor may choose to work with individuals or groups to help them self-identify their giftedness—and to accept it. Some young people, having always attended school with numerous able students, consider themselves average, when in fact they are quite capable compared to the general population. Knowing this may give such students the confidence to try out for a competitive academic scholarship or to apply to a college known for its high academic standards.

Another kind of problem may emerge when a student attends an elite university or becomes part of a specialized program within a university. In such a group the student may no longer stand out as particularly gifted, and the competition is fierce. Some able students who have breezed through their academic work in high school may be in for quite a shock upon entering college. One semester may jolt them into awareness that they cannot proceed successfully through college the way they did through high school. Earnest effort may ensue.

Sometimes, though, failure, or lack of success, is so traumatic that the student drops out, afraid to compete. Or, if the student's financial aid is contingent on maintenance of high grades, one semester of low ones could cause the student to lose the scholarship and thus be forced to drop out. So, it is better to engage college-bound students in frank discussion of their strengths and weaknesses, and what they can do to build on their strengths and compensate for weaknesses. Students who have achieved nearly all their lives do not take well to failure, and whatever the counselor can do to ward off failure in college is worth attempting.

Vocational Choice

Another challenge for the counselor of gifted students lies in the area of vocational choice. Because very bright people often have many interests, picking one or two possible career areas may be difficult. Without failing to encourage their intellectual breadth through course selection, counselors should also use the tools available to them to help students narrow down their choices. In addition to vocational tests, counselors should administer tests that "provide information about a student's pattern of abilities, current level of achievement, and interests, rather than a global estimate of general intelligence" (Fox & Pyryt 1979, 186). Because students' career choices have more impact on their lives than almost any other decision they make, time and effort spent helping gifted youth focus on a career is well spent.

After some testing and guided discussion, attempts should be made to get these students "out into the field," that is, working, if only briefly, in the areas in which they are interested. For example, if a vocational inventory indicates that a gifted high school boy leans toward an occupation that involves working with people, and if his academic strengths are verbal—writing and speaking—then he might be interested in a career in city promotion, city planning, or city management. The local chamber of commerce may be persuaded to arrange an internship with one of the directors. If a long-term internship is not feasible, then possibly the student could shadow the professional to speaking engagements and meetings for several afternoons and evenings.

When students get out into the workplace, not only do they see jobs that they might or might not be interested in, but they make valuable contacts as well. For example, if the young man in the previous example decides that he wants to aim for a career with the chamber of commerce, the person he shadowed could possibly arrange for exciting summer internships in related but scarcely known fields. Such experiences are invaluable to the gifted, who, as we saw in chapter 2, aim to do original things in their vocations. It is important to have people from many different fields come to the school to visit with students, for the majority of young people have no idea of what occupations are available other than doctor, lawyer, teacher, mayor, and the like. Students may know which field they want to major in but then have no concept of what job options are available in that field. So the job of counselor involves narrowing some gifted students' fields of vision and broadening others!

Conflicts with Teachers

Conflicts between gifted children and their teachers occur often enough to present a perennial problem to counselors. Teachers may love the gifted—or let them know that they are a bane to their existence. When a student approaches a counselor concerning a teacher, the situation must be handled carefully, sensitively, and prudently. In a few paragraphs, it is impossible to explore all the possible roots of gifted student–teacher problems, but a few possibilities and solutions will be offered.

Rarely is any problem all one party's fault, and this goes for conflicts between gifted students and their teachers, too. But a student who asks a counselor for help, either directly or indirectly, needs an advocate, especially considering the problems that bright students traditionally have with their teachers.

Too often, very able students are perceived as threats by teachers who are insecure about their own knowledge and ability. Bright students who ask questions generated by their knowledge and curiosity are frequently put down by such teachers. Rather than admitting that they do not know the answer, which is a perfectly acceptable response to a question, these teachers squash the students' enthusiasm as a cover-up for their own lack of knowledge. When "teachers lambast students for asking . . . questions, gifted teens may develop self-doubts or become cynical about anything that goes on in the classroom" (Johnson 1981, 27).

When such hostile situations occur (and they do, from kindergarten through graduate school), there are basically two avenues open. First, the student can be removed from the class. In severe cases, this is the only option. No student should be subjected to a year's worth of put-downs—whether for an hour a day in high school or all day in elementary school. Students in a classroom quickly adopt their teacher's perceptions of other students, so it is highly likely that a student slighted and degraded by the teacher will soon receive the same treatment from peers. Whether the expression of hostility is overt or masked, the student, particularly a sensitive gifted student, can discern it and be affected by it, and should be removed from such a situation.

In some cases the counselor can provide another avenue for the gifted student who has a personality conflict with a teacher. Whether to use it depends upon the severity and type of the conflict and the maturity of the child. For many highly able youth, presenting the situation realistically and planning possible strategies to improve the situation is a legitimate guidance technique. Gifted children and youth tend to be highly perceptive. They are usually able to determine that the reason for conflict with their teacher(s) is the threat their giftedness poses. What they often need help with, then, are ways to deal with the situation positively. Many students act negatively, reciprocating the antagonism. In junior high and high school classes, more than in elementary classes, this not only gets back at the teacher but may increase the antagonizing student's status among classmates. However, the strategy is totally nonproductive for either the students or the teacher.

The counselor can try to point out the unproductiveness of such behavior. A group of students having the same problems may develop alternatives through modeling or role playing. Depending on the counselor-teacher relationship, a three-way conference could be held with the student to try to resolve their differences. A judicious counselor could determine the chances that such a plan would work.

Boredom

Another frequent complaint by gifted students is that they are bored in class. The problem may begin in first grade, when a student who can already read is forced to go through the preprimer. Sumption and Luecking point out that

> no child who has learned to read, and who has read for himself
> in the interesting books that are being published for beginning
> readers, can be expected to be satisfied for any length of time to
> read about a dog and a cat, or a boy and a girl, whose conversa-

tion consists of "Oh!" "Look!" "See!" and other such absorbing comments. (1960, 352)

Boredom is present when a mathematically gifted student is restrained
in a class plodding through eighth-grade general math because her
school does not believe in accelerating students beyond their grade
level, nor does it provide qualitatively different courses of study for the
highly able.

Boredom may be present when a student who has been intrigued by
marine biology since he was a young child, and has pursued that interest, is required to list the parts of a plant on a ditto sheet. Boredom may
rear its ugly head when a student, capable of thinking at a higher level,
is expected to answer questions that tap only literal-level comprehension, nothing more. Gifted students can be expected to generalize and
synthesize material presented to them and for this reason, require a
qualitatively different curriculum (see chapter 6, "Academic Curriculum for the Gifted"). The students in the examples are bored either because the material itself is far below the level where they are capable of
working or because the presentation method is below their learning
threshold. Sometimes, though, gifted students are bored because they
refuse to become involved, or because they have been legitimately
bored in school for so long that the phrase "I'm bored" rolls off their
tongue whether it is justified or not. (It is a good pity-inducer for parents: "You poor thing—you're so smart and have to sit there all day,
listening to those boring teachers.")

It requires a perceptive counselor to determine which type of boredom the student is experiencing. If the boredom is legitimate, then
working with the student's teachers is expedient. If not, then some
time needs to be spent with the student, encouraging the discovery
that a subject is boring because the student is refusing to enjoy it. By
accomplishing this, the counselor opens a portion of life to a student
who might otherwise have missed it because it was "boring."

SPECIAL SUBGROUPS OF THE GIFTED

Three subgroups of the gifted have special needs that deserve separate
discussion. They are (1) gifted females, (2) gifted children who are also
handicapped or learning disabled, and (3) the creatively gifted.

Gifted Females

Although both genders of gifted students benefit from the help of a
counselor, for a few more years at least, gifted girls will need more

help. They often lack the opportunism or aggressiveness that under-lies the ambition shown by males. Some of Wolleatt's (1979) findings point to the conclusion that women develop competitive behavior later than men do. Even though male and female roles are changing, the old attitudes remain powerful enough to cause girls to experience conflict between the traditional female role and the new one—which tends to attract them.

Wolleat's perception of the counseling and guidance needs of gifted females may be summarized as follows:

1. Purposeful, deliberate affirmative action strategies must be im-plemented with gifted females.
2. A multimodal counseling approach is required, since the under-lying causes of gifted females' failure to utilize their potential are complex.
3. Counselors must examine their own assumptions regarding gifted females.
4. Male and female students need intervention regarding assump-tions about gifted females.
5. Besides academic challenges, gifted girls need experiences that will develop their autonomy, self-esteem, self-confidence, toler-ance for ambiguity, willingness to compete, and assertiveness.
6. Gifted females need help broadening their goals beyond the nar-row set of occupations traditionally considered appropriate for women.
7. Gifted females need help seeing the value of a background in math and science.
8. Gifted females should be encouraged to make plans—to utilize their talents, to investigate various life-styles with which they could be satisfied, and to determine their educational and career goals. (Wolleat 1979, 341–42)

Counselors need to inform themselves about the unique characteris-tics of gifted females and then determine strategies to encourage their development to full capacity. For an extensive bibliography on gifted girls and women, see Rodenstein 1977. Another good place to start is the section entitled "Women" in Colangelo and Zaffrann (1979) which includes several excellent articles for counselors.

Handicapped/Gifted and Learning Disabled/Gifted

Just as some people consider "underachieving gifted" to be an oxymo-ron, some cannot imagine that handicapped/gifted or learning disabled/gifted are terms that can be collocative. Whitmore defines the gifted/handicapped child as

> One who requires special educational programming (*a*) to accommodate one or more handicapping conditions and (*b*) to fully develop his or her potential for exceptional achievement in one or more areas in which he or she may be gifted or talented. (1981, 107)

Whitmore estimates that there are between 300,000 and 450,000 handicapped children in the United States who could also be classified as mentally gifted (this number is 5 percent of the 6 to 9 million handicapped children and youth). Because of the methods conventionally used to identify the gifted—teacher nomination, group achievement scores, group intelligence scores, and previously demonstrated accomplishments (Stefanich & Schnur 1979)—it is doubtful that even 1 percent of the handicapped/gifted are being adequately served. One can see how these measures would keep many handicapped students from showing up as gifted. The counselor or teacher of the gifted and/ or handicapped must be informed of methods and instruments that will not exclude those students who are both gifted and handicapped. For a more extensive discussion of identification procedures for these students, see the chapter "Identification of the Gifted" and its annotated bibliography.

The dilemma of learning disabled/gifted students is that their giftedness often allows them to find ways to compensate for their disability. That is, the gifted are intelligent and self-aware and are therefore able to perceive their weaknesses and devise strategies for circumventing them. This "self-improvement" is usually not enough to make the gifted/learning disabled student evidently gifted, but it is enough to make him or her evidently average. This is a problem because, appearing to be average, the student does not receive enrichment for giftedness or remediation for deficits but becomes lost among the average students (Wolf & Gygi 1981).

In order to seek out these students, counselors should remain alert to new findings on their characteristics and new methods of identification. And when such students are identified, the counselor must "go to bat" for them. Many school personnel (including school-board members, administrators, and teachers) are neither cognizant of the co-occurrence of giftedness and disability nor informed about how best to educate such students. Without someone (counselor, teacher, or parent) pushing for appropriate education, it will never happen—and these students will never reach their potential.

Creatively Gifted

Some students, if and when they become bored, create their own excitement. These students, often quite creative, can disrupt entire classrooms and are rarely the joy of their teachers' days. An article by Davis and Rimm (1977) succinctly discusses the characteristics of creatively gifted children. The picture they paint allows the reader to see why such persons do not allow themselves to be bored for long. They are high in independence and self-confidence and have an unusually high energy level mixed with spontaneity. They tend to be playful and possess a good sense of humor (Davis and Rimm 1977). "Squelching" the creativity of children and youth who are creatively gifted not only robs them of a large part of their uniqueness but also deprives the society of the wealth these individuals have to offer. However, if such creativity is interfering with a successful school experience, the counselor may need to help the student learn to operate within the structure the school imposes—usually necessarily. For example, teachers generally expect assignments to be handwritten or typed on paper. If a creatively gifted child prefers turning in assignments on videotape—with the appropriate background music and visual effects—the counselor might make clear the teachers' reasons for wanting assignments to be completed on paper, while also attempting to point out to the teacher the merits of videotaped homework. Possibly a compromise can be worked out. Especially with highly creatively gifted students, though, when such compromises cannot be reached or when understandings cannot be established, the counselor needs to seek the option of placing them with teachers who appreciate, or at least tolerate, extraordinary creativity.

The key to counseling the gifted is forthrightness. The level of their intellect, the depth of their perception, and the degree of their sensitivity makes reasoning with the gifted both challenging and productive. Counselors can also be straightforward with gifted children and youth because they have not built up all the stereotypes and preconceived notions that many adults have. Such unconventionality is one reason working with the teachers and parents of gifted students may be difficult—but very necessary.

COUNSELING FOR TEACHERS

It will be assumed that teachers who work exclusively with the gifted have had training of one kind or another in gifted education—through special in-service training, courses in gifted education, or even an advanced degree in the field. Teachers of homogeneous classes for the gifted have their own needs for a counselor, and they will be addressed separately at the end of this section. The majority of the section will deal with counselors who work with teachers of heterogeneous classes.

Many teachers and administrators carry a lot of stereotypic baggage, and much of it is negative regarding the gifted. With such adults, counselors must take an indirect approach. A direct challenge may cause them to close their minds completely and thus thwart any efforts to inform them about gifted students and their needs. Counselors know their schools and the people who work in them, and they need to make individual decisions about how best to open up communication on the educational needs of the highly able.

Providing some in-service training for teachers is one possible beginning. This training can be conducted by the counselor, by a local teacher of the gifted, or by an outside expert. One session will not be sufficient, so a series should be planned for the year. It might prove helpful to appeal first to the interests of some of the leaders among the teachers. If leaders have a positive attitude regarding gifted education, less dissension among other faculty members can be expected.

In some schools, it may be more successful to conduct a quiet campaign through personal discussions with individual faculty members. If the local gifted association is holding a session that might interest a faculty member, that teacher could be invited to accompany the counselor. If a workshop conducted by an authority in the field is planned for a nearby area, the principal and a few teachers might be encouraged to attend. Their participation will certainly heighten their interest—and the information they share when they come back will stimulate others.

If certain teachers work particularly well with able students, the counselor should encourage them to propose a session at a local, state, regional, or national professional conference. The counselor may even provide the forms. The teachers not only get a morale boost, but they will pick up ideas at the conference to pass on to the staff at home.

One object of such tactics is to heighten teachers' awareness of the gifted students in their classrooms. Most teachers do not recognize the characteristics of giftedness. If they became familiar with the signs of giftedness, then they could identify students in their classes who need differential education.

Counselors must remember that teachers want to teach—very few of the "bad" or less-than-outstanding teachers are satisfied with their poor performance. Most of them want to do a good job, which means *teaching*. If teachers are truly informed about what children need and *how to provide it for them*, then they will do almost anything in their power to accomplish that end. Counselors can appeal to teachers' needs to be successful and their desire to provide appropriately for their students in order to inform them about how to best teach the gifted.

For example, many teachers have never tried using an independent study contract with a gifted student—and this is one effective way of providing for the able youngster in a heterogeneous classroom. It allows for acceleration, enrichment, and pursuit of the student's individual interest—all components of the differentiated education needed by able youth. Counselors could provide a brief introductory minicourse on setting up independent studies, which would be enough to allow the teachers to see the feasibility of such projects. Several sample contracts, management methods, and rationale articles should be available for the teachers. The counselor should also have other materials available for those whose appetites for teaching the gifted have been whetted.

Counselors are not expected to be experts in every curriculum area, but when a teacher comes to ask for help in planning for an able student, the counselor needs to be able to get that teacher some help. People in gifted education tend to be very helpful and willing to share— because they know that unless everyone involved continues to work and spread the good word, gifted education will fall by the wayside again. If no personnel are available to help, then professional publications should be recommended, with articles specified, for teachers seeking solutions to the challenge presented by students of superior capabilities.

One area where counselors are experts, and teachers generally are not, is the interpretation of tests. Few teachers have had more than one course in tests and measurements. Most cannot plan appropriately for students on the basis of a number such as IQ. Counselors can provide teachers with explanations of test scores, percentiles, and profile sheets. Testing is for naught unless results can be used by someone. One hopes that someone is the person who directly affects the student each day—the teacher.

Teachers who work primarily with gifted students also need help interpreting test scores, and they often need help relating to the other teachers in their building. In many, many schools, not only are the children identified as gifted the objects of hostility from regular teachers, but so are the gifted students' teachers. It is difficult to be the pariah in a school building just because one's job is serving gifted students.

There may be no one with whom to share successes because they are met with comments like, "Of course your kids are learning—you've got all the smart ones." A teacher in this type of situation also cannot share failures because many on the faculty are just looking for the program to fail.

Also, the gifted-program teacher who is the sole advocate for the gifted in a building may have to step on some toes and feelings in order to do what is best for the children. For example, the best option for a junior high school girl may be to accelerate her right through junior high to high school. But some bypassed teachers may see this action as an affront to their teaching abilities. Many teachers believe that they individualize enough that able, slow, and average students all get the education they need in one classroom. The role of advocate rarely endears teachers of the gifted to other teachers' hearts, but fortunately, most of them still do what they have to do.

The counselor in the school can be an ear or a shoulder for such a teacher, or a comrade in advocacy. Working together, they can begin to effect changes in a school's complexion, so that being gifted or teaching the gifted does not ensure ostracism. These two professionals can form a team that has as its goal full membership from the staff, so that all are working and providing for their exceptional students.

COUNSELING FOR PARENTS

Counselors, teachers, and parents of the gifted need to become a team from the outset. Only when family and school collaborate can the unique needs of the gifted be best met (Lester & Anderson 1981). Part of the counselor's task is to convince the others of this fact.

The myth that all parents believe their children are gifted is simply not true. Many parents whose offspring are gifted do not realize that fact—and some refuse to acknowledge it when the evidence is shown to them.

Several reasons could contribute to such rejection of facts. If the parents do not consider themselves bright, then they may have a hard time believing that they have produced a gifted child. Some parents may deny the facts because they do not *want* a gifted child. Despite some recent change, there are still many "good average folks" who just want to have a "good average child." Such an attitude stems from the stereotypes about gifted children and youth—that they are scrawny bookworms who are the social outcasts of the school and neighborhood. Thus, parents may be concerned that inherent in gift-edness is a life of loneliness and ostracism.

Such parents need to be given some literature (which looks inviting to read) about the characteristics of the gifted. They should learn about the various degrees of giftedness and the multiple areas in which children and youth manifest their gifts. Then, if possible, the parents should be taken to a school or classroom where gifted children or youth are working. This experience should amply demonstrate that stereotypes about the gifted are unfounded—and that joy, not fear, should be the reaction to discovering that one's offspring is gifted.

Whether or not they are surprised to discover that their child is gifted, virtually all parents of gifted children want and need answers to some questions. The counselor should not only be ready to answer them but should have available pamphlets and fact sheets from the National Association for Gifted Children (NAGC) or The Association for Gifted (TAG) (addresses are in the appendix). It would also be prudent to make sure that the local library purchases books and subscribes to magazines that deal with giftedness. Some schools maintain a professional library, which should contain some books of interest to parents of the gifted. Another possibility is to encourage the school's parent association to maintain a lending library for parents (for suggestions, see the annotated bibliography in the chapter "Parenting Gifted Children").

Some of the parents' questions cannot be answered by books, so counselors will need to be informed and ready to answer. For example, parents should know about the type and extent of their child's giftedness and how the child compares to others. They should be informed about any special needs their child has or will have (e.g., special training, camps, courses) so that they will have lead time to make financial and other plans. They may also need some suggestions regarding discipline—what works well with able children and what might be effective with their child in particular.

In families that include other children, parents may need guidance so that their home does not begin to revolve round the gifted child. Some parents need to be shown ways to accept and encourage each of their children's differences. Role playing might be an effective way to demonstrate these techniques. It may seem obvious that, although a child is gifted, he or she is first a child, with regular childlike needs—for love, affection, room to grow. However, many parents (and other adults) forget this fact about able children and young adults.

As is thoroughly discussed in the parenting chapter, parents of the gifted need to form support groups, for their own benefit as well as their children's. Counselors can help get such a group started, as either an independent organization or a branch of the school's parent association.

One group that a counselor can expect to see consists of parents of children who did not quite qualify for the gifted program. In some communities, it is prestigious to be labeled gifted—or to have one's child so labeled. Therefore, when a child does not meet the school district's criteria, some parents become upset and want to know why. No blanket statement can be made about how to handle this problem other than to be candid regarding the child's areas of strength and weakness. It is difficult to explain why one school district uses an IQ cutoff of 130, while another ten miles away uses 128—and why the parents in the counselor's office have a child who would be labeled gifted in another school district but not this one.

These parents, too, should be provided with material to read and the name of the local group for parents of the gifted. Although they may not be happy when they leave, these parents should at least be armed with some ways to nurture their child's abilities, providing stimulation and promoting readiness for self-fulfillment and service.

Working with parents is a significant part of the school counselor's job. Parents are vitally important in the education of their child, especially as they contribute to the child's motivation and feelings of self-worth. If the school situation is bad, as it sometimes is for gifted young people, parents can help buffer some of the negative responses their children are getting. If the school situation is good, parents can help reinforce the positive. To aptly aid their gifted children, parents need to know how to help, and the counselor can back up the parents. (See chapter 8, "Parenting Gifted Children.")

Much of counseling with the gifted and those surrounding them involves *helping*—to know, to provide, to serve, to reach, to attain. According to Rothney and Koopman (1958), counselors can do for most students what no one else is in a position to do because they generally have a more comprehensive view of the educational scene, including its vocational outcomes and possibilities and its social and domestic circumstances. Counselors with patience, wisdom, and training are needed by the gifted—because the gifted are needed by society.

A TEAM EFFORT: HELP
FOR THE GIFTED UNDERACHIEVER

If young people are the greatest natural resource of the world, then the gravest waste of that resource is permitting underachievement among the gifted. Gowan and Bruch (1971, 45) state that "as a group, gifted students are likely to be our most severely underachieving population." No one is more able to confront and solve the problems of the world than are the gifted; allowing them to underachieve will have repercussions of a magnitude beyond what can be imagined.

Strong statements will be made in this section on the underachieving gifted, but one hopes that vehement statements will lead to firm stands, which will lead to decisive actions. Without such actions, the gross waste of this precious resource will continue—which must not be allowed.

To most teachers of the gifted, there is no need to establish the existence of underachieving gifted students. It is a rare classroom of highly able students that does not include underachievers. Almost every teacher who works with the gifted laments students who score at or near the top on achievement and aptitude tests but rarely do classwork, turn in homework, or participate in school-related extracurricular activities.

The picture painted by these teachers seems paradoxical to many. People who do not work closely with gifted students often find the idea of underachievement among that population difficult to accept. Most lay people and many educators see gifted students as constantly seeking to please their teachers—for example, by doing extra-credit reports even though their average is already A+. Such students may or may not be gifted, and even when they are not, they are often recommended for gifted placement because of their productivity. The only label that can be placed with assurance on these children is "productive"—not necessarily gifted.

Zilli (1971) delineated five groups of underachieving gifted students:

1. Students with low grades and high achievement-test scores (i.e., students who score well on yearly achievement tests but whose grades do not reflect the same achievement).
2. Those with high grades and low achievement-test scores (i.e., students whose hard work and/or abilities enable them to earn high grades but who, because of lack of interest, poor test-taking ability, or other problems, are unable to exhibit their learning on achievement tests).
3. Cases of chronic underachievement (i.e., students whose performance is consistently below their measured aptitude or potential for academic achievement.

4. Situational underachievement (i.e., students whose under-achievement can be directly or indirectly traced to a particular set of circumstances, such as the death of a parent).
5. "Hidden underachievement" (i.e., students who, in the teacher's judgment, are holding back or deliberately underachieving).

Consideration of such categories, including subgroups within each category, is necessary in order to successfully address the problems of underachievement. A phrase synonymous with underachievement is "not working up to potential." Just as cancer is treated differently depending on the type, treatment of the malady of underachievement begins with identifying the particular type experienced by the student. To expect only one type of underachievement from members of a group as diverse as the gifted would be ludicrous: giftedness manifests itself in numerous ways, and so too does the underachievement of gifted persons.

According to Barrett (1957), individuals underachieve either because they cannot adequately utilize their inner resources or because they choose not to. Gifted individuals may be underachieving because their inner resources (1) have atrophied due to disuse, (2) have been numbed by expectations of convergent production, (3) have been squelched by ignorant teachers or parents, or (4) have been blocked because all attention and energy have been diverted to handle a tough situation. Also, gifted individuals may choose to underachieve in order to (1) better "fit in" with their age-mates, (2) meet family expectations, or (3) rebel against the achievement emphasis of our culture. Whatever the reason for able students' underachievement, professional help must be provided. Hoping that students will "grow out of" an underachievement "phase" is like hoping that a child will grow out of having bad teeth. Neglecting the condition only makes it worse, until finally the damage becomes irreparable. Neglecting a gifted child's underachievement almost ensures at least a partially "decayed" life and life-style.

The professional help needed by underachieving gifted students may be provided by counselors, teachers, parents, peers, or others in the community. The number of people and the extent to which they must become involved depends on the degree of underachievement, and how long it has been allowed to continue—how firmly it has taken root. Shaw and McCuen claim that many types of underachievement in the gifted can be detected in the first grade—and, "while counseling with underachievers may prove successful at all levels, it requires less time with younger students" (1960, 107). The longer underachievement continues, the more firmly entrenched it becomes in the child's habits, attitudes, and behaviors. Underachievement must be discovered early and corrected early!

Who should be responsible for recognizing the signs of underachievement? The responsibility lies with those adults who spend the most time with the youngster—parents, teachers, and counselors. In order for them to detect the beginnings of underachievement, they must be informed about its characteristics. The task of disseminating information regarding the underachieving gifted rests with anyone who possesses this knowledge. Counselors and teachers familiar with underachievement among gifted individuals should share the information with their colleagues and with parents. Parents, either independently or through parent organizations or gifted-advocacy groups, should disseminate the information to other parents and parents-to-be, and to the schools. The information can be shared informally, over coffee; formally, through workshops or lectures; or by passing on books, pamphlets, or articles. Community members also need to be made aware of the tragedy of gifted underachievers, so that they too can offer support when needed.

The characteristics of underachievement vary, but the certain indication is a discrepancy between expectation and performance. As noted in Zilli's list of categories, the discrepany is not always in the direction of high expectations and low performance, although this is the type most often associated with underachievement. The discrepancy may lie in the other direction—low expectation and high achievement. Ironically, the misnomer *overachievement* is usually applied to this phenomenon. But, just as one cannot extract two cups of water from a one-cup jar, neither can a child produce more than he or she is capable of. There is however, the viable concept of *underexpectation*, which is often mislabeled overachievement. When this happens, in the case of low test scores combined with high grades, there actually is underachievement on the test, and this condition deserves attention by a counselor or other trained professional.

Counselors, classroom teachers, and parents must keep in mind the watchword "discrepancy between expectations and performance" as they maintain their vigilance against underachievement. Much of the vigilance entails awareness—knowing what is normal and then constantly being watchful for what is abnormal. For example, a teacher who has taught first grade for seventeen years knows the rate at which most first graders learn to read and also knows the relative percentage of children who come to school already able to read. This teacher also knows generally what those early readers' achievement-test scores are likely to be. Therefore, when a child comes to school reading and is an avid learner, but then scores miserably on standardized tests, the aware teacher recognizes that something is amiss.

Likewise, an experienced and aware junior high school science teacher is alert to clues of underachievement when a ninth grader, who has been the top science project winner for three years in a row, and an active member of the science club, suddenly drops out of the club, fails a major science test, and refuses to complete the science portion of a standardized achievement test. The teacher knows that not only is this abnormal for this student, but the abnormality is negative.

Similarly, a high school English teacher knows that a problem exists when a student who consistently uses sophisticated language when speaking, and scores at the ninety-ninth percentile in all areas of aptitude tests, refuses to participate in *any* class activities or to complete *any* class assignments and has a longstanding reputation for failing everything except tests. This teacher shares what the aforementioned teachers have—awareness of what is normal and what is an aberration in student performance. Two factors influence this awareness: experience and a conscious decision to remain aware.

A teacher's (or counselor's, or administrator's, or parent's) experience can be broad or deep or both. The breadth stems primarily from the diversity of experience and the length of service. Depth of experience comes from strong involvement with students. School personnel who become intimately involved with students gain a much deeper perspective than do those who are just "putting in their time."

Some educators "naturally" become closely involved with students. Others must make a conscious decision to be more receptive and responsive. Counselors, teachers, administrators, and parents must also make some sort of willful determination to be attentive to the young people around them. They must decide whether this attentiveness is going to include their physical, mental, and/or emotional needs. In order to effectively detect and ward off underachievement among the gifted, school personnel must know not only the normal range for the age group they serve but also the range the individual student operates in most efficiently and comfortably. Then, those associated with the student must remain vigilant to ensure that if and when a gifted student deviates from the range of normality, something is done immediately. Keeping one's head in the sand is totally unacceptable as a means for contending with underachievement.

Given that underachievement exists, and given that it can be recognized by the disparity between what is expected and what is performed, what can be done to alleviate the syndrome among gifted children and youth? Any of the following suggestions will be most effective and will require less effort if instituted early in a child's underachievement. Many believe that if underachievement is allowed to continue until a student is in high school, it will never be overcome, and except in rare cases, the student will never approach the level that could have been reached if abilities had been fully utilized.

As in the previous section of this chapter, we will make suggestions for the counselor, but teachers and parents may also find them helpful. In order to be most effective, these suggestions should be carried out jointly by the underachieving child's counselor, parents, and teachers.

As mentioned earlier, one must keep in mind the different types and causes of underachievement. Just because one intervention has worked with an underachieving gifted student in the past does not mean it will necessarily work in all cases. Some remedial teachers get into a rut, using one treatment as a panacea for all problems, and being often disappointed at its ineffectiveness.

Many highly able children are placed, and must remain, in "regular" first grade classrooms in their local schools. Schooling alternatives may not be available for a variety of reasons, such as parents' limited budgets, local school officials' unawareness of a need for gifted education, or lack of recognition of the child's giftedness. Then, more often than not, these gifted children do not receive an appropriate education. They are underchallenged at best and discouraged at worst. And the stage is set for the beginning of underachievement.

In order to avoid annoying the teacher by always finishing first, some gifted children will play the game of "averageness." They are smart enough to learn the acceptable pattern in the classroom, which they then mold themselves to fit. They purposely tone down their inquisitiveness and learn to do just enough to "get by." Anything that lies unused long enough will begin to atrophy, including the ability to think and function at a high level. If gifted youngsters spend several years enduring classrooms that neither challenge nor encourage their abilities, chronic underachievement often results.

The very best "treatment" for this type of underachievement is *prevention*. Teachers, especially kindergarten and first grade teachers, need to be educated so that they can recognize signs of giftedness. They then need to be further trained and motivated to meet the educational needs of those students in their classrooms who are extraordinarily able.

Many teachers—good teachers—do not know what methods they can use to teach and continually challenge their gifted students. Too many primary teachers hold the notion that the best they can do for their able students (who can already read, are doing their own science experiments, and/or compose original music) is to let them "mark time" until the rest of their age-mates catch up with them. The able students "mark time" by being "teacher's helpers," by vegetating in average reading groups, by helping slower students, or by doing reams of work sheets at a higher grade level. Needless to say, little or no positive learning takes place.

Elementary school counselors should spend a great deal of time with primary teachers to help adequately serve the gifted students in their classes. The counselors may find it most effective to work with teachers on an individual basis, or one grade level at a time. These encounters could involve sharing methods for enrichment, acceleration, or differentiation that work with gifted students. If this help is offered in a nonjudgmental way, virtually all teachers will appreciate and respond to the suggestions. They will recognize that using them will enhance the quality of teaching in their classrooms, which is exactly what teachers want.

On the other side of the coin, what if no counselor is available for the primary grades? And, what if a gifted child has endured five years of underexpectation and underchallenge so that now, as a fifth grader, he or she has limited desire to perform in school and seems satisfied to be complacent regarding learning? The task of reversing the underachievement is infinitely more difficult than prevention would have been—but still possible. In order not to become discouraged, one should keep in mind that the reward for this effort is an achieving, happier child.

The first step is to establish the *actual* level of the child. This may be done "in-house" by the school counselor or, if no counselor or psychometrician is available, the testing may have to be done by an independent professional. A series of tests and interviews rather than a single measure will yield the truest picture of the student's abilities.

Once this is established, the child should be informed, if not specifically, at least generally, about the results. Too many gifted students have no idea how bright they are, and it stands to reason that this is even more true of underachieving gifted students because they have not competed to see how they compare to other students. Knowing the extent of their abilities could contribute to their recovery from underachievement. Some gifted persons, in their desire to excel, will not even attempt certain things for fear of failing. If such persons discover that they are indeed highly capable in a particular area (or areas), that fear may be removed, or at least lessened. It is possible that teachers and parents can then provide enough encouragement that the students will make the effort in the previously avoided area.

After determining the abilities of an underachieving ten- or twelve-year-old, and informing the student about those abilities, the next step is to match that student with a teacher who is enthusiastic about learning and teaching. Each month that an underachieving gifted student spends in an unstimulating environment deepens the rut of underachievement. The most lively teacher at, or just above, the child's current grade level should be entrusted with the student. The teacher should be one who makes learning exciting for all students—whether of low, average, or high ability. This teacher should also be willing to go the extra mile (or two or three) that it will take to recover the underachieving gifted student. Just as not all students are created equal, neither are all teachers. Special-ability students need special-ability teachers.

Whether a classroom change in the middle of the year is deemed necessary in order to best meet the needs of the underachieving gifted child, or whether the change takes place more routinely at the beginning of the year, the parents must be called in to become partners with the school. Turning an underachieving gifted youngster around is not impossible without the parents' cooperation, but it is immeasurably more difficult. Rescuing an underachieving gifted student requires consistency from the school, from the home, and from the home and school in tandem. Inconsistency on either side undermines the efforts of the other—and lengthens or destroys the process.

Deliberately and thoughtfully interweaving the parents and school personnel will be time-consuming. At least one side will need educating—about teaching the gifted, about underachieving among the gifted, and about how to help the underachieving gifted student. Either the parents or the educators may need convincing concerning the efficacy and urgency of rescuing this young person who has so much potential but is allowing it to fade away. In short, the task of entwining parents and teachers will not be without effort, but it is vitally important to the success of the endeavor.

Next, through a cooperative effort, the child's most intense interests must be found and cultivated. No single method necessarily yields this information, but one way that should at least be included with others is to ask. Ask the child what he or she finds the most intriguing or the most fascinating. The answer may provide at least a clue to the direction that the next step should take.

The next step is to find some one person with whom the gifted child can identify. This may entail a trial-and-error process, but it is an important step for the gifted student who has been underachieving for a number of years. This one person may be a relative, a teacher, an older young person (high school or college student), a professional in the community, a retired person, or it could be anyone who can share an affinity with the child. Although their areas of interest do not necessarily have to coincide, that is often the attraction that initially serves to bring them together. A common interest will not *hold* them together, however, nor will it serve to lift the young person out of underachievement. This can only be accomplished by sincere caring, commitment, and willingness to be both friend and taskmaster when required. One hopes that this relationship will develop to the point that the youngster will make the extra effort in school because of the "significant other's" inspiration (Abraham 1962). Then, once the cycle of effort and success has begun, and the underachievement syndrome has been broken, one hopes the kinship will continue—but the achievement should continue with or without the relationship. This turnaround takes time—but it is time which will bestow benefits on each person who contributes.

The time and effort involved in salvaging underachieving elementary school youngsters is far less than that which must be spent retrieving those gifted youth who are still underachieving in junior high and high school. At this point, some would consider the task insurmountable—and it nearly is. For the student who is highly able and has been performing at an average or below-average level for five to ten years, the pattern is set in rapidly hardening cement. This pattern could include exerting little or no effort, being settled into a lethargic stance concerning achievement, and displaying a lackadaisical attitude toward college and later career goals. Retrieving underachieving gifted high school students involves a drastic, strong, and concerted effort by all those involved: parents, teachers, counselors, administrators, community members, and peers.

For adolescents, no one group is more influential than their peers. A prudent counselor will utilize that peer influence for all it is worth in order to help the underachieving students change their course. Gowan recommends group therapy for the gifted underachiever:

> Because this type of young person feels insecure and is likely to lack a real peer group . . . (the group) may at least lead to confidences and possibly friendships among people, leading ultimately to improved social adjustment . . . (and) stronger worth-while personal attitudes. (1955, 270)

Counselors may choose to form counseling groups that include only gifted underachievers, or a minority of gifted underachievers and a majority of gifted achievers. Mixing gifted and nongifted students would be of doubtful benefit.

In conjunction with group counseling, the steps outlined earlier should be utilized, too: determine ability, inform the student, place with an enthusiastic teacher, cultivate intense interests, and foster a relationship with a significant other. It is possible that drastic schooling alternatives will need to be provided at this point. Some students cannot learn in traditional situations, and rather than writing these students off, multiple alternatives must be conceived of and offered. These alternatives must in some way provide the outlets into which the underachieving gifted can plug, thereby electrifying their minds so that neither they nor those around them continue to operate in the dark.

Should gifted persons be expected to be performance machines—reaching new heights on every project they undertake? No, the point of this section is not to advocate pushing and pulling gifted youth in every direction so that they achieve and then achieve some more. The point is that gifted youth should be *allowed* to achieve, not kept from it by their own laziness or by the languidness of those who have been entrusted to educate these bright spots of the present and the future. Underachievement is one of the stumbling blocks that could keep the gifted from reaching their potential—and it is one that can be prevented or removed should it occur. Regarding a decision to help an underachieving gifted child, Abraham said,

> The choice is a relatively simple one to express. Do it, and help meet society's major ills with the skilled personnel capable of working toward these goals; or ignore it, and delay solution of our medical, social, and other problems, lose the major contributions of potentially qualified personnel to their nation and community, and condone the frustrations of many who for their entire lives operate on a plane below their capabilities. (1962, 468)

The prevention and removal of underachievement will entail effort, but it is effort worth the cost to parents, teachers, counselors, and gifted students themselves. Not making the effort is incalculably more costly than can be borne by present or future generations.

SELECTED BIBLIOGRAPHY

The bibliographic categories are sequential in relation to the information discussed in the body of the text. Generally the headings are the same as those used within the text. If a source is cited in more than one category, it will be annotated in the first entry and all subsequent entries will indicate the category under which it is annotated.

Characteristic Problems
of Gifted Students

Allan, Susan Demirsky, and Fox, Donna K. "Group Counseling the Gifted." *Journal for the Education of the Gifted* 3:83–92 (1979).

Authors say that the gifted need group counseling, not because of common personality traits but because of their common collection of problems. They provide a rationale for group counseling and outlines of several successful programs to integrate group counseling.

Altman, Reuben. "Social-Emotional Development of Gifted Children and Adolescents: A Research Model." *Roeper Review* 6:65–68 (November 1983).

Altman's model for generating and integrating research on the social and emotional development of the gifted is presented. The model is depicted as a cube with three major categories of variables: sources of the research data (e.g., child, teachers, parents); the social-emotional traits being investigated (e.g., self-concept, personality traits); the demographic variables being investigated (e.g., sex, age, economic level).

Andron, Sandy. "Our Gifted Teens and the Cults." *G/C/T* 26:32–33 (January/February 1983).

Andron warns that the gifted are actively recruited by cults. She says the characteristics of gifted youth make them ripe for being taken in by cults. Her solution is to fill the vacuum so there will be no reason for the gifted teenager to search elsewhere for answers.

Beery, Richard G. "Fear of Failure in the Student Experience." *Personnel and Guidance Journal* 54:190–203 (December 1975).

This four-part article profiles high-achieving and gifted college students. Beery posits that many are motivated by fear of failure. He provides good verbal illustrations of this type of student.

Brode, Diane S. "Group Dynamics with Gifted Adolescents." *G/C/T* 15:60–62 (November/December 1980).

Brode's article explains some of the problems that gifted adolescents experience. She offers several group activities that counselors could use with gifted students.

Burnside, Lenoir H. "Psychological Guidance of Gifted Children." *Journal of Consulting Psychology* 6:223–28 (July/August 1942).

Although written more than forty years ago, the article is basically relevant today. As necessary provisions for the gifted, the author recommends (1) early recognition, (2) a challenging educational program, (3) individual student guidance, (4) parent guidance, and (5) community cooperation.

Colangelo, Nicholas, and Lafrenz, Nancy. "Counseling the Culturally Diverse Gifted." *Gifted Child Quarterly* 25:27–30 (Winter 1981).

The article provides a model for meeting the counseling needs of culturally diverse gifted students. The authors state strongly their belief that culturally diverse gifted students have a definite need for counseling different from that provided for mainstream (white) gifted youth. Counselors should familiarize themselves with the cultures of their students, and they need to affirm the fact that all cultures have gifts and no culture is better than another. The article and model could be used as part of an in-service training program for counselors or in a counselor-education class.

Colangelo, Nicholas, and Pfleger, L. R. "A Model Counseling Laboratory for the Gifted at Wisconsin." *Gifted Child Quarterly* 21:321–25 (Fall 1977).

The article briefly describes the Research and Guidance Laboratory, which has conducted longitudinal research with populations of gifted and talented students since 1958. The address is included for those who wish to contact the laboratory for further information.

Colangelo, Nicholas, and Zaffrann, Ronald T., eds. *New Voices in Counseling the Gifted.* Dubuque, Iowa: Kendall/Hunt Publishing Co., 1979. 521 pp.

This large volume contains chapters by persons recognized in the field and by relative newcomers. By reading the entire volume, one gains a rich perspective concerning the task of counseling the gifted. The book is divided into ten sections: Perspectives, Identification, Counseling, Creativity, Career Development, Special Issues, Women, Families, Programming, and Consulting. It should be a well-worn part of every counselor's library.

Culross, Rita R. "Developing the Whole Child: A Developmental Approach to Guidance with the Gifted." *Roeper Review* 5:24–26 (November 1982).

Culross's article lists ten guidance and counseling needs unique to the gifted—for example, the need to work independently and to participate in decision making, the need to set realistic goals and to evaluate realistically, and the need to be challenged. Next, she makes ten accompanying recommendations for gifted programs. The author makes a good case that gifted children need developmental counseling—not just crisis counseling.

Delisle, Jim. "Preventive Counseling for the Gifted Adolescent: From

Words to Action." *Roeper Review* 3:21-25 (November/December 1980).

The author says that "what is needed is the introduction of counseling as a preventive intervention rather than as a crisis strategy." He lists four areas in which the gifted may experience specific adjustment problems. Under each problem area, the author describes several group activities to increase the students' awareness and ability to deal with difficulties. Teachers who work with junior high or senior high school gifted students should read this article and adapt and incorporate some of the suggestions into their classroom activities.

Dirkes, M. Ann. "Anxiety in the Gifted: Pluses and Minuses." *Roeper Review* 6:68-70 (November 1983).

Dirkes says that giftedness is fertile ground for anxiety, which can have either negative or positive effects, depending on how the gifted are taught to respond to it.

Exum, Herbert A. "Key Issues in Family Counseling with Gifted and Talented Black Students." *Roeper Review* 5:28-31 (February 1983).

Exum clearly discusses several issues of import to counselors working with gifted black students: (1) family structure, (2) family psychosocial orientation, (3) general concerns of black parents, (4) biracial families. He makes excellent recommendations that could be useful for developing in-service training for counselors.

Gowan, John C., and Bruch, Catherine B. *The Academically Talented Student and Guidance.* Boston: Houghton-Mifflin, 1971. 107 pp.

This book is based on the notion that academically talented students are not able to solve all their problems alone and that they do need adequate guidance. In this easy-to-read text, the authors convince the reader of this idea and provide well-founded suggestions for how to counsel the gifted. An extensive bibliography is provided.

Harris, Pearl, and Trolta, Frank. "An Experiment with Underachievers." *Education* 82:347-49 (February 1962).

Nine counseling sessions were conducted with a group of eight underachieving seventh graders. The article presents some interesting insights into the underachiever. The authors believe the time spent with these young people was worthwhile.

Harvey, Steven, and Seeley, Kenneth R. "An Investigation of the Relationships among Intellectual and Creative Abilities, Extracurricular Activities, Achievement, and Giftedness in a Delinquent Population." *Gifted Child Quarterly* 28:73-79 (Spring 1984).

The authors found that approximately 18 percent of their subjects—youth who entered the Colorado Juvenile Justice System—

were gifted in some way. An excellent synthesis of related literature is presented to support the study and its implications.

Kaplan, Leslie. "Mistakes Gifted Young People Too Often Make." *Roeper Review* 6:73–77 (November 1983).

The author, a high school guidance counselor and director of a program for intellectually gifted adolescents, says that gifted youth who have mistaken notions about the meaning and role of giftedness in their lives risk becoming unable to deal with normal problems. She discusses their misunderstandings in several areas: (1) what giftedness really means, (2) what to expect from themselves, (3) views of themselves.

Kenny, Adele. "Guidance and Counseling for the Gifted/Talented: ABC's for Helpers." *G/C/T* 27: back cover (March/April 1983).

This clever ABC block design has one maxim for each letter of the alphabet.

Klima, Melissa. "A Neglected Option for the Gifted: Group Counseling." *G/C/T* 31:19–21 (January/February 1984).

The article describes a successful group counseling program for gifted junior and senior high school students in the Bellevue, Nebraska, Public Schools. It would provide a good model for other school districts.

Lajoie, Susanne P., and Shore, Bruce. "Three Myths? The Over-Representation of the Gifted among Dropouts, Delinquents, and Suicides." *Gifted Child Quarterly* 25:138–43 (Summer 1981).

The authors give numerous chilling statistics regarding dropouts, delinquents, and suicides among the gifted. Their eighty-four-item bibliography would be invaluable for those planning classes or training sessions for counselors, teachers, and others who work with gifted students. The authors conclude that gifted or high ability dropouts, delinquents, or suicides exist, but at an "average" proportion. They believe their review should help dispel the notion that gifted youth require no extra help.

Leaverton, Lloyd, and Herzog, Steve. "Adjustment of the Gifted Child." *Journal for the Education of the Gifted* 2:149–52 (Spring 1979).

The authors conducted a study using 113 exceptionally bright students in third through fifth grade (IQ 140+). Average ranking on a social-confidence scale was twenty-fifth percentile and on the Self-Acceptance Scale, the thirty-second percentile. They recommended that a higher priority should be given to meeting the needs of gifted children—educational and adjustmental.

Lester, Carol F., and Anderson, Rebecca S. "Counseling with Families of Gifted Children: The School Counselor's Role." *School Counselor* 29:147–51 (November 1981).

This clearly written article delineates the role of the school counselor in working with the parents of gifted children. The counselor should promote understanding, provide information, and motivate parent involvement.

Manaster, Guy J., and Powell, Philip M. "A Framework for Understanding Gifted Adolescents' Psychological Maladjustment." *Roeper Review* 6:70–73 (November 1983).

The authors address potential maladjustment problems of gifted adolescents. They propose that these problems are due to their being *gifted* and *adolescents*. Three conditions exist: being (1) out of stage, (2) out of phase, or (3) out of sync. The authors expand on the three conditions in three very helpful tables, with pertinent research cited.

McCants, Gayle. "Suicide among the Gifted." *G/C/T* 38:27–29 (May/ June 1985).

McCants identifies ways that parents, teachers, and counselors can detect indications that stress is affecting a gifted child to the point that he or she is considering suicide. She says that gifted children "and all other children who find life so stressful must be given the guidance that will allow them to develop the wisdom to seek alternative solutions to their problems."

Merrill, Janet L. "The Gifted Child: A Guidance Dimension." *Texas Personnel and Guidance Journal* 7:19–23 (Spring 1979).

This article encourages schools to have counselors to work with the gifted. It gives reasons that gifted children need counseling along with differential schooling.

Morton, Jerome H., and Workman, Edward A. "Insights: Assisting Intellectually Gifted Students with Emotional Difficulties." *Roeper Review* 1:16–18 (December 1978).

This good article offers the conclusions reached by the authors in working with gifted students experiencing emotional and behavioral problems. It emphasizes that all three areas of a child's ecological system must be dealt with—family, school, and inner self.

Ogburn-Colangelo, M. Kay. "Giftedness as Multilevel Potential: A Clinical Example," In *New Voices in Counseling the Gifted,* edited by Nicholas Colangelo and Ronald T. Zaffrann. Dubuque, Iowa: Kendall/Hunt Publishing Co., 1979.

Written for counselors or persons who possess a background in counseling, this chapter presents the theory of positive disintegration as a framework for identifying and counseling gifted individuals. Included is a case study of one person which demonstrates the usefulness of this model.

Ostrom, Gladys. "Imagery and Intuition: Keys to Counseling the

Gifted, Talented and Creative." *Creative Child and Adult Quarterly* 6:227–33 (Winter 1981).

The author provides a brief rationale for creative imagery as a technique to use in counseling the gifted and then gives a script to employ using this technique.

Parker, Margaret. "Bright Kids in Trouble with the Law." *G/C/T* 9:62–63 (September/October 1979).

This hard-hitting editorial says that everyone who works with gifted students must take part of "the rap" when gifted juvenile delinquents emerge, unless they have been part of the solution to the problem. Parker illustrates how highly able youth, continually rejected by society, can resort to crime or antisocial behavior in order to have an outlet for their intelligence and creativity—and to find appreciation for those traits.

Patterson, Patricia, and Starcher, Sherolyn. "Encounter Program." *G/C/T* 33:12–14 (May/June 1984).

The authors describe the Encounter Program, which is designed to help students age twelve to fourteen understand their social, emotional, and academic needs. The program also stresses the need to incorporate differentiated, developmental guidance counseling for highly able youth into the middle school curriculum. The authors point out that traditional counseling is not sufficient for gifted youth and that the persons who will provide appropriate counseling are likely to be the students' teachers, who therefore need to be prepared for that task. The model presented is worthy of further exploration and utilization.

Rothney, J. W. M., and Koopman, N. "Guidance of the Gifted." In *Education for the Gifted,* Part 2 of *Fifty-Seventh Yearbook, National Society for the Study of Education,* edited by N. B. Henry. Chicago: Univ. of Chicago Pr., 1958.

The authors believe that counseling the gifted, although not differing in nature from counseling other students, does make different demands upon the counselor. These demands are related to the greater educational and occupational opportunities available for the gifted, the gifteds' early abilities to self-appraise and self-conceptualize, and the unusual pressures exerted on the gifted by family, teachers, and peers.

Rothney, J. W. M., and Roens, Bert A. *Guidance of American Youth: An Experimental Study.* Cambridge: Harvard University Press, 1950. 269 pp.

This book reports on a study conducted at Harvard in 1936–42. The counselors worked closely with adolescents over the five-year period and were able to see marked development due to their guidance efforts. Although the study was not limited to gifted youth, many highly able young people were counseled in the guidance program.

Rothney, J. W. M., and students. "Annotated Bibliography. Published Research Reports: Research and Guidance Library, University of Wisconsin." *Gifted Child Quarterly* 21:412–20 (Fall 1977).

Forty reports of research conducted at the University of Wisconsin Research and Guidance Laboratory are annotated. Anyone doing research with gifted students would find the article worth skimming.

Safter, H. Tammy, and Bruch, Catherine B. "Use of the DGG Model for Differential Guidance for the Gifted." *Gifted Child Quarterly* 25:167–74 (Fall 1981).

The authors present an outstanding synopsis and explanation of the Differential Guidance for Gifted model (DGG), which is comprised of variables (categories of giftedness, socioeconomic status, value orientation, and developmental stage/grade). Each of these variables is discussed so that a counselor could use this model in guiding the gifted. The authors include a way that guidance personnel trained in gifted education could work with district-level personnel and teachers within schools to implement appropriate curriculum, since most districts will not fund a budget for a sufficient number of counselors. An extensive bibliography is included.

Sanborn, Marshall P. "Counseling and Guidance Needs of the Gifted and Talented." In *The Gifted and the Talented: Their Education and Development*, Part 1 of *Seventy-Eighth Yearbook, National Society for the Study of Education*, edited by A. Harry Passow. Chicago: Univ. of Chicago Pr., 1979.

This article stresses that gifted children are unique individuals and that counselors need to help each gifted student discover that uniqueness. He illustrates this idea with several case studies.

Seeley, Kenneth R. "Perspectives on Adolescent Giftedness and Delinquency." *Journal for the Education of the Gifted* 8:59–72 (Fall 1984).

Seeley summarizes the research that indicates a relationship between giftedness and delinquency (creativity and delinquency, IQ testing among delinquents, school environment, etc.). He discusses two opposing perspectives on the relationship between giftedness and delinquency: (1) gifted children are more vulnerable to environmental factors because of greater perceptual acuity and ease of learning; and (2) gifted children are protected against delinquency because of greater ability and insight.

Thompson, Susan H. "Refining the Children of Gold: The Gifted and Talented Personality Pyramid." *G/C/T* 31:5–8 (January/February 1984).

Thompson posits that some gifted or talented children "lose their luster" because their social and emotional needs are neglected. Thompson discusses the Gifted and Talented Personality Pyramid as a viable model for meeting the personality needs of students.

Tomer, Margaret. "Human Relations in Education—a Rationale for a Curriculum in Inter-personal Communication Skills for Gifted Students—Grade K-12." *Gifted Child Quarterly* 25:94-97 (Spring 1981).

Tomer offers sound reasoning behind promoting interpersonal communication skills among gifted students. She uses Krathwohl, Bloom, and Masia's "Taxonomy of Educational Objectives—Affective Domain" as the basis for her plan for curriculum change, which would include communication skills.

VanTassel-Baska, Joyce. "The Teacher as Counselor for the Gifted." *Teaching Exceptional Children* 15:144-50 (Spring 1983).

The author contends that for a number of reasons, the teacher of the gifted may be the person most able to meet the counseling needs of the gifted. She presents her rationale and a number of suggestions for teachers who may be serving in this role.

Walker, JoAnn J. "The Counselor's Role in Educating the Gifted and Talented." *School Counselor* 29:362-70 (May 1982).

The author sees the functions of the counselor for the gifted as (1) identification of students, (2) consulting with teachers, (3) counseling students and parents, (4) coordinating services to enhance the education of the gifted, and (5) evaluation and research regarding the gifted. She sees counselors as vital to the implementation of appropriate education for the gifted.

Williams, Andrea. "Teaching Gifted Students How to Deal with Stress." *Gifted Child Quarterly* 23:136-41 (Spring 1979).

Williams discusses a three-year project that involved eighteen gifted seventh graders in developing a coping model to integrate with independent study. No specific results are given, but descriptions of the activities used in the coping model are provided.

Yadusky-Holahan, Mary, and Holahan, William. "The Effect of Academic Stress upon the Anxiety and Depression Levels of Gifted High School Students." *Gifted Child Quarterly* 27:42-46 (Winter 1983).

This article reports on a study undertaken at a residential school for highly able and motivated high school students. The results indicated that stressors on these students included unrealistic goals, high expectations from significant others, being in residence, a demanding academic work load, and change in social status (from being the brightest in class to being average). This interesting article should be required reading for counselors and teachers at residential schools for able students.

Zaffrann, Ronald T. "Gifted and Talented Students: Implications for School Counselors." *Roeper Review* 1:9–13 (December 1978).

The author views the role of the school counselor (and others who interact with gifted students) as having three functions: counseling, consulting, and research and evaluation. The article includes several models of forms that counselors could use when working with and for gifted students (discussion topics, independent study contracts, etc.).

Zaffrann, Ronald T., and Colangelo, Nicholas. "Counseling with Gifted and Talented Students." In *New Voices in Counseling the Gifted*, edited by Nicholas Colangelo and Ronald T. Zaffrann. Dubuque, Iowa: Kendall/Hunt Publishing Co., 1979.

This chapter looks at three aspects of counseling the gifted and talented. The authors see the gifted and talented as needing a developmental guidance program that is differentiated to meet their special needs. They also believe that mental health and creativity can be facilitated through the affective domain. This is a good basic article.

Ambivalence over Upward Social Mobility

Gowan, John C. "The Organization of Guidance for the Gifted." *Personnel and Guidance Journal* 39:275–79 (1960).

Gowan stresses the important role of the counselor, who should be bright, interested in children, have broad educational training, and be a suitable role model for able students.

Academic Choices

Gowan, John C., and Demos, George D., eds. *The Guidance of Exceptional Children: A Book of Readings*, New York: David McKay, 1965. 404 pp.

The book is divided into nine major sections. Section 2 is about gifted children, and Section 3 is about underachievers, including gifted underachievers. All the articles are written by people considered experts in the field. Most are reprints of journal articles.

Griggs, Shirley A. "Counseling the Gifted and Talented Based on Learning Styles." *Exceptional Children* 50:429–32 (February 1984).

Griggs discusses the implications for school counselors of each of six learning-style preferences: independent, internally controlled, persistent, perceptually strong, nonconforming, and highly motivated.

Moore, G. D. "Counseling the Gifted Child." *School Review* 68:63–70 (1960).

This good general article encourages counselors to inform gifted students about their giftedness, especially as they prepare for college—so that they have high enough, but still reasonable, expectations.

Perrone, Philip A. "Giftedness: A Personal-Social Phenomenon." *Roeper Review* 6:63–65 (November 1983).

Perrone defines giftedness "as the amount of reserve or surplus in conceptualization skills, motivation, task commitment, and divergent thought processes existing within the individual given the demands of the learning environment (school), work, family, or community." He provides support for ensuring that gifted students receive differentiated attention for both their cognitive and personal abilities.

Yadusky-Holahan and Holahan 1983. *See* Characteristic Problems of Gifted Students

Vocational Choice

Culbertson, Susan. "Career Guidance for the Gifted." *G/C/T* 38:16–17 (May/June 1985).

Culbertson says there are five pitfalls in the career decision making of gifted students: multipotentiality, expectations of others, high self-expectations, need for extended education, and social isolation. Suggestions for counselors are made.

Delisle, James R. "Reaching toward Tomorrow: Career Education and Guidance for the Gifted and Talented." *Roeper Review* 5:8–11 (November 1982).

This excellent article spells out clearly the problems of gifted students regarding career choices—and the crying need for counseling in this area. Delisle not only provides much support for his view, but also includes suggestions for teachers, schools, and school districts. This is must reading!

Fox, Lynn H., and Pyryt, Michael C. "Guidance of Gifted Youth." *Educational Forum* 43:185–92 (January 1979).

The authors discuss the need for counselors to be knowledgeable regarding all the alternatives available to gifted youth and the ways to guide students into the appropriate pathways.

Frederickson, Ronald H. "Career Development and the Gifted." In *New Voices in Counseling the Gifted*, edited by Nicholas Colangelo and Ronald T. Zaffrann. Dubuque, Iowa: Kendall/Hunt Publishing Co., 1979.

Five issues related to gifted students' career development are dis-

cussed in this chapter: society's expectations, premature career decisions, frustration of multiple career options, no one best occupation,
and identification of gifted in many areas of competence. The author
recommends that career counseling progress through five stages
with the gifted: readiness, awareness, exploration, reality testing,
and confirmation.

Conflicts with Teachers

Johnson, Christopher. "Smart Kids Have Problems, Too." *Today's Education* 70:26–27, 29 (February/March 1981).

Johnson says that often, gifted students may see their giftedness as
a mixed blessing—"a blessing that allows them to make perceptions
that others miss, a curse that causes them to question school, parents, and themselves." He explains the ways that gifted students begin to underachieve when ridiculed by students and lambasted by
teachers.

Youngs, Sally L. "Look Who's in the Counselor's Office." *G/C/T*
5:22–25 (November/December 1978).

This tongue-in-cheek article makes the point that counselors need
to work with teachers to help them recognize and accept the various
learning styles of students.

Boredom

Sumption, Merle R., and Luecking, Evelyn M. *Education of the Gifted.*
New York: Ronald Pr., 1960. 499 pp.

At the time it was published, this was one of the few comprehensive books on gifted education. It covers a whole range of topics related to the gifted, such as research, a historical overview, preschool
programs, and college programs. Chapter 5 is "Guidance of the
Gifted."

Special Subgroups of the Gifted

Gifted Females

Colangelo and Zaffran 1979. *See* Characteristic Problems of Gifted Students

Fox, Lynn H., and Richmond, Lee J. "Gifted Females: Are We Meeting
Their Counseling Needs?" *Personnel and Guidance Journal* 57:256–59
(January 1979).

This excellent article summarizes research on gifted females and its
implications—for example, gifted female students need counseling
regarding career interests and expectations, they need to be in-

volved with others (especially high-achieving female professionals), and early identification is essential.

Grau, Phyllis Nelson. "Counseling the Gifted Girl." *G/C/T* 38:8–11 (May/June 1985).

Grau presents eight psychosocial barriers to the career achievement of the gifted girl: (1) psychological construct of femininity is not consistent with achievement, (2) women's self-hatred, (3) socialized need for affiliation, (4) motherhood mandate, (5) home and hearth mandate, (6) female reliance on external sources of control and praise, (7) male or female labeling of occupations and professions, (8) lack of nontraditional female role models.

Hollinger, Constance L. "Counseling the Gifted and Talented Female Adolescent: The Relationship between Social Self-Esteem and Traits of Instrumentality and Expressiveness." *Gifted Child Quarterly* 27:157–61 (Fall 1983).

The author hypothesized that gifted or talented females classified as high on both self-assertiveness and nurturance would score significantly higher on social esteem than gifted or talented females classified otherwise. This was borne out in her research.

Hollinger, Constance L., and Fleming, Elyse S. "Internal Barriers to the Realization of Potential: Correlates and Interrelationships among Gifted and Talented Female Adolescents." *Gifted Child Quarterly* 28:135–39 (Summer 1984).

The authors found that gifted or talented adolescent females who were diagnosed as possessing one or more internal barriers to realization of potential (e.g., nonassertiveness, fear of success) were characterized by a unique profile of personality correlates. There are numerous implications for counselors.

Rodenstein, Judy. "Bibliography on Career and Other Aspects of Development in Bright Women." *Gifted Child Quarterly* 21:421–26 (Fall 1977).

The bibliography concentrates on research concerning women and achievement, sex-related differences among the gifted, and career development for girls and women. Seventy-six references are included.

Wolleat, Patricia L. "Guiding the Career Development of Gifted Females." In *New Voices in Counseling the Gifted*, edited by Nicholas Colangelo and Ronald T. Zaffrann. Dubuque, Iowa: Kendall/Hunt Publishing Co., 1979.

"The purpose of this chapter is to review the literature towards the ends of (1) delineating the differences between gifted females and gifted males; (2) examining the differences between gifted and non-gifted females; (3) identifying the unique career development characteristics of gifted females; (4) setting forth some assumptions around which counseling and guidance strategies can develop; and (5) identifying some specific counseling and guidance strategies which will address the gifted female's unique needs." The author fulfills her purpose.

Handicapped/Gifted and Learning Disabled/Gifted

Stefanich, Greg, and Schnur, James O. "Identifying the Handicapped-Gifted Child." *Science and Children* 17:18–19 (November/December 1979).

The authors make a case for revising the identification procedures so that students who are handicapped and gifted will not be excluded. Quotes from several handicapped scientists add credence to the article.

Whitmore, Joanne R. "Gifted Children with Handicapping Conditions: A New Frontier." *Exceptional Children* 48:106–14 (October 1981).

Written by one of the foremost experts on "exceptional" gifted children, this article expresses strongly the growing conviction held by those experienced in gifted education—that the least served segment of the gifted population includes the handicapped gifted. Whitmore provides a historical perspective on the problem, suggestions for identification procedures, and a challenge to educators and parents concerning the handicapped gifted or talented. This is an excellent article!

Wolf, Joan, and Gygi, Janice. "Learning Disabled and Gifted: Success or Failure." *Journal for the Education of the Gifted* 4:199–206 (Spring 1981).

This article reports lucidly on the paradox of being learning disabled and gifted. The authors report on characteristics, identification, programming problems, and possible solutions to the difficulty in identifying and serving these youth. It should be required reading for all teachers and counselors.

Creatively Gifted

Davis, Gary A., and Rimm, Sylvia. "Characteristics of Creatively Gifted Children." *Gifted Child Quarterly* 21:546–51 (Winter 1977).

The authors paint a brief portrait of the creative person—very descriptive and very clear. They then describe five personality-based creativity measures, going into some depth on the GIFT—Group Inventory for Finding Creative Talent, a measure developed for use in the elementary school. This is a good ready-reference article.

Counseling for Parents

Delisle, Jim. "Striking Out: Suicide and the Gifted Adolescent." *G/C/T* 24:16–19 (September/October 1982).

This is a fairly straightforward article regarding why gifted teenagers commit suicide. Delisle recommends four preventive steps parents can take: respect, awareness, tolerance, and participation. Parents should read this article and some others listed in the references.

Lester and Anderson 1981. *See* Characteristic Problems of Gifted Students

Rothney and Koopman 1958. *See* Characteristic Problems of Gifted Students

Schatz, Eleanor M. "Determinants of Guidance within the Home." *G/C/T* 27:59–60 (March/April 1983).

Schatz says the four determinants of guidance are materials, modeling, space, and time. She explains the value of each of these.

Treffinger, Donald, and Fine, Marvin. "When There's a Problem in School: Some Guidelines for Parents and Teachers of Gifted Children." *G/C/T* 10:3–6 (November/December 1979).

The article presents two somewhat parallel sets of guidelines for parents and for teachers regarding parent-teacher conferences. The guidelines suggest how to prepare for the conference, how to conduct the conference, and how to follow up on the conference. A counselor could use this model in an in-service for teachers and for a presentation to the local parent organization.

Walker 1982. *See* Characteristic Problems of Gifted Students

A Team Effort: Help for the Gifted Underachiever

Abraham, Willard. "Motivating the Gifted Underachievers." *Education* 82:468–71 (April 1962).

Abraham provides seven recommendations for solving the problems of lack of motivation and/or underachievement in gifted students.

Bachtold, Louise M. "Personality Differences among High Ability Underachievers." *Journal of Educational Research* 63:16–18 (September 1969).

Personality characteristics of achieving and underachieving bright fifth graders were studied. Credulity, self-confidence, and self-control were components of successful female achievers. Emotional stability, seriousness, and sensitivity were successful male achievers' components. Underachievers differed in personality factors ac-

cording to their types of underachievement. In remediating underachievement, one should consider the type of underachievement.

Barrett, Harry O. "An Intensive Study of Thirty-Two Gifted Children." *Personnel and Guidance Journal* 36:192–94 (November 1957).

The author reports on a preliminary study conducted in Toronto in
preparation for a comprehensive long-term project designed to determine the underlying causes of underachievement. Although the
results are based on a small sample, the research was fairly exhaus-
tive. The article reports patterns of intellectual achievement and ability, patterns of home background, patterns of school attitude, and
patterns of personality.

Briscoe, Joyce. "Independent Study for the 'Tuned Out.'" *Adolescence*
12:529–32 (Winter 1977).

Briscoe recommends independent study as a way of rekindling underachieving gifted students' interest in learning.

Compton, Mary F. "The Gifted Underachiever in the Middle School."
Roeper Review 4:23–25 (April/May 1982).

Compton presents the idea that underachievement among gifted
middle school students may be at least partly, if not wholly, due to
their developmental stage. She cites and discusses the following reasons for underachievement: brain-growth periodization, nutrition,
peer influence, burnout, boredom, family relations, inappropriate
curricula, and incorrect identification. She suggests individualiza-
tion, flexible curricula, teacher preparation, and guidance as features of effective middle school programs that help make school
meaningful for gifted early adolescents.

Delisle, Jim. "Learning to Underachieve." *Roeper Review* 4:16–18
(April/May 1982).

Delisle posits that "underachievement is a complex web of learned
behaviors" and that "underachievement is learned because it is
taught." He makes a strong case that the child is not to blame for
underachievement, but rather the people around the gifted youngster are to blame. This article would make a great discussion starter
at a parent or teacher meeting.

Dowdall, Cynthia B., and Colangelo, Nicholas. "Underachieving
Gifted Students: Reviews and Implications." *Gifted Child Quarterly*
26:179–84 (Fall 1982).

This is a concise review of the literature from the past twenty years
concerning underachieving gifted students. The review is divided
into these categories: definitions, identification, causes, characteristics, interventions, and conclusions/implications. The authors concluded that more confusion and circularity than clarity and direction
had resulted from the last two decades of research. They called for a

functional definition and long-term interventions that begin early—
before the pattern is set.

Fearn, Leif. "Underachievement and Rate of Acceleration." *Gifted
Child Quarterly* 26:121–25 (Summer 1982).

Fearn describes the San Diego Unified School District's Gifted Education Program for underachievers. The district's premise is that
underachieving gifted students need acceleration in academic or
basic-skill development. The evidence indicates that problems of
underachievement in these areas can be solved.

Fine, Marvin J., and Pitts, Roger. "Intervention with Underachieving
Gifted Children: Rationale and Strategies." *Gifted Child Quarterly*
24:51–55 (Spring 1980).

The authors have drawn on research and on their own experiences
to compile this article, which lists and discusses eleven dynamics of
underachievement (e.g., parent-school conflicts, defense tactics,
low self-esteem, motor deficiency). They also provide a plan for intervention. This article provides good general reading on underachievement among the gifted.

Golicz, Heidi J. "Use of Estes Attitude Scales with Gifted Underachievers." *Roeper Review* 4:22–23 (April/Mary 1982).

The author recommends use of the elementary form of the *Estes
Attitude Scales: Measures of Attitudes towards School Subjects* as a means
of detecting early the attitudes among gifted children that may lead
to underachievement. The test is described, and various support is
given for its use.

Gowan, John C. "The Underachieving Gifted Child—a Problem for
Everyone." *Exceptional Children* 21:247–50 (1955).

This article summarizes unpublished research of the fifties concerning gifted underachievers. Good suggestions for counselors of
gifted underachievers are given.

Gowan and Bruch 1971. *See* Characteristic Problems of Gifted Students

Hall, Eleanor G. "Recognizing Gifted Underachievers." *Roeper Review*
5:23–25 (May 1983).

This article describes the results of a characteristics checklist given
to eighty-four teachers enrolled in beginning gifted education
courses. Although the checklist (which is included in the article) included descriptions of underachieving gifted students, these were
seen as descriptions of low achievers. Hall suggests using the checklist during teacher training to point out to the teachers how they can
be fooled by some concomitant traits of gifted youngsters—
especially underachieving gifted. The article would be useful to
someone planning a workshop on gifted identification.

Hoffman, Jeffrey L., Wasson, Frances R., and Christianson, Betsy P.

"Personal Development for the Gifted Underachiever." *G/C/T* 38:12–14 (May/June 1985).

The authors present a program that works with gifted underachievers. Personal development activities are described. Enough information is given that counselors and teachers could work together to adapt this idea for their own school situation.

Jackson, R. M. "In Support of the Concept of Underachievement." *Personnel and Guidance Journal* 47:56–62 (1968).

This article reviews the literature regarding the concept of underachievement. The author then describes a study of 1,078 fourth graders. The comparisons done among this group indicated significant differences between underachievers and achievers or overachievers. Thus, Jackson states, underachievement is a valid concept.

Karnes, Merle, McCoy, George, Zehrbach, Richard, Wollersheim, Janet P., and Clarizio, Harvey F. "The Efficacy of Two Organizational Plans for Underachieving Gifted Students." *Exceptional Children* 29:438–46 (May 1963).

This article reports on a study that investigated the efficacy of placing a small proportion of gifted underachievers in homogeneous classes (by IQ) with high achievers, as compared to placing gifted underachievers in heterogeneous classes. The investigation was longitudinal (three years). The findings seem to suggest that placing underachieving gifted students in homogeneous classrooms with high achievers has merit.

Karnes, Merle B., McCoy, George F., Zehrbach, Richard Reid, Wollersheim, Janet P., Clarizio, Harvey F., Costin, Lela, and Stanley, Lola S. "Factors Associated with Underachievement and Overachievement of Intellectually Gifted Children." *Exceptional Child* 28:167–75 (December 1961).

The authors tested seven hypotheses regarding the differences between overachieving and underachieving gifted. Only two proved out: overachievers had a higher degree of perceived peer acceptance and higher scores on four scales that measured creativity. The article goes on with recommendations regarding administrative planning, instructional methods, teachers, and materials.

Rimm, Sylvia. "Underachievement . . . Or If God Had Meant Gifted Children to Run Our Homes, She Would Have Created Them Bigger." *G/C/T* 31:26–29 (January/February 1984).

Rimm defines underachievement and discusses its characteristics and possible home roots. Several "rituals" engaged in by families with underachieving gifted children are presented. These rituals typify the relationships between underachieving gifted children and their parents (e.g., "Daddy is a dummy" or "Mommy is an ogre").

The article would be helpful to parents or to counselors working with parents of gifted underachievers.

Saurenman, Dianne A., and Michael, William B. "Differential Placement of High-Achieving and Low-Achieving Gifted Pupils in Grades Four, Five, and Six on Measures of Field Dependence–Field Independence, Creativity, and Self-Concept." *Gifted Child Quarterly* 24:81–86 (Spring 1980).

This article reports on research conducted with ninety-six fourth-, fifth-, and sixth-grade gifted children, half high achieving and half low achieving. The purpose of the study was to determine differences and interrelationships between the two groups' scores on measures of field independence–field dependence, creativity, and self-concept. They found that the high achievers tended to be more field independent, more creative in divergent production, and more interested in academic achievement.

Shaw, Merville C., Edson, Kenneth, and Bell, Hugh M. "The Self-Concept of Bright Underachieving High School Students as Revealed by an Adjective Check List." *Personnel Guidance Journal* 39:193–96 (November 1960).

This article reports on a study of four groups: male achievers, male underachievers, female achievers, and female underachievers. Students completed the Sarbin Adjective Checklist. Major findings were: (1) differences in self-concept exist between achievers and underachievers; (2) male underachievers have more negative feelings about themselves than male achievers; (3) female underachievers tend to be ambivalent regarding their feelings toward themselves; (4) data did not indicate whether differences in self-concept were the cause of, or the result of, underachievement.

Shaw, M. C., and Grubb, J. "Hostility and Able High School Underachievers." *Journal of Counseling Psychology* 5:263–66 (1958).

The authors report on a study undertaken to determine whether hostility characterizes bright underachievers at the high school level. They found that bright male underachievers did score significantly higher on three hostility scales than did a group of bright male achievers. Implications are that demanding more and/or better schoolwork may have a detrimental effect on scholastic underachievement.

Shaw, M. C., and McCuen, J. T. "The Onset of Academic Underachievement in Bright Children." *Journal of Educational Psychology* 51:103–8 (1960).

The authors studied groups of achievers and underachievers with IQ's over 110 and compared them on the basis of GPA at every grade

level from one through eleven. They found evidence of underachievement beginning in first grade and recommend early identification of underachieving gifted.

Vriend, R. J. "High-Performing Inner-City Adolescents Assist Low-
Performing Peers in Counseling Groups." *Personnel and Guidance
Journal* 47:897–904 (1969).

Vriend reports on a study demonstrating that achieving disadvantaged students could be trained as peer leaders and serve as models
for fellow students of lower achievement—to help them develop attitudes and behaviors that improve school performance.

Whitmore, Joanne Rand. "The Etiology of Underachievement in
Highly Gifted Young Children." *Journal for the Education of the Gifted*
3:38–51 (1979).

The author reports the findings of her study of twenty-seven
young highly gifted underachievers. She found three categories of
causal factors that seem to explain why highly gifted children may
become underachievers or nonproducers in primary classrooms: (1)
psychological or personality characteristics, (2) physical or developmental characteristics, and (3) the social and academic environment
of the school. She discusses these categories in depth and makes recommendations for educational intervention.

Whitmore, Joanne Rand. *Giftedness, Conflict, and Underachievement.*
Boston: Allyn and Bacon, 1980. 462 pp.

Judging from her writing and from the amount that her writing is
quoted, Whitmore is recognized as the foremost expert on underachievement in this country. Her well-written and exhaustively researched book is divided into five major sections: An Overview of
the Field; Identification and Definition of the Problem of Highly
Gifted Underachievers; Gaining an Understanding of the Problem;
Conceptualization and Implementation of a Special Program for
Highly Gifted Underachievers; and Results and Recommendations.
It should be read cover to cover if one wants to gain a sense of the
problem and of solutions to gifted underachievement.

Wilhelms, Fred T. "The Importance of People: Gulliver and Other Underachievers." *Educational Leadership* 16:369–72 (March 1959).

Wilhelms draws an analogy between the ropes that held Gulliver
down and the restraints put on the gifted.

Zilli, Marie G. "Reasons Why the Gifted Adolescent Underachieves
and Some of the Implications of Guidance and Counseling to This
Problem." *Gifted Child Quarterly* 15:279–92 (Winter 1971).

Zilli provides a brief but broad review of research concerning underachieving gifted students. The article would be good reading for
those working with gifted students.

CHAPTER 5

Programming for the Gifted

Just as all educators do not agree that the gifted should receive a differentiated education, neither is there agreement among the proponents of differentiated gifted education concerning the type that should be provided. This chapter will explore several aspects of gifted education. Although they will be divided up for the purposes of discussion, these aspects generally work best in conjunction with other components.

Which components a school district selects—and the degree to which any one component is implemented—depends on the size of the school district. Size determines the number of gifted students to be served and the personnel, space, and financial resources available for their education.

For example, a large urban school district with a student population of more than 800,000 will have approximately 20,000 to 40,000 able students to serve, roughly half of them in the elementary schools and half in the middle and secondary schools. On the other hand, a school district that serves 20,000 students will have approximately 500 to 1,000 able students to provide for. The size of the large urban school district's gifted population justifies the creation of separate schools for some of the gifted in addition to special classes within heterogeneous schools. Special training can be provided for all teachers who will serve able learners as part of their normal classroom load. However, the smaller school district cannot consider separate schools—at least within the school district. Creative cooperation between several smaller school districts may be necessary in order to provide adequately for the gifted. In general, the larger the school district, the more easily many options can be offered to gifted students. Mid-size and smaller school districts should not hide behind their size in order to shirk their duty to provide appropriate options for gifted learners. However, success will require more creative planning.

ACCELERATION

According to the *American Heritage Dictionary*, to accelerate means ''to make or become faster or to cause to happen sooner.'' Acceleration programs for the gifted are indeed intended to enable intellectually talented children and young adults to become all they can be—both faster and sooner than would normally happen in the traditional lockstep of public education. The forms that educational acceleration can take are limited only by the innovation and resourcefulness of the persons involved with the gifted—counselors, parents, teachers, and administrators. A number of these forms will be discussed in this section, although the options available in acceleration go far beyond the discussion (see Stanley 1978a, 57, 60–62).

Historically, there have been two types of acceleration: double promotion (grade skipping) and completion of the normal amount of work in less than the normal amount of time (Justman 1956). Although these two options are still available, variations and innovations of these two have multiplied with the recent upsurge in attention to the gifted.

Many gifted children exhibit their abilities quite early. Parents, nursery school personnel, babysitters—all may notice the apparent precocity of such children. Sometimes, even strangers comment on highly able children's extraordinary command of the language and the unusual confidence with which they present themselves. To expect these children to be challenged when they are enrolled at age five in a regular kindergarten is absurd. One alternative is to enroll them in a special school for the gifted. This may be either prohibitively expensive or physically impossible due to the lack of such a facility nearby. Another alternative is to hire a special tutor or to teach the child at home. A third is to enroll the child in school a year early.

Early enrollment is forbidden by some school districts and by some state laws, no matter how precocious the child. When this is the case, and no other public or private school options are available, then enrolling the child at the ''proper'' age, meanwhile providing a great deal of stimulation outside of school, is suggested. Then, once the child is enrolled, obtaining acceleration (grade skipping) past kindergarten or first grade may be possible (thereby circumventing the ban against early enrollment). Schools may not advertise that this option is available, but to meet the needs of some gifted children, it is worth investigating and pursuing.

Many persons who are ignorant of the benefits of acceleration would question why highly able young children, just entering school and eager to learn, would need to be accelerated at the beginning of their school career. Some might say, Why not let them "settle in" and get used to being in school for a couple of years before "forcing" them ahead? A careful look at the question reveals the answer: highly able children are eager to learn when they first enter school, and there is no faster way to squelch that eagerness than by forcing them to take part in minutia (such as skill drills) with their less able age-mates in kindergarten or first grade.

DeHaan (in Horne & Dupuy 1981, 105) pointed out that "if novelty of learning motivates the learner, brighter students need novel experiences at a quicker pace." If bright students do not get an ample supply of new experiences, then a school-related apathy is likely to be what will "settle in" (see section on underachievement in chapter 3). Waiting for two or three years to accelerate very bright children is almost asking them to begin to underachieve. Stanley says,

> The oft-sounded fears that educational acceleration will hurt the social and emotional development of intellectually highly talented youths in the United States who want to move ahead faster than their agemates are groundless. On the contrary, frustrating the natural pace of highly apt students can cause serious academic and emotional damage. (1978a, 3)

For many capable youngsters, putting them a grade or more ahead of where they chronologically "should" be, thereby associating them with their mental peers, will help avert underachievement because the students will have more of an academic challenge as they begin their school life. Rather than harming a young gifted child, acceleration is usually helpful. Laycock (1979, 12) states, "The exceptions, whom we all know—the persons who suffered from acceleration, socially and otherwise—are indeed exceptions." Studies of children admitted early to school show that few if any of the early entrants suffered adverse affects (see Daurio 1979). The practice of early admission deserves more research, particularly concerning identification methods that can be used inexpensively with preschoolers. Many young children are not identified early and do not get the chance to accelerate during their early schooling, at least partially because schools cannot afford to administer a battery of tests to all the preschoolers they are expected to serve.

Since cost is, and must be, an issue with local school districts, acceleration should be seen as a financially attractive method of providing for academically able students. Because there is no need for costly special teachers or equipment, grade-skipping can be provided by small and large school districts alike. Also, if some children are able to complete six years of elementary school in five years or less, that too saves the school district money, because for every year accelerated, one less "child year" must be staffed. One would hope that school districts would want to provide for gifted students in whatever ways were best, regardless of the cost, but realistically, such an altruistic stance is not possible. Therefore, presenting acceleration as both a money-saving and educationally sound method of providing for the gifted may ensure its trial and acceptance.

Grade-skipping, or double promotion, is the least disruptive means of acceleration and therefore requires the fewest concessions from the schools and school districts involved. Often, it may be left up to the building principal to decide whether to double promote a child. No interschool agreement or cooperation would be required.

However, grade skipping is not the only way to accelerate young gifted children, and other options do require some cooperation. For example, some elementary schools allow and encourage able students to move through the regular curriculum at their own rate—thereby shortening the time spent in elementary school so that the students will be able to tackle advanced work sooner. In order to accomplish this goal, several important considerations must be met by the whole school district:

1. Are all the elementary schools in the district organized to accommodate the ungraded acceleration? For example, if a child is progressing rapidly through the intermediate grades, covering all the material in two years instead of three, and moves in the middle of the second year, will the other elementary schools in the district also allow the student to progress rapidly, or will she be placed in a regular fifth grade because of age?
2. Do the junior and senior high schools accept advanced students, and are they willing to allow these students to continue their acceleration? If a student completes six years of elementary school in five years, will the junior high school accept him even though he is twelve instead of thirteen—and can the student continue to accelerate instead of reverting to a lockstep progression?
3. Are the schools (elementary, junior high, and senior high) able to provide a flexible schedule for students accelerated in one area

but not in another? Can a fourth-grade student highly able in mathematics take ninth grade algebra during the first period and spend the rest of the day in regular fourth-grade classes?

4. Is the school district in contact with colleges and universities who will accept younger-than-average students? When talking with parents and students about acceleration, can the counselor provide names, requirements, and living facilities of colleges and universities that are not only willing, but anxious, to take accelerated students?

Acceleration must be coordinated throughout the school system if it is to be successful. Schools and school districts that establish and support a flexible acceleration program for gifted students will need to do a great deal of planning before beginning the program and will need to continually monitor the program once it is established to ensure its effective coordination.

Because middle schools (junior high schools) and high schools tend to be larger than elementary schools, they can usually be more flexible in their scheduling. Even though seventh graders traditionally take general mathematics courses, schools that support acceleration could enroll able seventh graders in ninth-grade algebra or geometry while they also took regular seventh-grade English if necessary.

For the extremely able students, it is often not enough to place them in a regular course that is one to two years ahead of the normal course progression.

> Our experience with acceleration reveals that when we accelerate by moving courses downward, this alone does not meet the challenge that these students need. Thus, the geometry course taught in the ninth grade must be more comprehensive than the traditional high school plane geometry course. (King 1967, 73)

Extreme examples of such enrichment can be seen in the work of Julian Stanley and others with the Johns Hopkins Study of Mathematically Precocious Youth (SMPY). Through this program, which Stanley (1978a, 56) characterizes as "resolutely interventional, longitudinal, and accelerative," unusually able students are being radically accelerated in mathematics and often through their entire junior and senior high school program. The SMPY and other similar programs use the Scholastic Aptitude Test (SAT) (normally given to high school seniors) as a screening instrument for gifted seventh and eighth graders. The students invited to take the SAT must rank in the top 3 percent nationally for their age group in mathematics. These young students take the test, and if they score at or above a designated score (usually some combination of the SAT-Math and SAT-Verbal), they are invited to take part in specially designed courses at Johns Hopkins.

The results of this program have been phenomenal (see, e.g., Brandt 1981; Eisenberg & George 1979; Olson 1981; Solano & George 1976; Stanley 1978b, 1980). Although the SMPY is a unique program for extraordinarily gifted youth, it embodies the possibilities that acceleration can extend to the gifted. The research generated from this program and others like it demonstrates that acceleration may be the most effective educational route for academically talented students. In fact, acceleration may be a misnomer; "accelerated learning is not really accelerated for the brighter student; it is accelerated only in comparison with average students" (Horne & Dupuy 1981, 105). Since one of the cognitive characteristics of the gifted is their ability to learn rapidly, it makes sense that what might be fast paced for average students is "just right" for the superior students.

Not only will "fast paced" courses allow gifted students to finish their elementary and secondary schooling early, or at least enable them to begin college at a higher level, but it appears that acceleration causes them to be better learners during the shorter time they are in school. Johnson reported that

> there is experimental evidence to indicate that acceleration itself also contributes something to the scholarship of bright pupils. Apparently, curtailment of the years of tedious drill in tool subjects and the increased motivation that comes from self-evident accomplishment sometimes results in an enhancement in scholarship beyond that attained by equally bright but unaccelerated students. (1943, 78)

What acceleration alternatives are available for the highly motivated, advanced high-school-age student? Basically, there are three categories from which to choose: Advanced Placement courses and tests, concurrent enrollment, and early admission to college.

The Advanced Placement (AP) program was established during the 1950s to try to remove the sharp delineation between high school and college (see Cornog 1980; Hanson 1980; Marland 1976). Able high school students may take AP tests in any of seventeen different subject areas. The tests are graded by AP teachers and college professors and are given scores from one to five. Depending on the score and on the college's requirements, students are granted a certain number of college hours in that area, thus allowing them to enroll in advanced-level courses in their areas of proficiency instead of freshman-level courses.

Although many high schools offer AP courses, which are good preparation for the tests, the courses are not a mandatory prerequisite. Students who are unusually adept in a particular field may elect to take the AP test in that field without the preparatory course. Such a student may also want to take any one of the CLEP (College Level Examination of Proficiency) tests, which also allow students to earn college credit through examination. The AP program can save students time and money in college (fewer courses must be taken and paid for), gives able students a chance to stretch their minds, and removes the barrier between the twelfth and thirteenth grades.

Another way to breach the barrier between high school and college is to be concurrently enrolled in both. Laycock says that in some ways, attending college while still in high school

> is superior to AP because it is more realistic: the student actually goes to the campus, learns about its facilities and mores, the level of demand and competition—in a dose that is less concentrated than a full schedule in the regular freshman year. (1979, 11)

Another advantage to taking college courses as opposed to other forms of acceleration is that students can take the courses at night and/ or in the summer while still participating in their high school activities. This way, able youths can interact with intellectual peers but still maintain a social relationship with their age-mates.

Another benefit to dual enrollment in college and high school is the advanced standing that will be afforded these students when they enroll in college full time. Most colleges that allow able students without high school diplomas to take courses will hold those credits in "escrow" until the students are graduated from high school (Solano & George 1976). If the student decides to go to another college or university, these credits will transfer just like those of full-time students who transfer. This policy of accepting college credits earned while still in high school is becoming more widespread as colleges and universities compete for the highly able students. A gifted student who has earned twelve to twenty-four hours (or more) while still a high school student is very appealing to higher education institutions.

Voorheis (1979) points out an advantage of concurrent enrollment that benefits the enrollee's school and all its students: the top students, the ones who are able to take college courses while still of high school age, are also very likely the leaders in the school—officers of student government, yearbook editors, band majors, etc. If a school refuses to allow or encourage these extraordinary students to get the extra work they need, then they may elect to drop out of high school and enroll full time at a college in order to receive adequate intellectual stimulation. Therefore, it behooves everyone to support those students capable enough to take college courses but who also elect to remain in high school.

For some superior students, concurrent enrollment is not enough; for them, early admission into college is best. More and more colleges and universities are accepting (and welcoming) bright youth who have not finished high school. Students whose abilities exceed those of most of the regular college students with whom they will attend classes, and whose motivations for learning and achieving are high, can succeed in college in spite of being younger than average. For many students who would otherwise be doing nothing more than marking time in high school, early admission to college is the answer.

The idea of early admission to college often meets with a great deal of resistance even though research consistently supports it. Entering college early also means exiting college early, thus getting an early jump on career and life after school—which seems to be a good idea.

Acceleration will not add two years to the life of all students; it is not a panacea for educational ills. Just as a doctor cannot categorically prescribe one treatment for all patients, neither can one method—acceleration—be prescribed for all gifted children. However, a voluminous amount of research points to acceleration as a highly successful course of action, and its effectiveness cannot be denied. Morgan, Tennant, and Gold (1980, 57) state "Whatever the method, the evaluations of acceleration have been uniformly positive." It is a method far too infrequently explored in the search for the best alternatives for academically talented students—much to their loss.

ENRICHMENT

Daurio (1979) reviewed the literature on acceleration and enrichment and concluded that almost no studies of "so-called" enrichment found it to be as effective as acceleration. Just the same, not all courses can or should be accelerated. Acceleration works best in those subjects that are linear-sequential in content and which therefore build on previous skills and knowledge (Lewis 1984). For highly capable students, such courses as mathematics, physics, chemistry, and linguistics can be learned in rapid-pace format. Other courses, such as history, English, economics, and logic, can also be accelerated—if one considers their content nothing more than a compilation of facts. But if such courses are perceived as containing the core of human culture and thought, then a presentation method other than acceleration must be utilized for academically superior students. For many gifted youth, enriching some or all of their courses will differentiate their education so that they can make maximum use of their capabilities.

In considering enrichment as an alternative for the gifted, we find Lessinger's definition a sound one:

> Enrichment is a process of systematically organizing, relating, and generalizing a given subject matter around selected inter-disciplinary concepts having maximum subject matter clarification, transfer of training properties, and general knowledge integration potential. (1963, 120)

If this definition were used as a benchmark, many of the so-called enrichment programs that receive so much criticism would be eliminated. These programs, which usually involve the pull-out format (pulling the students out of their regular classes), often entail busy-work combined with irrelevant horizontal academic enrichment.

In this sort of program, students have no idea of the purpose of the class and often take themselves out of the program because, while they see few advantages in participating, they see several disadvantages (e.g., missing regular classes that must be made up, disruption of teacher-student and peer relationships). Generating and maintaining parental support is difficult because no real goal is set toward which parents can see their children working. Administrative support is often weak because of lack of purpose and because of the additional headaches caused by teacher complaints (e.g., "I'm sick and tired of these gifted kids trooping in and out of my room every Tuesday and Thursday. Isn't there some way they could leave during lunch and come back at the end of recess?") Intraschool encouragement may be lacking because regular classroom teachers do not perceive the purpose of the program, and they resent the disruption caused when *some* students miss *some* classes on *some* days. Lastly, often even teachers of enrichment programs for the gifted are unsure of their task—and so, although they support the concept of differentiated education for the gifted, they are not sure whether they are accomplishing that goal.

Therefore, without student, parent, administrator, and teacher support, the success of such a program is questionable. In order to garner and maintain the support of students, parents, administrators, and teachers, an enrichment program for the gifted cannot be a busywork, pullout, totally separate entity in a school. It must be an integrated part of the curriculum, involving all of those persons named above in its planning and ongoing assessment.

Gifted students typically find their regular classroom experiences dull and less than challenging. Although some rare teachers detect the gifted child's spark and do everything they can to fan it to a flame, the majority of gifted students sit in schools for twelve years experiencing precious little challenge and motivation. Sanders says,

> Enrichment implies that the typical classroom diet is inade-
> quate for the academically talented child. It is a means of pro-
> viding learning activities that challenge the child and expand
> and deepen his understanding. (1961, 69)

Sanders' final phrase, "challenge . . . expand . . . deepen . . . un-derstanding," provides key words by which to measure enrichment programs and activities. Doing logic problems may be a challenge to gifted students, but after a while, if those logic problems do not lead to a deeper understanding of thought and organization, were they en-riching or were they just an activity done in the name of teaching think-ing skills?

Likewise, "independent projects" (researching a particular topic for presentation) are a favorite focus of gifted programs. Although the process and product of the IP may be a valuable part of the enrichment program for some gifted persons, for others, it is not. Worcester (1979) states that when enrichment is real and adapted to the child, it is highly valuable, but when all of a group is "required" to experience the same enrichment, they merely move from one lockstep to another. For some able children, getting locked in to doing research on a topic and then being required to present the information in a certain way is neither challenging nor expansive. Many gifted students find such projects ir-relevant to their lives and goals and therefore find little inner motiva-tion to participate in the gifted enrichment classes that require such ex-ercises.

While it is true that gifted children and youth tend to be inquisitive and usually have highly developed interests in individual areas, not all the areas are researchable in a library, nor can the information always be presented in a traditional way (e.g., a report, a slide show, a poster). Enrichment planners must guard against convergent thinking regard-ing requirements for gifted students.

On the other hand, when enrichment opportunities broaden and in-tegrate students' knowledge, enabling them to fill in gaps and to fol-low special interests, then interest and dedication to the enrichment program should result. For example, imagine that a young gifted girl

has seen a special news broadcast reporting on illegal dumping of res-
taurant waste in her community. She is not only interested because of
her concern for the environment, but her strong sense of right and
wrong causes her to be incensed that violators are fined only $200
when caught, even though they are saving themselves thousands of
dollars by not disposing of the waste properly. When this child tells her
enrichment class teacher that she would like to further explore this
breach of justice, and the idea is okayed, the two draw up a plan. It
covers objectives, ways to meet those objectives, resource persons and
places, and alternative plans of action.

For the next several months, this student communicates with the in-
vestigative reporter who broadcasts the story, does library research using methods the reporter teaches her, and contacts businesses named
as violators of the dumping law. During this period, the girl's teacher is
monitoring her activities and progress and is providing guidance and
encouragement as they are needed. Finally, when the student feels
that she has amassed enough expertise to speak knowledgeably on the
subject, she prepares a slide show and pamphlet to display at a local
mall during an environmental awareness week. Her slides and pamphlets will also be used in a presentation at a city council meeting when
a new city ordinance concerning illegal waste disposal is to be considered.

Has this project been a challenge? Has this project expanded the student's knowledge? Has it deepened her understanding of city government, reporting, and laws? Obviously, the answer to all three questions is yes. This type of project would be classified as a Type III
enrichment activity according to the schema of Renzulli's Enrichment
Triad Model (see Maker 1982 for a concise explanation, Renzulli 1977
for a more extensive description and discussion). Students involved in
Type III enrichment activities are neither bored nor do they see their
efforts as futile busywork. In order to be successful, enrichment programs must be attractive and valuable to students; if they involve challenge and a sense of purpose, they will be.

While enrichment programs must be attractive and valuable to students, they must also appeal to parents. Parents can make or break a
program for gifted students. Since the parents of gifted children pay
the taxes that support the public schools, and since parents are the
ones who have to provide financial support for many of the extras in
gifted programs (materials, transportation, etc.), they justifiably want
their money's worth! Enlisting and sustaining parents' support must
begin by informing them about the program—its purposes, its goals
and objectives, and how the school purports to reach them. The pur-

poses, goals, and objectives should be strongly undergirded with research—information that will not be required by every parent but should be readily available to those who ask. The purposes, goals, and objectives will probably be easier for most parents to swallow than will some of the methods employed to get there.

For example, if one goal is to enable the gifted children to more freely express themselves, and one of the activities involves having the students act like different vegetables cooking, some parents will have trouble seeing the connection. And, without some substantial backing from experts in creative expression, most parents will see little reason for their gifted children to miss social studies twice a week to participate in this "enrichment" class. If the parents are not involved in some pre-enrichment education of their own, and then all they hear about the program is bits and pieces of the activities going on in the classroom (e.g., counting the number of hairs on a square inch of forearm), the likelihood is that they will not be supportive of the effort.

If, however, the parents know that the goal of freer self-expression is to be met by having each student in the gifted class find and interview a family from one of the foreign cultures being studied in social studies so that each child can then become like a member of that family at school for a day (in dress, dance, song, etc.), more of the extension aspect of enrichment will be perceived. By and large, parents want their gifted children learning what everyone else is learning. If parents are sure that their children are, then they find expanding beyond that perfectly acceptable. Enrichment programs that supplant the regular curriculum need to cover the objectives of the course being supplanted and then do something more.

It is possible to cover the regular curriculum and then go beyond it because of the extraordinary learning capabilities of gifted children. The students in an enrichment program that meets twice a week during social studies can learn the material their regular teacher planned to cover in much less than an hour. Their enrichment class teacher can then fortify that subject matter with activities designed around the able students' learning abilities. Enrichment classes for the gifted should provide "experiences for which the average or below average child lacks either the time, the interest, or the ability to understand" (Worcester 1979, 98). These experiences must have a purpose defensible to all those concerned with the gifted children in the program.

Special populations and all the things inherent to them are the bugaboo of many local and district administrators. How much easier it would be for principals if all the children in their buildings were members of that nebulously termed group—the average. But no school is comprised wholly of an "average" population. Students with special needs all along the continuum are present in every school—whether or not they are acknowledged. One would think that administrators would be pleased and proud to identify and serve the above-average students, but that is not necessarily the typical scenario. Serving the gifted within a comprehensive school can cause all kinds of administrative problems involving scheduling, finances, special rooms, parents who want their children in the program, and regular classroom teachers who want their students "exempted" from going to the gifted class. All of these hassles are real, and unless the principal or other administrator can also recognize strong positive attributes of the gifted program, he or she will do little to support it and may do a great deal to undermine its very existence.

The persons most responsible for developing and sustaining the building administrators' support are the teachers of the gifted and the gifted program supervisor(s) (or their counterparts). Just as the parents of the gifted students need to be educated regarding the program and then involved in its development, so too do the administrators. Once the program is under way, administrators should frequently be invited to participate—view productions, to serve as resource persons, or even to become mentors for one or more gifted students.

Ideally, building principals should drop by each classroom each day. Over a period of months, progress should be apparent. If the "enrichment" activities in April are the same as the ones in September, the administrator will hold a less-than-positive regard for the merits of the program. An administrator who sees nothing going on that could not be happening in regular classrooms will also be less than impressed. And, if the activities seem unworthy of being called educational, then the future of the program is dubious.

Unlike traditional acceleration (grade skipping) as a means for serving the gifted, enrichment does cost the school district money. If separate classes are offered, teachers, classrooms, materials, and sometimes transportation must be provided—and paid for. If regular classroom teachers are expected to enrich their course content for the gifted who are mainstreamed into regular classes all day, then *extensive* training must be provided to enable those teachers to adequately differentiate their curriculum (see Hannigan 1984; Perry & Hoback 1984; Williams 1979).

Whichever option is chosen, there will be considerable expenditure. Therefore, results to justify that expenditure will be expected. Utilizing Renzulli's Triad Model or some variation of it will help ensure the results expected by administrators, parents, students, and teachers.

Classroom teachers tend to be very protective of their domain, which includes their subject matter, materials, time, and students. This is not necessarily an undesirable trait, but it is one of which to be aware, nevertheless. Classroom teachers as a group will be the hardest to convince that the time spent by a gifted student in special education is time well spent, but, once convinced, classroom teachers will be the strongest proponents of gifted education. Although part of the persuasion may be verbal, results will do most of the talking. Classroom teachers will only happily relinquish some of their guarded time with a student if they believe that student is benefitting more by being elsewhere.

Results will not be instantaneous, but teachers do not expect that they will be. They do expect change over a period of time, and they do expect that students removed from their classrooms are receiving something substantial, or they should not be removed.

Enrichment programs that are well designed, closely monitored, and updated will have substance and produce positive results. Sanders (1961, 68–69) states that "In itself, enrichment is not an organizational device but the very core of any program for the gifted, regardless of the organizational plan used." A viable program for the gifted cannot be *all* enrichment, just as it cannot be *all* accelerative. The two are not, nor should they be, mutually exclusive. The foremost proponent of acceleration, Julian Stanley, says that "properly conducted acceleration tends to be enriching and appropriate enrichment is deliberately accelerating" (1980, 9).

A solid enrichment program for the gifted in the public schools should support and expand upon the curriculum. It should not be a totally separate program. By tying the enrichment in with the curriculum, one identifies a base of content to explore. If this content is thoroughly explored, students, parents, administrators, and classroom teachers can all feel secure knowing that no child is missing out on knowledge by participating in the enrichment program. The content can either be covered rapidly, leaving time for going beyond it, or it can be covered slowly, with enrichment each step of the way. Thus, content is made more meaningful to the gifted, and as they begin to participate in the various portions of the program, the desired results will begin to appear, and again, students, parents, administrators, and teachers can feel satisfied and pleased with the program.

Some school districts will never give enrichment a try and will not know the satisfaction and pleasure that can result. When this is the case, alternatives must be sought. Many communities have found that Saturday, after-school, or summer programs are their answer. These programs are extracurricular and therefore have no limit to the scope they can cover. They may be offered through community colleges, universities, public agencies, private schools, or by any other group or individual interested in and committed to special education for the gifted of this nation.

Even though such sponsored programs do not have to be restricted to public-school content, the same criteria should apply: the programs should provide experiences above and beyond those that the less-than-gifted can appreciate. *Quality* instruction should be provided—both by persons trained in gifted education and by persons who are experts in their field but may never have had experience teaching the gifted.

Whether provided outside the public schools or within the public schools, and whether provided in classes specifically for the gifted or by well-trained regular classroom teachers, enrichment should be part of a differentiated curriculum for the gifted. Gifted learners, like all learners, have various learning styles and needs. For many, enrichment will match their learning style and meet their learning needs.

SPECIAL PROGRAMS

Each time in this century that there has been a resurgence of interest in the education of gifted individuals, a plethora of programs emerges. Some programs appear virtually overnight, are based on a current popular notion, and exist only to serve that notion. The majority of these fade out when the popular sentiment to serve the gifted fades out.

Other programs, however, only come to fruition after careful planning and research have laid the groundwork for the conception to become an educationally sound reality. These are the programs more likely to outlive the periodic swings of attention away from the gifted individual's best interests. Their proponents are continually involved in the process of evaluation and improvement, and longevity attests to success in that process.

In a few pages, it would be impossible to even briefly discuss the exemplary programs that currently exist in the United States. Therefore, the reader is referred to the annotated bibliography of this section for references that report on these successful programs.

Two definitions will aid readers as they peruse the references that discuss exemplary programs.

Magnet schools were first heard of in the 1960s, when educators and legislators were attempting to prevent "white flight" from large urban school districts. These magnet schools were intended to attract students back into the school district by offering unique programs not traditionally available. The term magnet school is still used primarily by large urban school districts to refer to schools that offer programs tailored to meet the educational needs of students with particular talents, interests, or vocational aspirations. For example, magnet schools exist for students talented in the arts, gifted in academics, interested in business, or aspiring toward a law career. Magnet schools are sometimes called *vanguard schools* or by a specific name—for example, Governor's School for Science and Mathematics.

Comprehensive high schools are also known as traditional high schools. They offer courses in all areas of the curriculum, with no one area emphasized over any other. Gifted students are sometimes provided for in comprehensive high schools through special classes or programs that group several classes together. For example, one suburban school district in Texas offers a humanities-based program for its gifted high school students. Students take history and English courses specially designed to meet their intellectual and creative abilities and needs.

SPECIAL CLASS GROUPING

Grouping students according to their measured ability has been tried for many years. Various reasons for the practice have been cited, but little research during this century has found positive results. This being the case, is there justification for including ability grouping as a topic in this chapter?

Yes. The overwhelming majority of grouping that has been done has divided youngsters into "high," "middle," and "low" groups. Generally, the research has found that the students in the low and middle clusters were harmed academically and emotionally by being so grouped and that those in the high group experienced no particular harm *or* benefit from membership in that group. This section will provide a rationale for grouping gifted students into special classes. These special classes would contain *some* of the same students who would be considered "high" in the high, middle, low configuration, but a high group could not go intact as a gifted class because not all its members would be considered gifted.

Though it is possible that grouping could be efficacious for all students, we will consider only those who are gifted. According to the

Dictionary of Education (cited by Passow 1962), homogeneous grouping is "the classification of pupils for the purpose of forming instructional groups having a relatively high degree of similarity in regard to certain factors that affect learning." Reducing the variance among the students is one of the positive aspects of grouping able children and youth with their intellectual peers (Keating 1979). When a teacher has thirty pupils whose abilities may range from mentally handicapped to mentally gifted, it is impossible to meet all their instructional needs, especially if the top students have abilities that exceed those of the teacher in particular areas. Placing highly able students together limits that range of ability somewhat—although homogeneous grouping does not mean that all the students are the same! The teacher of such a class should not expect all the students' abilities to lie in the same areas nor that they be operating at the same level.

Having been trained in gifted education, a teacher of such a specially clustered class would not expect the students all to be alike. This kind of knowledge on the part of the teacher is another major reason for gifted students to be specially grouped. They need a teacher who is sensitive to their emotional and mental needs as gifted students. Brink discounted the part teachers play in educating gifted students when he said "the brighter pupils will do pretty well with any kind of teacher, or perhaps with none at all" (1932, 429). In fact, this is simply not true. The role teachers play is crucial to the success of gifted education. That is why specially screened and trained teachers should be charged with the facilitation of gifted students' learning. In special grouping, this can happen more readily than when gifted students are primarily mainstreamed into regular classes and only attend the gifted class once or twice a week for an hour or two each time.

When a full-time class for the gifted is established, many problems— ones that often lead to criticism of programs for the gifted—are averted. Mirsky (1984, 25) says that a full-time special class for gifted students avoids the "mental gymnasium where children meet twice a week for problem-solving games that may be challenging but have no lasting pedagogical value." In the elementary school, a self-contained gifted class allows the teacher to plan for continuity in the students' learning. The teacher can carefully integrate the subjects so that the learning will be neither piecemeal nor fragmented. Gifted students are already adept at seeing relationships, and when subject matter is deliberately interwoven by their teacher to demonstrate the interconnectedness of various disciplines, their ability to make connections is augmented, thus facilitating their learning. Fox states that "the goal of any program for the gifted should be to provide meaningful learning experiences in the most efficient and effective way in order to minimize boredom, confusion, and frustration'' (1979, 126). A gifted class grouping, with a specially trained teacher as the primary planner and facilitator, is one way to meet this goal.

In secondary schools, this goal can also be met using special classes for the gifted. Keating (1979) points out that at the high school level, special classes are more flexible and more practical than special schools for highly able students. In high school, because a large variety of classes and scheduling options are available, able students can enroll in some courses designed for the gifted and some regular or honors courses, depending on their own particular areas of strength and weakness.

Part of the success of gifted classes will stem from the positive influence that the gifted members of the class have on each other. The students will provide an intellectually stimulating environment for each other and, for the first time for many students, being bright will be not only acceptable but desirable. Academic ability will form a common bond that will link the students into a support system for each other.

Another first for many will be a situation where they are not the ''smartest kid in the class.'' This is a hard, but necessary, experience. Although some people argue that special classes for the gifted will produce snobs, if there is any cause-effect relationship at all, it is more likely to be the opposite. An attitude of superiority may develop in some gifted students when they are members of mixed-ability classes. This may happen because they very often have the right answer—and they know they do and their classmates know they do. In a class full of academically able students, no one has the right answer all the time, and there is in fact less likelihood of feeling superior or snobbish.

Cornell, in the thirty-fifth NSSE yearbook, observed that

> the results of ability grouping seemed to depend less upon the fact of grouping itself than upon the philosophy behind the grouping, the accuracy with which grouping is made for the purposes intended, the differentiations in content, methods, and speed, and the technique of the teacher, as well as upon more general environmental influences. (1936, 304)

Schools that decide to use special class groupings as one component of their gifted program will have to determine their goals first. Once established, the goals will serve to determine the entrance requirements for the program, the curricular modifications necessary, and the means of program evaluation. As with other aspects of a gifted program, careful advance planning is essential for gaining and maintaining support and for ensuring better chances of success in the endeavor.

Why go to all the trouble to have special classes for the gifted? The answer lies in the specialness of these learners and the fact that the gifted learn better and are more challenged by the rigorous, abstract, and problem-centered nature of a curriculum devised with their needs in mind. The gifted must have differentiated education in order to develop their abilities and then to reach the heights of those abilities.

SUMMARY

Gifted education is special education. One of the mandates of special-education laws is that exceptional students are to be placed in the least restrictive environment for learning. For virtually all groups of exceptional students, this means making every attempt to mainstream them as much as possible into regular classrooms. However, for the group of exceptional students who are gifted, this is not the case. "The least restrictive environment for the gifted child moves away from the regular classroom rather than towards it as is the case with other exceptionalities" (Bull & Otey 1984, 36).

This chapter has presented *some* of the alternatives to the standard lockstep model of education. There are others, and parents and teachers of the gifted should become familiar with as many as possible. Only in this way will the "least restrictive environment" be found for these young people whose minds need to be liberated.

SELECTED BIBLIOGRAPHY

The bibliographic categories are sequential in relation to the information discussed in the body of the text. Generally the headings are the same as those used within the text. If a source is cited in more than one category, it will be annotated in the first entry, and all subsequent entries will indicate the category under which it is annotated.

Acceleration

Alexander, Pauline J., and Skinner, Michael E. "The Effects of Early Entrance on Subsequent Social and Academic Development: A Follow-up Study." *Journal for the Education of the Gifted* 3:147–50 (1980).

The authors conducted a study to determine the social and academic progress of students who qualified for early entrance into kindergarten and who are now sixth, seventh, and eighth graders. They reported that with few exceptions, the students maintained good to excellent academic standing, had positive peer relationships, and were involved in extracurricular activities. Both parents and students gave an overall positive report of the experience.

Babbot, Edward F. "A Year Early: What 378 Colleges Say about Admitting Students Right after Their Junior Year of High School." *College Board Review* 87:7–10, 32–33 (1973).

According to the author's survey, the majority of colleges accept students at the end of eleventh grade, with or without a diploma.

Bartkovich, Kevin G. "A Dual Perspective." Morales, Arlene J. "Life in the Fast Lane." Cohn, Richard J. "Thoughts on Acceleration." In *Readings in Curriculum Development*, edited by David M. Jackson. Guilford, Conn.: Special Learning Corporation, 1980.

These three brief "testimonials" were written by accelerants in the SMPY. All see their acceleration as a positive experience.

Benbow, Camilla P., and Stanley, Julian C. "Constructing Educational Bridges between High School and College." *Gifted Child Quarterly* 27:111–13 (Summer 1983).

The authors present seven options for bridging the gap between high school and college which they have derived from their extensive experience working with the Talent Search Model. (1) Take stimulating high school courses and one or two college courses. (2) Take AP exams and credit. (3) Take college-level correspondence courses. (4) Accelerate subject matter. (5) Graduate one year early from high school. (6) Attend an early-entrance college in lieu of high school. (7) Enter college early without a high school diploma. Excellent rationales for these options are provided.

Braga, Joseph L. "Early Admission: Opinion versus Evidence." *Elementary School Journal* 72:35–46 (October 1971).

The article presents a great deal of research that supports the concept of early admission to school, including criteria for early admission and its effect on achievement and social and emotional adjustment. The forty-seven-item bibliography would be helpful to someone interested in early admission for able students.

Brandt, Ron. "On Mathematically Talented Youth: A Conversation with Julian Stanley." *Educational Leadership* 39:101–7 (November 1981).

This is a fascinating, lucid article regarding the whys of the Johns Hopkins Study of Mathematically Precocious Youth. Stanley, who is the director of the SMPY, answers the interviewer's questions directly and firmly. Any one interested in the SMPY should read the interview.

Cornog, William H. "The Advanced Placement Program: Reflections on Its Origins." *College Board Review* 115:14–17 (Spring 1980).

Cornog's article retraces the history of the AP program and presents reflections based on hindsight.

Cox, June, and Daniel, Neil. "Options for the Secondary Level G/T Student. Part 2. Concurrent Enrollment: School and College." *G/C/T* 27:25–27 (March/April 1983).

Reasons for encouraging concurrent enrollment are given along with key points for developing a concurrent-enrollment program.

Daurio, Stephen P. "Educational Enrichment versus Acceleration: A Review of the Literature." In *Educating the Gifted: Acceleration and Enrichment*, edited by William C. George, Sanford J. Cohn, and Julian C. Stanley. Baltimore: Johns Hopkins Univ. Pr., 1979.

The author conducted an *extensive* review of the literature in order to compile this chapter. His conclusions are: (1) Academic enrichment may be worthwhile for gifted and nongifted students. (2) No studies show that enrichment provides results superior to those of acceleration. (3) The resistance to acceleration is based on concerns about the socioemotional development of the accelerants, and these concerns are unfounded. (4) Accelerants perform as well as or better than "normal age" controls, both academically and nonacademically.

Eisenberg, Ann R., and George, William C. "Early Entrance to College: The Johns Hopkins Experience: Study of Mathematically Precocious Youth (SMPY)." *College and University* 54:109–18 (Winter 1979).

The authors address the effects of shortening the overall time for completing elementary school, high school, and college, and the performance of students who so accelerate. All the data are positive concerning acceleration for highly able youth.

Feldhusen, John, and Reilly, Patricia. "The Purdue Secondary Model for Gifted Education: A Multi-Service Program." *Journal for the Education of the Gifted* 6:230–44 (Summer 1983).

This article presents a model combining acceleration and enrichment opportunities with a counseling component to guide gifted secondary youth to the program services that best fit their needs, interests, and abilities. The model is well explained.

George, William C., Cohn, Sanford J., and Stanley, Julian C., eds. *Educating the Gifted: Acceleration and Enrichment*. Baltimore: Johns Hopkins Univ. Pr., 1979. 242 pp.

This book contains the "revised and expanded proceedings of the Ninth Annual Blumberg Symposium on Research on Early Childhood Education." Its three major sections are (1) Acceleration and

Enrichment: A Controversy in Perspective; (2) Enrichment: High-lights of the Literature; and (3) Acceleration: Highlights of the Litera-ture. Some of the individual chapters are original; others are reprints of journal articles. The editors say up front that, although they have attempted to make the book unbiased, they do believe that accelera-tion is superior to enrichment for gifted youth.

Goldberger, Nancy. "Simon's Rock: Meeting the Developmental Needs of the Early College Student." *New Directions for Higher Educa-tion* 8:37–46 (1980).

Simon's Rock Early College is an autonomous unit of Bard College, a small liberal arts college in New York state. It has been in existence since 1964, serving capable tenth and eleventh graders who enroll full-time to begin work toward an A.A. or a B.A. degree. The article explains the background of the school and the results of the pro-gram. It also provides support for the notion that able students do not need to stay in high school until they are eighteen.

Gregory, Estelle, and March, Eileen. "Early Entrance Program at Cali-fornia State University, Los Angeles." *Gifted Child Quarterly* 29:83–86 (Spring 1985).

This article describes the history of the California State University, Los Angeles, Early Entrance Program. Several case studies are pre-sented as evidence of the success of such a program.

Hanson, Harlan P. "Twenty-Five Years of the Advanced Placement Program: Encouraging Able Students." *College Board Review* 115:8–12, 35 (Spring 1980).

The author had directed the College Board's AP program for fif-teen years prior to writing this article. He provides an interesting up-date on the program.

Horne, Don L., and Dupuy, Paul J. "In Favor of Acceleration for Gifted Students," *Personnel and Guidance Journal* 60:103–6 (October 1981).

The authors review the advantages and disadvantages of enrich-ment and acceleration programs for the gifted. They conclude that, particularly for students who move frequently, acceleration is more advantageous.

Johnson, William H. "Program for Conserving Our Superior Elemen-tary School Student." *Educational Administration and Supervision* 29:77–86 (February 1943).

The author presents numerous reasons for accelerating bright youth. He discusses several studies and successful acceleration pro-grams. He warns against judging the value of acceleration by focus-ing on those who were wrongly accelerated.

Justman, J. "Acceleration in the Junior High School." *High School Jour-nal* 40:121–26 (1956).

The author presents proponents' and opponents' arguments regarding acceleration. He concludes that, although the research is relatively scanty, acceleration is a viable alternative for able students.

Karnes, Frances A., and Chauvin, Jane. "A Survey of Early Admission Policies for Younger Than Average Students: Implications for Gifted Youth." *Gifted Child Quarterly* 26:68–73 (Spring 1982a).

The authors report the results of a survey they conducted to ascertain the prevalence of colleges that admit younger-than-average students prior to their high school graduation. A thorough description of their survey and several informative tables are provided. Guidance counselors and high school teachers should know about the results of this survey in order to assess a young gifted student's chances of being accepted for early admission.

_____. "Almost Everything That Parents and Teachers of Gifted Secondary School Students Should Know about Early College Enrollment and College Credit by Examination." *G/C/T* 24: 39–42 (September/October 1982b).

The authors review five acceleration options: dual enrollment, early admission, Advanced Placement (AP), College Level Examination Program (CLEP), and the International Baccalaureate Program (IB). Addresses for the latter three are given.

Kearney, Katheryn. "At Home in Maine: Gifted Children and Homeschooling." *G/C/T* 33:15–19 (May/June 1984).

Two families who have chosen to educate their own children at home are the focus of Kearney's article. She discusses their reasons for making this somewhat radical choice and then interviews the parents and children regarding the homeschool experience. All feel it has been a positive move for them. Guidelines are provided. This is a good article.

Khatena, Joe. "What Schooling for the Gifted." *Gifted Child Quarterly* 27:51–56 (Spring 1983).

Khatena briefly discusses accelerative enrichment, process learning, individualized education, and curricular programs and special projects.

King, Fred M. "Student Attitudes toward Acceleration." *Education* 88:73–77 (September/October 1967).

This interesting article reports on a survey of nearly 600 accelerated high school students. Their overall opinion was that being accelerated met their needs by being both demanding and challenging.

Kirschenbaum, Robert J. "Examining the Rationale for Gifted Education." *Roeper Review* 7:95–97 (November 1984).

Kirschenbaum says that the "rationale for instituting special programs for exceptional children is that their educational needs can not

be adequately met in the regular classroom." He presents both sides
of several programming alternatives. He concludes that tracking students into minicourses with accelerated content is more prudent.
Students who are creatively productive in these minicourses should
then work on creative projects under the supervision of a teacher of
the gifted.

Klausmeier, Herbert J. "Effects of Accelerating Bright Older Elementary Pupils: A Follow-Up." *Journal of Educational Psychology*
54:165–71 (June 1963).

Klausmeier reports on a follow-up study of fifth graders who had
attended a five-week summer session that enabled them to skip
third grade. The author found no unfavorable consequences in comparing the accelerants with four types of control groups.

Laycock, Frank. "College Programs for the Gifted." *Roeper Review*
2:10–14 (September 1979).

Laycock reviews several specific college programs for gifted students and also gives some general descriptions of programs that
could be implemented. He provides support for the appropriateness
of accelerating gifted students.

Lewis, Gail. "Alternatives to Acceleration for the Highly Gifted
Child." *Roeper Review* 6:133–36 (February 1984).

Two highly gifted children who participated in a special summer
program are contrasted. Lewis makes the point that acceleration
alone is not sufficient to meet the needs of these children. She says
assessment, flexible scheduling, and counseling are essential components of a successful program for extremely gifted youngsters.

Marland, Sidney P. "Advanced Placement." *Today's Education*
65:43–44 (January/February 1976).

Marland, who was president of the College Entrance Examination
Board at the time of this article, explains the pros of the AP program.
He bemoans the fact that it is grossly underused and offers possible
reasons why this is the case.

Mirman, Norman. "Are Accelerated Students Socially Maladjusted?"
Elementary School Journal 62:273–76 (February 1962).

The author studied 128 high school seniors (half had been double
promoted, half had not) and found no real difference in their scholastic interests, vocational interests, participation in school activities,
or social adjustment. Mirman concludes that the impact of acceleration on social adjustment has been grossly exaggerated.

Mitchell, Charlotte. "Excelleration." *G/C/T* 33:29–31 (May/June 1984).

"Excelleration" is a "game" that has as its objective, "To be the first
to 'graduate' and at the same time learn about gifted students and

the ways in which they can be accelerated." This clever article would be fun to use at an in-service session on acceleration.

Morgan, Harry J., Tennant, Carolyn G., and Gold, Milton J. *Elementary and Secondary Level Programs for the Gifted.* New York: Teachers College Press, 1980. 70 pp.

This short book could be a "primer" for administrators and teachers designing curricular programs for the gifted. It is well written and can easily be understood by lay persons unfamiliar with gifted education.

Olson, Nancy S. "Youngsters Speed through Fast-Paced Summer Programs." *Educational Leadership* 39:96–100 (November 1981).

The article describes the three-week summer program sponsored by Johns Hopkins University. Over 200 eleven- to fourteen-year-olds participated in the 1981 program, pursuing courses in mathematics, science, and writing. The article is very readable and would be good for teachers or counselors who are encouraging highly able students to participate in such programs.

Parrot, Margot Nicholas. "A Parent Speaks Up for Acceleration: Acceleration Can Work. Eddie Is Proof Enough for Me." *G/C/T* 12:12–13 (March/April 1980).

Written by the mother of a gifted child, this article is personal testimony that acceleration is an alternative worth investigating. The author's son was accelerated from third to fifth grade and, although it was not a completely smooth transition, it solved many of his problems. She recommends enrichment to augment acceleration.

Paulus, Pat. "Acceleration: More than Grade Skipping." *Roeper Review* 7:98–100 (November 1984).

Paulus presents historical support for acceleration along with current research that indicates the value of acceleration as the most viable alternative for gifted students.

Pressey, Sidney L. "Educational Acceleration: Occasional Procedure or Major Issue?" *Personnel Guidance Journal* 41:12–17 (September 1962).

According to the author, his article "presents considerations arguing that acceleration is certainly the most advantage-yielding, and, on the whole, most sound method of dealing with talented youngsters, that the top fifth or more of all pupils might well progress faster than the usual lockstep pace, that acceleration may occur desirably anywhere from kindergarten to professional school—and presents the most rewarding of all opportunities for wise student personnel policy."

————. "Fordling Accelerates Ten Years After." *Journal of Counseling Psychology* 14:73–80 (1967).

Pressey reports on the progress and accomplishment of the recipients of the Ford scholarship who attended Oberlin College, University of Louisville, and Fisk University during the early 1950s. Of this group, the majority who graduated had also obtained advanced degrees, and many were already into outstanding careers. In answering questionnaires, the "Fordlings" indicated an overall positive view of their acceleration.

Rice, Joseph P. "Developmental Approach to Pupil Acceleration." *Clearing House* 40:216–20 (December 1965).

Rice discusses various viewpoints regarding acceleration but posits that it is *one* viable means for meeting able students' needs.

Robeck, Mildred C. *Acceleration: Programs for Intellectually Gifted Pupils.* California Project Talent, 1968. 174 pp.

This book is a report on California's Project Talent acceleration program. It explains the purposes and findings of the program and how a similar one could be implemented in other school districts. There are a number of forms that might be useful guides for schools designing their own. Administrators considering an acceleration program would benefit from skimming this book.

Roedell, Wendy Conklin, Jackson, Nancy Ewald, and Robinson, Halbert B. "Programs for Gifted Young Children." *Gifted Young Children,* New York: Teachers College Press, 1980. 107 pp.

The authors, experts regarding young gifted children, present a general description of how to identify young children who would benefit from special programs for the gifted and what should be expected from these special programs. They also describe several of the outstanding programs in the United States for young, able students. The book is well worth reading.

Solano, Cecilia H., and George, William C. "College Courses and Educational Facilitation of the Gifted." *Gifted Child Quarterly* 20:274–85 (Fall 1976).

The authors present evidence for encouraging gifted junior and senior high students to take college courses. They discuss experimental data and "commonsense data" concerning the efficacy of acceleration.

Stanley, Julian. "Educational Non-Acceleration: An International Tragedy." *G/C/T* 3:2–5, 53–57, 60–63 (May/June 1978a).

Stanley makes a strong case for acceleration as the "method of choice," particularly for those students who reason extremely well mathematically. The article is an updated version of the author's invited address to the second World Conference on Gifted and Talented Children. He reports on the progress of some of the SMPY's radical accelerants and lists and explains twelve ways to accelerate students who are able and motivated.

————. "Radical Acceleration: Recent Educational Innovation at Johns Hopkins University." *Gifted Child Quarterly* 22:62–67 (Spring 1978b).

This article is based on an informal talk given by the author at a JHU alumni meeting. He discusses several of the radical accelerants who have been discovered as a result of the SMPY. They have received, or are in the process of receiving, Ph.D.s from noted universities—years ahead of the norm. One must keep in mind that these students are extremely rare, but without radical acceleration they would be receiving their high school diplomas at age eighteen instead of their Ph.D.s.

————. "The Study and Facilitation of Talent for Mathematics." In *The Gifted and the Talented: Their Education and Development*, Part 1 in *Seventy-Eighth Yearbook of the National Society for the Study of Education* 78th, edited by A. Harry Passow. Chicago: Univ. of Chicago Pr., 1979.

Stanley provides a general overview and rationale for intervention in the education of those with an extraordinary facility in a particular area (e.g., mathematics).

————. "On Educating the Gifted." *Educational Researcher* 9:8–12 (March 1980).

Stanley speaks out strongly for acceleration as the means for teaching highly able youth. He believes much of the enrichment in gifted programs is a waste of time. He presents the idea of a longitudinal teaching team in the area of mathematics which would be responsible for helping students meet the criteria for mathematical competence. He believes this model could and should be extended to other subject-matter areas as well.

Stanley, Julian C., and George, William C. "Now We Are Six: The Ever-Expanding SMPY." *G/C/T* 1:9–11, 43–44, 50–51 (January/February 1978).

This article is based on the "Sixth Annual Report to the Spencer Foundation concerning its support of the Study of Mathematically Precocious Youth during the period 1 September 1976–31 August 1977." It relates one success story after another and should be read, along with all the other SMPY publications, by those interested in or fascinated by acceleration for highly gifted youth.

Tobin, Dianne. "Accelerated Mathematics for the Gifted." *G/C/T* 9:48–50, 78 (September/October 1979).

The author, a research associate of the Intellectually Gifted Child Study Group at the Johns Hopkins University, describes her son's experiences in an accelerated mathematics class. The class was held on Saturday mornings for two hours, and the students were given homework to do during the week. Tobin said that an often over-looked benefit of the fast-paced mathematics courses is the gain in the participants' self-discipline and study skills. Her article is honest and would be worth reading for anyone whose child is considering a fast-paced course.

Voorheis, Greg P. "Concurrent High School–College Enrollments." *Educational Record* 60:305–11 (Summer 1979).

The author outlines the process that the University of Vermont went through to set up a concurrent enrollment program with local high schools. He presents the rationale for concurrent enrollment as opposed to early admission.

Williams, Marjorie. "Diamond in the Rough: A Story of Accelera-tion." *G/C/T* 33:21–23 (May/June 1984).

The author is a teacher of the gifted, and she documents the pro-cess she and others went through to accelerate a very bright child from second grade to fourth grade. The article is very readable, in-formative, and upbeat.

Witty, Paul A., and Wilkins, L. "The Status of Acceleration or Grade Skipping as an Administrative Practice." *Educational Administration and Supervision* 19:321–46 (May 1933).

The authors assert that acceleration for the gifted has never been given a real chance. They review the literature of the early part of the century which is, in their opinion, fragmentary and poorly de-signed. Their overall conclusion is that acceleration should be rec-ommended for the gifted.

Enrichment

Blanning, Jean M. "High School Students Undertake Study of Contro-versial Heroes." *G/C/T* 4:34–36 (September/October 1978).

The author describes a summer enrichment program funded by a Youth Grant in the Humanities from the National Endowment for the Humanities. The most significant idea to be gleaned from the ar-ticle is that an enrichment program can be positive for gifted youth when they work to produce quality products.

Carney, Fay M. "Another Look at Triad: Practical Considerations in Implementing the Model." *G/C/T* 17:40–43 (March/April 1982).

In this well-written article, the author does exactly what her title says—she gives specific "ins and outs" of using the Triad Model. Her article details factors related to student success and teacher suc-cess along with considerations for administrators. It should be read by all persons considering an enrichment program, particularly if the Enrichment Triad is the model to be used.

Carran, Mike. "Developing a Community Based Summer Enrichment Program." *Roeper Review* 6:81–82 (November 1983).

Carran discusses how a group of teachers and parents established a summer enrichment program for the gifted.

Clifford, Jerry Ann, Runions, Ted, and Smith, Elizabeth. "The Learning Enrichment Service (LES): A Multi-optioned Approach to Programming for Gifted Secondary School Students." *Roeper Review* 6:226–28 (April 1984).

LES (based on the Enrichment Triad Model and the Revolving Door Identification Model) is administered by a resource team that provides five enrichment services: screening, training, networking, counseling, and exchanging information. The authors explain the model and their current research supporting its use.

Daurio 1979. *See* Acceleration

Durr, William K. "Dimensions of Enrichment." *Exceptional Children* 26:202–6 (1959).

The author describes the three basic dimensions of enrichment: horizontal, vertical, or supplementary. He explores the pros and cons of each.

Gilbert, Janet P., and Beal, Mary R. "Music Experiences for the Gifted and Talented: Adapting the Renzulli Enrichment Triad Model." *G/C/T* 24:50–51 (September/October 1982).

The authors describe a way to use Renzulli's Enrichment Triad Model as a method for the exploration of music topics by gifted and talented students. One sample lesson is included.

Glass, L. W. "A Cooperative University–High School Project for Talented Students," *Gifted Child Quarterly* 23:523–37 (Fall 1979).

The author describes a program that allowed fifteen outstanding juniors to work with a scientist in their area of interest during a summer-long college course for which they received six hours of college credit. The experience was quite positive for the participants.

Hannigan, Irene. "Core-Explore-More: A Structure for Planning Enrichment Activities." *Roeper Review* 6:142–44 (February 1984).

The author describes the basis of her district's enrichment program, which is designed to help classroom teachers serve the gifted children who are mainstreamed in their classrooms. The ideas are good, but the actual differentiation between this program and any enrichment program for all students is fuzzy.

Hester, Joseph P. "The Gifted: An Enrichment Curriculum." *The Creative Child and Adult Quarterly* 7:43–48 (1982).

The author describes his enrichment curriculum, which provides a model for investigating one's essential humanness. It focuses on the question, What is human about humans? and is holistic in that it is comprehensive and multidisciplinary. The model has been field-tested in a resource setting with middle school and high school gifted students.

Horne and Dupuy 1981. *See* Acceleration

Jackman, William D., and Bachtold, Louise M. "Evaluation of a Seminar for Gifted Junior High Students." *Gifted Child Quarterly* 13:163–68 (Fall 1969).

The authors report on a seminar program for gifted students that was piloted and then established at a junior high school. The article recounts both the good and the bad about the program, along with suggestions for improving it. Students and teachers in the program evaluated it as a valuable learning experience.

Karnes, Frances A., and Gregory, Barbara. "Saturday Programs for the Gifted." *G/C/T* 12:49–51 (March/April 1980).

The authors briefly describe several well-established Saturday programs for gifted students. Persons interested in starting a Saturday program will find this article worth taking a look at. The authors provide some useful addresses for obtaining more detailed information.

Kolloff, Penny Britton, and Feldhusen, John F. "The Effects of Enrichment on Self Concept and Creative Thinking." *Gifted Child Quarterly* 28:53–57 (Spring 1984).

The authors report on their study of how an enrichment program based on the Purdue Three-Stage Model affected the self-concept and creative thinking abilities of gifted elementary students. They found that self-concepts were unaffected, but creative thinking abilities were improved.

Lazar, Alfred L., Gensley, Juliana, and Gowan, John C. "Developing Positive Attitudes through Curriculum Planning for Young Gifted Children." *Gifted Child Quarterly* 16:27–31 (Spring 1972).

The article describes an enrichment curriculum for gifted students, called Creative Americans.

Lessinger, Leon M. "Enrichment for Gifted Pupils: Its Nature and Nurture." *Exceptional Child* 30:119–22 (November 1963).

Lessinger discusses enrichment as a means for educating the gifted. Topics include considerations, definitions, illustrations, and the role of the teacher.

Lewis, Gail. "Alternatives to Acceleration for the Highly Gifted Child." *Roeper Review* 6:133–36 (February 1984).

This article focuses on two highly gifted five-year-olds (IQ 158+). The author posits that acceleration alone will not serve these extraordinary children. She recommends careful assessment, flexible scheduling, and counseling to accompany any program of acceleration for the highly gifted.

Maker, C. June. *Teaching Models in Education of the Gifted*. Rockville, Md.: Aspen Publications, 1982. 475 pp.

Maker examines Renzulli's Enrichment Triad Model in her book (p.207–36), reviewing its underlying assumptions, its elements, how it modifies the curriculum, and how the model itself can be modified. She also briefly discusses its development, research on its effectiveness, and its advantages and disadvantages. Her overall opinion of the model is positive.

Perry, Phyllis J., and Hoback, John R. "How to Put Your Gifted/Talented Programming in Gear." *G/C/T* 17:20–22 (March/April 1981).

The authors have drawn an analogy between going on a trip and establishing a gifted program. The article would be good reading for persons organizing others to inspire a school district to establish a program for the gifted.

_____. "Grid Planning: A Tool in Programming for Talented and Gifted Students." *Roeper Review* 6:139–42 (1984).

The authors explain how to use a grid as a framework when planning enrichment activities for able students. The side of the grid has the focuses of the unit and the top has Bloom's six levels. The authors state that their plan is efficient, comprehensive, flexible, integrative, and allows for individual differences.

Pringle, Robert G., Webb, Judith G., and Warner, Dennis A. "Innovative Education for Gifted Children in Rural Elementary Schools." *Elementary School Journal* 73:79–84 (November 1972).

The article describes an enrichment program established to serve several rural school districts. The rationale for the program and comments from parents and teachers are included.

Renzulli, Joseph S. *The Enrichment Triad Model: A Guide for Developing Defensible Programs for the Gifted and Talented*. Mansfield Center, Conn.: Creative Learning Press, 1977. 88 pp.

For anyone considering establishing an enrichment program for the gifted, or for anyone who already has one, this book is "must" reading. Whether or not one chooses to implement Renzulli's model in its purest form, many of its facets would enhance any program for the gifted.

Renzulli, Joseph S., and Smith, Linda H. "An Alternative Approach to Identifying and Programming for Gifted and Talented Students." *G/C/T* 15:4–11 (November/December 1980).

The authors provide a succinct explanation of their Revolving Door

Approach to identification and programming. Every planner of gifted programs should read this article. It presents the idea that different gifted children can be served during a year, depending on their needs.

Sanders, David C. *Elementary Education and the Academically Talented Pupil.* Washington, D.C.: National Education Association Project on the Academically Talented Student, 1961. 96 pp.

This book is an outgrowth of the 1959 invitation Conference on Elementary Education and the Academically Talented Pupil. The author has pulled together a number of the issues and concerns discussed at the conference. He covers planning a program, identifying the gifted, differentiated curriculum and curricular organizations, and administrative concerns.

Stanley 1980. *See* Acceleration

Tuttle, Frederick B., Jr., and Becker, Laurence A. *Program Design and Development for Gifted and Talented Students.* 2d ed. Washington, D.C.: National Education Association, 1983. 128 pp.

This concise book is divided into six sections: rationale for special provisions for gifted and talented students, program design, curricular models, teacher selection, program evaluation, and steps in initiating a program.

Weiner, Ann. "Beware of 'Enrichment' Programs for Your Gifted Child." *G/C/T* 4:13 (September/October 1978).

The author warns against the "new enrichment," saying it can often cause more problems that it is worth.

Williams, Frank E. "Williams' Strategies to Orchestrate Renzulli's Triad." *G/C/T* 9:2–6, 10 (September/October 1979).

In this article, Williams presents the idea of "marrying" Renzulli's Enrichment Triad with Williams' Interaction Model. He explains how using the two in harmony can create wonderful lessons for children—average and gifted. Two sample lessons are provided.

————. "Enriched Experiences for More Able Learners." *G/C/T* 29:2–5 (September/October 1983).

The importance to learning of "making connections" between old and new experiences is discussed. Williams gives several examples of enriched experiences that resulted in new connections.

Worcester, Dean A. "Enrichment." *Educating the Gifted: Acceleration and Enrichment,* edited by William C. George, Sanford J. Cohn, and Julian C. Stanley. Baltimore: Johns Hopkins Univ. Pr., 1979.

Worcester's brief chapter espouses enrichment for the gifted—if it is truly an expanding experience but not if it is busywork or just another lockstep program.

Special Programs

"The Alabama School of Fine Arts." *Gifted Child Quarterly* 23:543–50 (Fall 1979).

The article describes the Alabama School of Fine Arts, which "offers a six year curriculum of general academic studies and specialized fine arts studies harmonized to produce graduates with professional and vocational capabilities representative of both academic and fine arts disciplines."

Arnold, Allyn E., and Berro, Sandra. "Key to More Effective Programs for Gifted/Talented—The Right Evaluation." *Roeper Review* 5:34–35 (February 1983).

Arnold discusses the monumental task of trying to create educationally sound programs in 600 schools. He also discusses ways to evaluate so that the right changes can be effected.

Barbe, Walter B. "Evaluation of Special Classes for Gifted Children." *Exceptional Children* 22:60–63 (November 1955).

This article discusses the results of a questionnaire mailed to all the living, locatable graduates of the Cleveland Major Works Classes (1938 to 1952). Their overall opinion was that it had been a success and had had a positive effect on their lives.

Bassett, Patrick F. "Educating the Gifted: The Independent School Challenge." *G/C/T* 26:24–25 (January/February 1983).

Bassett posits that, in theory, private schools should be at the vanguard with revolutionary ideas and methods that require flexibility to implement and administer, since the size and independence of private schools allow such flexibility. On the other hand, public schools should lead the way in experimenting with ideas that require large populations and funding. Bassett says the two should work together in gifted education. He then presents an overview of the program for the gifted that his private school offers.

Blakeslee, Sandra. "A College for Kids," *Education Digest* 41:36–37 (September 1975).

The article, reprinted from the *New York Times,* reports on Marin County's College for Kids, which is held at a local junior high school. The program serves children from kindergarten through ninth grade. It is designed as an enrichment program, offering such courses as Marine Biology; Our Solar System; and Grasshoppers, Lizards, Ladybugs and You. The program has been very successful.

Bray, Jim. "The Governor's School of North Carolina (West)." *G/C/T* 8:47, 54–57 (May/June 1979).

The author, who had been director of the school since 1969, describes the program. He includes information on the reasons the school was started, how students are selected, the curriculum, and the outlook for the future. He believes the future looks bright!

Caffee, Barbara. "The Arkadelphia Secondary Gifted and Talented Program." *G/C/T* 17:55-57 (March/April 1981).

The author briefly describes a secondary program in rural Arkansas based on Renzulli's Enrichment Triad Model. She sees the program as a success.

Callahan, Carolyn, M. "Issues in Evaluating Programs for the Gifted." *Gifted Child Quarterly* 27:3-7 (Winter 1983).

Callahan says the issues that continually plague attempts to carry out meaningful evaluations fall into three categories: (1) legitimate and important issues, (2) illegitimate but important issues, (3) those not worth talking about. She addresses some of the issues in the first group, proposes some solutions, and offers implications for improved program evaluation.

Carter, Kyle R., and Hamilton, Wilma. "Formative Evaluation of Gifted Programs: A Process and Model." *Gifted Child Quarterly* 29:5-11 (Winter 1985).

The authors describe an evaluation process and model that they developed to help a Colorado school district assess the effectiveness of its programs for gifted and talented. The underlying philosophy of the model and a rationale for the evaluation process are clearly explained. This article would be very useful to schools.

Clendening, Corinne P., and Davies, Ruth Ann. *Challenging the Gifted: Curriculum Enrichment and Acceleration Models.* New York: R. R. Bowker Co., 1983. 483 pp.

This book would serve teachers, librarians, and curriculum consultants well as a reference book. The first part briefly describes how programs for the gifted should be designed and implemented. The second part, which comprises the bulk of the book, presents fifteen model programs for grades K-12. Some of the programs could be used just as they are, and others could be modified to fit the needs of an individual school or school district.

Coleman, Dona. "England's Saturday Clubs: An Answer for Our Gifted." *G/C/T* 17:46-47 (March/April 1981).

The author briefly describes her visit to one of the Saturday Clubs, which are designed to provide greater opportunity for self-fulfillment than is normally experienced by some gifted children. The article may provide some ideas for communities that want to start enrichment programs for their gifted students.

"Cooperation: The Gifted-College for School Kids." *Nation's Schools and Colleges* 2:23-26 (April 1975).

This article describes the highly successful Marin County (California) College for Kids program. In this program, gifted elementary school children attend local community college classes designed especially for them.

Cox, June. "Community-Based Programs." In *The Gifted and the Talented: Their Education and Development,* Part 1 of *Seventy-Eighth Yearbook of the National Society for the Study of Education,* edited by A. Harry Passow. Chicago: Univ. of Chicago Pr., 1979.

Cox, who has been involved in studying programs for the gifted all across the country, describes several community-based programs. She urges persons with gifted children not to forget the wealth of opportunity available in the community, which is sometimes "just for the asking" and at other times must be carefully planned and coordinated.

_____. "Advanced Placement: An Exemplary Honors Model." *G/C/T* 26:47–51 (January/February 1983).

Cox provides a look at the value of AP programs for highly able students. College policies, research data, teacher selection and training, grading, and motivation are discussed. A pilot project—a junior AP program—is also reviewed.

Cox, June, and Daniel, Neil. "Options for the Secondary Level G/T Student. Part 2. The International Baccalaureate." *G/C/T* 27:24, 28–30 (March/April 1983a).

The authors explain the requirements for the International Baccalaureate and present the IB program as it operates in one large school district. Key points for developing an IB program are given.

_____. "Specialized Schools for High Ability Students." *G/C/T* 28:2–9 (May/June 1983b).

Six schools are featured: Houston's High School for the Performing Arts; Cincinnati's Walnut Hills High School (College Preparatory) and School for Creative and Performing Arts; the Bronx High School of Science; North Carolina's School of Science and Mathematics and School of the Arts.

_____. "Programming for Excellence in the Summer." *G/C/T* 31:54–60 (January/February 1984a).

This article discusses several outstanding summer programs for gifted or talented students: National Music Camp at Interlochen, Michigan; National High School Institute at Northwestern University; Northwestern Talent Search; Duke Talent Identification Program; Governors' Schools in Arkansas, North Carolina, South Carolina, and Virginia. Other programs and pertinent information are listed in a helpful table.

_____. "Comprehensive Programs for Able Learners." *G/C/T* 32:47–53 (March/April 1984b).

Four school districts with successful programs for able learners are discussed. Each is different—but a commonality of vision and commitment is shared.

_____. "Comprehensive Programs: The Role of the State Agency and Other Partners in Education." *G/C/T* 33:57–60 (May/June 1984c).

Three people who hold central roles in their state agencies shared their concepts of their roles in education for the gifted and talented. Also, other agencies and institutions that cooperate with schools to provide for the gifted are discussed.

Dubner, Frances S. "IMPACT: A High School Gifted Program that Works." *Roeper Review* 7: 41–43 (September 1984).

IMPACT, which has been in existence for over twelve years and has been judged highly successful, is described.

Duckrow, Edward, and Bothmer, Richard. "Welcome to the Academic Challenge Bowl." *G/C/T* 26:22–23 (January/February 1983).

The authors discuss the Academic Challenge Bowl, which has a College Bowl and Whiz Quiz format. It is heard on a local radio station.

Ebmeier, Howard, Dyche, Barbara, Taylor, Patty, and Hall, Maud. "An Empirical Comparison of Two Program Models for Elementary Gifted Education." *Gifted Child Quarterly* 29:15–19 (Winter 1985).

The authors designed a study that had as its purposes: (1) to develop a gifted program that could be used by regular classroom teachers and (2) to compare the cognitive achievement outcomes when students identified as gifted were (*a*) taught in this program or (*b*) taught by a teacher specialist in gifted education. The study took two years to complete, and the results indicate that their concept is a viable alternative when a school district cannot afford to have gifted specialists in each elementary building.

Ehrlich, Virginia Z. "A Model Program for Educating Gifted Four- to Eight-Year-Old Children," *International Journal of Early Childhood* 11:115–23 (1979).

The article describes the Astor Program for Intellectually Gifted Primary School Children, which is located in New York at Teachers College, Columbia University. The author recommends that gifted children be given an early start in differentiated education.

Feldhusen, John, and Sokol, Leslie. "Extra-School Programming to Meet the Needs of Gifted Youth: Super Saturday." *Gifted Child Quarterly* 26:51–56 (Spring 1982).

The authors provide an extensive update on the Super Saturday program (see Feldhusen & Wyman, 1980). The program has grown to serve gifted children from preschool through twelfth grade, and some special courses are now offered in the afternoon and evening. The program continues to be successful.

Feldhusen, John F., and Wyman, Ann Robinson. "Super Saturday: Design and Implementation of Purdue's Special Program for Gifted Children." *Gifted Child Quarterly* 24:15–21 (Winter 1980).

The authors describe the program they direct on the Purdue University campus. The Saturday classes serve approximately one hundred students during each six-week session. They offer such courses as Creative Dramatics, Math and Computer Science, German, Photography, and Humor and Creative Expression. The authors have evaluated their program using attitude surveys completed by students, parents, and teachers. All three instruments are included. The results indicate generally positive attitudes towards this enrichment program.

Finkel, Estelle. "Convocations for the Gifted." *G/C/T* 26:18–21 (January/February 1983).

Finkel describes a way her school district provides for its EEP (Extended Enrichment Program) students. A CAPS day (Create, Advertise, Produce, and Sell) was set up as a "meeting of the minds" for EEP students. An excellent checklist for a school planning a convocation is included.

G/C/T International Issue: Gifted Education around the World. Issue 39 (July/August 1985).

The entire issue is comprised of articles about special programs in various countries around the world (e.g., India, China, Guam, Australia).

Gerencser, Stephen. "The Calasanctius Experience." In *The Gifted and the Talented: Their Education and Development,* Part 1 of *Seventy-Eighth Yearbook of the National Society for the Study of Education,* edited by A. Harry Passow. Chicago: Univ. of Chicago Pr., 1979.

The Calasanctius School in Buffalo, New York, was named after an innovative educator, Joseph Calasanctius (1556–1648). The school was founded in 1957 and now serves four-year-olds through young adults preparing for college. This article gives a fascinating picture of this innovative school. Its philosophy and curriculum are different from those of most comprehensive schools, and it is definitely proving successful in its endeavor to educate bright, motivated youth.

Gilberg, Jody A. "Formative Evaluation of Gifted and Talented Programs." *Roeper Review* 6:43–44 (September 1983).

The author defines formative evaluations as "assessments of worth focused on instructional programs that are still capable of being modified." She explains models and objectives of formative evaluation, obstacles that must be overcome, and steps to follow.

Ginsberg, Gina. "The Saturday Workshop." *G/C/T* 1: 30–34 (January/
February 1978).

The author is the director of the Gifted Child Society, which began
sponsoring Saturday Workshops in the late 1950s. She descibes the
program's eligibility requirements and gives other general information (courses offered, teacher training, costs, etc.). An address is
provided so that others can contact the author for more information.
She states: "Unlike most organizations, the Gifted Child Society
and its Saturday Workshops are working actively toward their own
demise. The membership hopes the day will come when their children can stay home on Saturday to play baseball . . . sleep late . . . or
contemplate the ceiling because their special learning needs are being met during the week in the classroom.

Girard, Barbara S., and Girard, James P. "College Bowl Competition
and the Gifted Student." *Roeper Review* 6:86–89 (Novemebr 1983).

The authors contend that college bowl competitions benefit students not only in the effective areas (for example, character building
as a result of teamwork), but also in terms of substantive, generaliz-
able skills of particular value to the gifted. They clearly support their
contention.

Gold, Milton J. "College Programs." In *The Gifted and the Talented:
Their Education and Development*, Part 1 of *Seventy-Eighth Yearbook of
the National Society for the Study of Education*, edited by A. Harry Passow. Chicago: Univ. of Chicago Pr., 1979.

Gold chronicles the change in the focus of colleges and universities
in the twenty years since the publication of the last NSSE yearbook
on the gifted. He notes that the focus changed from emphasis on the
highly able to emphasis on the less able in college, but it is now
swinging back. He discusses a number of programs (both generic
and specific) and recommends that each institution more clearly define its own mission rather than trying to create a whole new set of
institutions.

Hensel, Nancy. "A Cooperative University/School District Gifted Program." *Roeper Review* 7:220–222 (April 1985).

Hensel describes a program implemented when funds were cut so
drastically that the school district was unable to provide adequately
for gifted students. A nearby university bused the students to the
campus once a week for two hours. Children had three courses to
choose from—each taught by teacher-education students under faculty supervision. Advantages and disadvantages are discussed.

Hogan, Ralph E. "Georgia's GHP." *Today's Education* 62:34–35 (May
1973).

The author, who directs the Governor's Honor Program, describes the tenth summer session. During the eight-week program, students participated in classes in their particular areas of interest and strength. The experience was stimulating for all participants.

Karnes, Frances A., and Pearce, Norma. "Governors' Honors Programs: A Viable Alternative for the Gifted and Talented." *G/C/T* 18:8–11 (May/June 1981).

The authors give brief overviews of the Governor's Honors Programs in Arkansas, Florida, Georgia, Louisiana, North Carolina, Pennsylvania, South Carolina, and Virginia. Contact persons in each state are listed, with addresses.

Karnes, Frances A., and Peddicord, Herschel Q., Jr. *Programs, Leaders, Consultants, and Other Resources in Gifted and Talented Education.* Springfield, Ill.: Charles C. Thomas, 1980. 342 pp.

This book provides a wealth of information regarding people and programs in gifted education. Part 1 (pp. 3–117) is "Programs for the Gifted," and it is divided into five sections: preschool programs, elementary programs, elementary/secondary programs, secondary programs, and performing arts programs. For each of the individual programs the authors discuss, they present the name of the program, the contact person (with address), an overview of the program, a description of the program, and an evaluation of it. This is an invaluable book for persons starting or already involved in gifted education.

Laycock, Frank. "Bright Students and Their Adjustment to College." *Journal for the Education of the Gifted* 8:83–92 (Fall 1984).

Laycock briefly explores the different types of colleges, the pressures bright students experience regarding college selection and performance, and their reactions and adjustments to being college students.

Lupkowski, Ann E. "Gifted Students in Small Rural Schools Do Not Have to Move to the City." *Roeper Review* 7:13–16 (September 1984).

The author discusses several alternatives for rural school districts, which have special problems in serving their gifted populations. These include cooperative programs, innovative teaching, individualized instruction, counseling, community resources, and challenging courses.

Mulhern, John D., and Ward, Marjory. "Achieving Excellence through the International Baccalaureate Program: A Case Study of University–School District Cooperation." *Roeper Review* 7:226–27 (April 1985).

The authors describe the partnership between the University of South Carolina and Lexington School District #5, in which an International Baccaulaureate program was set up.

Rebbeck, Barbara J. "Chats with GATS." *G/C/T* 38:37–40 (May/June 1985).

Three gifted students who took part in a special summer institute cosponsored by school districts and universities in Michigan share their reactions to labels, role models, goals, etc. They are very insightful.

"Richardson Study Q's and A's." *G/C/T* 36:2–9 (January/February 1985).

G/C/T interviews Valieu Wilkie, executive vice-president of the Richardson Foundation in Fort Worth, Texas. The foundation has funded an extended survey of programming for the gifted in the United States. Reasons for and some results of the study are presented. A complete study report is forthcoming (1985).

Sawyer, Robert N. "The Duke University Educational Programs for Brilliant Youths." *Roeper Review* 7:103–9 (November 1984).

Sawyer, director of the Duke Talent Identification Program, explains the various facets of the program: Precollege Program for Rising High School Seniors; Summer Residential Program for Verbally and Mathematically Precocious Youths; By-Mail Program; Commuter Program.

Scruggs, Thomas E., and Cohn, Sanford J. "A University-Based Summer Program for a Highly Able but Poorly Achieving Indian Child." *Gifted Child Quarterly* 27:90–93 (Spring 1983).

Scruggs and Cohn describe a summer program designed for an eight-year-old Pima Indian boy who had superior reasoning abilities but poor academic skills.

Stalnaker, John M. "Recognizing and Encouraging Talent." *American Psychologist* 16:513–22 (August 1961).

Stalnaker describes the National Merit scholarship program and why it identifies and rewards talent as it does.

Tatarunis, Alphonse M. "Exceptional Programs for Talented Students." *Music Educators Journal* 68:55–60 (November 1981).

The majority of the article provides a rationale for special programs for the gifted. The final page briefly describes several special programs for children gifted in music.

Thom, E. Jean. "A Systemwide Program." In *The Gifted and the Talented: Their Education and Development*, Part 1 of *Seventy-Eighth Yearbook of the National Society for the Study of Education*, edited by A. Harry Passow. Chicago: Univ. of Chicago Pr., 1979.

Thom's article describes the Cleveland Major Works Program, which has been in existence since 1921. The reasons it has survived while other such programs have floundered are its broad base of community support and its adherence to the goals it set.

Tittle, Bess M. "Why Montessori for the Gifted?" *G/C/T* 33:3–7 (May/ June 1984).

Tittle says that gifted children's need to learn what will propel them toward independence from others can become an obsession. For this reason, the Montessori method is particularly suited to the education of the gifted. Her rationale is well explained, and a two-page chart that ties gifted characteristics to Montessori education is very helpful.

VanTassel-Baska, Joyce, Landau, Marsha, and Olszewski, Paula. "The Benefits of Summer Programming for Gifted Adolescents." *Journal for the Education of the Gifted* 8:73–82 (Fall 1984).

In an attempt to determine what gifted attendees might have gained from the 1983 Northwestern summer program, questionnaires were mailed to the students' parents and to the students' home schools. Responses are summarized in the article. The authors said, "the summer program experiences provided for gifted students through the search model appear to provide a systematic intervention at a critical stage in development that can propel students forward toward adult productivity in a way that benefits them personally, socially, and academically."

VanTassel-Baska, Joyce, and Prentice, Mary. "The Midwest Talent Search: Catalyst for Local and State-Wide Program Development on Behalf of the Talented." *Roeper Review* 7:167–70 (February 1985).

Using Indiana as an example of the positive changes that can occur, the authors point out the value of the talent search model in effecting change and programming growth for gifted education.

Ward, Virgil S. "The Governor's School of North Carolina," In *The Gifted and the Talented: Their Education and Development*, Part 1 of the *Seventy-Eighth Yearbook of the National Society for the Study of Education*, edited by A. Harry Passow. Chicago: Univ. of Chicago Pr., 1979.

The Governor's School of North Carolina, begun in 1963, is a summer residential school for gifted secondary youth. This chapter provides a brief overview of the program, which has served as a model for similar programs.

Weatherly, Myra. "Residential School for the Gifted." *G/C/T* 19:17–21 (September/October 1981).

The author describes the North Carolina School of Science and Mathematics, founded in 1980. It is believed to be the first public residential high school for students gifted in science and mathematics.

Wertz, Dan C., Landers, Lester, and De Sanchez, Jeannette S. "Gifted Students: Program Organization and Identification Techniques in an International Setting." *Roeper Review* 6:94–96 (November 1983).

All three authors are affiliated with the private Colegio Nueva Granada School located in the Andes Mountains in Bogota, Colombia. The school's enrichment program is described.

Wetherell, Nancy. "A High School Gifted Program: Staffing Makes It Work." *G/C/T* 27:44–45 (March/April 1983).

The author describes a unique staffing approach used by her school district: a five-person team of teacher-mentors. Advantages are clearly explained.

Willens, Anita J. "Montgomery County Summer School for the Performing Arts." *NASSP Bulletin* 63:58–60 (November 1979).

Willens describes an intensive summer program that offers advanced drama, music, and dance.

Special Class Grouping

Brink, Laurence B. "The Fallacy of Ability Grouping." *School and Society* 35:427–29 (1932).

Brink believes that the system of ability grouping breaks down on five counts: (1) statistical invalidity, (2) administrative difficulties, (3) unsatisfactory criteria, (4) inadequate curriculum adjustments, and (5) disadvantages of homogeneous grouping.

Bull, Kay Sather, and Otey, John W. "A Hierarchy of Services for the Gifted Child." *G/C/T* 33:36–39 (May/June 1984).

The authors present and explain a model of a hierarchy of services for the gifted based on three premises: (1) the regular classroom is the most restrictive environment for the gifted; (2) the more gifted the student, the less likely he or she can be served adequately in the regular classroom; and (3) the ultimate long-term learning environment is the "real world."

Colangelo, Nicholas, and Kelly, Kevin R. "A Study of Student, Parent, and Teacher Attitudes toward Gifted Programs and Gifted Students." *Gifted Child Quarterly* 27:101–10 (Summer 1983).

The overall results of this study indicate that the gifted program in the particular junior high school studied is valued as much as other academically oriented programs—none of which are valued very highly as compared to certain sports activities. The gifted students, however, did value the program and did desire to be a part of it.

Cornell, Ethel L. "Effects of Ability Grouping Determinable from Published Studies." In *The Grouping of Pupils,* Part 1 of *Thirty-Fifth Yearbook of the National Society for the Study of Education,* edited by Guy Montrose Whipple. Bloomington, Ill.: Public School Publishing Co., 1936.

The author wrote her article in an attempt to present the reasons for, or the conditions under which, researchers obtained conflicting results concerning the effects of ability grouping.

Cox, June, and Daniel, Neil. "The Pull-Out Model." *G/C/T* 34:55–61 (September/October 1984).

Several variations of the pullout model are presented along with its recognized strengths and weaknesses. The authors believe pullout programs have served their purpose, and it is time to move on.

Elman, Linda L., and Elman, Donald. "Mainstreaming the Gifted: An Approach That Works." *G/C/T* 26:45–46 (January/February 1983).

The article reports on the Kent State University School, which divides its 200 preschool through sixth-grade children into multiage units, which are further subdivided into demonstrated ability groups. The authors' children attend the school, and they are very satisfied.

Evans, Ellis D., and Marken, Dan. "Multiple Outcome Assessment of Special Class Placement for Gifted Students: A Comparative Study." *Gifted Child Quarterly* 26:126–32 (Summer 1982).

This study compared gifted students who had elected to remain in regular classrooms and gifted students who elected to accept placement in a special class for the gifted. No significant main effects were found for any of the five variables studied—higher cognitive skills, personal autonomy and responsibility for learning, positive attitude toward school, positive self-image, and extracurricular leadership and participation. An extensive discussion section provides possible explanations why differences were not found.

Fearn, Leif, and Owen, Jimmie Jean. "The Individual Education Plan for Gifted and Talented Students." *Roeper Review* 7:80–83 (November 1984).

The authors describe Project SPRING (the Special Program Responding to Intellectual Needs of Gifted). SPRING focuses on gifted students' intellect—defined as success in school content. IEPs were developed for the students, and the results were significant.

Fox, Lynn H. "Programs for the Gifted and Talented: An Overview." In *The Gifted and the Talented: Their Education and Development*, Part 1 of the *Seventy-Eighth Yearbook of the National Society for the Study of Education*, edited by A. Harry Passow. Chicago: Univ. of Chicago Pr., 1979.

Fox briefly discusses eleven different ways of providing for bright children's needs. A chart at the end of the chapter summarizes her points. It could be useful for illustrating various ideas in a presentation to a board of education.

Gray, Howard A., and Hollingworth, Leta S. "The Achievement of Gifted Children Enrolled and Not Enrolled in Special Opportunity Classes." *Journal of Educational Research* 24:255–61 (November 1931).

The authors say the biggest advantage to homogeneous grouping for gifted students is not greater achievement in the tool subjects, but enrichment of the students' school experience with additional intellectual opportunities.

Keating, Daniel P. "Secondary School Programs." In *The Gifted and the Talented: Their Education and Development*, Part 1 of the *Seventy-Eighth Yearbook of the National Society for the Study of Education*, edited by A. Harry Passow. Chicago: Univ. of Chicago Pr., 1979.

Keating discusses, in a general fashion, programs for gifted students at the secondary level. His conclusion is that two goals must be reached so that secondary gifted education can be improved: (1) a concerted effort to create a variety of appropriate opportunities, and (2) an equal effort to create a counseling system that can bring together these opportunities for individual gifted students.

Lamping, Ed. "In Defense of the Self-Contained Gifted Class." *G/C/T* 17:50–51 (March/April 1981).

The author, teacher of gifted students and father of a gifted child, gives his reasons for favoring self-contained classes for the gifted above other means of serving them. His reasons are sound. His number-one reason is that the teacher is trained to understand and serve highly able children and youth.

Miller, Bernard, and Miller, Betty. "Recognizing the Gifted: Is Differentiation Undemocratic?" *The College Board Review* 115:2–7 (Spring 1980).

The authors discuss the various prejudices that many hold toward the gifted. They also provide numerous reasons why educating the gifted is the most democratic for society. The article would be good reading for anyone who continually encounters resistance to educating gifted students differently.

Mirsky, Naomi. "Starting an Interage Full Time Gifted Class." *G/C/T* 33:24–26 (May/June 1984).

The author received a $3,000 federal minigrant to start a multiage "family" grouping of gifted children in grades one through three. Her article goes through the rationale for such a program, describing its inception, the steps toward its establishment, and its success. She is very positive toward the idea.

Oglesby, Krista, and Gallagher, James J. "Teacher-Pupil Ratios, Instructional Time and Expenditure Estimates for Three Administrative Strategies for Educating Gifted Students." *Gifted Child Quarterly* 27:57–63 (Spring 1983).

The authors compared the resource-room, teacher-consultant, and special-class strategies on the dimensions of instructional time provided, estimated expenditures, and teacher/pupil ratios. The highest ratio was in the resource room model, while the lowest was in the special class. In time spent per student, the least attention was provided under the teacher consultant model, while the most was spent in the special-class model. The median cost figure for the three models was 15 to 30 percent above the cost of educating the average pupil.

Orenstein, Allan J. "What Organizational Characteristics Are Important in Planning, Implementing, and Maintaining Programs for the Gifted?" *Gifted Child Quarterly* 28:99–105 (Summer 1984).

The author surveyed 104 school districts to determine the various organizational dimensions considered important for establishing program viability. Extensive results are presented with definite implications for other schools.

Passow, A. Harry. "The Maze of the Research on Ability Grouping." *Educational Forum* 26:281–88 (1962).

Passow says that the problems of equating and synthesizing the research on ability grouping stem from differences in the studies' (1) scope of aim and purpose; (2) number of students, groups, and size of classes involved; (3) duration; (4) adequacy of selection bases; (5) treatment; (6) deployment of teachers; (7) instruments and techniques used for evaluation; and (8) failure to assess effects of grouping on teachers and administrators.

Reis, Sally M. "Creating Ownership in Gifted and Talented Programs." *Roeper Review* 5:20–23 (April/May 1983).

Reis points out that teachers, administrators, parents, and other community members must all feel a sense of ownership if a program for the gifted is going to be successful. She discusses ways to accomplish this.

Worcester 1979. *See* Enrichment

CHAPTER 6

Academic Curriculum for the Gifted

Some may question whether a chapter on curriculum belongs in a book about the gifted. They may ask questions such as, Do not gifted students need to learn the same content as all other students? Should not parents of able children and youth expect that their youngsters will learn well and easily how to read and write and "cipher"? While it *is* true that gifted students do need to know the same content as other children and youth, and that most will be able to master the skills and content easily and well, it is *not* true that these skills and this content should be covered in the same way for the gifted as for other learners. By definition, gifted youth require a differentiated curriculum to adequately meet their learning needs.

As one reads material written about developing curriculum for the gifted, the term *differentiated* appears time and time again. What does *differentiated* mean when used in conjunction with *curriculum for the gifted*? Curriculum differentiated for the gifted is purposely made unlike or different from the "regular" curriculum; observers can perceive and implementers can express differences between it and the regular curriculum. In other words differentiated curriculum for the gifted has characteristics that distinguish it from regular curriculum for nongifted students.

Curriculum for the gifted cannot just be differentiated; it must be *qualitatively differentiated*. C. June Maker, author of *Curriculum Development for the Gifted* (1982a) and *Teaching Models in Education of the Gifted* (1982b), the two definitive works on curriculum for gifted students, states that the phrase *qualitatively different*

implies that the basic curriculum must be examined, and

changes or modification must be made so that the most appropriate curriculum is provided for the gifted students. Modification must be quality changes rather than quantity, and they must build upon and extend the characteristics (both present and future) that make the children different from non-gifted students. (1982b, 3)

Based on her own work and that of other experts in the field of gifted education, Maker (1982a, 1982b) makes several recommendations concerning how basic curriculum can be made more appropriate for gifted children and youth. She says modifications should be made in the areas of content, process, product, and learning environment. Her suggestions can be outlined as follows:

1. Content modifications
   a. Abstractness
   b. Complexity
   c. Variety
   d. Organization and economy
   e. Study of people
   f. Study of methods
2. Process modifications
   a. Higher levels of thinking
   b. Open-endedness
   c. Discovery
   d. Evidence of reasoning
   e. Freedom of choice
   f. Group interaction activities and simulations
   g. Pacing and variety
3. Product modifications
   a. Real problems
   b. Real audiences
   c. Transformation
   d. Evaluation
4. Learning environment modifications
   a. Student-centered versus teacher-centered
   b. Independence versus dependence
   c. Open versus closed
   d. Accepting versus judging
   e. Complex versus simple
   f. High mobility versus low mobility

At least sixty curriculum models exist, and probably a fourth of these are particularly appropriate for use in developing curriculum for the gifted. We have chosen to use three in this chapter to illustrate the benefit of using a structure to develop a curriculum for the gifted, rather than just put together a collection of activities and call it a gifted program. The three models were chosen because they emphasize three components that are vital in planning and developing curriculum for able learners:

1. *Bloom's Cognitive Taxonomy*, which emphasizes higher level thinking
2. *Williams's Teaching Strategies for Thinking and Feeling*, which emphasizes creativity
3. *Renzulli's Enrichment Triad*, which emphasizes products.

We will briefly describe each of the three models, including specific uses of the model within each description. All illustrative examples were created to enhance students' skills of characterization. Such similarity will allow readers to compare and contrast the variability available through the use of these three models.

Then, for each curriculum area presented in this chapter, appropriate application of the models will be discussed. As will be seen, not all models are appropriate in every area; that is, one area of study may lend itself more readily to Renzulli's Enrichment Triad, while another may lend itself more readily to Bloom's Cognitive Taxonomy, and yet another may best be served by integrating aspects of two or three models.

Bloom's Cognitive Taxonomy

Bloom's Cognitive Taxonomy is one of the better-known and more widely used models for creating curriculum for the gifted because of its emphasis on developing higher-level thinking. It is also relatively simple in design and is easily applicable by teachers with a minimum of training in its use.

As a taxonomy, Bloom's is hierarchical in nature, i.e., achievement at higher levels is dependent on success at lower levels. The following six levels comprise Bloom's Cognitive Taxonomy:

1. *Knowledge*, which is the lowest level, consists of remembering what has been read, seen, or heard, with no transformation of the information received.
2. *Comprehension* involves the lowest level of understanding and requires that a student be able to restate what has been read, seen, or heard in his or her own words and make use of the informa-

tion, although not relating the information to any other ideas already possessed or presented.

3. *Application* involves putting the new information to use in a different situation, without being told how to do so.

4. *Analysis* entails deconstructing the whole into its component parts so that the relationship betweeen the parts can be seen. This allows for more complete understanding of the underlying structure or basis.

5. *Synthesis* entails constructing a whole from constituent parts—although the new whole or pattern or structure is not the one from which the parts were taken.

6. *Evaluation* is the highest level in the taxonomy, and it involves making judgments about the value of something, for a particular purpose. Students must either develop their own criteria or be able to apply the criteria of others and use various types of evidence in order to make these critical, evaluative judgments.

Application of Bloom's Cognitive Taxonomy

As was stated earlier, all illustrative examples will be designed around curriculum created to enhance students' characterization skills. The following activities were designed using Bloom's Taxonomy as the model.

Knowledge

Read a character sketch to students. Ask them to recall adjectives used to describe the character.

Comprehension

Have students read the first chapter of a novel. After reading, students should write down everything they know about the characters who were introduced in the chapter—physically, mentally, and emotionally. Students should keep this description to compare to later impressions of the characters.

Application

Give students the following task:
Although the culture in the book you are reading is different from the one in which we now live, some of the roles played by men and women were similar. Note examples of women in nontradi-

tional roles (by our society's standards) and determine whether those roles are nontraditional for that culture.

Analysis

Give students the following task:
If you have brothers or sisters, then you know that sometimes the same event can be described in more than one way, depending on your point of view. Authors show us characters from a particular point of view. Jot down techniques that you notice the author using to give you a positive or negative feeling about a character. Then, from one of the books you are reading, choose an event that is written to portray the protagonist or another major character in a very positive or a very negative light. Retell the same event—portraying the character in the opposite light. Draw on some of the techniques you noticed the author using. Be prepared to discuss the techniques you used (adjectives, verbs, etc.).

Synthesis

Give students the following task:
Being strong does not make it easier to make decisions. The strong female protagonists in the books you and your classmates are reading are forced to make difficult choices. Record at least three decisions or choices the protagonist is forced to make. Tell what you know about the character based on her decision.

Evaluation

Give students the following task:
An appellation is a name, that is, the word by which a person, class, or thing is called and known. Sometimes an appellation, or nickname, is attached to someone cruelly—other times, endearingly. Still other times, it is as if the appellation emerges as a natural extension of the person because it is so representative of some characteristic. As you read, generate a list of appellations for the protagonist that are fitting to her personality. Try to imagine that you are friends with her. Decide which one you would most like to call her and which one she would most like to be called. Justify your choice(s).

Williams's Teaching Strategies for Thinking and Feeling

Whereas Bloom's model is a taxonomy—each level builds on the previous level—Williams's model is a morphological one—it has a three-dimensional structure. According to Williams, the three dimensions must interact in the proper mix for optimum learning to take place. Williams depicts his model as a 3-D box for which each of the three dimensions comprises one face. Listed below are the three dimensions which Williams sees as part of every teaching-learning situation:

1. Curriculum–subject matter content
2. Teacher behaviors and strategies or modes of teaching (to be explained below)
3. Pupil behaviors
   a. Cognitive
      (1) Fluent thinking: able to come up with many ideas, responses, solutions, questions, and ways of doing things
      (2) Flexible thinking: able to come up with many alternatives—a variety of ideas, solutions, and methods of attacking a problem
      (3) Original thinking: able to produce clever, innovative, unusual responses, questions, and ideas
      (4) Elaborative thinking: able to add to, embellish, and expand on the ideas, responses, or questions that have been produced
   b. Affective
      (1) Curiosity (willingness): the child is inherently inquisitive about nearly everything—people, places, events, and concepts
      (2) Risk taking (courage): Child is not afraid of making guesses and risking failure; can deal with uncertainty and lack of structure
      (3) Complexity (challenge): child is enthralled by complicated problems and concepts; prefers immersing self in the discovery of a solution to a problem
      (4) Imagination (intuition): child has strong visualization powers; thrives on fantasy, but does not become lost in it.

As stated earlier, Williams's model is based on the notion that all three dimensions interact in any teaching-learning situation. For the purposes of this chapter, Dimension 2: Teaching Behaviors and Strategies or Modes of Teaching, will be explained. Williams outlines eighteen such strategies that he says lead to more creative thinking:

1. *Paradox:* A seemingly contradictory statement that may nonetheless be true.
2. *Attribute:* A quality or characteristic belonging to a person or thing; a distinctive feature.
3. *Analogy:* A form of logical inference, based on a correspondence in some respect between people or things otherwise dissimilar.
4. *Discrepancy:* A divergence or disagreement, as between facts or claims; inconsistency.
5. *Provocative question:* Questions intended to excite and stimulate students' thinking and exploration of new ideas.
6. *Example of change:* A demonstration of how dynamic the world is or can be. Making provisions for activities that employ modifications or substitutions.
7. *Examples of habit:* Habits are a constant, often unconscious inclination to perform some act, acquired through frequent repetition. Activities for this strategy seek to provide examples that encourage students to avoid habit-bound thinking.
8. *Organized random search:* Developing a structure to lead randomly to another structure.
9. *Skills of search:* The development of methods to search for information. This might include trial and error, historical skills, or experimental skills.
10. *Tolerance for ambiguity:* Ambiguous situations are open to multiple interpretation. Activities for this strategy seek to present open-ended situations for discussion.
11. *Intuitive expression:* Intuition is the act of knowing without the use of rational processes. Activities for this strategy seek to encourage making guesses based on hunches and/or emotions.
12. *Adjustment to development:* This strategy seeks to enable students to develop or change rather than merely adjust to situations.
13. *Study of creative people and processes:* Activities for this strategy encourage students to look at people who are creative and explore the processes they utilize.
14. *Evaluation of situations:* Activities for this strategy encourage students to engage in prediction from the delineation of actions and ideas and to form conclusions based on careful consideration of consequences and inferences.
15. *Creative reading skill:* Using text as a stimulus for the creation of an idea or a product.

16. *Creative listening skill:* Encouraging students to respond to oral text in various ways that will allow them to develop ideas and respond to questions.
17. *Creative writing skill:* Encouraging students to express their feelings and emotions in clearly written passages.
18. *Visualization skill:* Activities for this strategy encourage students to form a mental image that includes an unusual or unique perspective.[1]

Teachers should seek to design activities that emphasize the thought processes required by these strategies. In other words, students should learn that paradoxes, analogies, and discrepancies, as well as opportunities for creative reading, listening, and writing, are present all around us. Also, they need to be challenged to think in divergent ways to search for and find them. To plan curriculum for gifted youth, Williams suggests that teachers ask the following four questions:

1. What is it that you want children to do? (lesson activity). Example: make a sensory time line of the future.
2. Where does this activity lead each child? (pupil behavior). Example: elaborative thinking, imagination.
3. What do you do to cause such behaviors? (teacher strategy). Example: intuitive expression, evaluate situations.
4. Within what subject should this occur? Where does this activity fit into the curriculum? (curriculum/subject matter content). Example: future studies, social studies, science.

As before, the following activities were designed to enhance students' characterization skills.

Paradox

Give students the following task:
Oxymorons are figures of speech in which opposite or contradictory ideas are combined. One could think of oxymorons as two-word paradoxes. For this activity, you are going to need to find a very fragile-looking girl or woman—who is anything but fragile. First, think of a fragile-looking girl or woman you know. Second, find out if she *is* fragile (it is up to you to determine what *fragile*

---

1. Definitions are derived from the *American Heritage Dictionary of the English Language* (Boston: Houghton Mifflin, 1981).

means). If she is, repeat the first step. If she is not, go on to the next step. Third, when you have done that, meet with one other member of the class who has done the same activity, and together, write a series of oxymorons describing this girl or woman. For example, "fragile steel." Be prepared to justify your choices.

Attributes

Give students the following task:
There are many kinds of strength that can be inherent in a person. Make a list of at least four types of strength. As you read, determine which type(s) is (are) possessed by the protagonist. Construct a chart to present your findings.

Analogy

Give students the following task:
In the book *Dark of the Moon*, the character Kindrie has special powers that can be used for deep healing:

> For each act of deep healing, the healer had to reach down to the very roots of his patient's being. At that level, it was possible to do much good, but even greater harm. The safest way was to discover what metaphor each patient was currently using, consciously or unconsciously, for his own soul. For those concerned with growing things, for example, the botanical image of root and branch often worked very well. On the other hand, scrollsmen could often be reached through the metaphor of a book, which must first be unlocked and then deciphered. Hunts, battles, and riddles were other common metaphors. Once the healer sensed which one to use, he could deal with his patient's illness or injury through it in a way that was at least compatible with the other's basic nature. (p. 274)

As you read, watch for and take note of phrases used by the main character that would indicate her metaphor for life. Explain that metaphor and be prepared to justify your answer.

Discrepancy

Give the students the following task:
The protagonists in the books you are reading share several commonalities—for example, they are all "outsiders"; somehow they are not part of the society, group, or family in which they live. Look for statements the characters make or thoughts they

have that indicate an awareness of their state. Record the gist of these statements or thoughts. When you finish reading the books, reflect on the impact that being an outsider had on the main character.

Provocative Questions

Give students the following task:
In *The Hero and the Crown*, Arlbeth, the king, tells his daughter, Aerin, "Royalty isn't allowed to hide—at least not once it has declared itself" (p. 100). Write an argument for or against the following rewording of that statement, as if you were the protagonist in the book you are reading. "Ability isn't allowed to hide—at least not once it has declared itself."

Examples of Change

Give students the following task:
Keep a running list of the major characters who appear in the books you are reading. Keep another list of occupations that these characters might have if they lived in the United States today.

Examples of Habit

Give students the following task:
Most of us have, at one time or another, dreaded telling someone something about ourselves—a habit, a personality trait, a family secret, whatever—for fear that this person would no longer like us. In *God Stalk*, Jame experiences this dread, but is surprised by her friend's response when she finally tells him her secret.

> The moment she had most dreaded was past. He knew the worst about her now, and it didn't seem to bother him at all. Either he was unusually tolerant or maybe, just maybe, it wasn't so terrible to be different after all. (p. 151)

Think about something that you have been dreading telling someone—and it is really eating at you. Write down the worst possible scenario if you tell. Then, weigh the risks and the benefits of ridding yourself of this dread. Do something about it.

Organized Random Search

Give students the following task:
In the book *Dark of the Moon*, Torisen, Jame's brother, comes across images on the wall:

> They were imus, symbols of a power so ancient that all but the name had been lost—or so most civilized men believed. (pp.38-39)

You will create an imu (a symbol of ancient power) that represents the power of the female protagonist in the books you are reading. As you are reading, make sketches and notes to record your ideas. Then, determine a way to display the imu you have created for the protagonist.

Skills of Search

Give students the following task:
The protagonists about whom you are reading all have some restrictions on them because they are women. Some of these are custom, while others are law. Find and list some restrictions that are put on women in our society. Indicate which ones are law and which ones are custom. Cite your sources.

Tolerance for Ambiguity

Give students the following task:
Strength and power have their costs. Many people envy others who possess strength and/or power. As you are reading, determine whether, in your opinion, the protagonist is to be envied. Cite specific examples to support your opinion. Expect that someone in the class will challenge you.

Intuitive Expression

Give students the following task:
The strong female protagonists in the books you are reading have normal, supernormal, and supernatural characteristics. Find several instances of supernormal and supernatural characteristics (sometimes the distinction may not be too clear between the two!). After you have finished reading the two books, look back at the list you have made. Choose one supernormal and one supernatural characteristic you yourself would like to have. Tell

which of the characteristics you now possess you would trade for these two. How would your life be different?

Adjustment to Development

Give students the following task:
In *The Hero and the Crown*, Aerin discovers a book about Damar, her country.

> The book with the interesting binding was a history of Damar. Aerin had had to learn a certain amount of history as a part of her formal education, but this stuff was something else again. The lessons she'd been forced to learn were dry spare things, the facts without the sense of them, given in the simplest language, as if words might disguise the truth or (worse) bring it to life. (p. 30)

Can you empathize with Aerin's sentiment? Explain. Do you have any suggestions to help education include the facts and the sense of them? Determine a way to implement your ideas.

The Study of Creative People and Processes

Give students the following task:
As far as readers of *God Stalk* and *Dark of the Moon* know, Jame has lost her past.

> What a cursed nuisance to have mislaid so much of her past
> . . . or to have had it taken from her. (*God Stalk*, p. 10)

Not knowing her past greatly troubles Jame. What effect would not knowing your past have on you? Do you need to know your past in order for it to have an effect on you? Be prepared to discuss your responses to these questions. Note at least three events, people, or circumstances in your past that have made you what you are now. Then, get a copy of *People* magazine. Read one of the profiles of a strong, successful person. Note references to how the person's past has affected his/her success. Compare your impressions with those of others in your class.

Evaluating Situations

Give students the following task:
In *The Darkangel*, Aeriel must be taken care of by a group of people, the Ma'a-mbai. One of the Ma'a-mbai, Orroto-to, tells Aeriel that the Pendarlon is not their ruler.

> He does not rule us. No one can rule us. No one can rule
> anyone who does not first agree to the ruling. . . . One must
> rule oneself. (p. 124)

List some of the characters in the books you are reading. Determine which ones understand the concept stated by Orroto-to and
which ones do not. What implications are there for present-day
governments?

Creative Reading Skill

Give students the following task:
In *The Blue Sword*, Luthe wanted to find out whether Harry was
"the sort of vessel that cracks easily." Are you? How would an
author relate this to a reader? Write one example.

Creative Listening Skill

Give students the following task:
In *The Blue Sword*, Harry was trained to compete in the laprun trials, even though she was a woman. Her mentor, Mathin, recognized the value in cultivating talent, regardless of gender. For the
next couple of weeks, listen to the people around you. Which
ones indicate, either directly or indirectly, that they see value in
cultivating talent, regardless of gender? Write down what it is
they say that gives you this impression. Later, you will list the
attributes of these people—and then compile a class list of these
attributes—to see whether you can come up with a composite.

Creative Writing Skill

Give students the following task:
Choose a significant event involving the protagonist. Write an expository piece in which you explain what happened and what
part the protagonist played in the occurrence. Take the position
of an objective observer—except that your bias lies in wanting to
portray women as weak/strong (pick one). Be sure the title or
headline reflects your bias (subtly, of course).

Visualization Skill

Give students the following task:
In *The Darkangel*, Aeriel must spin garments for the wraiths, us-

ing only a golden spindle. This tool is extraordinary. One does not use it to spin wool or flax—but rather

> . . . it spins from the heart—joy, sorrow, anger, hate. Whatever you feel in your heart this spindle will spin. . . . You must learn in your own way and in your own time how to use it, as well as what to spin. (p. 55)

Choose two relatively minor characters, preferably two who have quite different personalities. Imagine that each uses the golden spindle to spin from the heart. What would each spin? What would garments spun from this thread be like? Depict them in some visual way.

Renzulli's Enrichment Triad Model

The Enrichment Triad Model is one of the very few teaching-learning models developed specifically for use with gifted children. Renzulli developed this model after extensive experience working with, and evaluating programs for, gifted children and youth. He sought to design a model that could be used as a guide in developing "defensible programs for the gifted"—programs that are "qualitatively different." His model ties in closely with his conclusion about what constitutes giftedness. In his three-ring conception, giftedness resides at the intersection of three clusters of traits: (1) above-average general ability; (2) task commitment; and (3) creativity. Renzulli believes that the interaction of these three clusters is necessary for creative, productive accomplishment.

Accordingly, Renzulli's triad model includes three types of enrichment:

1. *Type I—General Exploratory Activities.* Type I includes "those experiences and activities that are designed to bring the learner into touch with the kinds of topics or areas of study in which s/he may have a sincere interest" (Renzulli 1977, 17). In enrichment of this type, children are given the opportunity to explore a wide variety of content with the intent of finding a topic for further, in-depth study (i.e., Type III enrichment).
2. *Type II—Group Training Activities.* Type II "consists of methods, materials, and instructional techniques that are mainly concerned with the development of thinking and feeling processes. . . . The objective of Type II Enrichment is to develop in the learner the processes or operations (the 'powers of the mind')

that enable him/her to deal more effectively with content" (Renzulli 1977, 24–25).

3. *Type III—Individual and Small-Group Investigations of Real Problems.* Type III enrichment is the real crux of this model and "consists of activities in which the youngster becomes an actual *investigator* of a *real* problem or topic by using appropriate *methods of inquiry*" (Renzulli 1977, 29). In other words, the gifted students become "professionals." Renzulli recommends that Type III investigations account for approximately 50 percent of the time a gifted individual spends in enrichment.

Like previous illustrative examples, the following instructions have actually been used with able students. The Type I and Type II activities were planned by the authors, and the Type III activities were planned or designed by the students with guidance from the authors. Instead of providing only one example for each category (as we did for Bloom's and Williams's models), we will include several in order to show the variety possible.

Type I—*General Exploratory Activities*

Tell students that the purpose of these activities is for them to determine the attributes of strong women and then to decide on a project involving strong females.

Give students the following task:
Many strong people are not aware of their strength nor of the effect that it has on others. Decide whether this is the case with the protagonist in the books you are reading. Cite your evidence.

Give students the following task:
Strong women have some inner force and/or inner wish driving them. For example, Aerin, in *The Hero and the Crown,*

> brooded about what, precisely she was setting out to do. Test the fire-repellent properties of her discovery. Toward killing dragons. Did she really want to kill dragons? Yes. Why? Pause. To be doing something. To be doing something better than anyone else was doing it. (p. 97)

Look for and discover clues to what drives the protagonist in the books you are reading. Record your ideas. Then, interview someone you consider a strong female. What drives her?

Give students the following task:

One trait shared by each of the strong female protagonists in the books you are reading is a feeling of responsibility toward other women. Think of the strong women you know. Do you think they feel any responsibility toward other women? Find out. Be prepared to report your findings.

Give students the following task:
In *The Darkangel* and *A Gathering of Gargoyles,* Aeriel is brave in numerous situations but does not see herself as brave. Neither does the darkangel.

> The darkangel shook his head then and laughed. "I suppose I should kill you," he said idly at last, "I did forbid you to go up on the tower—but I shall not. You are interesting. Not one of my servants was ever brave enough to go up amongst the gargoyles before, much less disobey me." He shook his head, frowned very slightly. "Strange. You do not look brave." (*The Darkangel*, p. 61)

What does *brave* look like? Decide—and determine a way to represent it.

Give students the following task:
Jame, as a Shanir, has certain characteristics—both physical and mental—over which she is struggling for control.

> I will *not* be used. Let me be a monster in my own right if I must, but not the puppet of some damned indifferent god. I will be responsible for my actions whatever prompts them. I will be free. (*God Stalk*, p. 158)

Each of the protagonists in the books you're reading feels used at some point. Chronicle the protagonist's realization of being used, her response to it, and how she deals with it. What parallels could you draw between her experience and your own or that of someone strong that you know?

Type II—*Group Training Activities*

These activities were designed as some students began to focus on their Type III investigations and the authors saw which skills they would need to begin them.

Give students the following task:
Authors who create well-developed characters enable us to know those characters. And, just as we can often predict the words and

actions of the people we know in real life, we can also predict the words and actions of the characters we come to know in the stories we read. Create a scenario in which the protagonist appears. Give it to someone else who has not read the books you have, and to someone who has. Have them complete the scenario. Compare their responses.

Give students the following task:
In *God Stalk* and *Dark of the Moon,* Jame is able to dance in a way that literally mesmerizes her audience. It is a "talent" that she is not sure she wants.

> Dally saw his companion grimace. "You still have reservations about dancing, don't you?" he said to Jame as they crossed the square.
> "Yes, more so all the time. I can't get over the feeling that I'm abusing a great and terrible ability, although what its proper use is I can't guess. . . ." (*God Stalk*, p. 110)

Do you know someone who may share this same feeling with Jame? Design an interview or some other method of determining what the ability is and in what ways its use or misuse is affecting the person.

Type III—*Individual and Small-Group Investigations of Real Problems*

The following are actual investigations completed by students taught by the authors.

One of the students, who is interested in male and female body-building, decided to investigate people's perceptions of physically strong women. She devised a pictorial survey form which she administered to friends, family, acquaintances, and strangers in a shopping mall. Using the results of her pictorial survey, she constructed an interview to obtain further information. She decided to write up her results for the newsletter of a national health club chain—and is currently awaiting word on her article's acceptance.

One student was struck by a statement made by one of the characters in the book she was reading. She designed an activity sheet much like the ones we had been using with the students. The statement occurred in *Dark of the Moon,* where Lyra explains to

Jame about her marriage contract and that she is hoping that her father will extend the contract to include children.

> Jame stared at her. "Don't you have anything to say about it?"
>
> Lyra stared back. "Of course not! Lord Caineron is the head of my family. Naturally, I have to do what he tells me."

Respond to the last statement.

Susan distributed this sheet to nearly 500 students at the elementary, middle school, and high school levels. When the sheets were returned to her, she began the process of sorting and categorizing and trying to make sense of her data. She found that the youngest girls were the ones with the most contempt for Lyra's statement, "Naturally, I have to do what he tells me." She is now in the process of tracking the television shows these girls watch, the books they read, and other features of their lives. She plans to compare the results to those for boys the same age, looking for variations related to the girls' feelings. She has already made arrangements with the child-development teacher at her high school to present her findings to classes.

Another student told us that he recognized that his "consciousness had been raised" by our Type I exploratory activities. He had been struck by a conversation between his little brother and another kindergartner, a girl. She had said that she was going to be a doctor, but our student's brother had told her that she could be a nurse, not a doctor. She had vehemently informed him that she could be anything she wanted, and she wanted to be a doctor because doctors made more money than nurses. Matt decided that his little brother and other young children needed their consciousness raised, so he envisioned a traveling talk show that would perform at local nursery and elementary schools. He devised several scripts about "Girls/Women Who Do Things" after reading a large number of children's books to find characters familiar to the children (e.g., *Brave Irene* by William Steig; *Tales of Amanda Pig* by Jean Van Leeuwen; *Flossie and the Fox* by Patricia McKissack; *Coco Can't Wait* by Taro Gomi). He and his troupe are making a videotape now to send to some schools because they cannot meet all the requests for their talk show.

We selected all the preceding examples from the literature area so as to illustrate the variety of lessons and strategies that can be designed.

These models will serve in all curriculum areas, as will be seen in the following sections of this chapter. For example, students in philosophy could focus on the discrepancy noted by Copernicus on the Ptolemaic theory (Williams's model); students in algebra could conduct an organized random search by examining various algebraic equations to arrive at a sound formulation (Williams); students in social studies could use creative reading skills to view the Constitution as an attempt to resolve the issue of power versus liberty (Williams).

This chapter serves as a cursory guide to curriculum development for able students. Teachers and others involved in curriculum development must go beyond this text in order to become well grounded in the theory and practice of the various models and curriculum areas. Speaking from our own experience, one can expect to spend a great deal of time preparing to write curriculum for the gifted. That preparation involves *teaching* able learners, *reading about* able learners, *attempting to write* curriculum, and *thinking* about the task. It is a process that cannot be hurried, although it can be facilitated through reading, thinking, and talking about the task.

Since this chapter on academic curriculum development for the gifted is only one part of a book about the gifted, the discussion of each topic must be relatively brief. Therefore, after reading the general introduction to this chapter, readers are invited to find those specific curriculum areas in which they are interested. For these areas, one should read the overviews and then explore the books, chapters, and articles that are annotated in order to prepare for developing particular curricula.

As the reader explores this chapter and some of the readings that are annotated, questions are bound to arise: Why are these specific recommendations made for teaching gifted students? Would not many of these methods and models also apply to other students, exceptional or otherwise? Often, the answer to the latter question is yes—the recommended model or strategy or program would also serve other students, particularly those who are above average but not necessarily gifted. However, because so many people view gifted children and youth as essentially capable of teaching themselves, it is necessary to explain, justify, and reiterate specific instructional models, programs, and strategies for teaching the gifted.

> Teaching some children is like molding clay; if a mistake is apparent, it can be remedied by some manipulation or adjustment before it is dry. Working with the gifted, however, because of their sensitive nature, is like sculpting fine marble; an error here or there is difficult to remedy, often irreparable; and the

value of the finished product is greatly altered. (Anderson 1961, 46)

Gifted children and youth offer our greatest hope for the future. From their ranks will come the scientists who find solutions to a diminishing world food supply, doctors who find cures for diseases hitherto considered incurable, teachers who instill in their students an affinity for learning, leaders who bring peace to a long-troubled world, and citizens capable of enriching the lives of those around them. Lessening the collective ability of the ranks of the gifted by diminishing or blocking the potential of even one person could have deleterious effects. Laird (1968) warns that, except for a few heartening exceptions, school systems not only fail to stimulate children's natural appetite for learning but actually dull and deaden their intellectual palate. In the recently published document *A Nation at Risk*, one of the indicators of risk was that in over half the population of gifted students, tested ability does not lead to comparable achievement in school.

Everyone who teaches gifted students has the responsibility to seek and find methods to tantalize their intellectual palate. This does *not* include leaving them to their own devices to acquire what they can as best they can; it does mean designing and delivering an excellent education with nothing left to chance.

READING CURRICULUM

There are several reasons to begin a discussion on curriculum development for the gifted with a section on reading. First, it is an apt starting point because reading is the foundation for virtually all other curriculum areas. A second reason is that most gifted students *are* able to read well. In fact, according to Johnson (1978, 103), "There is probably no single characteristic more consistent among gifted children than enhanced reading proficiency." So, since it is best to begin teaching from a learner's area of strength, a discussion of how best to teach gifted students should start with how best to teach reading. Third, there is a prevailing myth that holds that since gifted students tend to read well, they do not need reading instruction. Although the myth that the gifted can teach themselves is prevalent in all curriculum areas, nowhere is it more pervasive than in the area of reading. Differentiated reading instruction for the gifted is virtually nonexistent (Dawkins 1978; Mangieri & Madigan 1984; Switzer & Nourse 1979).

Before going on, it seems appropriate to address the myth that gifted students can teach themselves all they need to know about reading. Unless one believes that reading instruction is necessary for the gifted, justification for teaching in other areas will seem unfounded. Stevens states

> All too often, little attention in our classrooms goes into "getting the most out of" superior students. This is particularly true in the field of reading. As long as their reading performance is consistently above average, superior students are often considered to be doing "well" in reading. However, this overlooks the fact that such readers may still be performing far below potential. (1980b, 12)

In any subject, including reading, a child's need for remediation is determined based on the discrepancy between potential and performance. Using this same guideline, one can readily see that most gifted students are in need of remediation in reading. Being "on grade level" or even one or two grade levels above age-mates in reading is still far below the capabilities of most gifted students.

Olson and Ames agree. They state that most able readers, by the time they reach middle school or high school,

> are more retarded in reading than any other one group. In most cases, they are retarded not because they are reading below grade level, but because they are reading so far below their capacity level. (1972, 221)

How can teachers prevent retardation in reading among their gifted students? One way is to design curriculum that requires students to reach their capacity. All three of the curriculum models presented in the introduction are appropriate for developing reading curriculum for gifted students, and in fact we would encourage the integrated use of all three.

Since Bloom's Cognitive Taxonomy emphasizes higher-level thinking, it is an ideal resource for developing questions about material students are reading. It also works well in designing progressively more challenging activities.

Williams's Teaching Strategies for Thinking and Feeling also help in designing reading curriculum for able learners because they emphasize creativity and provide numerous examples. Reading material—both narrative and expository—lends itself well to activities designed around Williams's three dimensions.

Renzulli's Enrichment Triad can be seen as the overall model for reading instruction if one considers the following: (1) Assigned, guided reading can be considered part of Type I general exploratory activities. (2) Many activities based on Williams's model or Bloom's taxonomy can be considered part of Type II group training activities. (3) Nearly any Type III individual and small-group investigations of real problems will involve reading—of the sort that students may later use in professional work.

In using any or all of these models, however, teachers must remember that activities planned around a model will not suffice as a reading program. Instruction must also be provided (Barbe 1956; Bonds & Bonds 1983; Brown & Rogan 1983; Johnson 1978; Munson 1944; Sabaroff 1965; Switzer & Nourse 1979). This instruction must be specialized and related to the gifted students' characteristics and needs.

Which student characteristics should affect a reading program for the gifted, and what impact should they have? One obvious characteristic of the gifted is that many of them—from 20 to 50 percent, by various estimates—learn to read before entering school. Those who do not come to school already reading are likely to learn rapidly once the opportunity presents itself. Knowing this, kindergarten and first grade teachers must avoid the preprimers and primers that accompany basal programs. Sumption and Luecking (1960) point out that children who have learned to read and who have been exposed to good children's literature cannot be expected to like a book about a boy and a girl whose conversation consists of "Oh!" "Look!" "See!" and other similarly absorbing comments. While it is true that basal stories have improved since the 1960s, using primers with gifted children is ludicrous. Beginning in first grade, these children must have a literature-based program instead of the basal program (Brown & Rogan 1983; Flack & Lamb 1984; Schlichter 1984; Vida 1979). Teachers should have multiple copies of trade books for the children to read and discuss. Activities should be developed around "real" reading—trade books, magazines, newspapers, letters—rather than contrived reading—basal readers and their accompanying workbooks and worksheets.

Gifted children and youth who are using children's and young-adult literature as the basis for their reading program need to be in groups. Gifted children tend to be gregarious and enjoy the company and stimulation of others. Gifted students may be grouped across grade levels if necessary to accumulate adequate numbers for discussion. They may all read the same book, which has been carefully chosen by their teacher or by members of the group, or they may read books of one genre or by one author. Whatever the focus, the teacher must spend time with the group, offering guidance, providing instruction, and constantly assessing individuals' progress.

Proper instruction cannot be offered if the teacher does not know what the gifted reader can and cannot do. Diagnosis and prescription must begin in first grade (Bonds & Bonds 1983) and continue for as long as the student is attending precollegiate school. Standardized tests provide some information, but informal assessment through teacher-made tests, observation, and discussion provides much more—especially when the teacher is informed and knows what to look for.

Another reason gifted readers should not plod through a basal program is that most such series include seemingly endless skill drills. Gifted students do not like—nor do they need—such repetitive routine drills, and the worksheets are likely to be completed very carelessly or not at all. Rather than force students to repeat this work until they "do it right," teachers need to recognize that gifted learners do not benefit from repeated drill on such isolated skills as phonics or word analysis. Their ability to generalize allows them to learn these discrete skills through inductive processes—without extensive drill and practice.

Gifted students have an extraordinary ability to see relationships and to make connections, and to further enhance this valuable ability, the most appropriate instruction involves critical and creative reading. Although such reading should be a part of all reading programs, it must be the backbone of a program for the gifted.

Gifted readers must be guided and taught. They do not teach themselves the higher levels of reading and thinking. Direct teaching, both of critical and creative reading, is necessary (Bonds & Bonds 1983; Boothby 1979; Cramond & Martin 1981; DeBoer 1963; Dunn 1979; Martin & Cramond 1984; Miller 1982; Rupley 1984; Schuster 1984; Torrance 1963; Trezise 1977).

Critical reading requires the reader to evaluate the material—for truth, authority, and value (Cushenbery & Howell 1974). All readers need this skill, but for the gifted, it is particularly important: they tend to be voracious readers and so have a particular need to critically sort through the volumes of material they encounter.

> Critical thinking and critical reading must lead to conclusions upon which one can act. Creative criticism does not result in a vacuum or intellectual statement. (DeBoer 1963, 441)

Therefore critical reading leads to creative reading.

Creative reading involves an even higher level of reading and thinking than critical reading does (Barbe 1974). Witty says,

> We may consider creative reading to be a thinking process in which new ideas are originated, evaluated, and applied. Divergent and varied responses, not right answers, are goals as thinking transpires and conclusions are reached. Finally the

pupil evaluates his conclusions and seeks to extend and use them. (1974, 15)

Creative reading involves using the printed page as a springboard to thinking and action.

Reading curriculum for gifted readers must also take into account their extensive vocabulary, enjoyment of reference materials, curiosity, and affinity for independent learning. Teachers must bring in a wide variety of resources for such students. Reference books (encyclopedias, dictionaries, almanacs, atlases, readers' guides, record books), periodicals, and media should all be integral components of the program developed for gifted students.

The program should allow the gifted reader a great deal of freedom, including choice of reading materials. Stevens (1980a, 1980b) found that superior students' comprehension was positively affected by their interest in the material, whereas average and below-average students' comprehension was not so affected.

The freedom to pursue independent interests in reading also prevents gifted students from feeling that they are in a lockstep program. Sabaroff observed,

> Bright pupils resent stereotyped work. They react to it in several ways. They do the required work so easily, using only a small part of their minds and energy, that they become lazy and come to expect that all learning should come with great ease. Or, if they already know what is being taught, they become bored, and refuse to put in any effort—eventually falling behind in needed skill development. Later when they are confronted with a problem that requires full attention and sustained effort, they are unable to cope with it and are easily discouraged. (1965, 393)

Gifted students must be challenged if they are to continue to use their extraordinary capabilities.

Although most gifted students are good readers and have the potential to become outstanding, there are some exceptions. Some gifted pupils cannot read—and crisis is imminent unless immediate steps are taken. Munson believes that

> Early treatment is urgent since frustration from reading disability rises in direct proportion to the deviation between mental power and reading progress. Thus, the gifted child with reading disability suffers in proportion to his degree of intelligence. (1944, 46)

As soon as a reading problem appears in a gifted student, diagnosis leading to a prescription for instruction is warranted.

The goals of a reading program for the gifted do not differ from those of other reading programs as much in kind as in degree (Jacobs 1963). Two such long-term goals were put forth by Polette (1982, 39):

1. To create readers in the full, meaningful sense of the word.

An immeasurable quantity of material is available for reading. Highly able children and adults can make good use of this material because of their quick, assimilative minds and their potential for creative use of knowledge. Everyone in the society stands to gain when gifted students are instructed and stimulated so that they are *able* to read and *want* to read at their maximum level. The gifted must be enabled to read both for information and for pleasure.

2. To expand the child's reading, writing, speaking, and thinking vocabulary.

Gifted students tend to enjoy learning and using new words. With appropriate, creative instruction, however, their vocabularies can be functionally increased far beyond the level that would occur spontaneously. An extensive vocabulary allows one to understand more and to express more. This is a legitimate goal for able learners.

Cushenbery and Howell (1974) list other goals desirable for gifted readers.

1. The gifted should achieve reading fluency through mastery of decoding skills.

Because most young gifted students can generalize very well, intensive phonics drill is usually unnecessary. Instead, these children will detect similarities and differences among words and sounds with only a minimum of direct instruction. So that such decoding becomes automatic, gifted children need the chance to read, read, read.

2. The gifted need highly developed comprehension skills, which provide for deep insight, awareness of subtleties and nuances of meaning, and depth and breadth of knowledge in various areas.

Gifted students should be expected to comprehend text at higher levels—and earlier—than other students. Using Bloom's taxonomy as a model, gifted students should be instructed in analysis, synthesis, and evaluation of written material. With practice in using these higher-level comprehension skills, more knowledge will be acquired, and more avenues and resources will be available for applying it.

3. The gifted require the skill to evaluate reading matter for authenticity, validity, and objectivity so as to form an opinion or determine its usability.

Because able students can be expected to read and comprehend vast amounts of material, it is only sensible to instruct them so that they evaluate what they read rather than accept it at face value.

4. Teachers of the gifted should nurture the ability to differentiate between good and mediocre literature and a preference for better literature.

Although the gifted should not be restricted in their choice of reading matter, a concerted effort must be made to expose them to all genres (e.g., historical fiction, mystery, fantasy, science fiction, poetry, informational literature, biography) and to introduce them to the great works within each genre. From an early age, these students should be taught to recognize the motifs that differentiate one genre from another, and they should learn to evaluate by applying literary criteria.

5. The gifted should have the skill to efficiently and effectively compile and organize information from a variety of sources and the ability to locate materials on topics of particular interest.

Gifted students need to be able to locate and give structure to information readily. This facility will only come about through instruction and practice in using reference materials, books, magazines, and journals.

6. Through creative reading, gifted education should foster increased ability in creative thinking.

Creative reading involves higher-level thinking and results in action. Able students should be given the impetus, encouragement, and freedom to take creative action based on their reading.

7. Gifted students should come to use reading as a source of enjoyment.

Reading can provide a lifetime of enjoyment—as a release, as an escape, as exploration, as learning, as vicarious experience. Gifted students need to experience reading for all it is worth—by seeing it as a channel for the world, not as drudgery meant only to fulfill assignments.

Teachers and other curriculum developers must address each of these worthy goals in planning the reading program (K–12) for gifted children and youth. The goals mentioned above are not really different from those set for every child. The distinction comes from the

> depth of understanding sought, the experiences and activities used, the materials and teaching methods employed, and the rate for which learning is planned and achieved. (Cushenbery & Howell 1974, 55)

The first and last words of this statement are the most significant regarding goals for gifted readers. Academically talented and gifted readers should be expected to go far beyond "average" readers, and so their program must be developed to ensure that. And, they can be expected to achieve. In many reading programs, ultimate goals are set but very few students can or do attain them. But with gifted readers, students can and should attain the goals, and some will exceed them. Enabling gifted students to read better is a challenging, satisfying, fulfilling experience.

LANGUAGE ARTS CURRICULUM

The language arts are actually comprised of four distinct subjects: reading, writing, speaking, and listening. Because of the fundamental role of reading in acquiring knowledge, it was treated separately. However, the language arts are interrelated, and curriculum developers should consider this fact when planning for gifted youth (Biersdorf 1979; George 1972; Sebesta 1976).

For essentially the same reason as cited in the section on reading curriculum, all three models presented in the introduction are appropriate for use in developing language arts curriculum for the gifted. And, as before, we recommend integrating the three models for best results.

Bloom's Cognitive Taxonomy provides an excellent means for designing lessons to elicit higher-level thinking and production through written and spoken discourse, as well as higher level thinking and processing of aurally received discourse. Teachers can create opportunities for students to evaluate spoken discourse presented by another student as a means of synthesizing information gained through reading on a topic of interest. Students can use writing skills to display their comprehension of poetry recited as part of a speech contest. Their knowledge of parts of speech can be used to analyze each others' writing in their process groups.

Williams's Teaching Strategies for Thinking and Feeling are useful in designing curriculum in all the language arts areas, because divergent production is to be expected and encouraged. Able students must never see language as confining, but only as enabling. As may be seen from examples in the introduction, Williams's strategies can be used to evoke production in reading, writing, speaking, and listening.

It is wise to view Renzulli's Enrichment Triad as the overarching guide in language arts. Teachers of the gifted must continually be thinking of ways to get their students into real projects so that they can put their language skills to real use. A continual search must be undertaken for professionals willing to tell students how reading, writing, speaking, and listening are essential for success in their jobs and their lives. Also, teachers and parents need to look for professionals who are willing to allow students to hone their own language skills by working with them on various real projects.

Brown and Rogan (1983) cite several experts who point out that language is our primary symbol system and that "the ability to manipulate internally learned symbol systems is perhaps the sine qua non of giftedness" (p. 6). Because of the primacy of language, fluency in the manipulation of this symbol system is almost required for school and career success. Gifted students tend to have a proclivity for achievement in this area, but great progress is rare without instruction tailored to develop the verbal abilities of these students.

Writing

Just as many people assume that all gifted children are good readers, many also assume that all gifted children are good writers. But, just as gifted children need instruction if their reading is to become better than "good," good writers are not *born*. Rather, they *evolve*—through the instruction and guidance of teachers and other writers and through experience gained through both literary (narrative) writing and expository (content) writing.

Elementary

> I LV U (I love you)
> Wunsuponutim . . . (Once upon a time . . .)

Young children born into a literate culture have a desire to communicate both orally and symbolically. A child who can hold a crayon or some other writing instrument can be a writer. All that is necessary is a desire to communicate in writing, some rudimentary symbols, and someone willing to "read" or "listen to" what has been written. The notion that a child cannot write without acquiring proper handwriting, conventional spelling, correct punctuation, and other discrete skills is actually detrimental to the development of writers. A great deal of class time is spent on these discrete skills which could much more profitably be spent writing.

> The notion that creative writing is the end result of a backlog of skills learning does great disservice to the natural incentive to acquire skills created by the desire to be read. Creative writing is not the end result of other learning. It is a process within which a child begins to need to learn related skills as he wishes to be understood by others. (Beebe 1979, 27)

There is much that parents and teachers can do to encourage writing behavior in their young gifted children (Beebe 1979; Isaacs 1973; Torrance 1962). Several suggestions are made below.

First of all, opportunities to write must be provided. Teachers and parents can provide a stimulus for writing by reading a story aloud and then asking children to create a different ending to the story or to create their own story involving one of the characters (Williams: creative listening, creative reading, creative writing). Gifted children can also be given several stories of a similar genre and asked to write one that could be included in the group (Bloom: analysis, synthesis; Williams: attributes, creative reading, creative writing). Also, exposure to many types of poetry should be started early and continued throughout the grades. With opportunities to write and the right encouragement and modeling, gifted young poets can emerge in elementary school.

Second, the desire to write must be noted and nurtured as soon as possible. Some gifted children demonstrate very early that their talents lie in the area of written communication. Some prefer writing poetry, plays, stories, or reports more than other activities; other children do not appear to prefer writing but produce extraordinary gems of written material. Both groups should be given extra attention and incentive to continue their writing. Gifted young writers deserve to have their work read by others besides the teacher (e.g., principals, other authors, or community members interested in fostering a child's budding ability to write). Outstanding material should be submitted to contests and to publications that accept children's work (*Cricket, Highlights for Children, Stone Soup, Merlyn's Pen*) and later to publications that do not specialize in publishing the writing of children (Renzulli: Type III).

One can never be sure which word of encouragement or which act of affirmation is the one a gifted author will later cite as the *one* which compelled him or her to persevere in writing.

The majority of gifted children will not be gifted authors—what should their elementary writing curriculum entail? The objectives for elementary children gifted in writing are to allow them to develop their writing ability, their desire to write, and the discipline necessary to do so. By contrast, the objective for children gifted in other areas is to learn how to express themselves in writing—to serve their own personal purposes, so that writing is not the stumbling block that prevents their advancement but an ability that enables them to produce written accounts of their accomplishments in other fields. They should be given ample opportunity to become fluent writers, expected to write frequently and for many different purposes (Renzulli: Type II, Type III). Children who have written notes, stories, plays, lists, paragraphs, and responses as a matter of course will not be overwhelmed by a blank piece of paper and the direction to write something. This kind of block prevents many people from putting on paper what they have in their heads to say. Gifted children have too much to say to allow it to be blocked by fear of the blank page.

In order to allow gifted children to experience the personal value of writing, teachers should create opportunities for them to write for personal reasons: diaries and journals, letters, notes, lists, etc. This type of writing should never be graded or corrected; it is for *personal* use. Children need to see the value writing can have when it is exclusively for one's own use.

In addition to personal writing, gifted children in elementary school need to acquire the skills necessary for school success—clarity, sense of audience, punctuation, grammar, and neatness. The first two *cannot* be, and the latter three *must not* be, taught through drill and practice. Highly able students, especially highly able and highly creative students, tend to have little or no tolerance for skill drills and other mundane tasks. Therefore, teachers need to carefully formulate writing tasks (for real purposes and real audiences) that will entail instruction and practice in the target skills (Renzulli: Type II, Type III). For example, if the skill being focused upon is proper use of possessive markers, the following assignment could be to make an inventory of family members' favorite possessions. This inventory would include lists (John's favorite possessions) and narratives concerning these possessions written after interviews with each family member. The final product could be given to the family's insurance agent or locked in the safe deposit box to be used in case of fire or theft. Teaching gifted children skills in conjunction with putting the skills to real use is a key to their learning.

Finally, gifted children whose talents lie in areas other than writing need to learn how to share their expertise with others through the written medium. Beginning in kindergarten, an able child who pursues an area of personal interest or expertise should be expected to accompany it with a written "report." Its length and depth should vary with the child's age and experience and the stimulus project. As other children respond to the project, the notion of sharing interest and information through writing becomes implanted in the gifted child's mind.

Gifted elementary children must have instruction that provides the tools for better communication through writing. In addition, they must have the opportunity to write for, and be read by, real audiences.

Secondary

The writing curriculum for gifted secondary students has similar goals as those for elementary school, but its scope is expanded. Students gifted in writing should be actively prodded and promoted to further develop their talent. Those gifted in other areas should continue strengthening their expressive skills in writing so that their school and career success is not hampered by less than adequate writing ability and so that their expertise can be shared with others through writing.

Gifted young writers need the critical advice and instruction, not only of their classroom teachers, but also of experienced writers. Modeling and practice are important in many subjects but in none more so than writing. Verbally gifted children who have the potential to become accomplished writers must see and feel that writing is a process—a sometimes fun, sometimes laborious process (Daniel 1982; Fearn 1981; Finn 1981; Gilmar 1979; List 1983). They need to be encouraged in their strengths and strengthened in their weaknesses. Writing is an arduous endeavor; without encouragement during the early years, many aspiring writers—with talent—give up.

Young writers should have the opportunity to talk to real authors—journalists, novelists, poets, technical writers (Renzulli: Type II, Type III). These opportunities should be provided frequently and, if possible, on a regular schedule. Some of these writers, especially those who had their own mentors, may serve as tutors for students who are aspiring authors.

Other modeling can be provided by the teacher. The Bay Area Writers' Project concept has spread across the United States, so that there are writers' projects in most states now. Usually held in the summer, they are designed to give classroom teachers an opportunity to discover and explore their own ability to write. Small-scale writers' projects for gifted students could be set up in a classroom, in a school, or in conjunction with a university (Gilmar 1979; List 1983). Students could meet together to generate ideas, to share works in progress, to reveal finished products, and to create a support system. By responding to the writing of others and by having their own work discussed, participants may develop a sense of belonging to a writers' community and lose the feeling of being a writer—all alone. Such groups may be peer grouped or, if the students are sophisticated enough, they can cut across age boundaries.

Writers need an audience, and it should include people other than the teacher. Gifted students can write for younger students; they can write letters (real letters, not letters copied from a textbook to a bogus person residing at a bogus address); they can write in journals; they can write for publication. Real audiences can be found when real problems are addressed, and teachers can avoid assigning stilted, contrived writing tasks, so typical of many textbook lessons.

Speaking

Rightly or wrongly, lasting impressions are often based on a person's dress, carriage, and speech. No matter what a person's abilities, if he or she speaks unclearly, with hesitancy, without conviction, and with nonstandard grammar, many listeners will not attend to the message because of the medium. For highly able, highly creative children, youth, and adults to be ignored because of poor oral language skills is to squander abilities that are already in short supply. Such a waste can be prevented through proper instruction and experience. The goals of instruction in oral language should include:

1. Accurate articulation of words that appropriately convey meaning.
2. The fluent expression of ideas and information.
3. Logically organized presentation.
4. The ongoing appreciation and pleasure that accompany the efficient use of language. (Coody & Nelson 1982, 84)

These goals will be addressed in the following sections for elementary and secondary students.

Elementary

In the elementary school, particularly in the primary grades, oral language should be the predominant mode of expression. Young children must be given ample opportunities to speak—in conversations, in responses, and in presenting information. Direct instruction, modeling, and practice of clearly enunciated spoken language should be provided. Gifted children can be expected to observe and reenact real-life incidents where communication has broken down or a poor impression was made because of inarticulate speech. Enacting how the same incident might have gone if correct speech had been used reinforces effective speaking to obtain a positive effect (Williams: any number of the strategies, depending on the context; Renzulli: Type III).

Gifted children need to be taught to organize their thoughts and their speech so that their intended message is conveyed. Beginning in the primary grades, gifted students can be taught to prepare well-organized presentations of information they have acquired (Bloom: comprehension, application, analysis, synthesis, evaluation). These presentations can be delivered to classmates, other classes, clubs, or interest groups (Renzulli: Type III). Peer teaching provides practice for able students in preparing and presenting a talk on a given topic—and demonstrates the necessity of organization and clarity (children are very quick to point out that which does not make sense).

Language in and of itself, appeals to most gifted children, and this appreciation should be encouraged through poetry recitation, language play, word games, and oral reading. Instruction to enhance or perfect gifted students' oral language skills is required so that these students feel confident in expressing themselves and so that they feel compelled to continue mastering the art of speaking.

Secondary

The secondary school provides many more organized opportunities for verbally gifted students to practice the art of speaking. Speech, debate, and drama activities are ideal venues for students who actually want to perform by speaking. For students who are more interested in honing their speaking skills for effective conduct of their schooling and career, other arenas are more appropriate (e.g., campaigning for and serving as an officer in a school-related organization, serving as a guide at local places of interest, teaching minicourses for younger students, working for a local or state official).

Just as gifted students should be expected to compose a written piece to accompany explorations into their areas of expertise, they should also be expected to prepare an oral presentation. Sometimes, the two can be combined, as when a gifted student's writing is presented orally to an audience (Adalbert 1966) (Renzulli: Type III). Depending on the age and sophistication of the student, any number of audiences can be found. Middle school and high school teachers should cultivate contacts with local parent groups (such as PTA), service organizations (Lions, Rotary), and youth groups (Girl Scouts, Boy Scouts). Since many groups have a speaker at each of their meetings, many of them maintain a list of possible speakers and topics. Those verbally gifted students whose public speaking skills are well-developed could serve them as ideal speakers. Public relations benefits can accrue if the speaker is introduced as a student in the gifted program at a specific school.

Gifted students have a great deal to offer, and part of the school's responsibility is to make sure that they can say it—informedly, forcefully, and clearly.

Listening

The final portion of the language arts, and the most neglected, is listening. Listening is part of communication. Like the tree falling in the forest, if no one is hearing another's message, one must question whether any communication is going on. Keen listening skills are an essential element of communication. Effective leaders know when and how to listen.

Preparing gifted youth to be good listeners later in life is a legitimate long-term goal. However, the short-term goal of teaching students how to listen in school is just as valid. Planned, sequential activities for developing gifted students' listening abilities must be integrated into the language arts curriculum (Corpening 1984, 1985).

Listening can be subdivided into five categories: (1) passive listening, (2) listening for information, (3) listening for understanding, (4) critical listening, and (5) appreciative listening (DeHaven 1983). Each of the five will be discussed below, along with implications for elementary and secondary curriculum for the gifted.

Passive Listening

Hearing—receiving sounds—with little or no mental response is known as passive listening. For example, in a library one may be vaguely aware of sounds passing through the air, but they are not disruptive to reading or studying. Passive listening is not acceptable when one is in a classroom and only vaguely aware of the teacher's lesson. Unfortunately, it happens, and in fact, teachers must be particularly conscious of those students whose attentiveness is signified by their body position, eye contact, and frequent nodding—they may know that if they appear to listen, they will be left alone by the teacher. It behooves teachers to determine whether these students are really attending to the message actively—or only passively.

Listening for Information

One listening skill involves attending to information that is stated and concentrating on remembering what is said (Bloom: knowledge, comprehension). Since gifted students are usually able to recall information readily, sharpening this listening skill will enable them to radically increase their store of knowledge and information.

For *elementary* students, provide one oral direction to follow, then two directions, and so on. Over time, build up the number until they can recall long strings of directions (Bloom: knowledge). Later, students can be given several directions to follow—with the directions out of sequence. Before demonstrating their ability to remember the directions they have heard, they must put them in the correct order (Bloom: comprehension). Have students keep a chart of their own progress on these tasks.

Have *secondary* students listen to complex sentences from works of literature or from technical writing. Have them paraphrase these sentences orally or in writing (Bloom: comprehension). Students can also be asked to listen to a speech or a piece of written discourse for paradoxes, discrepancies, or analogies (Williams).

Listening for Understanding

To understand, the listener must make connections between various ideas and bits of information that are heard. Such connections allow the listener to solve a problem or to comprehend a formerly unclarified situation (Bloom: application; Renzulli: Type I, Type II, Type III). Able students are capable of seeing relationships, and teachers need to make sure that they are taught to apply this ability in listening.

Have *elementary* students determine a problem that exists in the classroom or the school and state it in writing on the chalkboard. Next, tell students to brainstorm steps that could lead to a solution. Tape record their answers. When all ideas have been generated, play the tape back to the students with the instruction to listen and determine a reasonable sequence or plan of action. Have them write their sequence on paper and then share it with others. Use one of the plans to attempt to solve the problem (Renzulli: Type III).

While *secondary* students are working on writing an essay or research paper, they should choose a partner, and each should read his or her paper to the other, one paragraph at a time. The listener should try to identify the main idea and the supporting details (Bloom: analysis). If the results are incorrect, then the pair should work together to assess the paper and improve its cohesiveness.

Critical Listening

This complex skill requires the student to listen for both information and understanding and to adopt an analytical, judgmental approach to the information being heard (Bloom: analysis, evaluation). Critical listening involves the higher-level thinking processes so necessary for gifted students to develop their extraordinary intellectual ability.

Tell *elementary* students that authors and speakers always have a purpose for composing the words that they do, in the way that they do (e.g., to inform, to explain, to convince, to entertain, to express feelings). Have students listen for and tape record examples of each. These tapes can be played for other members of the class to listen for speakers' intent (Renzulli: Type II). Next, interested students can set up a project to determine whether average listeners are aware of the intent of various advertisers—and whether their intent is working (Renzulli: Type II or III, depending on the eventual product).

After secondary students have chosen a topic for a research paper, tell them that prior to writing it, they will present brief speeches related to their topic. They are to slant their presentation very subtly toward one bias or point of view. The class will listen to the presentation and not only determine the bias but note its indicators in the speech (Bloom: analysis, evaluation; Williams: discrepancy, paradox).

Appreciative Listening

Also called creative listening, appreciative listening is the highest-level listening skill because it involves a personal response to what is heard. The listener may respond to the intonation of someone's voice, to the word choice in a poem, or to the melody of a symphony.

For *elementary* students, create a bulletin board or learning center entitled "Sounds I Like." Class members should bring in examples of their favorite sounds (e.g., a tape of the garage door opening, because it signals that a parent is home from work; a tape of a kitten mewing; a music box). These sounds can be shared with other class members. Also, the teacher could make a tape of sounds that often evoke a response (e.g., bacon frying, a baby babbling, a little child's laughter, thunder). As the tape is played, the teacher and children should discuss their responses to these sounds and the background of those responses (Bloom: evaluation).

Require *secondary* students to plan a multimedia presentation of a topic that interests them. Their presentation must include a component that appeals to the sense of hearing, and it must also reflect one of Williams's modes from Dimension 2 (e.g., analogy, examples of habit).

In designing language arts curricula for the gifted, one should keep the "big picture" in mind. Academically gifted students usually have extraordinary language capabilities. So, instead of being satisfied when they do above average work in the basic curriculum, make special provisions for expanding their capabilities to their limit. The majority of gifted learners can become capable—sometimes eloquent— writers; articulate—sometimes inspired—speakers; acute—sometimes perceptive—listeners; and critical—sometimes creative—readers. To render this possible, the language arts curriculum must be planned with care and attention from kindergarten through twelfth grade. Regarding such a program, Sebesta says that first it must have structure.

> The teacher, the core materials, and the curriculum guide for helping the gifted ought to possess a framework based on one or more language disciplines. It is not enough to have a collection of enticing but unrelated language ideas without an organizing framework. (1976, 19)

Higher-level thinking must be required, and quality products must be nurtured and demanded. Experts in gifted education, experts in the four language arts subareas, and experts in pedagogy should comprise the curriculum-development team that designs and then trains teachers to implement language arts curriculum. Although the curriculum is structured, freedom must also be built in, and teachers must understand how to offer this freedom to their gifted students who need it. Freedom, with guidance and instruction, will allow the gifted to attain heights that they could not reach were they lacking in verbal skills.

LIBRARY CURRICULUM

The importance of libraries to gifted children and youth cannot be overemphasized. Cummings (1982) quotes from an American Association for Gifted Children/American Library Association publication: "The library is the community resource best equipped to provide gifted children with needed help, inspiration, and guidance." What makes libraries so important for gifted youth is inherent in their function. Libraries serve as repositories and dissemination points for vast amounts of information, which becomes accessible to gifted children and youth as soon as they can read or listen or watch. The information in libraries is more readily available than, say, information that must be obtained from another person, who might not always be handy. Through books and other media, the gifted can explore ideas, places, jobs, emotions, philosophies, strategies, and lore that might otherwise never be available to them.

Gifted children should learn to use the library for exploration and research—not as an isolated skill but in conjunction with learning in other curriculum areas. Renzulli's Enrichment Triad is the ideal model for library curriculum development because of its emphasis on enabling students to become professionals. In the library, Type I Enrichment: General Exploratory Activities could involve teaching students about various sources that are available, providing impetus for their use, and making them accessible to children searching for alternatives for further study. Type II Enrichment: Group Training Activities could include such tasks as these: (1) Have students compare accounts of events from sources espousing completely different philosophies—for example, an Iranian newspaper and *The New York Times*—a task which would obviously also involve finding someone to translate from the Iranian newspaper. (2) Take a general topic, such as "Opinions of the American Educational System," and determine different, specific directions to take in investigating it. Students should explore a range of the sources available regarding the topic. Type III Enrichment: Individual and Small Group Investigations of Real Problems lends itself well to library curriculum development. Students who have determined the topic they want to investigate and the product they intend to create as a result of that investigation will need to use the resources of the library in the way that a professional does—and should determine in what ways that might be.

Elementary

From the time children are born, someone should be reading to them. From a very early age, children develop a concept of reading and books. If they have been comfortably introduced to books—for example, while curled up beside a family member—then their concept of reading will be positive. Reading will call forth feelings of inner warmth and pleasure, and they will know the benefits books can bring.

Children who have been exposed to books from birth will be ready at a young age to choose some books on their own. This will occur first at home or at the place where the child is typically read to. A child who has demonstrated an ability to make a preference known should be given the opportunity to select books at the library.

Some of the books chosen will be inappropriate for one reason or another—they may have no interest for the child, be too short or too long, have too few pictures or poor illustrations. However, such problems do not indicate that the child is not yet able to make selections—because adults often make inappropriate selections for themselves. (For example a book turns out not to be on the topic of interest, or a favorite author writes a book that does not appeal).

Gifted children—whose abilities and interests are far-ranging—should never be limited to the "children's section" of the library. Parents, teachers, and librarians should introduce them to all sections of the library and then provide guidance for library use.

For example, if students have been engaged in Type I: General Exploratory Activities in the area of conservation, they will already be familiar with some of the children's books on this topic, as well as articles in such children's magazines as *National Geographic World* and *Ranger Rick,* which stress prudent use of the environment. As students begin to determine an area of interest—that is, one which will lead to a Type III investigation—they will need to go beyond the children's section. They will be investigating as professionals and will need to acquire a professional's knowledge and skills to work in this way. A student who wants to test the water in a creek near his home (which is downstream from a paper plant) needs to know what chemicals are used in the paper-making process, how to test for the presence of those chemicals, what effect particular chemicals have on fauna and flora. If he finds dangerous levels of chemicals, the student will need to know how other conservationists have presented their findings to the companies causing the damage. Learning how and what and why will entail use of magazines, journals, government documents, directories. Students will need some help in making sense of the materials they find, but just as adult professionals do not understand every single word they read, neither will these young professionals.

Gifted children in elementary school need to know how to use the card catalog, which may either be on cards in long drawers or on a computer. Because of gifted children's ability to make connections and categorize information, the Dewey Decimal system and the Library of Congress system for categorizing informational books can be introduced much earlier than with other children. Young gifted children must be taught how to use the resources that will allow them to find and retrieve information as they need it.

For example, if a bright third grader is fascinated with whaling and decides she wants to know more about it, she should have already learned, or be taught now that she needs the knowledge, how to proceed to find out about whaling. While the encyclopedia is one resource, it is not the only one. A card catalog search under the subjects WHALES and WHALING should lead her to a few titles. Once she explores those, she may find the names of several countries where whaling is an industry—for example, Japan and Russia. Another trip to the card catalog will yield the location of books on Japan and Russia. She can then use the tables of contents or the indexes of these books to determine whether they contain information pertinent to her topic. And the search goes on. . . .

The librarian is a key to gifted students' effective use of the library. Cummings says that

> The public library can function as a haven, a source of endless materials to be devoured according to the child's special interests and appetites. The librarian, adopting the role of facilitator, connects that young patron with references of all types while teaching by example the basic skills of information retrieval. (1982, 57)

In order to better serve the gifted, school librarians and public librarians should have some education regarding gifted children—especially their characteristics and how best to nurture those characteristics through the services of the library. They need to realize that the thirst for information is not age bound and that libraries should be open places where students can secure materials of any level. Gifted children and youth must not only be allowed to use all sections of the library, but they must be taught how to use them. Librarians should be familiar with the underlying concepts of Renzulli's Enrichment Triad and should participate actively in curriculum development for the gifted.

Highly able youth have a penchant for information, and if they

> are to have access to the full range of information within any given area or field of knowledge, then it is important that they learn about the existence, nature, and function of . . . reference materials. (Renzulli 1977, 59)

The librarian's primary function for the gifted is to serve as a guide and a liaison between them and the information they seek. This function may be served by individual contact with students or through programs meant to reach the larger community.

Secondary

By the time gifted students are in middle school and high school, they should have been taught to investigate topics of interest and concepts of concern. In the years beyond elementary school, gifted students should practice and perfect these skills so that they become capable of in-depth investigations—for satisfaction of personal curiosity, for school requirements, and for completion of Type III investigations. Gifted high school students should receive instruction in their school library, the local public library, and a nearby college or university library. The latter should be accomplished even if they must travel by bus or car for a fair distance.

Familiarity with the resources of the public and university library will remove the fear and sense of "untouchableness" or "impenetrability" that many students feel about libraries other than the small one housed within the school. As early as possible, gifted students should be introduced to, and receive practice using, the myriad of indexes, abstracts, bibliographies, and computer-accessible databases that can direct an interested person to virtually any information desired. This instruction and practice should be part of a planned library curriculum for highly able students that spans their secondary school career.

Gifted students and librarians are natural partners. As in any mature partnership, the more one knows about the other, the more solid and lasting the relationship.

FOREIGN-LANGUAGE CURRICULUM

At present, gifted students are not being provided adequate foreign-language instruction. Bartz (1982) points out that this neglect is a cause for serious concern because the gifted are the ones who "will assume leadership roles in our nation's business, governmental, and educational sectors" (p. 329). If one can speak at least one foreign language and comprehend other cultures, one's ability to be effective outside national boundaries increases greatly.

To plan foreign-language curriculum for able learners, teachers can use the models suggested in the language arts section. Once students have learned the rudiments of the target language, they need to begin thinking in the language, and this will only happen as foreign-language teachers require students to think. Teachers can ask questions and expect answers that employ the upper levels of Bloom's Cognitive Taxonomy. Williams's Teaching Strategies for Thinking and Feeling can be used to create opportunities for creative thinking.

Teachers can instill the necessity of knowing (a) foreign language(s) by guiding students to Type III investigations regarding foreign language.

In order to accomplish the latter most effectively, teachers should spend some time with business and political leaders, educators, and scientists when designing the curriculum. These contacts will be useful later when students are searching for professionals to learn from and emulate.

Elementary

The gifted, especially the verbally gifted, should begin to receive foreign language instruction at a very young age. The earlier children are exposed to a foreign language, the more native their pronunciation and diction will be. Therefore, gifted preschool children should have the opportunity to be exposed to a foreign language. If a full-time foreign language teacher for the program is not feasible, then a search to locate a willing and capable volunteer instructor must be conducted.

In much the same way that children acquire their first language, these early lessons should involve learning a basic vocabulary and ordinary requests, commands, and responses, A one-hour "lesson" two or three times a week is enough to entice gifted preschoolers into acquiring a foreign language.

When gifted children begin elementary school, more formal instruction can begin—still, however, retaining a relaxed atmosphere. These children can begin to learn sentences, brief response sets, short poems, and stories. As the children advance through elementary school, this instruction should proceed rapidly and should extend into a second foreign language as soon as a student is relatively proficient in one (Bartz 1982). Highly motivated students could do much of the work independently, using an approach such as the SILP method (Pontillo 1977). Independent study and/or working with a private tutor (paid or volunteer) may be necessary if no other program is available.

Another excellent option for able youngsters is an immersion program, in which children are taught half the day in their native language and half the day in their target language. These programs are most effective in the preschool and primary grades.

Secondary

Secondary foreign-language programs for gifted students can and should proceed more rapidly than those for the nongifted. In addition to learning the language quickly, gifted students should be expected to read the literature of the culture, write critical essays on the literature, attend cultural events presented in the target language (plays, movies, operas), find and converse with a native or fluent speaker of the language, and become knowledgeable about mores and social customs of those cultures that use this language.

Leaders in business, education, and government should be enlisted to help convince local school districts that accelerated, enriched foreign language programs should be provided, beginning in elementary school. Such community members are likely to know the value of having more than one language, and their influence may ensure that gifted students are not cheated by a lack of opportunity to learn languages.

PRESCHOOL CURRICULUM

If one age category among the ranks of the gifted is ignored more than any other, that group would have to be preschoolers (Karnes & Bertschi 1978). Very young gifted children, those from ages three to five, rarely have an appropriate education provided for them. Kitano cites several experts in preschool gifted education who point out that this lack of support during the early years is "one source for the devastatingly wasteful underachievement of many gifted adolescents" (1982, 14). There are a few programs specifically for preschool gifted youngsters (Delahanty 1984), but unfortunately these are the exception, not the rule.

While some would argue that giftedness is not yet evident in preschool children, those who have worked with young children for any length of time would quickly argue to refute that misconception. Roeper (1963b) states that, in general, gifted preschool children are "high energy" children, both physically and mentally. They acquire many skills early and are unusually proficient with language. Gifted preschoolers have exceptionally good memories and are very curious, rarely reticent about asking questions. They thirst for and acquire knowledge across a broad spectrum of areas but are usually more informed in one specific area. Their sense of humor is much better developed than their age-mates', and they form friendships easily.

As early as kindergarten, gifted children should spend some time with an intellectual peer group (Malone 1974) comprised of children who are the same age. They need the intellectual stimulation provided by other gifted children, but since there is often disparity of size and coordination between children of different ages, it is better for the youngsters to be of approximately the same age. This peer group may be present in a gifted child's preschool program, but if it is not, then parents need to seek out other able children and establish a peer group for their child (see the chapter "Parenting Gifted Children").

When one analyzes traditional preschool programs, several commonalities become apparent. Virtually all programs have an art component (cut and paste, paint), a music component (sing-alongs, finger plays), a reading component (stories are read to the children and/or a phonics program is "taught"), a play component (blocks, dress up), and an "experiential" component (taking walks, going to see new things). There is nothing inherently wrong with a program of this nature except that it is limited, but the last thing preschool children need is to have their learning limited. This is, of course, even more true for gifted young children.

Hanninen (1979) says that the emphasis in teaching preschool children should be on challenging their thinking processes. The curriculum must be planned so that the gifted children have an opportunity to go far beyond the confines of the typical preschool program. For example, if the class of four-year-olds is going to visit a train station, the typical plan would include reading the class books like *The Little Engine That Could* by Watty Piper and *Freight Train* by Donald Crews. Children would also be encouraged to draw or paint trains, or to construct a picture of a train from some construction paper shapes precut by the teachers (so that everyone's looks alike). A game might be organized where each child holds onto the waist of the preceding child and the "train" goes around the playground. The class could sing "I've Been Working on the Railroad" and could listen to train sounds on a record the teacher has checked out from the library. Finally, the class would visit the train station and see some of the engines and hear real trains.

Have the gifted children in this class been mentally stimulated by this experience? Yes, but only to a limited extent—and to an extent far short of their capabilities and thus far short of the goals their teachers and care givers should be planning. Such provisions as a wide variety of books, magazines, and manuals (for model trains) should be made available to the children. Whether or not they can read is of no consequence. For the children who express an interest in mechanical aspects of trains, someone who has a model train set could come to the class and explain the switching system. The teacher could do a guided fantasy with the children and have them imagine that they are a train travelling across the country at night—what would they see? The able children should also be encouraged to dictate stories to be written by an older child or adult or to write their own stories about trains. They could also be given the task of making a tape of train sounds, and since no trains are readily available in a preschool, the children would have to experiment with various objects to find ways to create their own trainlike sounds. The list of possibilities is endless, but the key to educating preschool gifted children—with their seemingly endless energy and curiosity and potential—is to plan experiences and activities that are broad in scope and range, watch for the tiniest spark—and then fan that spark until it flames.

As stated earlier, the curriculum must be planned to encourage and enable gifted preschoolers to go far beyond the confines of a typical preschool program. Of the models presented in this chapter, Bloom's Cognitive Taxonomy is most appropriate to use as a *guide* in planning. Figure 6.1 is taken from Isabel E. Blomberg's booklet *In Pursuit of Bloom's: A Primer to Guide You through Bloom's Taxonomy*, one of the most helpful publications on this subject. The six different questioning levels are like six floors in a building. Here is a quick reference for the process words written at the six different levels. These process words are the major "occupants" of the thinking building. Anyone who has been in a preschool or kindergarten and looks at the words at the "Knowledge" level of the chart, recognizes those as indicative of the majority of tasks given to young children. Little children are constantly being asked to identify and label objects, to match colors, to name shapes, and so forth. There is nothing wrong with these tasks except that they are far too limiting for gifted youngsters. These children need to be asked to complete tasks at higher levels of the taxonomy. For example:

1. Interpret a story (comprehension).
2. Explain a project they have completed (comprehension).
3. Conduct and observe several experiments illustrating the same principle, draw conclusions based on the results, and state the rule or principle illustrated (application).
4. Find out information to answer their own questions or the questions other children pose (application).
5. Categorize, not just by color or size, but by color and size, or by mammal/nonmammal, or by ugly sounds/pleasant sounds. Explain the categorizations (analysis).
6. Compare dissimilar objects or people or sounds and tell how they are similar (analysis).
7. Find a new way to organize the block area or the family living area (synthesis).
8. Invent, create, and construct new ideas, new machines, new tasks—which the class can try out (synthesis).

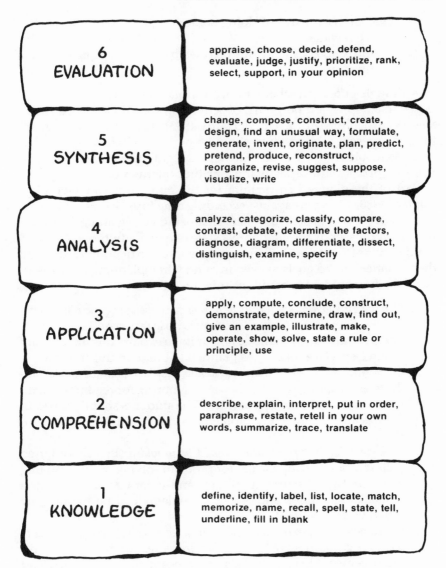

6 **EVALUATION**	appraise, choose, decide, defend, evaluate, judge, justify, prioritize, rank, select, support, in your opinion
5 **SYNTHESIS**	change, compose, construct, create, design, find an unusual way, formulate, generate, invent, originate, plan, predict, pretend, produce, reconstruct, reorganize, revise, suggest, suppose, visualize, write
4 **ANALYSIS**	analyze, categorize, classify, compare, contrast, debate, determine the factors, diagnose, diagram, differentiate, dissect, distinguish, examine, specify
3 **APPLICATION**	apply, compute, conclude, construct, demonstrate, determine, draw, find out, give an example, illustrate, make, operate, show, solve, state a rule or principle, use
2 **COMPREHENSION**	describe, explain, interpret, put in order, paraphrase, restate, retell in your own words, summarize, trace, translate
1 **KNOWLEDGE**	define, identify, label, list, locate, match, memorize, name, recall, spell, state, tell, underline, fill in blank

Fig. 6.1. The Six Levels of Questioning in Bloom's Taxonomy

SOURCE: Isabel E. Blomberg, *In Pursuit of Bloom's: A Primer to Guide You through Bloom's Taxonomy* (Phoenix: Thinking Caps, 1981). Reprinted with permission of the author.

9. Evaluate two ways of doing something and justify the better choice (evaluation).
10. Prioritize jobs or activities or rules by self-determined criteria (evaluation).

Although gifted preschoolers need a planned curriculum (as opposed to a haphazard potpourri of activities), they do not need a *compulsory* curriculum (Ehrlich in McHardy 1983). Teachers who are planning the preschool curriculum should have a plan to fall back on, but when valuable learning experiences for the gifted lie outside that curriculum, *freedom* and *flexibility* must be the watchwords.

Part of the planned curriculum for the gifted must involve play. Kaplan (1980, 12) warns against excluding time for play in a gifted program because of a mistaken "belief that being young and gifted automatically transcends the child into a state of quasi-adulthood." Gifted young children need a challenging, balanced curriculum to develop their abilities. Broad goals to keep in mind when planning the curriculum for gifted students should include the following:

1. *Use the gifted child's interests as a basis for developing learning activities and experiences.* A gifted student who is fascinated with panda bears should be given the opportunity to explore this interest and to have special experiences planned to build on this interest.
2. *Opportunities for learning academic skills should be planned for able students.* If the gifted preschoolers are clamoring for reading or math instruction, it should be provided. The students should be stimulated academically but not forced beyond their interest or maturity.
3. *Problem-solving opportunities should be provided.* Preschool gifted children can develop facility for problem solving at a very young age—through discussion, action, and creative thinking. Both gamelike situations and real-life problems can be handled by gifted young children.
4. *Gifted young children should be encouraged to make discoveries and to use these discoveries as a basis for their learning.* For example, have a math center where numerals are present in many forms and number concepts are available for discovery in many different ways. Give the able students time to *play* at this center and encourage them to share discoveries with adults or other able students.
5. *Creativity should be fostered.* Great pains should be taken not to repress it. Able students should have opportunities to be verbally, artistically, and intellectually creative.

Teaching gifted young children provides an opportunity virtually unparalleled anywhere else in education:

> Very young gifted children provide educators with an, as yet, untapped resource. They give us a map for extending the educational horizons of tomorrow. These children, whose behavior is still only minimally overlaid with social repression, give us a way to study the characteristics of success. From them, we can learn about promoting growth rather than remediation. Through them, we can participate in the new interest in looking at "wellness" rather than at pathology. (Malone 1979, 25)

Roeper (1963a) says that parents and teachers of highly able young children have a twofold task: (1) to find ways to develop and nurture the special abilities of preschool children and (2) to correctly interpret their behavior and reactions in order to work with them most effectively. This is a tall order, but one that must be filled for our smallest gifted citizens.

MATHEMATICS CURRICULUM

John Kemeny, in speaking to the forty-seventh annual convention of the National Association of Secondary School Principals, stated:

> There is no other field of knowledge where there is as great a difference between the most talented and least talented students as in mathematics. There is something in the very nature of the subject matter that brings out extreme ability or lack of ability in the human mind. (1963, 31)

Thus, identifying students who are mathematically gifted is easier than identifying students gifted in other areas. From a very young age, even before going to school, mathematically gifted children are more interested in numbers and abstract numerical concepts than other children are. They ask questions about numbers and become frustrated when a nonmathematical adult dismisses a question as "silly." These young children enjoy working mathematical puzzles and reading and hearing about mathematical concepts—and they should be given many opportunities to do so. Such children learn mathematics facts very quickly and can apply the knowledge beyond the expected realm for their age group (Chen 1981). From early on, they perform well on standardized achievement and aptitude tests.

Although Kemeny's statements were made twenty-five years ago, it would seem that they either fell on deaf ears or on the wrong ears. Little differentiation is apparent in secondary schools today. At most, some students are assigned to Algebra II and Geometry (and maybe Trigonometry), while others are limited to Fundamentals of Mathematics and Algebra I. This situation must change, and soon, if the nation is to cultivate the incredible mathematical potential that lies fallow in the minds of its able students.

The learning of mathematics differs from other content areas for several reasons: (1) mathematics follows a clearly defined sequence of courses; (2) the sequential nature of mathematics means that the material in a given math course builds upon and utilizes the concepts learned in the preceding courses of the sequence; (3) understanding mathematics does not depend on life experiences associated with students' age (Bartkovich & George 1980).

However, as traditionally taught, the mathematical curriculum gives more attention to mastery of computation (drill), with less attention to mathematical reasoning. Such a curriculum is almost totally unsuitable for the gifted, who naturally exercise their ability to generalize and transfer ideas, coupled with their mental agility and flexibility in handling data (Greenes 1981). When forced into the conventional lockstep mathematics course of study established in most school systems, mathematically gifted students waste untold hours and run the risk of finding learning itself repugnant.

Bloom's Cognitive Taxonomy serves as an excellent model for mathematics curriculum development for able learners because of its hierarchical nature. Curriculum designers would also do well to include certain aspects of Williams's Teaching Strategies for Thinking and Feeling: paradox, attributes, analogy, discrepancy, provocative questions, examples of change, examples of habit, organized random search, skills of search, intuitive expression, studying creative people and processes, evaluating situations, visualization. Also, particularly for those students who may pursue careers in the physical sciences, Renzulli's Enrichment Triad is appropriate.

Elementary

In the elementary school mathematics curriculum, gifted children should have the opportunity to acquire computation skills but should have more challenging work than page after page of drill. In addition, their instruction in problem solving should have a different emphasis than that of traditional programs (Payne 1981). According to Chen (1981), to properly challenge gifted elementary students and build a solid foundation of concepts and skills, six ideas should be considered:

1. Curriculum should be condensed. Students should prog-

ress through the levels of mathematics at their own pace, without as much repetition as most students require.

To promote rapid progress by gifted students, the school should provide for some individual instruction from the student's classroom teacher, from a classroom teacher of a higher grade, from an older mathematically gifted student, or from a parent or community volunteer. Independent work on the part of the student will also be involved; often, these students can read and work through all or part of various mathematics books on their own. A third component should involve some group instruction with students of similar capability. This may occur during the school year, when the student goes to the middle school or high school for one period a day, during an after-school or Saturday program, or during a summer program. Highly able mathematics students *must not* be forced to endure the same pace of instruction as other students.

2. Students should learn the basic mathematics terminology.

Because mathematically gifted children are fascinated with the subject and sophisticated in their thinking about it, they deserve to be taught as intelligent mathematicians. From the beginning, the correct terminology should be used in instruction. They do not need any kind of watered down curriculum or "cutesy" enticements to enjoy mathematics. They will only be insulted.

3. Not only should students acquire concept, strategy, computational, and relational skills, but should also recognize their application to daily life.

As has been stated frequently, gifted students need real experiences that exemplify their learning. Instead of doing pages of drill concerning hypothetical measurements, these students should go out and actually measure something—obtaining needed information, not just numbers to be written down and dealt with arithmetically (Renzulli: Type III).

4. Mathematically gifted children may need to learn how to express mathematical reasoning in writing. Even though they are good at mental reasoning and computation, they may not be clearly aware of the steps involved in reaching solutions.

As frustrating as it is for bright students to have to explain *how* they arrived at an answer, they should be required to do so. This practice will not only clarify and strengthen their reasoning processes, but it will also teach the discipline required by the professions in which they can apply their mathematical knowledge.

> 5. Mathematical instruction should encourage gifted students to sense commonalities. They should learn to see the underlying principle of converting everything in a mathematical problem into a common system, as is done, for example, in adding unlike fractions.

Computation is often so easy for mathematically gifted students that they do not search for the underlying principle. However, as they get into algebra and geometry and beyond, these underlying principles become important. Teachers must be sure that their own amazement at the computing and reasoning ability of these children does not prevent them from teaching the connections necessary in later mathematics.

> 6. Mathematical instruction should promote the development of independent exploratory behavior. Students should be learning by discovery, with special projects to stimulate the exploration of problem solving. They should be encouraged to discover formulas, to generate problems, to look for patterns, to organize the data, and to express the relationships. (Chen 1981, 10)

Since mathematically gifted children do not need to spend as much time learning the rudimentary aspects of mathematics, they have more time available to apply their knowledge and curiosity. They should be allowed to design their own problems and should be challenged to solve problems at a much high lever than would normally be expected (Bloom: analysis, synthesis; Williams: skills of search).

Secondary

According to a Johns Hopkins University report, for students of high mathematical ability, the best time to intervene is at the end of sixth grade—prior to formal instruction much beyond arithmetic (Waters 1980). In other words, from seventh grade on, students gifted in mathematics should not be in regular mathematics classes, because these classes move too slowly, do not delve deeply into pure mathematics, and require no more than a fraction of the gifted student's abilities to reason mathematically.

Most school districts have only a handful of students so gifted in mathematics that only a program like the one at Johns Hopkins University will properly challenge and teach them. However, most school districts do have enough students in the top 5 to 20 percent of their mathematics classes to warrant providing separate classes for them. Such classes should replace the regular mathematics class, not serve as an "add on." Keller (1980) states that if students are capable of being in a special class for gifted and talented youth, then that should be their regular class. (This should also hold true if the special class is at a local college or university.)

The major goals of a secondary mathematics curriculum for the gifted should include some or all of the following:

1. To teach students to reason for themselves. (Kemeny 1963)

Gifted students should be given difficult problems to solve—with as little guidance as necessary in order to allow them to develop and hone their reasoning skills. Gifted mathematics students can certainly be expected to tackle college-level problems while still in middle school or high school. Working in pairs or teams facilitates the solution of such problems and also helps to develop the reasoning process: students will have to think and argue and support and question their own and others' ideas as they approach a solution.

2. To increase students' interest in mathematics and their understanding and appreciation of both our number system and other numeration systems. (Flagg 1962)

Gifted mathematicians have an understanding of more than just numbers and how those numbers operate in one system. Students need to learn about earlier mathematical systems, systems used by primitive cultures today, systems used by different disciplines, as well as systems which may be adopted in the future. Many resources— human and otherwise—will be tapped in order for students to gain this kind of understanding.

3. To develop problem-solving skills—including the identification of problems to investigate.

As has been emphasized over and over in this chapter, able learners must constantly be learning—and applying that learning to real situations. Mathematics is problem solving, and it lends itself to this type of approach in curriculum development. Students should learn to identify, to formulate, and to articulate problems and ways to search for solutions. The training must involve application of this skill to situations outside the classroom—ideally in what may serve as a student's future workplace (Bloom: Evaluation; Renzulli: Type III).

4. To explore advanced topics in mathematics.

The typical high school mathematics curriculum is far too limiting in scope and sequence, to serve students gifted in mathematics. They must be exposed to and challenged by topics normally reserved for college students and sometimes even for graduate students in mathematics. Curriculum planners must leave part of the curriculum open-ended so that as new students enroll and new resources become available, new challenges can be presented.

> 5. To develop logical-analytical ability. (Hersberger & Wheatley 1980)

The mathematics curriculum must include a substantial component of logical-analytical training, as well as opportunities for application of this training. Youth who are gifted in mathematics tend to be strong in logical ability, which should be fostered so as to serve as a starting point for more advanced instruction in analysis (Bloom: analysis).

> 6. To teach students to accept mistakes and learn how to benefit from them. (Wavrik 1980)

This goal could be a component of nearly any discipline's curriculum, but in mathematics, there are many opportunities for mistakes. The recognition, analysis, and acceptance of these mistakes will promote growth in mathematics—and in other areas (Williams: examples of habit).

> 7. To develop the human mind capacity to understand and interpret numerical, spatial, and logical situations and to approach such problems with a scientific, questioning, and analytic attitude. (Fehr 1974)

This goal almost sums up the others; however, the last line is particularly significant. Budding mathematicians must value the scientific method and the questioning and analysis it engenders. Teachers' attitudes can go a long way in helping to develop this attitude in students (Bloom: analysis, synthesis, evaluation; Williams: provocative questions).

In sum, because mathematics is such a rapidly growing field, the goal of a mathematics curriculum for the gifted must be to develop students' abilities to think mathematically rather than just to increase their store of mathematics information (Wavrik 1980).

Curriculum for the mathematically gifted must move more quickly than for average students, and it must involve active rather than passive problem solving (Wavrik 1980). A solid foundation of mathematical theory and computational fluency must undergird the program.

Standardized testing should be used to determine, not only students' areas of strength, but also their points of weakness, so that the latter can be strengthened. Teachers who are highly trained in mathematics and sensitive to their own and their students' strengths and weaknesses will be most effective with the gifted. For those students who are extremely able, mathematicians, pure or applied, should be found to serve as mentors to guide both exploration and learning. Even though a great deal of effort must be expended to find and arrange mentorships or other means of enriching or accelerating the mathematics curriculum for the gifted, none of this effort will be wasted. In fact, without it, mathematical genius is wasted.

SCIENCE CURRICULUM

The launch of *Sputnik* in 1957 caused those in government and education to take a long, hard look at the quality of education provided in the sciences. For the next several years, money and attention were lavished upon those in the scientific fields—new programs were developed, grants for research were awarded, scholarships were established for students showing promise in the sciences, and science fairs were entered with renewed fervor. Unfortunately, this attention did not last long, and the idea that students with demonstrated aptitude for science should be nurtured did not become firmly entrenched in the minds of school boards, curriculum directors, and teachers. The need for well-educated, conscientious, and creative scientists is even greater now than in 1957. Widespread interest in science education must be restored.

Like children gifted in mathematics, those gifted in science often exhibit distinctive behaviors very early. Following is a comprehensive checklist for identifying these students, along with implications for curriculum.

1. Interest in science during the preschool years.
2. Curiosity as to what makes things work.
3. Ability to understand abstract ideas at an early age.
4. Strong imagination in things scientific.
5. A love of collecting.
6. Abundance of drive—willingness to work on a science project for long periods of time in the face of difficult obstacles.
7. Better than average ability in reading and mathematics.
8. Unusual ability to verbalize ideas about science.
9. High intelligence; IQ of 120 or more.

10. Tendency to think quantitatively—to use numbers to help express ideas.
11. Willingness to master the names of scientific objects.
12. Tendency to write stories about science, including the writing of science fiction.
13. Creativity in science projects and delight in studying science for its own sake.
14. Evident discontent with reasons for things scientific that other children readily accept.
15. Exceptional memory for details.
16. Willingness to spend long periods working alone.
17. Ability to generalize from seemingly unrelated details.
18. Ability to perceive relationships among various elements in a situation. (Marshall 1961, 137)

A well-designed curriculum is necessary to challenge and enhance scientific abilities. All three of the curriculum models discussed in this chapter are appropriate for use in developing science curriculum for able learners. (1) Bloom's Cognitive Taxonomy requires students to use their abilities at the lower levels to progress to the higher levels; this is what one expects to happen in a well-designed science curriculum. (2) Williams's Teaching Strategies for Thinking and Feeling foster creative thinking, which is essential for outstanding performance and productivity in science. (3) Renzulli's Enrichment Triad allows for the development of skills and their application to projects students have deemed worthwhile and interesting; such opportunities often encourage and inspire scientifically able students.

Hurd (in Edwards & Fisher 1977, 26–27) offers eleven characteristics of the scientifically literate person. These are the characteristics that the curriculum should seek to engender and develop.

Powers and Limits of Science

1. The student has faith in the logical processes of science and uses its modes of inquiry, but at the same time recognizes their limitations and the situations for which they are peculiarly appropriate.

Gifted students need to be taught and encouraged to have critical, questioning attitudes toward all facets of life—including science. That is, they should recognize that even science cannot provide ultimate answers. Rather, the structure of the scientific process provides a framework for exploring scientific phenomena.

Elementary students can apply knowledge of hypothesis formation by creating hypothesis boxes. These are real boxes containing objects, and other students formulate predictions concerning their identification. They can use clues relating to size, shape, weight, movement within the box, smell, and any written clues that might be provided (Bloom: analysis, synthesis).

In order to demonstrate that science cannot provide all the answers, have *secondary* students pose questions stimulated by articles in scientific or popular journals (Williams's provocative questions). Such questions might include: At what price comes the cure for cancer? Since cloning is scientifically possible, should it be allowed, and who should make the decisions regarding who or what should be cloned? Once students have posed questions, they should delineate those aspects of the question that go beyond scientific consideration.

The Pleasures of Discovery

2. The student enjoys science for the intellectual stimulus it provides, for the beauty of its explanations, the pleasure that comes from knowing, and the excitement stemming from discovery.

Many people consider science and scientists devoid of excitement and interest. Students need to know of the excitement that comes with discovery—creating a new idea, or seeing years of work come to fruition.

For *elementary* students, excellent biographies of scientists have become available in recent years. These books examine, not only career highlights of scientists, but also the drama of discovery and the effect it has on the discoverer and society. Students should read biographies of scientists and then create a display expressing the value of the discovery to the scientist (Williams: creative reading).

Secondary students often appreciate such journals as *Scientific American*, such books as *The Double Helix*, and such television programs as "Nova" and "Connections." These present specific aspects of science and also portray the invigorating satisfaction of pursuing an idea. Have students identify a recent discovery and, either through reading accounts by the scientist or through personal correspondence, determine the personal triumph that is the reward for the years of sacrifice and work (Williams: creative reading; Renzulli: Type II). Information could be shared through class presentations, either oral or written.

The Interrelatedness of Natural Phenomena

3. The student has more than a commonsense understanding of the natural world.

Gifted children and youth are capable of seeing the relationships that undergird the natural world. As civilization has become more of a global village, it is imperative for gifted youth to realize that small, local actions often have far-reaching implications for the world at large.

Elementary students could explore the world of nature by examining legal restrictions placed on hunting and fishing. Local laws govern the dates of hunting and numbers of animals that can be killed, national laws prohibit hunting and fishing in national parks, and international laws govern such industries as whaling. Often, such codes are controversial. Gifted students could select one law and explore its many ramifications: the need for protection, ethics, economics, human emotions (Renzulli: Type I and Type II). Findings could be submitted to the local newspaper as a feature story (Renzulli: Type III).

Environmental issues also interest *secondary* students. We are constantly altering our environment, and the changes may be viewed as progress or as harmful. Students may concentrate on a controversial local issue—a building project on park land, replacing a historic building with a parking lot, flooding an area to create a lake. They should study all sides of the issue, concentrating first on facts, then on emotions. Representatives of such groups as the corps of engineers and preservation societies should be invited to speak to the class; field trips to the site should be conducted; similar projects and the outcomes should be investigated (Renzulli: Type II). A slide show or debate presenting both sides of the issue should be produced and presented at local service clubs, the library, or similar locations (Renzulli: Type III).

The Interaction of Science and Technology

4. The student appreciates the interaction of science and technology, recognizing that, while they both reflect and stimulate social and economic development, they do not progress at equal rates.

Since society is a composite of social, cultural, economic, scientific, political, religious, intellectual, and esthetic elements, effective leaders of society must understand the interrelationship of these elements. Making connections between science and technology and the other aspects of society will promote such understanding and allow the gifted to grow into their roles as leaders with the strength resulting from sound knowledge.

Elementary students may learn about science and technology by studying the development of the microchip. This tiny element has made possible advancements ranging from the personal computer to space flight. The students could investigate the people who discovered the microchip, those who applied this knowledge, the social effects of various applications of this knowledge, and the related proliferation of competition and technological espionage (Renzulli: Type I). A comprehensive investigation will yield information that can be presented in a variety of ways: a display at the local public library or shopping mall; articles for the school newspaper; a videotape of interviews with people whose lives have been affected by the microchip (Renzulli: Type III).

Secondary students might identify and investigate an example of the paradoxical phenomenon that science and technology do not progress at equal rates. (For example, medical scientists and researchers have determined that some treatments will at least arrest the progress of AIDS. Some of the drugs are slow in being approved—and funded for distribution on a wide scale) (Williams: paradox).

Concepts, Laws, and Theories

> 5. The student is in intellectual possession of some of the major concepts, laws, and theories of several sciences.

Science is more than memorization of rules and rote replication of experiments. Scientifically gifted students should be introduced to the theoretical underpinnings of science and should be expected to explicate the knowledge that provides the scaffolding for the research they are pursuing.

Rival Viewpoints

> 6. The student understands that science is not the only way of viewing natural phenomena, and that even among the sciences there are rival viewpoints.

Gifted students are able to think critically and evaluatively. In order to do so effectively, they must recognize the necessity of investigating all sides of an issue. They must realize that no scientific statement is an absolute truth.

Gifted *elementary* students tend to be very interested in language as an object of reflection. Since numerous theories of the origins of language have been proposed, the exploration of some of these theories and the plausibility of them, would be both instructive and fascinating. Have students interview both peers and adults to determine their view of how language began (Renzulli: Type II). Ask the class to group these suggestions into categories. Then have students read about the theories put forth by linguists (e.g., bow-wow theory, pooh-pooh theory, yo-he-ho theory). Discussion could ensue about the plausibility of these theories. Inviting a linguist to come to the class would serve as an effective culminating activity.

Gifted *secondary* students could be given the task of investigating all dimensions of the evolution/creation debate, one of the more controversial curriculum issues of the 1980s. Issues might include the various theories espoused by different groups, the stance taken by textbook publishers, the position of such organizations as People for the American Way, political ramifications, and the local climate influencing this debate. Students could present the results of their study at a public forum—local climate permitting (Renzulli: Type I, Type II, Type III).

Scientific Revisionism

7. The student appreciates the fact that scientific knowledge grows, possibly without limit, and that the knowledge of one generation "engulfs, upsets, and complements all knowledge of the natural world before."

Scientific knowledge cannot be contained within rigid boundaries because it is amorphous. For this reason, it is ideal as an arena for fostering creativity. Gifted students have a proclivity toward creative thinking and action, which must be encouraged to reach its full potential.

Have *elementary* students break into nine small groups, each choosing a planet for intensive study. Group members are to go to the library for books, encyclopedias, and magazines from the 1940s, 1950s, 1960s, 1970s, and 1980s. Each group should note the significant discoveries about their planet during each decade. Students will see the advances that have been made in only five decades. As a way to demonstrate how rapidly knowledge about the planets is being revised during the 1980s, each group should read accounts of the information gathered by *Voyager II*. A two-tier time line should be devised by each group, the top tier to present information known during each decade and the bottom tier providing information regarding the same phenomenon that is now known or speculated (Williams: examples of change).

Secondary students can identify the knowledge that has resulted from the discovery, in the 1930s, that splitting atoms could start a chain reaction. This breakthrough has caused some of the most revolutionary changes in scientific thought. The social-emotional-moral consequences of the application of this knowledge should also be examined by the able students (Bloom: analysis, synthesis, evaluation).

Cutting-Edge Concepts and Popular Understanding

8. The student appreciates the essential lag between frontier research and the popular understanding of new achievements, as well as the importance of narrowing the gap.

Scientific research is always expensive—in both time and money. In order to garner the resources to support this research, the populace must be convinced of its value. Science-gifted students will need to know how to obtain this support.

Elementary students have heard news reports of heart transplants, whether with human hearts or mechanical devices. The risks of such operations for patients and difficulties in obtaining and allocating donor organs have led doctors and the public at large to raise questions of ethics. Students should investigate the research being done concerning the heart, the long-term goals of such research, and the possible benefits of the publicity. A poll could be conducted to determine public and medical response to both the research and the publicity (Renzulli: Type II).

Secondary students who have watched space launches may know that the National Aeronautics and Space Administration (NASA) has fluctuated in popularity with both the public and the politicians who approve funding for it. Students should trace the history of NASA along three avenues: the scientific discoveries, the social/economic/political climate, and the popular programs (Williams: attributes, organized random search). The interaction of these should lead to conclusions that can form the base for an oral or written presentation.

The Proper Uses of Science

9. The student recognizes that the achievements of science and technology, properly used, are basic to the improvement of human welfare.

The scientifically gifted must learn to be not only scientists but humanists. Teachers and/or scientific mentors need to stress the connection between discoveries of science and technology and improvements in everyday life.

Have *elementary* students choose one discovery of science around which to trace a web of influence. For example, chemical fertilizer is linked with food supply, nutrition, and social patterns (Williams: evaluate situations).

Secondary students, who will be adult citizens in the late twentieth century and early twenty-first century, need to consider the ramifications (both positive and negative) of nuclear energy. Have students invite guest speakers, write to government agencies and private sources for documentation concerning nuclear energy, and read the popular and scientific magazines on this topic. A class bulletin board, display, or journal should be kept to chronicle the propaganda used by both proponents and opponents of nuclear energy. Students should also record changes in their own beliefs, if any (Williams: adjustment to development).

Process and Product

10. The student recognizes that the meaning of science depends as much on the inquiry process as on its conceptual patterns and theories.

Able students tend to enjoy learning for its own sake. The sciences hold possibilities for discovery that may or may not serve humankind—but are valuable nonetheless, because of the addition they make to knowledge.

The Culture of Science

11. The student understands the role of the scientific enterprises in society and appreciates the cultural conditions under which they thrive.

Gifted children and youth are probably better able than others to understand that nothing exists free of connections to the society.

In order for *elementary* students to recognize that the economic climate of the United States promotes scientific discoveries, they should choose a technological advance in which they are interested (cameras, plastics, telephones). Each student should investigate the progression of each invention and the role played by competition.

As *secondary* students pursue their investigation of space research, they may learn that Carl Sagan and others believe the most efficacious plan for space exploration to be a joint effort amongst technically advanced countries. Have students extrapolate about the possibilities for achievement if these countries worked together—sharing knowledge and resources (Williams: evaluate situations, intuitive expression).

Often, gifted children enter school with, or acquire very rapidly, scientific information exceeding the knowledge of their elementary teachers. Herein lies one reason that teachers of the gifted need to be self-assured—so that, rather than being threatened by students who know more than they do, they can marvel at them, and direct them to people who are more informed in each particular area of interest. Scientifically gifted children need science teachers who are knowledgeable about science and who are excited about their subject (Anderson 1961; Martin 1979).

Children gifted in science, or potentially gifted in science, need an abundance of "real" experiences with the discipline. These experiences could involve serving as a student docent at a science museum (Ryder 1972), pinpointing and investigating a real-life problem (McCauley 1984; Strobert & Alvarez 1982), sending experiments on a space shuttle mission (Saunders et al. 1979), participating in a science fair (Boyd 1968; Wiszowaty 1961), or having hands-on experience at a science center (Cooper 1973; Davis 1981; Kegley et al. 1984; LaSalle 1979). Scientifically gifted children and youth usually have several interests in the area of science, and a wise teacher will guide those interests and provide opportunities for them to flourish and develop.

When school districts do not provide for the gifted in science, then it is up to parents and other community members to grab the reins and make sure that something is available outside of school to encourage scientific talent. Such a program may be offered during the summer (see McTighe 1979), or it may be provided on weekends or evenings by members of the community who recognize the need for abundant opportunity to learn in the field of science (Pinelli 1977).

Although one may not think of science as a creative field, it is, and this is one reason that those gifted in this area need much stimulation and encouragement, from the time they first express an interest. In order for science to go beyond what is already known, scientists must be divergent thinkers; they must be willing to take risks and break the bonds of rigid thinking. Helping youngsters who are interested in science become more creative may well further their scientific accomplishment (Kopelman et al. 1977; Pinelli 1977).

In a science curriculum designed for gifted students, the key word is *freedom*—freedom from textbooks, freedom from classrooms, freedom from pattern-bound thinking, freedom from restrictions of time, money, and support. Able students need to see and experience the work of scientists—they need to participate with researchers who may spend hours watching a cell, who may spend days logging methods and conclusions of an experiment, or who use tiny brushes to clean specimens from an archaeological "dig." In short, these gifted students need to be scientists in training. In no other academic field is the notion of apprenticeship so apt.

All gifted students are not gifted in science, but those who are must be nurtured and challenged and encouraged from the beginning of their schooling (which could commence before they enter a formal school setting). The nation and the world need the answers these young people can grow up to find. People, time, and resources should be allocated to ensure that these "science gifted" are able and motivated to search for those answers.

SOCIAL SCIENCE CURRICULUM

> social: 1. of or having to do with human beings living together as a group in a situation requiring that they have dealings with one another.

As defined by *Webster's Deluxe Unabridged Dictionary* (Simon & Schuster, 1983), the term *social* has a broad meaning; likewise, social science, or the study of society, encompasses a broad collection of disciplines. Traditionally, social science has included, at the very least, sociology, history, civics, and economics. In a less narrow sense, social science, or social studies, may be defined as the study of people and how they live together, including the structure of their society and members' functions within that society. In this sense, it can be seen that, in addition to the disciplines listed above, social studies may also include future studies, anthropology, psychology, philosophy, and the humanities—which in turn includes a broad range of subjects, such as English, music, and art.

In part of one chapter, it is impossible to adequately treat curriculum development for a branch of knowledge as global as social science, which comprises so many interrelated disciplines. Thus, many generalizations will be made concerning curriculum in this area. Readers interested in the specifics should refer to the extensive bibliography for this section.

According to Joyce, the social studies curriculum and method of instruction can influence three different aspects of education:

1. Intellectual education, which has as its purpose "to introduce children to the modes of thinking of the social scientist." (1972, 2)
2. Social education, which has as its purpose "to prepare citizens who can perpetuate and improve their society." (1972, 4)
3. Personal education, which has as its purpose "to help the child sort out the confusion of the social world and thus find meaning for his/her life." (1972, 7)

These three aspects are compatible with each other and can serve as reference points for implementing the curriculum and the activities designed for use in teaching the social studies. In addition, Bloom's Cognitive Taxonomy, Williams' Teaching Strategies for Thinking and Feeling, and Renzulli's Enrichment Triad can (and should) all be used in planning and implementing social studies curricula for able learners.

The following statements represent an attempt by Ellis to iterate some general goals of social studies instruction and thereby to provide a rationale for this area of the curriculum.

1. Social studies should help learners to come to a greater awareness of themselves, to clarify and examine their values, and to establish a sense of self-identity.
2. Social studies should provide learners with an understanding of past events and persons and of their roles in shaping present-day lives.
3. Social studies should promote in learners a concern for the development of an understanding and acceptance of others with different values and life-styles.
4. Social studies should provide learners with a knowledge of human systems in the areas of economics, government, and culture.
5. Social studies should provide learners with the skills necessary to carry out the independent investigation of problems and to react critically to the solutions posed by others.
6. Social studies should provide learners with an awareness of possible futures and the roles they might play in shaping those futures.
7. Social studies should provide learners with an appreciation of people's efforts to improve the human condition through creative expression and problem solving.
8. Social studies should provide learners with an understanding of the decision-making processes involved in human interaction and with the skills necessary to become effective decision makers.

9. Social studies should provide learners with the ability to utilize both cooperative and competitive circumstances for the achievement of goals.
10. Social studies should provide learners with a sensitivity toward their own potentials and toward the potentials of their fellow human beings. (Ellis 1977, 17)

Obviously, social science presents virtually unlimited possibilities for teaching and learning. Gifted students may explore their own nature, their place in society, and others who make up that society. Herein lies the need for well-developed social studies curriculum for gifted students: they should become vital, vibrant components of society, and understanding social dynamics will enhance the part they can play.

As with subject areas discussed in previous sections, the key to social studies curriculum for the gifted lies in challenging these students to draw on their extraordinary abilities to generalize and see connections between various events, people, and situations. To help in curriculum planning, we will restate the ten goals cited above, add related commentary, and suggest ideas that incorporate the key notion—first for elementary and then for secondary students.

Self-Awareness

1. Social studies should help learners to come to a greater awareness of themselves, to clarify and examine their values, and to establish a sense of self-identity.

Highly able students need to be aware of who they are, including their potentials and limitations, and they need to define the morals and values by which they will live. A strong sense of self will not only enable them to be happier and more productive members of society but will also counteract the enticements of cults and drugs.

Have *elementary* students create a webbing that illustrates their relationship to others—their place in others' lives and the effect that they have on others. This activity has as its purpose to demonstrate to the children their significance as members of society and their potential impact (Renzulli: Type II).

Require *secondary* students to investigate some cult that is presently active in the United States. Their research should include determining the groups' goals and objectives, tactics of enticing members, difficulty with which members can "quit" the group, and the characteristics of those targeted for recruitment. This information could be shared with other classes or with the entire student body (Renzulli: Type III). Students should be asked to assess themselves and their vulnerability to a group such as those reported on.

Past and Present

2. Social studies should provide learners with an understanding of past events and persons and of their roles in shaping present-day lives.

Gifted children should study creative people, the events that shaped their lives, and the events they helped to shape. The students need to see connections between the people and events of the past with the people and events of the present.

Have *elementary* students read several biographies of a person who was a leader in a political, economic, or social movement. They should also find newspaper or magazine coverage regarding this same person. The various viewpoints should be noted by students, along with speculation concerning the variance discovered. As a framework for presenting the information gathered through reading, students should trace the web of people and events that shaped their focus on the person's life (Williams: creative reading, intuitive expression; Renzulli: Type II; Bloom: conceivably every level).

Secondary students should choose either one key historical event or one key person in history to investigate. If they choose an event, they should determine the effect this one event had on all the key people connected with it. If they choose a key person, they should do a time line showing the events and people that influenced this person. Students should speculate on how things might have turned out differently had a particular event or person been absent (Bloom: analysis, synthesis, evaluation; Williams: intuitive expression).

Multiculturalism

3. Social studies should promote in learners a concern for the development of an understanding and acceptance of others with different values and life-styles.

The United States is a conglomeration of races, cultures, value systems, religious beliefs, and life-styles. Tolerance, and indeed nurturance, of these differences is what makes our country unique and strong. Gifted students must develop their understanding and acceptance of cultural differences, because those whose leadership skills are developed have the potential to foster tolerance and open-mindedness among many citizens of the country, and in some instances, the world.

Have *elementary* students discuss the concept of stereotypes and brainstorm stereotypes they have heard about various groups of people (Renzulli: Type II). Type a master list and have students respond "agree" or "disagree" to each item. Have them administer this same checklist to each of their parents. They should compare the answers of their parents and then compare their parents' answers with their own. Have students hypothesize about noticeable similarities and/or differences between the ratings. Then, have each student choose one stereotype to check out for frequency (Renzulli: Type I or II).

Secondary students (or pairs of students) are to choose any race, religion, culture, or life-style different from their own and investigate it in depth through a combination of library research, interviews, and observations. This information is to be presented to the class primarily in some form other than a written report. Depending on the teacher's guidance, this activity could involve many levels of Bloom's schema, numerous teaching strategies of William's, and all of Renzulli's types.

Economics, Government, and Culture

4. Social studies should provide learners with a knowledge of human systems in the areas of economics, government, and culture.

Highly able students make connections and see interrelationships more readily than do other students. Their exposure to and exploration of economic, government, and cultural systems should always be comparative and contrastive: How are these similar? How are these different?

As *elementary* students study different countries, have them keep a chart concerning various aspects of the government—with headings such as Type; Governing Body (name and function); Head of State (function); No. of Years This Type of Government Has Existed.

This chart could be kept as a class project (Bloom: comprehension, application, analysis). Individual students would be expected to draw on their knowledge of a country and the conditions there so as to write a page or two summarizing the effect of this type of government on the country and its people. Students could be asked to hypothesize about what effect a different type of government would have on the particular country.

Secondary students could be taught about various economic systems that have existed in the last millenium. In addition to reading and discussing these systems, they may be required to conceive of and develop a three-dimensional visual model to demonstrate various similarities and differences between these numerous economic systems (Bloom: analysis; Williams: visualization).

Research and Evaluation

5. Social studies should provide learners with the skills necessary to carry out the independent investigation of problems and to critically evaluate the solutions posed by others.

This objective ties in with Renzulli's concern that gifted children need to be involved in finding solutions to real problems, not in expanding energy to solve bogus, contrived problems.

Elementary students could concentrate on their own "real world"—their school. It is fairly rare to find a school that is not in need of some type of equipment or service that is beyond the range of its budget. Students who pinpoint a need could learn about politics, leadership, economics, and organization by leading a campaign to obtain a needed item or service. For example, if students wanted software that the school could not purchase, and they decided that they were willing to work very hard to make sure the money was raised to buy it, a real situation would exist—with a real problem and a real solution (Renzulli: Type III). Learning experiences might come about (1) as students tried to convince other students, parents, teachers, and administrators of the need; (2) as possible ways to earn money were suggested, discussed, accepted, or rejected; (3) as accepted avenues were explored; (4) as tasks were delegated and those given the tasks encouraged in their duties; (5) as money began to come in and had to be accounted for; (6) as shopping for the software was conducted; (7) as those dissatisfied with the purchase had to be placated.

Gifted *secondary* students' verbal abilities lend themselves to immersion in the social studies. Extensive reading—from sources far beyond the textbook—should be expected. Gifted students in a history class should have the experience of ferreting out and reading original documents and other primary sources (Renzulli: Types I and II). They should conduct interviews and collect oral histories. Historical fiction, if not already enjoyed by these students, should be introduced, and its reading encouraged. The class should have opportunities to write for real audiences; history clubs, explorer groups, and historical preservation societies would enjoy having bright, young, enthusiastic members to contribute to their newsletters, brochures, or magazines, or to speak to members at a meeting (Renzulli: Type III).

Teachers should enlist the aid of these groups in finding other "real" experiences for their gifted students. For example, if a group is planning to go to an archaeological dig site, and space is available for two more people, a call to a history teacher at the local high school or to the sponsor of the high school archaeology club could give two young people the opportunity to experience a dig.

Real experiences such as these also have implications for gifted students' career choices. That is, since most people have the Hollywood notion that archaeologists discover ancient ruins and unearth golden pitchers and bracelets, the image of an archaeologist seems rather exciting and glamorous. However, by going on a real dig, students can see the months of careful planning, the days of backbreaking work, the hours of tedious classification, and the meticulous minutes of using tiny brushes to gently uncover a shard of a vase—all balanced by the thrill of learning more about other peoples and cultures.

Future Studies

> 6. Social studies should provide learners with an awareness of possible futures and the roles they might play in shaping those futures.

Future studies focus on our most vital concern—tomorrow, the place where we are all going to spend the rest of our lives (Flack & Feldhusen 1983). Properly planned, a future-studies course or unit can serve as an hourglass for gifted students: information, philosophy, and experience gathered through broad exposure in the social studies are channeled through a narrow passage and then run unfettered through the large expanse of the bulb to be used in solving real problems of the future. Many school districts employ a future-studies component as part of their gifted curriculum. This component may or may not include participation in the Future Problem-Solving Bowl (see, e.g., Hoomes 1984), which began in one high school in Georgia in 1974 and has now expanded to over 100,000 participants nationwide.

Gifted students who take part in future-studies activities and projects that are part of a well-designed and thoughtfully planned curriculum are motivated to think creatively, to read, to write, to ponder, to produce—in other words, to become involved in their learning. Students involved in their learning are likely to learn more and are likely to remain learners.

Have *elementary* students create a "Future _____" bulletin board (e.g., "Future Food," "Future Clothing," "Future Government"). Students should do research concerning the focus of the bulletin board and construct a display related to their findings. (For example, soft drinks will not be in aluminum cans because all the aluminum will be gone. Instead, containers will be made from _____). Students should create a model wherever appropriate (Bloom: synthesis, evaluation).

Have *secondary* students read articles from *The Futurist* or some other "futures" magazines. A list of real concerns for the future should be generated and students allowed to form groups based on common interests in these concerns. As a means of gaining insight into the problem and the solutions being considered, students should contact professionals who are addressing the problems and/or the issues related to these problems (e.g., transportation, housing, food, garbage disposal) (Renzulli: Type I, II, and III). Articles for the school or local newspaper could be based on this research.

Humanities

7. Social studies should provide learners with an appreciation of people's efforts to improve the human condition through creative expression and problem solving.

A multidisciplinary opportunity for learning about other peoples and cultures is provided through the humanities. Lindsay defines the humanities as "the study of the natural interrelationships of several different human endeavors, intellectual, social, spiritual, perhaps even aesthetic" (1981, 6). Because the gifted are able to make connections and see relationships, the humanities provide a marvelous focus for their studies, especially in secondary school. An entire gifted program could be developed using the humanities as the core (see Perdue 1980). Lindsay states emphatically:

> The Humanities is the manifestation of the human spirit, the conduit through which Man enters, lives in, and leaves the world. Ultimately, Man is spiritual; the Humanities is the embodiment of that spirit. Through the Humanities, Man understands himself, his environment, and all the creatures in it, his culture, his planet, his cosmos. Through the Humanities, and only through the Humanities does man become ultimately educated. (1981, 9)

The gifted need to be ultimately educated—both for their sakes and for the sake of the rest of society.

Elementary school teachers should actively work to provide their young students with the opportunities to attend plays, musicals, symphonies, and art galleries. Classes could sometimes attend such a function as a group, but more desirable would be to arrange for one or two children to attend with someone who is an aficionado of the arts. In this manner, children are more likely to get the flavor of involvement in such activities (whereas attending with a whole class becomes more of an outing, with a field trip atmosphere). Prior to attending the symphony, for example, the students should be expected to find out about the composer, the period during which the music was written, and the social impact of its presentation. (Depending on the requirements, this could involve any number of Williams's Teaching Strategies and virtually any level of Bloom's Taxonomy.)

Whether in a *secondary* school class entitled Humanities or one entitled English or Social Studies, when gifted students study a particular period, they should be exposed to as many of its aspects as possible—the literature, the art, the social movements, the music, the people. This type of instruction helps able students see relationships and make connections (Williams: analogy, examples of change).

Decision Making

8. Social studies should provide learners with an understanding of the decision-making processes involved in human interaction and with the skills necessary to become effective decision makers.

Making judicious decisions and defending those decisions is part of mature adult life. Decisions that have to be made range from determining what time to get up in the morning to deciding whether to push the button that could trigger world destruction. Able students should be given practice making and defending real decisions—and in projecting themselves into possible scenarios where they make and defend hypothetical decisions.

As a group, elementary students could decide upon guidelines for classroom conduct. Depending on the ages and desires of the students, consequences for infractions could be predetermined, or members of the class could be chosen to determine the consequences on a case-by-case basis.

Secondary students who are interested in various professions could find people working in those professions to interview regarding the decisions they have to make. Students should be encouraged to probe deeply, particularly concerning what factors are weighed and the consequences of an incorrect decision. This information could be presented to career education classes or run as a series of articles in the school newspaper (Renzulli: Type I, II, and III).

Cooperation and Competition

9. Social studies should provide learners with the ability to utilize both cooperative and competitive circumstances for the achievement of goals.

In the quest to attain one's goals, both cooperation and competition are inherent. For highly able children and youth not to strive for high goals is to waste their extraordinary ability.

Have *elementary* students choose two states apiece. The students are to find out the capital of each of these states, learn the information themselves, and convey it to other members of the class. At the end of a week or ten days, students will be tested on their ability to name the capital of each of the "sponsored" states. Each student's grade will be based, not only on individual scores, but also on how well everyone else knew the capitals he or she was teaching. Students will achieve the goals of learning the states' capitals and of receiving high grades through both competition and cooperation.

During a political campaign, have *secondary* students choose a local, state, or national politician. After listening to the words of the candidate, the students should be expected to determine three to five personal or professional goals that have been espoused (Williams: creative listening). Next, students should determine how these goals can be reached, using a form such as the one illustrated below.

Goal:_____

_____

Cooperation necessary	Competition necessary
_____	_____
_____	_____
_____	_____
_____	_____
_____	

If at all possible, students should contact their candidate for a reaction to their assessment.

Human Potential

> 10. Social studies should provide learners with a sensitivity to-
>   ward their own potentials and toward the potentials of
>   their fellow human beings.

Gifted children and youth need to have an accurate concept of their own capabilities so that they neither underestimate nor overestimate their ability. And, likewise, they need sensitivity to the potential of others so that in their personal and professional dealings with other human beings, optimum performance can be expected and elicited from those persons with whom they come in contact, both profession-ally and personally.

Have *elementary* students work with a partner on the following proj-ect. Instruct them to elicit their partners' strengths through means other than question and answer (Bloom: analysis, synthesis). Each stu-dent is then to design a unique way to present the partner to the class so that all members can recognize and encourage each others' strengths.

Have *secondary* students write an in-depth autobiography in which they delve into such questions as the following: (1) What are my strengths, and do I capitalize on them? (2) What are my weaknesses, and how can I either compensate for them or transform them into strengths? (3) In what ways do I influence those around me—and is my influence emanating from my strengths or from my weaknesses? After completing this exercise, students should represent themselves metaphorically on a flag or banner that can be displayed in the room or library (Williams: analogy).

In order for society to go on—to be available for study—learning must continue so that answers to problems can be found—peacefully. Strong social science education for the gifted must be provided.

COMPUTER CURRICULUM

The field of computer technology—uses, functions, design, program-ming—is changing and growing so rapidly that nearly anything writ-ten about computers is dated before it is published. The uses of the computer in education are expanding just as rapidly. Keeping up with the changes and trying to design curriculum to adequately serve stu-dents' future needs involves an attempt to hit a moving target. It is nec-essary to aim where it will be, not where it is, judging the speed of the target in relation to the speed of the projectile (Kibler & Campbell

1976). This phenomenon alone should provide the impetus for schools and school districts to provide students with the tools to become computer literate.

Computer literacy involves a high "level of knowledge derived from the combination of a philosophical and social understanding of computers and a significant amount of hands-on experience with computers and computer programs" (Pantiel & Petersen 1984, 11). Computer literacy is therefore much more extensive than mere computer awareness, which refers to a "very rudimentary understanding of computers, including basic definitions of hardware, software, the components of a computer system, and the mechanics of how to turn the machine on and access information" (Pantiel & Petersen 1984, 11). Computer literacy—not just computer awareness—is required "to function effectively in a society increasingly dependent on computer and information technology" (Coburn 1982 in Roberts 1985, 37). Beginning in the late 1980s, students who graduate from high school without basic computer literacy skills will be at a similar, albeit a less severe, disadvantage as students who graduate unable to read and write. It is imperative that gifted students not be at any kind of disadvantage as they enter postsecondary education and their ensuing careers.

As in other academic disciplines, able learners must go beyond the normal curriculum in computer education. They must be expected to think and perform at high levels, to be creative, and to prepare for challenging educational opportunities and careers. Any or all of the three curriculum models discussed in this chapter can serve as guides for those people responsible for curriculum development. Bloom's Cognitive Taxonomy is appropriate because it requires progression in higher-level thinking and performance. Williams's Teaching Strategies for Thinking and Feeling can be used to design particular lessons, although it would not be appropriate as the sole model. Renzulli's Enrichment Triad is ideal because of its emphasis on developing thinking and production skills that lead to the creation of real products. Able students who are learning to use the computer, and those who are learning subject matter with the aid of a computer, need to develop skills that will serve as tools to further both their learning and their productivity.

Elementary

As anyone with a preschooler and a computer at home can attest, three- or four-year-olds are not too young to begin using a computer.

Just as young children's "writing" more closely approximates adult writing as the children mature, so too does children's "writing" on the computer. For example, the gifted daughter of a friend of the authors' began writing on the computer by pushing down one key and holding it. Next, she put a space between groups of the same letter. Her next step was to type spaces between groups of different letters. (She is not yet three years old). It can be expected that, before too long, she will type words she knows mixed in with groups of letters. Gifted pre-schoolers, if at all possible, should have the opportunity to use a computer, even though at first they do not view it as anything other than a toy.

Beginning in elementary school, school districts must offer computer courses for their young gifted patrons (Fiday 1983; Kirk 1983). If they do not already have the knowledge, they should learn the rudimentary aspects of computers (using prepared game and educational software). Simple programming should follow immediately so that children begin to develop a sense of the logic involved in "telling a computer what to do." Once these children have mastered the elementary aspects of the computer, they should quickly be taught the more advanced programming languages and techniques (Hampton 1980; Wiebe 1981).

Another facet of computer use that should be introduced and stressed is word processing. Although some adult authors (who have always written longhand on legal paper, or whatever) refuse to switch to word processing—or find themselves unable to switch—many have found word processing much more satisfactory and efficient for both composing and revising. For young children whose major aversion to writing stems not from lack of ideas but from the effort necessary to get the ideas from head to pencil to paper, word processing is a boon that should not be withheld. Typing one's story or report into a computer, being able to revise on the screen or from hard copy, and then printing out a final clean copy is definitely preferable to the previous alternatives. Gifted students, whose minds often race far beyond their hands' ability to write, can be more productive if they use word-processing software proficiently.

Whenever possible, gifted students should be instructed in separate classes because generally they will be able to progress more quickly than others. In addition, their instruction should be designed to enhance their creativity and problem-solving ability (Jensen & Wedman 1983). Dirkes (1985) points out that computers aid in the development of problem-solving skills because students are given the opportunity (1) to select the problems they want to solve; (2) to produce divergent solutions; (3) to try out alternatives; and (4) to evaluate these alternatives.

Anyone who doubts that the computer can be used to enhance logical thinking, problem solving, and analytical reasoning need only peruse such software-review columns as "Bytes for Brights" (*G/C/T*) or go to a full-scale software store and ask about the "game" and educational software available. Careful reading of the books available would also serve to convince the nonbeliever that the computer offers endless possibilities for enhancing the abilities of gifted students.

Secondary

At the secondary level, the possibilities for instruction are virtually boundless for gifted students. During high school, able students' strengths and areas of interest are solidifying. A computer educational plan that takes this fact into consideration is necessary. For example, students whose expertise and interest lie in the hard sciences need exposure to and experience with computer programs that handle scientific data. Although software is available for personal computers, it is desirable for scientifically gifted students to work with chemists, physicists and others who use large computers in a university or corporate setting. Nearly every field utilizes computers in one capacity or another, and able students who are headed toward a career in a particular field should have the chance to begin to specialize their computer skills.

One aspect of learning about and with computers that needs to be addressed in the curriculum is the question of ethics. Should all computer programs become part of the public domain? Should companies buy one software package and then duplicate it for all their employees to use? Should friends share software programs that they have purchased with one another? Should punitive action be taken against students who "break into" large companies' computers? The topics of a "computer ethics" course lend themselves well to the creation of Renzulli's Type III products by gifted students: letters to the editor (of computer periodicals), ethics guidebooks for high school computer users, a minicourse for younger gifted students on the "rights" and "wrongs" of computer privacy, suggestions to software manufacturers for ways to prevent users from infringing on copyrighted material.

The computer curriculum for gifted students needs to begin early and to provide for rapid advancement. Once students attain basic literacy, a great deal of individual freedom to advance and develop in their own areas of interest should be allowed. For mature students, an ethics component should be included along with continued instruction and freedom of exploration. If career education is a part of the school's curriculum, the computer department should be involved so as to make sure that students are well-informed regarding the almost infinite ways computer technology meshes with and is required by various careers. Gifted young adults, as they enter the workplace, need to be forward-thinking, competent, and responsible users of computers. An appropriate curriculum will ensure this.

CAREER EDUCATION

In this era of budget cuts, incessant cries of getting "back to the basics," and feverish attempts to pare down the curriculum to its essential elements, advocates of career education must stand firmly together or their programs will be sliced off along with other so-called "extraneous" curricula. The irony of this situation is that career education enhances "the basics," because when students understand the need for these skills in adult roles, learning them becomes more meaningful (Fox 1976). Because of its emphasis on real situations and real life, Renzulli's Enrichment Triad is the most appropriate curriculum model for career education. Nearly every example given in this section is designed to have students explore careers, develop the skills needed for a particular career, or begin work in a chosen field. In other words, the ideas are either Type I, Type II, or Type III.

OrRico and Feldhusen (1979) define career education as a process that helps individuals recognize and understand their interests, abilities, and motivations as these relate to occupations. Herr (1976) reviewed the appropriate literature and concluded that the term *career education* has come to include at least the following nine notions. (Each of the nine is followed by a statement regarding career education for the gifted.)

Academic and Vocational Correlation

1. Career education involves an effort to diminish the separateness of academic and vocational education.

Many highly able students see little or no connection between their schooling and their other interests, including career aspirations. Career education, which involves taking gifted individuals' areas of strength and interest into consideration, can do much to indicate the connection between school and work.

Some gifted young children already know "what they want to be when they grow up," but of course, many do not, nor should that be a goal of elementary career education. A special bulletin board could be set aside in elementary classrooms for the sole purpose of indicating relationships between skills being learned in class and various jobs and careers. Highly able students could be put in charge of the research needed to keep this bulletin board current and interesting. For example, if addition is being taught, then the able students would make a list of jobs where knowing how to add is important. For example, business people have to add up their expense accounts, grocery store managers have to add the number of hours their employees are working, real estate agents have to add up all the costs involved in buying a house. Sometimes, the relationship will be obscure and the students will have to use more of their resources to make the connections.

By the time students are in high school, many will have at least a vague idea of future career intentions. For a career education project, they could keep a log of all the skills they have learned or honed during one month in school. Then they should attempt to determine how these skills will enable them to function more effectively in their chosen career. If they are unable, they should go to the teacher in whose class the skill was taught and ask for help in making the connection.

Starting Early

2. Career education is an area of concern that has some operational implications for every educational level or grade from kindergarten through graduate school.

Because of the potential for extraordinary accomplishment possessed by highly able students, kindergarten is not too early to begin talking about various jobs and what they entail. Teachers must not assume that, since they themselves have found their career niche, their students have. And, today, there are more different kinds of jobs available than ever before. Undergraduate school is too late to begin to explore the possibilities.

Employability

3. Career education should ensure that every person exiting the formal educational system has skills in a job of some type.

In this portion of career education, gifted students may evaluate their areas of expertise and interest so as to decide whether they should lead to a vocation or an avocation. For example, a verbally gifted student who is enamored of medieval English literature and decides to pursue that interest in college needs to be aware that, while there are job opportunities for someone with a bachelor's degree of this sort, they are very limited if what one wants to do is continue exploring this field. But if the student recognizes this fact and decides to sacrifice long enough to complete a Ph.D. in this specialty, then it can be both a vocation and an avocation. On the other hand, a student who decides that the risk of finding a job perfectly suited to so narrow a specialization is too great may opt for a degree in English, focusing on linguistics, with the intention of pursuing a career in audiology, meanwhile continuing to enjoy reading the favored literature and possibly organizing a group of other enthusiasts to discuss their mutual interests.

Individual Choice

4. Career education involves a direct response to the importance of facilitating individual choice making so that occupational preparation and acquisition of basic academic skills can be coordinated with developing individual preference.

No one, least of all gifted individuals, should feel locked into either a career choice or a particular job. This can be prevented through adequate introduction to the available options and through explorations of those options that prove appealing. In many instances, this introduction is primarily an expansion of the students' horizons, which may be limited due to parental expectation (or lack thereof).

Making Studies More Meaningful

5. Career education is a way of extending relevant or meaningful education to greater numbers of students.

For students at the secondary level, school is often seen as little more than a babysitting service or a place to "put in one's time" before college or a job. Especially for gifted students who are not receiving differentiated education, high school is seen as a restraint—preventing them from doing what they really want to do. Far better if a means can be set up to help students assess their abilities and interests and apply them toward preparation for their life's work. Courses or projects could be set up to help them learn what will be necessary in their chosen career. Also, teachers can be made aware of their students' interests and can make a conscious effort to demonstrate how their lessons are applicable.

Opening the School to "Second-Chance" Students

6. Career education is a design to render education an open system in that school leavers, school dropouts, and adults can reaffiliate when their personal circumstances or job requirements make this feasible.

Students who leave school come from every social strata and intellectual level. It is a misconception that only below-average students from poor homes drop out of school. There is a high incidence of school leaving among highly able and/or creative students—often because their schooling has been totally inappropriate and has therefore been seen as a waste of time and effort.

Some of these students either begin to work in a job related to their area of interest, or they get a job far below their ability or far removed from their area of giftedness. Fortunately, many then realize that until they complete their education, their opportunities for advancement (in position, responsibility, and knowledge) and/or their possibilities for convergence on their area of expertise are limited. When this realization leads to action—that is, seeking out opportunities for school re-entry—the facilities and personnel need to be available so that these students can finally receive education appropriate for their abilities, schedules, and career aspirations.

Community Involvement

7. Career education involves a structure whose desired outcomes necessitate cooperation among all elements of education as well as among school, industry, and community.

To be most effective, career education should be a joint effort between students, the school, and the community (which includes representatives of business, industry, professional, and service jobs and careers). Teaching about careers without introducing students to the physical reality of those careers is like teaching about basketball without allowing students to see and touch a real basketball. Those school persons primarily responsible for career education must cultivate relationships with community members—from jobs that span the whole spectrum of careers. These people, especially those in personnel and management, realize the need for potential employees to be trained as fully as possible. Most will not only take time from their schedules but will also help make arrangements for site visits, class speakers, and internships. Community members know (or need to be informed) that the effort they expend now will be repaid by more productive, better prepared, happier employees later.

New Technologies

    8. Career education is an enterprise requiring new technologies and educational materials, such as individualized programming and simulations.

Career education should not include haphazard, slapdash instruction. Teachers committed to the concept of career education for the gifted should be hired and should be given the resources and the freedom to create a curriculum that is current and appropriate for the students and community being served. The movements toward more service jobs and more work involving technology must be reflected in the courses and overall curriculum.

Educational Worth

    9. Career education is a form of education for all students.

Consider the following theses:

    a. The primary function of education is to prepare students to live full productive, satisfying lives.
    b. Life satisfaction, for most American adults, is at least partially if not totally contingent upon vocational and avocational satisfaction.
    c. A prudent decision concerning career choice is more likely to be made by a person who is informed about various careers and their respective requirements.
    d. Career education is "a joint effort of the education system and the broader community aimed at helping individuals acquire and utilize the knowledge, skills, and attitudes necessary for each to make work a meaningful, productive, and satisfying part of his or her way of living." (Hoyt 1978, 9)

If one accepts these four premises, then one also must accept the following conclusion: career education has a vital place in the curriculum—for all youngsters, not excluding the gifted.

Fox (1976) sees three stages in career education. The first, which should be a part of the elementary school curriculum, involves helping students develop an awareness of the world of work. The second, which is appropriate for the middle school curriculum, entails career exploration—finding out about a broad cross-section of careers, with in-depth investigation of a few. The third stage, which has its place in the secondary curriculum, is career preparation. Students at this stage are actually pursuing the courses that they have determined are necessary in order to enter their prospective career. (Such choices are made with significant guidance from counselors, teachers, and persons working in said career.) At this point, also, students should be actively searching out the postsecondary schools that will best prepare them for their chosen vocation.

All three of the previously stated stages should be part of any comprehensive career education program. The differentiation for the gifted should come at each stage. For example, at stage one, gifted elementary students should be introduced to the broadest possible range of careers, with a heavy emphasis on those that require high-level intellectual and creative ability. This broad exposure is necessary because, when asked to name jobs, the vast majority of children can only cite the jobs held by their parents in addition to familiar ones such as doctor, teacher, nurse, police officer, fire fighter, and grocery store clerk. So, through planned field lessons, visiting speakers, books, newspaper articles, and private or class discussions, gifted elementary students should be introduced to vocations that are highly specialized, thereby requiring gifted individuals to perform them.

At the second stage, the exploration process must entail a careful examination of all aspects of particular vocations. It is not sufficient for a gifted teenager to want to be an astronaut. Also needed are answers to such questions as: What do astronauts really do in addition to blasting off into space? What is the difference between the tasks of a space shuttle's commander and those of its mission specialist? What selection process determines which applicants can become astronauts? What are the long-range predictions for the number of astronauts needed in the twenty-first century? What college course of study would best prepare one for a career with NASA? What time commitments do astronauts have to make to the program? Is it possible to maintain a family and a career as an astronaut? It should be clear that all these questions, and countless more, must be probed by a student before a prudent decision can be made to pursue a career as an astronaut. Teachers cannot do the exploring for their students, but they can serve as channels of information—suggesting people and ways to contact them, books, magazines, programs—all facilitative to gifted youth trying to make decisions that will affect the rest of their lives.

Feldhusen and Kolloff (1979) stress that an important aspect of the exploration phase of career education is for the gifted to acquire an understanding of the educational requirements of those higher-level careers in which they are interested. Thoroughness during the exploration phase will allow students to make the most efficacious use of the career preparation phase. They will know whether to take an extra physics course, or whether to enroll in an advanced computer-programming course during the summer, or whether they should do some intensive preparation for the SAT so they can attain the 720 math/650 verbal required by the university of their choice.

Clearly, the stages overlap to an extent. Students will still be discovering new careers as they explore others, and they will be exploring some as they begin to make preparations for others. The key, though, is *not* to wait until high school to begin making students aware of careers. Career choice should involve a thoughtful, long-term, informed choice. Gifted persons have so much to gain and offer if they make the right career choice. Career education is one step toward enabling this choice to be made.

ARTS CURRICULUM

It is impossible to explain why some children can read when they are three, why others can calculate square roots of four-digit numbers in their heads when they are six, why others can write poetry and prose that evoke strong, sensitive images when they are twelve, and why still others have organizational and leadership ability such that children twice their age happily take direction from them. Likewise, it is impossible to explain why some children possess such ability in the arts that their dancing is otherworldly, their music stirs the inner person, their dramatic interpretations bring life to flat words, and their visual art reaches far beyond the canvas, or the clay, or the metal. Although inexplicable, these children and youth retain creative insight and ability which, if properly nurtured and developed, can add beauty, substance, clarity, and *raison d'être* to the world in which we live.

Young people gifted in the arts may or may not also be intellectually gifted in the academic sense. Miller says that

> Creativity is not necessarily associated with the highest intelligence, but artistic products of highest value are probably associated with unusual intellectual gifts. (1962, 494)

As was pointed out in previous sections, before students can benefit from a specially designed curriculum, they must be identified as needing it. The same holds true for the artistically talented, and we are probably even less likely to recognize talent in this area than in others. Carlisle reminds readers that

> artistic genius in children is a reality. It is a precious treasure, but as a public society, we are not adept at identifying it nor predisposed to nurturing it. (1979, 22)

Such oversight—whether conscious or unconscious—needs to be corrected.

There are various ways to identify children who are artistically gifted (Duffy 1979; Edmonston 1981; Isaacs 1963; Lally 1967; Schmidt 1981; Stalker 1981), and this subject is covered more thoroughly in chapter 3, "Identification of the Gifted." However, there are several clues that should hint of a child's artistic gifts.

In a general sense, a first sign to adults may spring from a young child's unusual interest in a particular area of art, such as ballet, sculpture, violin, or poetry, especially if that particular interest seems to spring from nowhere—no role models are readily available and other family members do not share the interest.

Other clues are more specific to the particular art field. For example, a young child who is musically talented may exhibit a remarkable ability to transpose music designed for one instrument into music suitable for another, or may have the ability to play one or more instruments quite well at a very young age, with uncanny proficiency. These characteristics, or others that indicate an extraordinary interest and ability in music, should lead parents or teachers to have the child's ability assessed by a music professional.

Another area in which young children may exhibit precocious tendencies is in visual art. A young child who includes details in drawings, exhibits a sense of perspective, or chooses unusual objects to draw, paint, or sculpt may be artistically gifted. These children may prefer painting to passing a football, drafting ornamental facades to drafting reports on the presidents, or forming cubes from clay to finding the cube root of 398. Such tendencies, in conjunction with the ability to dedicate prolonged periods of time to art projects, is indicative of unique native ability.

Whenever a child or youth is willing to dedicate prolonged attention to anything, it should be considered unusual. So, if a young girl or boy spends a great deal of time dancing—practicing particular steps, choreographing dance numbers, reading books about the dance—and if this interest continues over several months and even years, then one should explore the possibility that the child is gifted in the specialized psychomotor field of dance.

Another specialized artistic field in which young people may distinguish themselves is drama. Dramatically gifted children may or may not be natural extroverts. Some are only outgoing through their characters, while others are "on stage" all the time. Their dramatic play goes far beyond that of other children; they actually want to put on plays and may constantly be rounding up neighborhood children to be either in the plays or in the audience. Children with a propensity for acting may be able to exhibit a whole range of emotions if the "part" calls for them—and some parents may tire of always serving as the audience for their able children's thespian pursuits.

At the beginning of this section, we said that artistic talent often goes unrecognized and unencouraged. This is due, in no small part, to our society's lack of recognition of value in the arts. Parents are much more likely to feel pride in their child's academic or sports accomplishments than in their child's artistic achievements. "My son got first place in the citywide art contest" does not garner the same "Ahhh!" of recognition as "My son threw the gamewinning touchdown" or "My son is valedictorian of his class." While this is unfortunate, it is a fact of late-twentieth-century American culture. Therefore, those segments of our society that do recognize the inherent worth in art must work doubly hard to promote a positive, accepting attitude in others.

The schools are a logical place to begin. When budgets are cut, or back-to-basics trumpets are sounded, invariably the first programs eliminated are art and music, beginning in the elementary school. This is not only a mistake for all young people but a tragedy for the gifted. Early exposure and training are virtually mandatory for talent to flourish. Beginning in the elementary school, and continuing through high school, art programs must find and develop the talents and gifts of the children in their charge. This must be done very deliberately—not through a mass screening process, as when searching for children with learning problems or visual deficiencies, but rather through constant vigilance by teachers and other school personnel.

Before these adults can be watchful for evidence of talent, they must be sensitized and trained to recognize it. In the middle school and high school, art, music, dance, and drama teachers should all be highly trained in their particular fields and therefore more likely to recognize talent. In the elementary school, however, teachers are usually generalists and less likely to recognize artistic talent. This weakness can be partially remedied through in-service training.

A school district's supervisor of visual or performing arts or an arts curriculum coordinator could team up with a leader of gifted education to plan and implement in-service workshops for all levels of classroom teachers, which would serve three purposes:

1. To sensitize teachers to the value of art and artistic talent.
2. To train teachers to recognize signs of artistic talent.
3. To present methods of encouraging artistic talent.

In addition, a workshop that included teachers from all levels of a public school system could put some networking into place (Carlisle 1979). For example, high school teachers could identify artistically gifted students to serve as "junior mentors" for younger artistically gifted children (see Szekely 1981, 1982).

While it is not very realistic to recommend that public school systems develop visual and performing arts curricula designed specifically for artistically talented students, it is realistic to recommend some changes in the arts curricula to better serve all children as the gifted are better served. The changes we recommend can be categorized using the four elements of creativity: fluency, flexibility, originality, and elaboration.

Fluency

Fluency refers to a person's ability to generate a large number of ideas, both rapidly and smoothly. It can be likened to individual brainstorming: the number of ideas generated is of more interest than the worth of each individual idea—the evaluation comes later. Fluency is a creative skill that can be taught. Strategies that reflect a curriculum designed to enhance fluency are as follows:

1. *Visual art.* Give students one color of paint and explain that their task is to generate as many different ways of applying that paint to paper as possible. Ways that are readily available should be demonstrated (chalk, fingers, tissues); others should be listed (egg, necklace, spray nozzle).
2. *Dance.* Tell students that they have ten minutes to create and demonstrate as many ways to "dance" across the stage as they can.
3. *Drama.* Tell students that using only their hands and feet, they are to experiment with ways to communicate joy to an audience.
4. *Music.* Have students choose any instrument in the bandroom. Ask them to make as many different soft sounds as possible— using any and all parts of the instrument.

Flexibility

Flexibility refers to a person's ability to adapt one idea or one part of an idea into another, different idea. The ability to be flexible in one's thinking is important in many aspects of life, including creativity in art. Like fluency, flexibility can be learned—and opportunities for practice must be provided.

1. *Visual art.* Have each student choose a print of a well-known painting. Direct students to recreate the paintings—but on a different-shaped canvas. If the painting they chose was originally rectangular, they are to redo it on a square canvas. An extension of this activity is to have students redo a two-dimensional picture as a three-dimensional object.

2. *Dance.* Tell each student to choose a recording of music from a ballet. They are to choreograph a square-dance number to that same music. They must teach other members of the class the dance and then perform it for the entire group.

3. *Drama.* Have students rewrite a scene from a play. Tell them that they may choose to adapt the scene: (*a*) from one type of drama to another (e.g., from tragedy to comedy); (*b*) for more or fewer actors; (*c*) for a different setting; or (*d*) for a different audience.

4. *Music.* Instruct students to sing an upbeat song in a tragic way or to play a slow, deliberate, heavy melody with a light touch.

Originality

If any of the four elements of creativity is most often associated with the notion of being creative, it is originality. In fact, one of the definitions of *originality* is "creativity." Other definitions include "freshness," "newness," "unusualness," and "inventiveness." Unfortunately, the arts curricula currently in place in most school systems do little to promote originality—and much to destroy it. How many elementary schools display thirty versions of the same art project outside their classrooms? How many students' only exposure to drama is to read the plays in the basal reading series? How many fourth graders nationwide learn the very same song on the recorder? It is no small wonder that creative teachers bemoan the lack of original thinking displayed by their students. However, with modification, the arts curricula can do much to promote originality.

1. *Visual art.* Have students cut out identical sets of squares, triangles, circles, and rectangles. Each student is to produce an origi-

nal design. (No two designs should even vaguely resemble each other!)

2. *Dance.* While students are listening to music, have them close their eyes and move in any new ways they can create. Encourage them to go beyond the confines of traditional movements and dance steps.

3. *Drama.* Expect and encourage students to write their own plays, and then to cast and produce them.

4. *Music.* Students who play instruments that do not traditionally go together (e.g., trumpet and viola) should be encouraged to play together and to create new arrangements that include both their instruments.

Elaboration

The last of the four elements of creativity is *elaboration,* which refers to a person's ability to extend or go beyond an idea. Students can be encouraged to elaborate upon their own or others' ideas.

1. *Visual art.* Obtain pictures of sculpture and have students choose one. Tell them that their task is to isolate one portion of the sculpture, which they are to recreate and elaborate upon. Once this is done, they may create a whole new sculpture around their recreated segment.

2. *Dance.* After students go to a live ballet, have them choose one dancer or character to investigate. They are to find out all they can about the person they have chosen and then write a fictionalized biography, elaborating on what they know. They may or may not choose to contact the dancer to check the accuracy of their description.

3. *Drama.* Building upon the notion of unrequited love, ask students to create a scene that demonstrates the agony of such love.

4. *Music.* Provide students with the opportunity to hear improvisational jazz. Invite jazz musicians to come to class, and encourage students to play with them.

Creativity is a key in appropriate arts curricula for academically and artistically gifted youth. It is imperative that divergency not only be allowed—but fostered. This work should begin when children are young, since that is the best time to nurture creative impulses (Baskin & Harris 1982; Simons 1979), but it should not stop them when they become less young.

Encouragement of divergence does not mean neglect of structure.

Gifted and talented children need to know the fundamentals of whatever they are learning but then must be freed to go beyond those fundamentals in their own creative production.

What about those children who are truly prodigious in their artistic ability? They need specialized instruction and guidance, which is often not available within the public school, except in rare instances. For elementary and secondary children and youth, private lessons with an experienced artist, dancer, musician, or actor are to be desired. If the cost is prohibitive, private or civic organizations may provide aid. Although lessons can often be taken after school or on weekends, there may be times when an artistically talented child needs to miss school. Parents and teachers who recognize extraordinary talent will be willing to make allowances when necessary—in the interest of the child's talent development.

As the talented children grow into talented adolescents and their potential for remarkable achievement in the arts becomes more evident, it is often wise to seek out a special school devoted to the development of talent (see Carroll 1976; Churchwell 1981; Cox & Daniel 1983; Gatty 1976; Gibberd 1966; Isaacs 1963; Maddy 1963; Stone 1976).

Some facet of the arts touches our lives every day. When one considers the generally low status accorded artists, and the odds that they therefore struggle against, it is no wonder that many become discouraged or are never discovered. With teachers, parents, and communities better educated regarding the arts, discouragement and lack of discovery should no longer prevent talent from being developed.

SELECTED BIBLIOGRAPHY

Introduction

Akers, Diane. "Why Programs for the Gifted Miss the Point." *G/C/T* 24:52 (September/October 1982).

The author says that the one characteristic common to all identified gifted children is their ability to learn whatever is presented to them faster than their age-mates. Therefore, they need less drill, less repetition, less review. Those who design curriculum for the gifted and those who teach them need to figure out how to reduce some of the drill and repetition, thereby allowing more time for alternative programming.

Anderson, Ross H. "Arousing and Sustaining the Interest of Gifted

Children in the Study of Science." *Gifted Child Quarterly* 5:35–41 (1961).

The author exhorts teachers and parents to do everything possible to encourage gifted children's interest in science. He suggests a wonderful group of experiments on heat for elementary students.

Bergman, Jerry. "Twenty Suggestions for Teaching the Gifted." *G/C/T* 19:34–35 (September/October 1981).

Bergman's suggestions are not geared toward any particular subject area, but rather address several areas. Elementary and secondary gifted teachers could adapt the ideas to fit their subject area and students.

Brown, Martha M. "The Needs and Potential of the Highly Gifted: Toward a Model of Responsiveness." *Roeper Review* 6:123–27 (February 1984).

Because of their very giftedness, highly gifted children typically experience more than the usual social and emotional pressures from everyday living. Brown says that programming for them must consider this interplay of nonintellective and cognitive factors if it is to be truly responsive to the unique needs of this subset of the gifted population. She believes Renzulli's three-ring definition of giftedness may exclude some highly gifted youth. This is a very interesting article.

Datnow, Claire. "The Cumulative Learning Effect: A Model for Coordinating Educational Opportunities for Gifted Students." *G/C/T* 14:54–57 (September/October 1980).

The model presented in this article is an attempt to create for gifted children learning experiences that are woven into a meaningful whole, rather than simply a number of disjointed pieces. Given a coordinator who can get the school district and community to work cooperatively, this model has a great deal of merit. It proposes an interaction of the regular curriculum with related explorations and with in-depth investigations that grow out of the explorations. The author describes two such programs that worked in Alabama.

Dunn, Rita, Bruno, Angela, and Gardiner, Barbara. "Put a Cap on Your Gifted Program." *Gifted Child Quarterly* 28:70–72 (Spring 1984).

"CAPS" (Contract Activity Packages) are self-contained units that teach a specific topic or theme. An example is given along with a rationale for using them with gifted students.

Evans, Malcolm D. "A Simple Statement of Beliefs." *Educational Leadership* 39:127 (November 1981).

The author relates the way that his local faculty committee prepared a philosophy of education statement from which goals could be derived for a program for gifted and talented children.

Fearn, Leif. "Do Adult Curricular Priorities Mislead Gifted Learners?" *G/C/T* 12:19 (March/April 1980).

Fearn raises legitimate questions concerning adults' messages to gifted youth: Are we telling them to perceive themselves one way because of the curricula we are developing? This brief article reports some of the findings from a study designed to compare descriptors of gifted children, as self-reported by those who deliver and consume direct gifted education services. Gifted students see themselves differently than adults say they see them.

Firestien, Roger L., and Treffinger, Donald J. "Creative Problem Solving: Guidelines and Resources for Effective Facilitation." *G/C/T* 26:2–10 (January/February 1983).

The authors say that the purpose of their article "is to provide some practical information and techniques for classroom teachers who are interested in increasing their effectiveness in using Creative Problem Solving." They do just that. Even teachers unfamiliar with CPS could begin to infuse this strategy into their gifted curriculum.

Gardiner, Barbara. "Stepping into a Learning Styles Program." *Roeper Review* 6:90–92 (November 1983).

The author explains how she used the results of a *Learning Style Inventory* that she administered to her class of gifted students. She was able to teach the students and allow them to learn based on their preferred style, and the results were very positive.

Griggs, Shirley A., and Dunn, Rita. "Selected Case Studies of the Learning Style Preferences of Gifted Students." *Gifted Child Quarterly* 28:115–19 (Summer 1984).

The authors cite over fifty studies regarding learning style preferences of gifted students. They conclude that, although the learning style model is based on the premise of individual differences, gifted/talented learners actually demonstrate a unique pattern of personal traits. This pattern is briefly discussed. The bibliography is invaluable for anyone interested in learning styles of the gifted.

Jackson, David M. *Readings in Curriculum Development for the Gifted.* Guilford, Conn.: Special Learning Corp., 1980. 216 pp.

This collection of readings has drawn from the major journals concerned with the education of gifted children and youth. School districts and/or libraries unable to subscribe to these journals may want to purchase the book for their collection.

Johnson, Roger A., and Yarborough, Betty H. "The Effects of Marks on the Development of Academically Talented Elementary Pupils." *Gifted Child Quarterly* 22:498–505 (Winter 1978).

The authors did an ex post facto study to compare an experimental group of gifted students who had attended a nongraded school for six years and three control groups of gifted students who had attended traditional, graded elementary schools. The researchers administered a battery of tests and concluded: "Collectively, the results of this study suggest that academically talented pupils may be less favored in a nongraded environment than in a graded environment. The control (graded) pupils in this study appeared to be more well adjusted; to relate more effectively to their peers; and to have more positive attitudes toward school, their families, and other adults in their lives than the experimental (nongraded) pupils."

Kaplan, Sandra N. "Myth: There Is a Single Curriculum for the Gifted!" *Gifted Child Quarterly* 26:32-33 (Winter 1982).

Kaplan says just as there is not a single prototype of a gifted learner, neither can there be a single curriculum for the gifted.

Karnes, Merle B., Linnemeyer, Susan A., and Denton-Ade, Cynthia. "Differentiating the Curriculum." In *The Underserved: Our Young Gifted Children*, edited by Merle B. Karnes. Reston, Va.: The Council for Exceptional Children, 1983.

Following an excellent overview on differentiating curriculum for young gifted learners, the authors give many sample lesson plans, which could be used as models for creating other plans suitable for gifted youngsters.

Laird, A. W. "Are We Really Educating the Gifted Child?" *Gifted Child Quarterly* 12:205-14 (Winter 1968).

Laird strongly questions what school districts are doing to provide for the gifted.

Maker, C. June. *Curriculum Development for the Gifted*. Rockville, Md.: Aspen Systems Corp., 1982a. 392 pp.

This book, along with Maker's *Teaching Models in Education of the Gifted*, is a *must* acquisition for every curriculum director and gifted education coordinator. In *Curriculum Development for the Gifted*, Maker sets out "to provide teachers and prospective teachers of the gifted with a comprehensive handbook of theoretical and practical approaches to teaching these special children." The book is divided into three sections: (1) an introduction to the general principles underlying curriculum development for the gifted; (2) ways for developing a program; (3) examples of four integrated approaches. The book is written well enough that readers can digest much of the material on their own, or it would make an excellent textbook for a course on curriculum development.

_____. *Teaching Models in Education of the Gifted*. Rockville, Md.: Aspen Systems Corp., 1982b. 475 pp.

This book presents eleven different teaching/learning models that can be used successfully in developing curriculum for the gifted. The models presented are Bloom's Cognitive Taxonomy; Krathwohl's Affective Taxonomy; Bruner's approach; Guilford's Structure of Intellect; Kohlberg's Stages of Moral Reasoning; Parnes's Creative Problem Solving model; Renzulli's Enrichment Triad; Taba's Teaching Strategies; Taylor's Multiple Talent Approach; Treffinger's Model for Self-Directed Learning; and Williams's Strategies for Thinking and Feeling. Anyone who teaches gifted students and is planning lessons and curriculum must be familiar with this book.

McAleer, Franny F. "TIE-ing It Together for Our Gifted Students: The TIE Challenge." *Roeper Review* 7:111–13 (November 1984).

The TIE model is explained. The model emphasizes exploring, experiencing, and expressing as the best opportunities for learning for gifted students.

Nasca, Donald F. "Creating Concepts for the Gifted." *G/C/T* 15:47–48 (November/December 1980).

Nasca distinguishes between "teaching" concepts and "creating" concepts. The former serves to increase students' stores of concepts, while the latter assists them in adopting "a process for organizing heterogeneously organized stimuli into discrete groups, creating a definition that establishes parameters of the groups, and assigning a label to the definition and its class of exemplars." Creating concepts serves the gifted by requiring the use of higher-level thinking skills.

Passow, A. Harry. "The Four Curricula of the Gifted and Talented: Toward a Total Learning Environment." *G/C/T* 20:2–7 (November/December 1981).

Passow says that the "issue is not whether gifted and talented children need differentiated programs and services but rather what constitutes a differentiated program and differentiated services?" He believes that the four curricula all students experience, and which must be considered when developing curricula for the gifted, are: (1) general education curriculum, (2) specialized curriculum, (3) subliminal/covert curriculum, and (4) nonschool educative settings curriculum. He explains these four curricula and how they should affect planning for the gifted.

Plowman, Paul D. "Programming for the Gifted Child." *Exceptional Children* 35:547–51 (March 1969).

Plowman says the trend in the fifties and sixties shifted from viewing gifted students as commodities to concern for their individual development. He discusses changes in programming that resulted from this shift.

Renzulli, Joseph S. "A Curriculum Development Model for Academically Superior Students." *Exceptional Children* 36:611–14 (April 1970).

Renzulli describes a curriculum model based on a team approach in which educators and scholars from various disciplines work together.

_____. *The Enrichment Triad Model: A Guide for Developing Defensible Programs for the Gifted and Talented.* Mansfield Center, Conn.: Creative Learning Press, 1977. 88 pp.

This book clearly explains the Enrichment Triad Model developed by Renzulli. He relates its background and offers ways that the model can be used in classrooms and schools. All teachers of the gifted should own or have ready access to this book.

_____. "What Makes a Problem Real: Stalking the Illusive Meaning of Qualitative Differences in Gifted Education." *Gifted Child Quarterly* 26:147–56 (Fall 1982).

Renzulli states that if gifted education is going to survive and prosper as a specialized field of knowledge, "we must become as adept at defining those things for which we stand as we have been in dealing with the educational practices we oppose." Renzulli lists the following characteristics of a "real" problem: (1) A real problem must have a personal frame of reference, since it involves an emotional or affective commitment as well as an intellectual or cognitive one. (2) A real problem does not have an existing or unique solution. (3) Calling something a problem does not necessarily make it a real problem for a given person or group. (4) The purpose of pursuing a real problem is to bring about some form of change and/or to contribute something new to the sciences, the arts, or the humanities. Renzulli goes on to provide examples of real problems.

Roberson, Terry G. "Determining Curriculum Content for the Gifted." *Roeper Review* 6:137–39 (February 1984).

Roberson points out the need for a more comprehensive curriculum design for gifted students. The suggested curricular framework features a structure for coordinating *core* experiences (necessary for gifted youth) with *content areas* (which have been reorganized around contemporary themes). Three very helpful charts depict the basic curricular framework, the regrouped/reorganized content areas, and guides for selection and development of instructional materials.

Schroeder, Ella F., and Van Norden, Leslie. "An Integrative Curriculum for Gifted Junior High School Students." *Roeper Review* 5:35–38 (April/May 1983).

The authors explain how programs for gifted students can be developed, based on Clark's Integrative Educational Model. This model "incorporates an integration of all human functions, including logical, rational thought; the important avenues of sensing; the emotional, feeling functions; and the power of intuitive knowing.'' The article notes changes to be made in the classroom environment, possible courses, and scheduling considerations. The authors believe that this model meets the requirement of providing qualitatively different instruction for the gifted.

Scruggs, Thomas E., and Mastropieri, Margo A. ''How Gifted Students Learn: Implications from Recent Research.'' *Roeper Review* 6:183–85 (April 1984).

The authors review several recent investigations into how gifted students learn and under what conditions they learn best. They conclude that gifted students spontaneously produce learning strategies that are more effective than nongifted students. For example, in order to memorize the pair ''effort-hunger,'' a gifted student might generate the sentence, ''It is an *effort* for an anorexic to experience *hunger*.'' A nongifted student might just practice saying the words over and over. They suggest that teachers can help gifted students by presenting some material in a spatial fashion and using mnemonic devices.

Singleton, H. Wells, and Nelson, Murry. ''Alternative Forms of Objectives for the Gifted and Talented Learner in School.'' *G/C/T* 15:49–51 (November/December 1980).

The authors suggest that since the gifted and talented learners tend to have certain learning characteristics, behavioral objectives should be augmented with expressive objectives and emergent objectives. They explain and give examples of the latter two types. Although they seem to be addressing social studies teachers, other content-area teachers could adapt the ideas.

Swicord, Barbara. ''Curriculum Development for Gifted Children in Salt Lake City—an Evolving Door.'' *Roeper Review* 6:144–45 (February 1984).

The author, teacher, and curriculum director for the Salt Lake City gifted program, reports on the improved quality of the program—due in part, she feels, to the increased use of thematic approaches, program developed curriculum, and administrative assistance specific to gifted curriculum.

Tremaine, Claire D. ''Do Gifted Programs Make a Difference?'' *Gifted Child Quarterly* 23:500–17 (Fall 1979).

The author compared seventy-four gifted students enrolled in special programs or courses with fifty-nine gifted students who were never enrolled in such programs or courses. She also administered a questionnaire to gifted graduates of three different school districts.

She found that enrolled gifted had higher GPA's and SAT scores. They elected more challenging classes in high school and won three times as many scholarships. Other findings were that enrolled gifted had higher educational goals and more regard for teachers and schools. They were also more involved in school and community activities and had a wide variety of friends. She concludes that gifted programs do make a difference—a very positive one!

Walling, Donovan R. "Hidden Talents: Process/Product Perspectives in Gifted Education." *G/C/T* 19:7–9 (September/October 1981).

Walling suggests three perspectives teachers of the gifted should adopt regarding the products their students generate: (1) products are viewed nonjudgmentally; (2) product does not presume process; (3) products suggest standards and expectations. He says. "To approve without judging, to support without restraining, to assist without impeding—these are the difficult but enormously important perspectives that teachers of talented youngsters must master."

Reading

Alexander, Patricia, and Muia, Joseph. "Gifted Reading Programs: Uncovering the Hidden Potential." *Reading Horizons* 20:302–10 (Summer 1980).

The authors present a procedure that is an alternative to current identification models. It identifies gifted students from both dominant and subdominant cultural groups. An extensive checklist has been compiled for use with this model, and it is included in the article.

Barbe, Walter B. "Problems in Reading Encountered by Gifted Children." *Elementary English* 33:274–78 (May 1956).

The author draws on his experiences working with gifted students to write this article. He says the biggest problem faced by teachers of the gifted is materials too easy for the students.

————. "Ingredients of a Creative Reading Program." In *Creative Reading for Gifted Learners: A Design for Excellence,* edited by Michael Labuda. Newark, Del.: International Reading Association, 1974.

Barbe says that teachers must aid children in going beyond merely learning how to read—they must help involve the children in the reading process. He provides a rationale for teaching creative reading, the skills necessary for creative reading, and resources and materials essential to a creative reading program.

Barbe, Walter B., and Norris, Dorothy E. "Reading Instruction in Special Classes for Gifted Elementary Children." *Reading Teacher* 16:425–28 (May 1963).

The authors describe the two major components of the reading program in the Cleveland Major Works Program for gifted children.

Bonds, Charles W., and Bonds, Lella T. "Teacher, Is There a Gifted Reader in First Grade?" *Roeper Review* 5:4–6 (February 1983).

The authors discuss how to identify the gifted early readers and how to provide optimum instruction for these children. This article would be a good addition to a packet of articles to be read by new first grade teachers.

Boothby, Paula. "Tips for Teaching Creative and Critical Reading." *Roeper Review* 1:24–25 (May 1979).

In her brief article, Boothby presents ideas for encouraging young children to read critically and creatively.

_____. "Creative and Critical Reading for the Gifted." *Reading Teacher* 33:674–76 (March 1980).

Boothby presents ideas for teaching critical and creative reading to both gifted and average readers.

Brown, Wesley, and Rogan, Joseph. "Reading and Young Gifted Children." *Roeper Review* 5:6–9 (February 1983).

In this excellent article, the authors make a case for differentiated reading instruction for young gifted readers. Along with the rationale, they discuss identification of these youngsters and how to best provide for them—for example, through encouragement for wide reading, creative reading, and critical reading.

Caldwell, Sarah T. "Highly Gifted Preschool Readers." *Journal for the Education of the Gifted* 8:165–74 (Winter 1985).

Caldwell reports on her study of twenty-four preschoolers who participated in a summer program for highly gifted children at the University of Georgia. She discusses the tests used and compares them to the tests often used by kindergarten screening programs. She also looked at twelve reading basal series to determine what recommendations they made for instructing young children who are reading when they enter school. Virtually no such recommendations were made. Implications for teachers and programs are presented.

Carter, Betty. "Leisure Reading Habits of Gifted Students in a Suburban Junior High School." *Top of the News* 38:312–15 (Summer 1982).

Carter studied forty-four students' reading habits (twenty-two gifted, twenty-two not gifted). She found that the gifted, as compared to the control group, read almost twice as much, including more science fiction and fantasy books and fewer realistic fiction books. The study should be replicated with several different populations so that the results can be generalized.

Cassidy, Jack. "Inquiry Reading for the Gifted." *Reading Teacher* 35:17–21 (October 1981).

Cassidy defines inquiry reading as "an approach which allows able students to research independently some area of particular interest to them." He provides a rationale for why inquiry reading gives able students a chance to apply their reading skills in a practical situation. A four-week plan for implementing inquiry reading with gifted youngsters is described.

Cassidy, Jack, and Vukelich, Carol. "Do the Gifted Read Early?" *Reading Teacher* 33:578–82 (February 1980).

The authors report on two studies done to determine what percentage of a given population of gifted children read before entering kindergarten and to determine what effect prekindergarten reading instruction would have on gifted children. They found that only a small percentage (17 to 23 percent) of their gifted sample read as preschoolers and that instruction seems almost fruitless until the child perceives reading as a functional skill.

Cramond, Bonnie, and Martin, Charles E., Jr. "A Parents' Guide to Creating a Creative Reader." *G/C/T* 18:55–57 (May/June 1981).

The authors posit that parents are in a very good position to promote creative reading among their gifted children. Fifteen activities and some general guidelines are provided to help parents nurture creative reading.

Cushenbery, Donald C., and Howell, Helen. *Reading and the Gifted Child: A Guide for Teachers.* Springfield, Ill.: Charles C. Thomas, 1974. 181 pp.

The authors have compiled an excellent book on the subject of reading and the gifted. The main text is clearly written and helpful. The appendices will also be quite useful to teachers. Cushenbery and Howell present ideas for preschool readers, enrichment, content area reading, evaluation. An appendix provides information concerning suitable periodicals, starting book clubs, games, books for teachers. This is a valuable resource and would make a good text for a gifted reading methods course or a supplementary text for a general reading methods course.

Dawkins, Betty Jo. "Do Gifted Junior High School Students Need Reading Instruction?" *Journal for the Education of the Gifted* 2:3–9 (September 1978).

The author describes the diagnostic-prescriptive reading program in place at her school. The research indicates that "Yes, gifted junior high school students do need reading instruction."

DeBoer, John J. "Creative Reading and the Gifted Student." *Reading Teacher* 16:435–41 (May 1963).

The author states that creative reading shares one purpose with other types of creative behavior: "To combine and recombine the materials of language to achieve a meaningful result. This means that (1) the creative reader is an active agent, not merely a passive recipient; (2) he is a seeker and an experimenter; (3) he is both a builder and a leveler." The article describes the major components of a creative reading program.

Devall, Yvonna L. "Some Cognitive and Creative Characteristics and Their Relationship to Reading Comprehension in Gifted and Non-Gifted Fifth Graders." *Journal for the Education of the Gifted* 5:259–73 (1983).

From her research, Devall draws several conclusions that have implications for instruction. Reading programs for the gifted should offer guidance, individualized instruction, student-set goals, and a creative production element.

Dole, Janice A., and Adams, Phyllis J. "Reading Curriculum for Gifted Readers: A Survey." *Gifted Child Quarterly* 27:64–72 (Spring 1983).

State and national leaders in gifted education and reading education were surveyed regarding the essential distinctions that differentiate reading curriculum for gifted readers. The questionnaire and an analysis of the results are included. Results indicate that reading curriculum for gifted is not vastly different from developmental reading curriculum, but it should emphasize certain elements more for gifted than for nongifted.

Dunn, Sharon. "The Gifted Student in the Intermediate Grades: Developing Creativity through Reading." *Reading Horizons* 19:276–79 (Summer 1979).

The author makes a strong case for *teaching* creative reading to able students.

Durkin, Dolores. *Children Who Read Early.* New York: Teachers College Press, 1966. 174 pp.

This book reports on Durkin's longitudinal research in California and New York on first graders who learned to read before entering school.

Flack, Jerry D., and Lamb, Pose. "Making Use of Gifted Characters in Literature." *G/C/T* 34:3–11 (September/October 1984).

This excellent article should be read by librarians and teachers who work with gifted students. The authors have reviewed many books that have gifted children as characters and have created activities to extend and enrich the reading of these books.

Harris, Karen, and Baskin, Barbara. "Reading Guidance for Gifted Children." *Top of the News* 38:308–11 (Summer 1982).

The authors make a case for helping gifted students broaden and deepen their reading selections.

Jacobs, Leland B. "Books for the Gifted." *Reading Teacher* 16:429–34 (May 1963).

Jacobs makes recommendations regarding the types of books gifted children should read. He states that the book collections to which the gifted have access should be "widely diversified in content, authorship, levels of difficulty, and type of genre."

Johnson, Joseph. "Giftedness: A Handicap to Reading Proficiency." *Creative Child and Adult Quarterly* 3:103–5 (Summer 1978).

Johnson points out that reading proficiency and giftedness are highly correlated—although excellent reading does not necessarily indicate giftedness. He calls for a sequential developmental program, tailored to individual gifted children's needs.

Krippner, S., and Hearld, C. "Reading Disabilities among Academically Talented." *Gifted Child Quarterly* 8:12–20 (1964).

The authors discuss their study of gifted students who have reading disabilities and average students who have reading disabilities. They suggest possible causes and possible types of remediation which could be provided.

Mangieri, John N., and Madigan, Faye. "Reading for Gifted Students: What Schools Are Doing." Roeper Review 7:68–70 (November 1984).

The authors present results of a study they conducted. They sent a 14-item questionnaire to 150 school districts and their analysis of responses received revealed five major findings: (1) key focus of reading programs for the gifted is enrichment; (2) teacher recommendation is of primary importance when selecting students for a gifted program; (3) the same basal series is used with gifted as with nongifted students; (4) regular classroom teacher is responsible for gifted students' reading instruction; and (5) a high degree of communication was reported between the schools and the parents of gifted students.

Martin, Charles E. "Why Some Gifted Children Do Not Like to Read." *Roeper Review* 7:72–75 (November 1984).

Martin surveyed 124 sixth-, seventh-, and eighth-grade students who were classified as either below-average, average, or gifted readers. Based on the information he obtained about their reading habits and interests, Martin makes recommendations to teachers in four areas: selecting reading material, designing prereading activities, providing challenging material, identifying attitudes and interests. This is a good article for teachers!

Martin, Charles E., and Cramond, Bonnie. "A Checklist for Assessing and Developing Creative Reading." *G/C/T* 32:22–24 (March/April 1984).

The authors provide a rationale for teaching creative reading. They also explain the twenty-item checklist (which is included).

McCormick, Sandra, and Swassing, Raymond H. "Reading Instruction for the Gifted: A Survey of Programs." *Journal for the Education of the Gifted* 5:34–43 (Winter 1982).

The authors report on the results of their nationwide survey of school districts, which was undertaken to determine how districts are providing reading instruction for their gifted students. Although many claim to be making provisions, the overall impression one gets is that nowhere near enough is being done (e.g., nearly half the gifted are provided for within the regular classroom—probably through the "top" reading group).

McIntosh, Margaret E. "Reading Instruction for Gifted Secondary Students." *Centering Teacher Education* 1:19–21 (August 1984).

Using a survey she conducted as support, McIntosh makes a case that secondary school gifted students need reading instruction. She makes recommendations for teachers and school districts that are planning to implement a reading program for their gifted students.

Miller, Margery Staman. "Using the Newspaper with the Gifted: An Everyday Opportunity to Enhance Critical Thinking/Reading Skills." *G/C/T* 23:47–49 (May/June 1982).

Miller provides a rationale for using the newspaper with gifted elementary and middle school students. She says the newspaper is a nation's and a community's mirror of internal and external forces. Helping gifted children recognize these forces through critical reading and thinking will promote their active participation in the nation and the community.

Munson, Grace. "Adjusting the Reading Program to the Gifted Child." *Journal of Exceptional Children* 11:45–48 (November 1944).

This fine article calls for a special reading program for the gifted that will not only promote growth but also provide remediation where necessary.

Noyce, Ruth. "Resources for Teaching the Gifted Reader." *Gifted Child Quarterly* 21:239–45 (Summer 1977).

Noyce provides a bibliography of resources to assist teachers in planning reading programs to stimulate gifted readers. Her list is divided into seven categories: creative reading activities, critical reading activities, identifying the gifted reader, individualizing reading instruction, learning centers, questioning, teaching strategies. Reading and/or gifted education coordinators could plan an entire in-service series using the materials listed here.

_____. "Try the Enrichment Triad in Reading Class." *Journal of Reading* 24:326–30 (January 1981).

Noyce presents a specific example of how to apply Renzulli's Enrichment Triad to reading instruction.

Olson, A. V., and Ames, W. S. *Teaching Reading Skills in Secondary Schools.* Scranton, Pa.: International Textbook Co., 1972. 233 pp.

Chapter 12 is "The Reading Needs of Special Groups." The authors devote a small section to reading for gifted secondary students.

Pennington, Cynthia Raker. "Evaluating Books for the Gifted Reader." *G/C/T* 34:15–18 (September/October 1984).

Pennington has briefly synthesized some of the literature on reading for the gifted and has developed a checklist based on identified desirable characteristics of literature for the gifted. The checklist is presented and explained.

Polette, Nancy. *Three R's for the Gifted: Reading, Writing, and Research.* Littleton, Colo.: Libraries Unlimited, 1982. 180 pp.

Polette provides a strong rationale for establishing and maintaining reading, writing, and thinking programs for the gifted. Only a portion of the book is text; the rest presents various learning modules that incorporate the three R's.

Rogers, Wanda, and Ryan, Susan. "Extending Reading Skills into Today's World." *Teaching Exceptional Children* 5:58–65 (Winter 1973).

The authors present a multiage program for accelerated readers based on "today's changing world." They briefly discuss units on study skills, the newspaper, speech, poetry, short stories, social studies, science, and drama.

Rupley, William H. "Reading Teacher Effectiveness: Implications for Teaching the Gifted." *Roeper Review* 7:70–72 (November 1984).

Rupley interprets four categories of effective reading teacher behaviors in terms of how they should affect the teaching of reading to the gifted. The categories are: (1) diagnosing students' reading strengths and weaknesses; (2) using a teacher-directed instructional format; (3) providing students opportunities to learn and apply their reading skills in actual reading tasks; (4) keeping students engaged in learning tasks.

Sabaroff, Rose E. "Challenges in Reading for the Gifted." *Elementary English* 42:393–400, 402 (April 1965).

Sabaroff discusses the various components that should comprise a reading program for the gifted.

Salzer, Richard T. "Early Reading and Giftedness—Some Observations and Questions." *Gifted Child Quarterly* 28:95–96 (Spring 1984).

The author reports on a study in which he interviewed over fifty children reported by their parents to be early readers. Several commonalities emerged: *early* interest in the alphabet, early and regular watching of "Sesame Street," self-assured behavior. The children differed in their ability to write.

Sanacore, Joseph. "Selecting and Guiding Academically Gifted Readers." *NASSP Bulletin* 56:55–61 (December 1981).

Sanacore describes the Hauppauge Middle School reading program for gifted readers, which serves 3 percent of the student population. The program has been highly successful.

Savage, John F. "Reading Guides: Effective Tools for Teaching the Gifted." *Roeper Review* 5:9–11 (February 1983).

According to Savage, a reading guide is "an assignment sheet, a set of questions and activities that structure a reading assignment." In his article, he explains how a teacher can design reading guides for use by gifted readers.

Schlichter, Carol L. "Using Books to Implement Triad Activities with Elementary Students." *Roeper Review* 7:75–79 (November 1984).

Schlichter's purpose was to identify a variety of resources in children's and young adult literature which elementary students could use in carrying out Triad activities. She provides an annotated bibliography of good books, divided into the following categories: "Books to stimulate Type I enrichment activities" (handbooks, biographies, fictional stories, authors and illustrators as models); "Books to support Type III enrichment activities" (how-to-do-it books, reference books); and "Resources for teachers in locating Type I and Type III support materials."

Schuster, Edgar H. "An Opportunity for Divergent Thinking in the Classroom: Students against the Text." *G/C/T* 34:30–33 (September/October 1984).

Schuster presents a set of ideas for gifted students to use in evaluating their textbooks. Several purposes are served: students have to read critically, they think divergently, and they recognize that textbooks are fallible.

Stank, Laurie A. "Reading Programs for the Gifted: A Necessity!" *G/C/T* 28:39–41 (May/June 1983).

The author provides a rationale for a reading program for the gifted, at both the elementary and secondary levels.

Stevens, Kathleen. "The Effect of Topic Interest on the Reading Comprehension of Higher Ability Students." *Journal of Educational Research* 73:365–68 (July/August 1980a).

The author found that interest significantly affected the comprehension of the higher-ability students but not the middle- or lower-ability students.

————. "The Effect of Interest on the Reading Comprehension of Gifted Readers." *Reading Horizons* 21:12–15 (Fall 1980b).

The author's research with ninety-three students (thirty-one superior, sixty-two average) indicates that interest does have a positive effect on reading comprehension—but only for the high ability group.

Sumption, M. R., and Luecking, E. M. *Education of the Gifted.* New York: Ronald Pr., 1960. 499 pp.

This book covers topics ranging from identification of the gifted to administration of gifted programs to college programs for the able. It was designed as a handbook for in-service or preservice teacher training.

Swaby, Barbara. "Questions Parents Ask about Reading and the Gifted." *Teaching Exceptional Children* 15:141–43 (Spring 1983).

The author has pinpointed six questions that parents of gifted children most often ask concerning reading. Her answers are succinct and lucid.

Switzer, Calvina, and Nourse, Margaret L. "Reading Instruction for the Gifted Child in First Grade." *Gifted Child Quarterly* 23:323–31 (Summer 1979).

The authors provide a good review of literature concerning reading instruction for gifted children. They conclude that (1) gifted readers are often neglected in the educational system; (2) special instructional practices are necessary if gifted readers' needs are to be met; (3) information to help aid teachers plan and implement the differentiated instruction is limited.

Torrance, E. Paul. "Helping Gifted Children Read Creatively." *Gifted Child Quarterly* 7:3–8 (Spring 1963).

Torrance presents reasons why creative reading should be and must be encouraged in children. He provides several excellent suggestions for helping children develop their creative reading skills.

————. *Gifted Children in the Classroom.* New York: Macmillan, 1965. 102 pp.

This small book contains a great deal of information. The chapters include emerging concepts of giftedness, goals in teaching the gifted, identifying and motivating gifted students, curriculum provisions, and creative reading for the gifted.

Trezise, Robert L. "Teaching Reading to the Gifted." *Language Arts* 54:920–24 (November/December 1977).

This good article provides ideas to help teachers encourage their gifted students to read more widely, more critically, and more creatively.

_____. "What about a Reading Program for the Gifted?" *Reading Teacher* 31:742–47 (April 1978).

Gifted children are different and require a differentiated reading program. The author makes recommendations that will not be termed "too costly."

Vida, Louisa. "Children's Literature for the Gifted Elementary School Child." *Roeper Review* 1:22–24 (May 1979).

The author describes an enrichment program for gifted sixth graders, centered around children's and young adult biography, realistic fiction, poetry, and tragedy. The rationale for each genre is given along with an overview of the activities.

Witty, Paul A. "A Balanced Reading Program for the Gifted." *Reading Teacher* 16:418–24 (May 1963).

Witty reviews characteristics of the gifted that should affect their reading program.

_____. "Rationale for Fostering Creative Reading in the Gifted and the Creative." In *Creative Reading for Gifted Learners: A Design for Excellence,* edited by Michael Labuda. Newark, Del.: International Reading Association, 1974.

Witty's chapter and the rest of this book are "must reads" for anyone working with gifted students, whether of elementary school or high school age. It is the only book available devoted to creative reading.

_____, ed. *Reading for the Gifted and the Creative Student,* Newark, Del.: International Reading Association, 1971. 63 pp.

This small book, written by experts in the field of gifted education, contains chapters on characteristics of gifted students and their needs for reading experience, innovative reading programs for the gifted, the role of parents and teachers in the reading education of gifted students, and a look at the future of gifted education.

Witty, Paul A., Freeland, Alma M., and Gothberg, Edith H. *The Teaching of Reading: A Developmental Process.* Boston: D. C. Heath, 1966. 434 pp.

Chapter 15, "Reading Programs for the Gifted," includes ways to identify the gifted, ways to guide the reading of the verbally gifted, and a case study of a verbally gifted child.

Wooster, Judith S. "Reaching through Reading." *G/C/T* 5:35–37 (November/December 1978).

Wooster presents several activities to expand gifted students' creative thinking abilities through reading.

LANGUAGE ARTS

Adalbert, Sister Mary. "Language Arts and the Gifted." *Catholic School Journal* 66:47–48 (March 1966).

The author recommends that the gifted participate in "depth reading," dramatics, writing, and public speaking.

Alexander, Patricia A. "Training Analogical Reasoning Skills in the Gifted." *Roeper Review* 6:191–93 (April 1984).

Alexander describes a training program in analogical reasoning based on Sternberg's component process (encoding, inferring, mapping, and applying). Session one explains to students the goals of the program and defines analogies. Session two provides direct instruction in the component processes applied to linguistic analogies. Session three provides instruction in analogies that are incorporated into the larger text. It focuses more on reading and how successful reading requires the same component processes as listed above. Data indicate that the program is effective directly and indirectly.

Bailes, Lee. "Film Making as a Creative Vehicle for Individual or Small Group Projects." *G/C/T* 11:54–58 (January/February 1980).

Bailes says that "one of the most obvious ways to effect creative learning is to offer a curriculum replete with opportunities for creative behavior." The author uses the rest of the article to explain how film making offers such opportunities. There are six steps, which are well-explained: introducing the equipment, planning the movie, shooting the picture, editing the film, recording the sound track, and presenting the finished film to an audience. If one's school district has some extra funds for film equipment, this article might indicate ways to spend it!

Barell, John. "Reflective Thinking and Education for the Gifted." *Roeper Review* 6:194–96 (April 1984).

The author defines reflective thinking as "using information as resources to search for meaning." The article is based on questions asked by a gifted twelfth-grade girl in a class in world history. This interesting account has many implications for teachers of the gifted.

Beebe, Rosalie Lake. "Creative Writing and the Young Gifted Child." *Roeper Review* 1:27–29 (May 1979).

Beebe exhorts teachers and parents to encourage creative writing among their young gifted children (ages three to seven). The article includes numerous samples of children's writing—which illustrates their early capability.

Bellanca, Jim. "Can Quality Circles Work in Classrooms of the Gifted?" *Roeper Review* 6:199–200 (April 1984).

The quality circle is a method developed by Japanese industrialists and scientists that purports to improve productivity, motivation, and quality of workmanship. It has been adapted for use in the United States and has recently been used with gifted students in the Chicago area. This article explains how this model compares with Future Problem-Solving Groups and why school districts may want to investigate it for use in their schools.

Bergman, Jerry. "Creative Writing." *G/C/T* 12:9–10 (March/April 1980).

Bergman provides a score of creative writing activities that have been used successfully with gifted students. They look like fun!

Biersdorf, Margot Peterson. "Further Adventures in Language Arts." *Roeper Review* 1:19–21 (May 1979).

The author stresses that teachers must *teach* reading, writing, speaking, and listening in an integrated fashion. All students, including gifted students, must recognize that reading is but one aspect of communication, writing is but one aspect, and listening is but one aspect. Biersdorf makes a good case for this stance.

Bosma, Jeannine, and Schultz, Carol. "Learning to Review Literature: Two Books Worthy of Assessment by *G/C/T* Young Adults." *G/C/T* 6:12–13 (January/February 1979).

And This Is Laura and *A Gift of Magic* are the two books recommended for creative reading activities with gifted youth. Suggestions for a format are included.

Brown, Jean E. "Supplementary Materials for Academically Gifted English Students." *Journal for the Education of the Gifted* 5:67–73 (Winter 1982).

The author has annotated periodicals suitable for use with gifted high school students. The annotations are divided into six categories: literary anthologies; cultural and historical heritage; humor; literary; literary, political, and social review; and news. This book would be quite useful for English teachers, department heads, and/or librarians.

Brown and Rogan 1983. *See* Reading

Buescher, Thomas M. "Language as Play: A Case for Playfulness in Language Arts for Gifted Children." *Language Arts* 56:16–20 (January 1979).

Buescher recommends that a language arts curriculum be based on five basic assumptions: (1) learning comes through experiential interaction with the world; (2) the best learning is "playful" learning; (3) conceptualization is heightened through play with symbols systems; (4) imagination facilitates cognitive, expressive, and conceptual ability; (5) "playfulness" in language arts precludes lockstep curriculum.

Burrows, Alvina Treut. "Encouraging Talented Children to Write." *Education* 88:31–34 (September/October 1967).

The author explores ways that all children can be encouraged to write and ways that meet the special needs of the gifted.

Caulfield, Jane. "A Key to Creativity: Children Write for Children." *G/C/T* 34:35–38 (September/October 1984).

The author, a teaching librarian, tells about a writing program she developed and implemented with three students at her school. The final product for each student was a book to present to children aged five to seven.

Cioffi, Diane Harper. "Writing Is a Thinking Process: A Back to Basics Model for the Gifted." *G/C/T* 34:13–14 (September/October 1984).

The author argues that writing is a logical process. She compares Donald Murray's Thinking-Writing Process with Bloom's Taxonomy, Parnes's Creative Problem-Solving Method, and Treffinger's Self-Directed Learning Model.

Clark, Wilma. "Twenty Hours of Activities in Vocabulary Building for High Potential Students." *English Journal* 70:16–21 (February 1981).

Clark offers a collection of very usable ideas. Middle school and high school teachers in English or other content areas will be able to adapt them for use with their bright students.

Coleman, Dona R. "Effects of the Use of a Writing Scale by Gifted Primary Students." *Gifted Child Quarterly* 27:114–21 (Summer 1983).

Coleman investigated the effects of using a creative writing scale (the Sager Writing Scale) as an evaluative and instructional tool for gifted primary age students. The scale consists of four subscales: vocabulary, elaboration, organization, and structure. Her results indicate that the students' writing abilities and attitudes towards writing were positively affected.

————. "Use of Literary Models in Writing for the Gifted: With My Own Words." *G/C/T* 34:22–23 (September/October 1984).

Coleman explains why using literary models is valuable when teaching children how to write. She provides several examples along with her rationale.

Coody, Betty, and Nelson, David. *Teaching Elementary Language Arts: A Literature Approach*. Belmont, Calif.: Wadsworth, 1982. 390 pp.

An excellent resource for teachers of elementary and middle school students. Since their notion of how to teach language arts is through literature, it is particularly appropriate for able learners.

Corpening, Dodie K. "What Page Did You Say That Was?" *G/C/T* 34:39–42 (September/October 1984).

Seven sequential activities presented are designed to improve students' listening skills. It appears that if teachers used these and followed the author's other instructions, the need to repeat directions would be decreased.

_____. "All Right Class, Let's Discuss It." *G/C/T* 35:27–29 (November/December 1984).

The author presents a series of lessons she has used to teach gifted students how to communicate ideas through discussion.

_____. "Intelligent Listening." *G/C/T* 36:15–17 (January/February 1985).

Corpening suggests two activities that will improve students' skills in listening to other students' reports. She suggests that they prepare questions which they expect to have answered during the report, and/or complete a form evaluating the student giving the report. A copy of the form is included.

Costa, Arthur L. "Thinking: How Do We Know Students Are Getting Better at It?" *Roeper Review* 6:197–99 (April 1984).

Costa says that teachers can observe their students and determine whether they are becoming better thinkers. Such behaviors as the following indicate better thinking during problem solving: perseverance, decreased impulsivity, flexibility in thinking, metacognition, checking for accuracy, problem posing, drawing on past knowledge and experiences, transference beyond the learning situation, precision of language, enjoyment of problem solving, an "I can" and "I enjoy" attitude.

Crittenden, Mary R., Kaplan, Marjorie H., and Heim, Judith K. "Developing Effective Study Skills and Self-Confidence in Academically Able Young Adolescents." *Gifted Child Quarterly* 28:25–30 (Winter 1984).

The authors' study focused on early adolescents who had succeeded in elementary school but were underachieving in junior high school (based on a determination of potential indicated by standardized test scores). Sixteen students participated in a short course designed to improve self-concept, study skills, and written language skills. All improved.

Cutforth, Nancy B. "A People Fair." *G/C/T* 35:54–55 (November/December 1984).

Cutforth explains the "Successful People Fair" presented by the second through sixth grades in the school's academically talented program. She gives an overview of the eight-week preparatory schedule, a rationale for such a fair, and activities for investigating successful persons for a people fair (based on Bloom's Taxonomy).

Daniel, Neil. "The Challenge of Writing: Tactics for Teaching Gifted Students." *G/C/T* 21:53–56 (January/February 1982).

Daniel posits that, rather than telling children that writing is important, teachers should tell them that writing is fun, stimulating, and the essence of thinking and learning. He recommends journal writing (as young as age three or four), letter writing, and word play as means to encourage children to take up the challenge of writing.

DeHaven, Edna P. *Teaching and Learning the Language Arts.* 2d ed. Boston: Little, Brown, 1983. 540 pp.

DeHaven has designed her book to provide sound practical teaching ideas, based on the latest research and theory. Very useful for teachers.

Fearn, Leif. "Writing: A Basic and Developmental Skill for Gifted Learners." *G/C/T* 17:26–27 (March/April 1981).

The author defines writing as "an expression of disciplined creative thinking and problem-solving skills manifest in the face of procrastination." Fearn believes that the majority of gifted students are writing far below their capabilities—mostly because of lack of instruction. He provides several suggestions taken from a book he cites.

Ferris, Mary Patricia. "Developing Higher Level Thinking Skills in Gifted Students Using Structuring Communication Activities." *G/C/T* 19:42–43 (September/October 1981).

Using the newspaper, the author developed activities to bring her gifted students from lower-level to higher-level thinking skills.

Finn, Jacqueline L. "Sowing the Write Seeds: Creative Writing for the Gifted." *G/C/T* 18:51–53 (May/June 1981).

The author, a teacher of elementary gifted children, believes that young writers must have a curriculum that fosters a love of writing and provides the skills necessary to write. She also states that young writers need to realize and develop the "true behaviors of the writer." The article includes a good rationale for this stance along with numerous sources for teachers to use in preparing their writing programs for gifted students.

Frazier, Virginia. "What Beginning English Teachers Need to Know about the Talented and Gifted: We Lay Waste Their Powers." *English Education* 10:227–32 (May 1979).

The author has written a very lucid article—which should be made available to beginning English teachers.

Frey, Diane. "The Use of Metaphors with Gifted Children." *G/C/T* 34:28–29 (September/October 1984).

The author posits that using metaphors with gifted children is effective, since many such children enjoy thinking abstractly. She then briefly discusses universal and prescriptive metaphors.

Frith, Greg H., and Mims, Aquilla A. "Teaching Gifted Students to

Make Verbal Presentations.'' *Gifted Child Quarterly* 28:45–47 (Winter 1984).

The authors identify and describe selected procedures that gifted students can use to make effective verbal presentations. Their suggestions should be very useful for classroom teachers.

Frith, Greg H., and Reynolds, Freddy. ''Slide Tape Shows: A Creative Activity for Gifted Students.'' *Teaching Exceptional Children* 15:151–53 (Spring 1983).

The authors elaborate on seven steps for developing a slide presentation: select a topic, write a script, develop graphics, take pictures, develop audio, choose music, integrate slides and audio.

George, John C. ''Language Arts for the Gifted.'' *Elementary English* 49:582–84 (April 1972).

The author gives a brief description of his language arts class for gifted students in fourth, fifth, and sixth grade. He utilizes reading, researching, writing, and listening.

Gilmar, Sybil. ''What If They Just Want to Write?'' *G/C/T* 9:8–10 (September/October 1979).

Gilmar relates the experience of the fifty students enrolled in the Challenge Program in her school district. The gifted students, ages seven to fifteen, all wanted to write. In order to accommodate their wishes and still provide an enriched program for them, the teachers set up their classes as ''writing workshops.'' Students belonged to one of three groups, depending on the type of writing they wished to do. The program appears to have been quite successful. A good bibliography for teachers who want to implement such a program in their gifted classroom is included.

Hanke, Jeannette J. ''Filmmaking—Some Experiences with the Gifted.'' *English Journal* 60:121–25 (January 1971).

The author relates her experiences with Honors and AP students who made a film as part of her course. She recounts their successes and tribulations—but is emphatic about the ultimate value.

Hershey, Myrliss, and Kearns, Phyllis. ''The Effect of Guided Fantasy on the Creative Thinking and Writing Ability of Gifted Students.'' *Gifted Child Quarterly* 23:71–77 (Spring 1979).

The authors conducted a study with fifty-one gifted students in fourth, fifth, and sixth grade to determine whether participation in sessions emphasizing relaxation techniques and guided fantasy would positively affect students' abilities to be creative, as measured on Torrance Tests of Creative Thinking and a writing exercise. The results demonstrated that guided fantasy can profitably be used to stimulate creative thinking prior to having students write.

Iarusso, Marilyn Berg. "Creative Children: Children as Filmmakers." *Top of the News* 28:60–67 (November 1971).

The author, a storyteller and group-work specialist with the New York Public Library's Office of Children's Services, believes that films are an ideal medium of self-expression for talented children, particularly for disadvantaged children, who often are nonverbal, lack in confidence, and may face a language problem as well. She visited four filmmaking centers in Manhattan to talk to children and adults producing eight-millimeter and super-eight-millimeter films. Her discoveries are related here.

Isaacs, Ann F. "What to Do When You Discover a Child Is Gifted and Interested in Language." *Gifted Child Quarterly* 17:144–49 (Summer 1973).

The secondary title for this article is "One Hundred Ways to Tickle Your Fancy with Language and Linguistics." The author has listed marvelous suggestions that parents and teachers can and should utilize with able children who are fascinated with language.

Jensen, Julie M. "Do Gifted Children Speak an Intellectual Dialect?" *Exceptional Children* 39:337–38 (January 1973).

The author studied and compared forty average boys and girls with forty superior boys and girls. Language samples were obtained for both a "casual style" and a "careful speech style." Significant differences occurred on 38 of the 147 comparisons.

Job, Beverly J., and Campbell, Patricia B. "Language Arts Resources for the Gifted: An Annotated Bibliography." *Gifted Child Quarterly* 20:205–23 (Summer 1976).

The authors evaluated materials according to six criteria: (1) Did the materials challenge the students to further investigation? (2) Did activities challenge the students to think critically and/or creatively? (3) Were questions and suggested activities open-ended, with no "right" answer? (4) Were materials adaptable for use by students of various abilities and interests? (5) Were materials designed for independent use? (6) Did materials present sex-role stereotypes? Using these criteria, the authors selected and annotated scores of materials for use in the language arts. The annotations are divided into six categories: creative writing, dramatics, thinking skills, humanities, values clarification, professional, and miscellaneous.

Johnston, James W. "Dialectic for Gifted Elementary Students." *Roeper Review* 6:47–48 (September 1983).

Dialectic is "a discussion by dialogue for the investigation of truth by analysis" and "a method of scientific investigation concerning the science of ideas or of nature and the laws of being." Johnston provides a rationale for dialectic and explains a dialectic teaching program at the Key Largo School during the 1980–81 and 1981–82 school years.

Kenny, Adele. "Guiding the Gifted: Self-Awareness through Creative Writing." *G/C/T* 23:9–11 (May/June 1982).

The author recommends using specifically designed creative writing activities as a point of departure for self-awareness sensitivity training. She lists and explains several writing activities in each of three categories: introductory, developmental, and concluding.

Kent, Suzanne, and Esgar, Lavelle. "Research Techniques for Gifted Primary Students." *G/C/T* 28:28–29 (May/June 1983).

The authors teach at an independent school, and they explain their program for enriching their second- and third-grade gifted curricula. They designed a program, emphasizing comprehension strategies, to allow students to be creative readers and to use their reading as a basis for extending their learning. General activities are presented.

Kingore, Bertie W. "Droodles." *G/C/T* 32:36–38 (March/April 1984).

Kingore presents a brief rationale for using droodles (drawings that symbolize a word or phrase) to stimulate divergent thinking and written expression. She then exemplifies the rationale with numerous droodles and activities involving droodles.

Larrick, Nancy. "Poetry Is for Everyone." *Gifted Child Quarterly* 20:42–46 (Spring 1976).

Larrick recommends using poetry with able children. She provides numerous titles that teachers and parents may obtain as they plan poetry encounters for children.

Lengel, Alan L. "Classroom Debating in the Elementary School." *G/C/T* 28:57–60 (May/June 1983).

Lengel presents a method for involving all members of a class in some aspect of a debate situation. He has used the method successfully with gifted/talented fifth and sixth graders.

Lewis, George L. "Speech: A Challenge for the Gifted." *Gifted Child Quarterly* 4:23–26 (1959).

The author posits that, since speech is the basic element in the communicative process, much more time and effort needs to be expended by schools in improving students' abilities to communicate orally. He believes a speech program for gifted students serves their needs in an ideal fashion: it allows them to explore, to solve problems, and to develop leadership skills.

List, Karen L. "Writing: The Journey and the Dance." *G/C/T* 26:26–31 (January/February 1983).

When this article was written, List was cofounder and director of the Young People's Institute, a seven-day summer program for gifted and talented youth held at the University of Connecticut. The participants ranged in age from nine to fourteen. The program was built on Renzulli's Enrichment Triad Model, so it included general exploratory activities, group training activities (emphasizing Murray's seven major aspects of writing), and a final product—*Journey's Dance,* an anthology of the work created by the participants. Several samples are included in the article.

Malone, Charlotte E. "Cost Little (or Less Than That): Creative Teaching Ideas." *Gifted Child Quarterly* 19:68–70 (Spring 1975).

Malone presents some good ideas for teaching evaluation skills, skills of search, attribute listing, divergent production, and questioning.

Master, Doris Leff. "Writing and the Gifted Child." *Gifted Child Quarterly* 27:162–68 (Fall 1983).

Master describes a developmental program designed to improve and develop gifted children's writing skills. Her presentation is excellent.

Mindell, Phyllis, and Stracher, Dorothy. "Assessing Reading and Writing of the Gifted: The Warp and Woof of the Language Program." *Gifted Child Quarterly* 24:72–80 (Spring 1980).

The authors have developed an ongoing process for evaluating gifted students' reading and writing abilities. Several of the instruments are included, along with the rationale behind the concepts and instruments. The authors operate under four premises: (1) The goal of the language program for the gifted is to enable them to think and act creatively. (2) Creative thought and action are predicated upon a basic language education that emphasizes both skill and advanced thinking ability in all aspects of reading and writing. (3) The first step in setting up such a program is to evaluate each student's functional abilities in each aspect of reading and writing. (4) An ideal vehicle for such a program is the unit, which permits basic skills to be taught within a meaningful context.

National Council of Teachers of English. *English for the Academically Talented Student in the Secondary School.* Washington, D.C.: National Education Association, 1969. 109 pp.

Nine essays concerning teaching English to gifted high school students comprise the text of this book.

Patterson, Patricia, and Starcher, Sherolyn. "Characteristics of Culturally Diverse Gifted Students: With Implications for Language Arts Programming and Design of Learning Materials." *G/C/T* 21:6–8 (January/February 1982).

The authors review several studies which have indicated that culturally diverse children have different learning styles. They offer several suggestions for modifications and changes in language arts curriculum.

Perry, Phyllis J., and Hoback, John R. "Independent Study: The Second (or is it the third) Time Around?" *G/C/T* 27:39–41 (March/April 1983).

The authors point out that, although not a new idea, independent study with middle school gifted students is valuable. Six stages of development are presented along with a discussion of Renzulli's Enrichment Triad Model as a framework for developing independent study activities.

Pilon, A. Barbara. "Non-Stereotyped Literature for Today's Bright Girls," *Gifted Child Quarterly* 21:234–38 (Summer 1977).

Pilon provides a great annotated list of books that present a nonstereotyped view of girls.

Quisenberry, Nancy L. "Developing Language Fluency in the Gifted Culturally Different Child." *Gifted Child Quarterly* 18:175–79 (Fall 1974).

The author warns against measuring culturally different or disadvantaged children's intellect by their dialect, which may cause teachers to overlook some gifted students.

Reis, Sally M., and Cellerino, Margaret. "Guiding Gifted Students through Independent Study." *Teaching Exceptional Children* 15:136–39 (Spring 1983).

The development of one student's independent project exemplifies the value of having gifted students work on independent studies.

Reynolds, Ben. "College Level Writing Skills for the Early-Adolescent Verbally Gifted: Philosophy and Practice." *G/C/T* 16:48–51 (January/February 1981).

This article is about the Writing Skills (WS) workshops held by the Johns Hopkins University Program for Verbally Gifted Youth. This program is the verbal counterpart of the JHU Study for Mathematically Precocious Youth. However, the workshops, since they are addressing the verbal skill of writing, are set up quite differently from the accelerated program of the SMPY. Students are divided into small groups of between six and fifteen, with a professional writer assigned to each. The groups function as writers' workshops, with members critiquing each others' work. A fine bibliography and reference list is provided for those interested in further reading.

Roody, Sarah I. "Teaching Conrad's *Victory* to Superior High School Students." *English Journal* 58:40–46 (January 1969).

The author describes a unit plan she has used successfully in preparing superior students to take the AP English examination. The plan is well organized and well explained.

Rowe, Ernest R. "Creative Writing and the Gifted Child." *Exceptional Children* 34:279–82 (December 1967).

The author provides some ideas for stimulating creative writing among gifted middle school students. These were used successfully by him during one school year.

Royer, Regina. "Creating Writing Assignments for the Gifted." *G/C/T* 21:28–30 (January/February 1982).

Royer states that although educators have developed curriculum based on Renzulli's Triad Model and Bloom's Taxonomy of Educational Objectives, "these teaching methods have not been fully utilized in composition programs." She believes that writing assignments should focus on real problems and require thinking at the various levels of Bloom's taxonomy. A sample that illustrates her idea quite clearly is included.

Schuster, Edgar H. "An Opportunity for Divergent Thinking in the Classroom: Students against the Text." *G/C/T* 34:30–33 (September/October 1984).

Schuster suggests that teachers can help students learn to be critical thinkers by encouraging them to find inconsistencies in textbooks.

Sebesta, Sam L. "Language Arts Programs for the Gifted." *Gifted Child Quarterly* 20:18–23+ (Spring 1976).

Sebesta strongly suggests that a language arts program for the gifted must have a structure—it cannot be simply a hodgepodge of activities. He recommends intrinsic motivation rather than extrinsic "sugar on the slate" motivation for gifted students.

Seiger, Sydelle D. "Reaching beyond Thinking Skills to Thinking Strategies for the Academically Gifted." *Roeper Review* 6:185–88 (April 1984).

Seiger says that people developing thinking skills curriculum for gifted students need to ask themselves whether they want to produce students who have maintained, extended, and applied the thinking ability with which they were naturally endowed, or if they want to produce students who are consistently effective and autonomous in producing useful, apt, and unique thought products in whatever situation they find themselves and in evaluating their own and others' thought products. She says once this decision is made, then curriculum designers will know how to develop the curriculum. Seiger makes rich suggestions for the latter type.

Shachter, Jacqueline. "Learning about Authors in Person and in Mixed Media." *Gifted Child Quarterly* 24:69–71 (Spring 1980).

Shachter states that, since authors generally limit their personal appearances, most children will have little or no opportunity to hear real authors talk about their work—unless they have access to the wide variety of mixed media presentations of authors. She discusses several sources, including books, tapes, movies, filmstrips, and videotapes. Many teachers will find this an enlightening article.

Sisk, Dorthy A. "Communication Skills for the Gifted." *Gifted Child Quarterly* 19:66–68 (Spring 1975).

Sisk presents two activities designed to encourage students to contribute and to build on others' ideas.

Stewig, John W. "I Absolutely Refuse to Be an Onion." *Gifted Child Quarterly* 20:31–39 (Spring 1976).

Stewig defines creative dramatics and then gives numerous suggestions for their use to encourage expressive, communicative, social, and creative behavior.

Stoddard, Elizabeth Pelton, and Renzulli, Joseph S. "Improving the Writing Skills of Talent Poor Students." *Gifted Child Quarterly* 27:21–27 (Winter 1983).

Using as subjects fifth and sixth graders of above-average ability, the authors did a study to determine whether the students' writing ability could be improved using activities designed to enhance their writing maturity and creativity. A holistic assessment of the writing indicated an improvement in the treatment group over the comparison group. A four-point, four-characteristic scale indicated a significant difference in creativity. Syntactic maturity also showed improvement.

Swicord, Barbara. "Debating with Gifted Fifth and Sixth Graders—Telling It Like It Was, Is, and Could Be." *Gifted Child Quarterly* 28:127–29 (Summer 1984).

Swicord discusses the debate component that has been a part of her district's gifted/talented program "Horizons" for six years. She said the purposes it serves are: (1) to teach children to debate rather than to argue; (2) to make children aware that every issue has two sides; (3) to make children more aware of current and pertinent issues; (4) to provide them with a constructive means for participating in the resolution of these issues; (5) to teach a higher level of research skills than they had previously learned; (6) to build students' self-confidence in speaking before an audience.

Tomer, Margaret. "Human Relations in Education—a Rationale for a Curriculum in Inter-Personal Communication Skills for Gifted Students—Grades K-12." *Gifted Child Quarterly* 25:94–97 (Spring 1981).

Tomer uses the Krathwohl, Bloom, and Masia Taxonomy of Educational Objectives—Affective Domain as the framework for her communications model. Her model is divided into five sections: (1) Receiving—Impressions, Interpretations and Sensations; (2) Responding—Reach Out and Touch Somebody; (3) Valuing—Developing a Foundation for Choice; (4) Organizing a Value System—Freedom and Responsibility in Making Choices; and (5) Developing a Code of Behavior Based on Accepted Values—Making the Dream and the Deed One. She believes that the gifted must have effective communication skills.

Torrance, E. Paul. "Ten Ways of Helping Young Children Gifted in Creative Writing and Speech." *Gifted Child Quarterly* 6:121–27 (Winter 1962).

The author presents ten suggestions for parents to help encourage children gifted in writing and speech—for example, provide materials that develop imagination, encourage children to record their ideas, encourage children to play with words.

Tway, Eileen. "The Gifted Child in Literature." *Language Arts* 57:14–20 (January 1980.)

Tway discusses numerous books that have main characters who are gifted children. Librarians, teachers, and parents will want to make sure their libraries have these books.

Vining, Patricia Ferguson. "Fairy Tales: Literature 001: A Minicourse for the Young Gifted Child (K–3)." *G/C/T* 4:40–41 (September/October 1978).

The author presents several activities to use with young gifted children as they explore fairy tales.

Vrba, Suzanna. "How a Gifted Student Writes." *G/C/T* 20:43–47 (November/December 1981).

In response to a letter from a former teacher, the author, a tenth grader, explains how she writes. Also included are samples of her poetry, stories, essays, and reports.

Warnken, Kelly. "Hey, Why Don't We Send It to a Magazine?" *G/C/T* 9:64–66 (September/October 1979).

The author has compiled a list of twenty-five magazines that accept work written by children and young adults. The address for each magazine is included along with an annotation concerning its content. This is a valuable resource.

Wedman, John, and Jensen, Rita A. "The Neglected Role of Media in Gifted Education." *G/C/T* 28:50–53 (May/June 1983).

The authors encourage teachers of the gifted to use media with their students and to help them learn how to use media. Three levels of objectives are given for using video production and photo/slide production. Good resources are suggested in the bibliography.

Weinstein, Joshua, and Laufman, Larry. "Teaching Logical Reasoning to Gifted Students." *Gifted Child Quarterly* 24:186–90 (Fall 1980).

The authors propose that the teaching of logic is appropriate for gifted learners. They provide support from psychology (Piaget and Kohlberg) and from experimental data.

Wolf, Willavene, and Shigaki, Irene. "A Developmental Study of Young Gifted Children's Conditional Reasoning Ability." *Gifted Child Quarterly* 27:173–79 (Fall 1983).

The authors tested two hypotheses regarding young children's ability to reason conditionally (on syllogisms). The results are given, and the authors believe a data base has been established.

Workman, Brooke. "A Semester of Hemingway for Gifted High School Students." *Journal of Reading* 23:598–600 (April 1980).

The author relates the success of the in-depth seminars she offers for gifted students. Each semester, the seminar focuses on a different author.

Library

Baker, D. Philip, and Bender, David R. "The Gifted and Talented." *Library Media Programs and the Special Learner.* Hamden, Conn.: Library Professional Publication, 1981a.

The chapter is written from an understandably biased viewpoint. It extols the potential of the positive influence that librarians and media specialists may represent for gifted and talented students. Characteristics that mark the gifted are described along with suggestions of ways to capitalize on those characteristics. Descriptions of five exemplary programs are presented. The entire book should be read by all librarians and media specialists.

_____. "School Library Media Programs and the Gifted and Talented." *School Library Journal* 27:21–25 (February 1981b).

This article was adapted and excerpted from chapter 4, "The Gifted and Talented," of the authors' book *Library Media Programs and the Special Learner.* They present three exemplary library programs that serve gifted children and youth.

Cummings, Alysa. "Super Summer: The Haddonfield Public Library's Summer Enrichment Program." *G/C/T* 23:57–59 (May/June 1982).

Haddonfield (N.J.) Public Library offers an eight-week summer program for self-identified gifted children based on three considerations: (1) individual children's needs, interests, and talents; (2) current research; (3) process-oriented curriculum that is product-directed. Phase 1 of the summer program offers workshops, while Phase 2 offers independent-study opportunities.

Dameron, Jennie. "Media Center Projects for Elementary Students." *Journal for the Education of the Gifted* 3:111–16 (1979).

The author makes suggestions intended as springboards for what librarians and media specialists can do to better serve gifted students. The two categories she addresses are independent study and evaluation.

Dresang, Eliza T. "Philosophy Statement: Library Services for the Gifted." *Top of the News* 38:301–2 (Summer 1982).

Dresang agrees that libraries should serve all children and youth but points out that librarians must recognize the gifted patron's special needs, which differ from the norm in terms of both manner and degree of service.

Hertz, Karl V., and Janecek, Blanche. "Libraries Are Important for Gifted Students." *NASSP Bulletin* 62:120–21 (February 1978).

The authors succinctly express the need for libraries to embrace the gifted.

Impellizzeri, Anne E. "A Parent's View: A Personal Statement, Enhanced by Consultation with Numerous Parents of Gifted Children." *Top of the News* 28:53–54 (November 1971).

Librarians are asked to be sensitive to gifted children as individuals—and to help nourish their growth as individuals.

Marland, Sidney P., Jr. "The Gifted Child and the Library." *Top of the News* 28:27–28 (November 1971).

Marland briefly iterates the need for libraries to embrace and encourage the gifted.

Mullen, Eunice G. "A Librarian's View: Open Access: A Boon to the Gifted Child." *Top of the News* 28:55–57 (November 1971).

Mullen describes the Rochester, New York, library's one-card, open-access system. She urges other libraries to adopt the same policy.

Noyes, Naomi. "An Interview with Dr. Hilary Deason: 'Some Day I Am Going to Be a Scientist.' " *Top of the News* 28:58–59 (November 1971).

Deason recommends numerous ways librarians can encourage gifted students' interest in science.

Renzulli 1977. *See* Introduction

Roslak, Carole, and Deutsch, Robin. "Making Cross Connections: Serving Gifted Students in the School Media Center." *Top of the News* 38:303–7 (Summer 1982).

The authors say that media centers can function like a multiple outlet device by providing multiple connections to knowledge. They encourage librarians to become informed about the gifted and to cooperate with teachers of the gifted. They state that it is *not* true that the gifted can teach themselves all they need to know about the library.

Smith, Janice. "Media Services for Gifted Students: An Overview." *School Media Quarterly* 8:161–68, 177–78 (Spring 1980).

This article presents the role of the library media specialist as it pertains to one specific curriculum model: Carolyn Tennant's "Tennant Gifted Extension Model." Her model specifies four areas in which the gifted need a qualitatively differentiated program: content, process, output, and evaluation. The author examines each of the four components of the model as it relates to the library media specialist.

South, Jean-Anne. "Gifted Children among Minority Groups: A Crying Need for Recognition." *Top of the News* 28:43–46 (November 1971).

South gives a number of examples of minority gifted adults who received no recognition until they were adults, because they were not Caucasian. She states that librarians can (and must) help recognize and serve bright young minority students.

Walker, H. Thomas. "Media Services for Gifted Learners." *School Media Quarterly* 6:253–54, 259–63 (Summer 1978).

Walker briefly discusses the characteristics of gifted students, then presents his recommendations concerning media services for them. A good media center or library should provide these services: (1) instructional development and design, (2) evaluation and selection of media, (3) reading guidance, (4) media and library skills instruction, (5) media production.

Witty, Paul A. "The Librarian as a Talent Scout." *Top of the News* 28:34–37 (November 1971).

Witty offers ways that librarians can readily identify their gifted patrons—and encourages them to do so!

Foreign Language

Bartz, Walter. "The Role of Foreign Language Education for the Gifted and Talented Student." *Foreign Language Annals* 15:329–34 (October 1982).

This position paper was prepared by Bartz for the National Council of State Supervisors of Foreign Languages. Their position is that all students, but especially the gifted, must receive education in foreign language. They recommend that, for the gifted, this education should begin sooner and be accelerated, and that a second foreign language should be pursued as soon as the students gain proficiency in the first.

Carlson, Nancy N. "An Exploratory Study of Characteristics of Gifted and Talented Foreign Language Learners." *Foreign Language Annals* 14:385–91 (December 1981).

The author studied the characteristics of gifted and talented foreign language learners and lists them in this article. She also includes some discussion of differences in the perceptions of students by French, German, and Spanish teachers.

Keating, L. Clark. "Languages for the Gifted." *Gifted Child Quarterly* 3:47–48+ (1959).

The author states that foreign languages are readily learned by young students—especially gifted ones. He suggests that gifted children can, and possibly should, be expected to learn two foreign languages simultaneously.

Pontillo, James J. "A Self-Instructional Language Program on the High School Level." *Foreign Language Annals* 10:284–87 (May 1977).

The author explains how a SILP (Self-Instructional Language Program), originally designed for college students, can be used at the high school level with linguistically gifted and highly motivated students. Foreign language department heads should explore this idea.

Rebbeck, Barbara J. "Foreign Language Techniques for the Gifted, or Watch Your Bloomin' Language!!" *Roeper Review* 4:31–33 (April/May 1983).

The author explains how to challenge gifted students in foreign language classrooms by structuring some opportunities for exploration using Bloom's Taxonomy.

Soffietti, James P. "Foreign Languages." In *Curriculum Planning for the Gifted*, edited by Louis A. Fliegler. Englewood Cliffs, N.J.: Prentice-Hall, 1961.

Soffietti advocates early instruction in the foreign languages. His belief is that the nation's future leaders—today's gifted students—must have knowledge and understanding of other cultures, including their languages, aspirations, and ways of thinking.

Preschool

Camp, Louis T. "Purposeful Preschool Education." *Gifted Child Quarterly* 7:106–7 (Autumn 1963).

The author, principal of Hunter College Elementary School (for gifted children), relates the philosophy of the school concerning preschoolers and their learning. He urges teachers of preschool gifted children to use activity units that stress meaning and purpose in learning.

Caruthers, Margaret. "Some Observations about Gifted Preschool Children." *Gifted Child Quarterly* 7:116–18 (Autumn 1963).

Caruthers, who directs her own nursery school, says that gifted preschoolers are purposeful about their learning, are constantly ready to explore new ideas and places, and need wise encouragement from parents and teachers.

Delahanty, Rebecca. "Challenge, Opportunity, and Frustration: Developing a Gifted Program for Kindergartners." *Roeper Review* 6:206–8 (April 1984).

The author describes her experience with a school district in designing and implementing an identification system and program for gifted kindergartners. She offers a rationale, explains the background research done, and outlines the design of the program. Although the program was deemed very successful, because of budget cuts it was discontinued—hence the frustration mentioned in the title.

Follis, Helen D., and Krockover, Gerald H. "Selecting Activities in Science and Mathematics for Gifted Young Children." *School Science and Mathematics* 82:57–64 (January 1982).

The authors stress that gifted preschoolers must be actively involved in their learning. Teachers must select activities that encourage peer interaction, provide opportunities for discovery learning, foster independence in learning, and include the cognitive, affective, and psychomotor domains of learning. Examples of such activities are given.

Fox, Ann E. "Kindergarten: Forgotten Year for the Gifted?" *Gifted Child Quarterly* 15:42–48 (Spring 1971).

The author, who obviously feels very strongly about the travesty of gifted children's education in kindergarten, provides numerous examples to illustrate the reasons for her strong feelings. Although it deserves to be read, the author's tone may put some kindergarten teachers on the defensive—especially if they recognize themselves.

Gallagher, James J., and Ramsbotham, Ann. "Early Childhood Programs for the Gifted." *Educational Horizons* 56:42–46 (Fall 1977).

The author discusses early manifestations of giftedness and how to accommodate them. They mention parent counseling, early admissions, and special programs.

Gensley, Juliana. "The Pre-School Gifted Child." *Gifted Child Quarterly* 17:219–20 (Fall 1973).

In this brief article, the author suggests that parents (and teachers) work to ensure that gifted children have the concepts to match their vocabulary.

Hanninen, Gail. "Developing a Preschool Gifted/Talented Program." *G/C/T* 9:18–19, 21 (September/October 1979).

Hanninen describes the Sunburst School (otherwise known as the Rural Preschool Gifted and Gifted/Handicapped Model Project), including the criteria it uses to identify gifted preschoolers and the learning environment it offers. This article would be a good reference for anyone interested in education for gifted preschoolers.

Kaplan, Sandra N. "The Role of Playing in a Differentiated Curriculum for the Young Gifted Child." *Roeper Review* 3:12–13 (November/December 1980).

Kaplan defines play for young gifted children as an instructional strategy designed to meet particular learning needs. She offers a strong rationale and a way for teachers of young children to determine ways of using play in their differentiated curriculum for the gifted.

Karnes, Merle B., and Bertschi, Jane D. "Identifying and Educating Gifted/Talented Nonhandicapped and Handicapped Preschoolers." *Teaching Exceptional Children* 10:114–19 (Summer 1978).

The authors describe the RAPYHT Program (Retrieval and Acceleration of Promising Young Handicapped and Talented), which operates in Illinois. They explain how children are screened by the program and then compare two different ways they might be served—through either the SOI (Structure of Intellect) Model or the Open Classroom Model.

Karnes, Merle B., and Shwedel, Allan M. "Assessment of Preschool Giftedness." In *The Psychoeducational Assessment of Preschool Children*, edited by Kathleen D. Paget and Bruce A. Bracken. New York: Greene and Stratton, 1983.

This apparently well-written book includes a chapter, "Assessment of Preschool Giftedness," which should be required reading for early childhood courses. Three good examples of gifted preschoolers are described. The authors stress the need for more research because very little has been done in this area. Several good instruments are included in the appendix.

Karnes, Merle B., Shwedel, Allan M., and Kemp, Polly B. "Maximizing the Potential of the Young Gifted Child." *Roeper Review* 7:204–8 (April 1985).

The authors give several reasons why preschool gifted children are rarely served. They then present an overview of the University of Illinois Program for Young Gifted Children: goals, objectives, recruitment, identification, and programming. They also discuss five principles of learning upon which the program is built: (1) learning is developmental; (2) learning involves the child in decision making;

(3) learning integrates knowledge; (4) learning is based on dialogue; (5) learning involves acting on the environment.

Karnes, Merle B., Shwedel, Allan M., and Lewis, George F. "Long-Term Effects of Early Programming for the Gifted/Talented Handicapped." *Journal for the Education of the Gifted* 6:266–78 (Summer 1983).

The authors report on a follow-up study of elementary children who participated in the RAPYHT (Retrieval and Acceleration of Promising Young Handicapped and Talented) program as preschoolers. Indications are that early identification and programming pay off for gifted/talented children who are also handicapped.

_____. "Short-Term Effects of Early Programming for the Young Gifted Handicapped Child." *Exceptional Children* 50:103–9 (October 1983).

The authors present research supporting the use of RAPYHT. The model looks very promising.

Karnes, Merle B., Shwedel, Allan M., and Williams, Mark. "Combining Instructional Models for Young Gifted Children." *Teaching Exceptional Children* 15:128–35 (Spring 1983).

The authors discuss their use of an instructional model that resulted from combining the open framework model of the British Infant School and the SOI model. They present the goals, rationale, and specific examples of how to implement the model with preschool children.

Kitano, Margie. "Young Gifted Children: Strategies for Preschool Teachers." *Young Children* 37:14–24 (May 1982).

Kitano reviews the literature on gifted young children and makes six specific recommendations for their curriculum. The article is clearly written and would serve as a good basis for preservice or inservice training of preschool teachers.

_____. "Issues and Problems in Establishing Preschool Programs for the Gifted." *Roeper Review* 7:212–13 (April 1985).

The issues and problems in establishing preschool programs for the gifted that Kitano has identified are (1) the absence of longitudinal data, (2) parent expectations, (3) effects on confidence and self-concept, (4) children's interests versus school demands, (5) maintaining consistency with an established model.

Malone, Charlotte E. "Early Childhood Education of Gifted Children." *Gifted Child Quarterly* 18:188–90 (Fall 1974).

This brief article discusses the need for intellectual peer grouping as early as kindergarten for gifted children.

_____. "Gifted Children in Early Childhood Education." *Viewpoints in Teaching and Learning: Early Childhood Education and Perspective* 55:25–28 (Summer 1979).

Malone reviews the characteristics of young gifted children and discusses curricular modifications based on these characteristics.

Mathews, F. Neil. "Parental Perceptions of a Preschool Gifted Program in a Public School System." *Roeper Review* 6:210–13 (April 1984).

Louisiana's 1981 Education for All Exceptional Children law mandated special education services for all gifted/talented youth, including those of preschool age. Although the programs are mandated by the state, the enrollment in the preschool programs is optional. Therefore, positive parental attitudes are crucial to the success and survival of the program. Mathews describes parental evaluation of a public school preschool gifted program and points out issues that could have implications for similar programs.

McHardy, Roberta. "Planning for Preschool Gifted Education." *G/C/T* 29:24–27 (September/October 1983).

This article is a dialogue concerning identification, curriculum, teacher preparation, evaluation, and parent participation in preschool gifted education. Those involved in the discussion are all nationally recognized experts in the field and were invited to participate in this special-interest meeting held at the twenty-ninth annual meeting of the National Association for Gifted Children, held in New Orleans.

Meyers, Elizabeth S., Ball, Helen H., and Crutchfield, Marjorie. "Specific Suggestions for the Kindergarten Teacher and the Advanced Child." *Gifted Child Quarterly* 18:25–30 (Spring 1974).

The article provides numerous suggestions for working with advanced kindergarten children.

Roeper, Annemarie. "Some Observations about Gifted Preschool Children." *Journal of Nursing Education* 18:177–80 (April 1963a).

Roeper is an expert in the area of gifted education. Her well-written article describes characteristics of preschool gifted children along with illustrative examples.

_____. "Planning for the Gifted: A New Task for Nursery School Educators." *Gifted Child Quarterly* 7:113–15 (Autumn 1963b).

The author urges that, in the endeavor to educate the whole child, nursery school teachers *not* underestimate the importance of intellectual development for gifted youngsters. Learning is anything but drudgery for them!

_____. "Gifted Preschoolers and the Montessori Method." *Gifted Child Quarterly* 10:83–89 (Summer 1966).

In a well-written article, Roeper compares the traditional nursery school method, the Montessori method, and the method used at the Roeper City and Country School.

Rosenbusch, Marcia H., and Draper, Dianne C. "Gifted Preschoolers: Learning Spanish as a Second Language." *Roeper Review* 7:209-12 (April 1985).

The authors describe Project Pegasus, which is designed to meet the intellectual and creative needs of gifted/talented preschool children. They also present an overview of the foreign language program, including the results that indicate that the program is a success.

Sherrod, Kathy. "Nurturing Creativity in the Preschool Child, or 'How' Is Worse than 'What.' " *G/C/T* 20:30-31 (November/December 1981).

The author offers several suggestions and an extensive list of suggested readings.

Shorr, David N., Jackson, Nancy E., and Robinson, Halbert B. "Achievement Test Performance of Intellectually Advanced Preschool Children." *Exceptional Children* 46:646-48 (May 1980).

The authors report on a study done to assess the feasibility of using an established achievement test, the Peabody Individual Achievement Test, with intellectually precocious preschoolers. Their results indicated that the PIAT is an appropriate instrument to use for assessing the academic skills of bright preschoolers.

Siegelbaum, Laura, and Rotner, Susan. "Ideas and Activities for Parents of Preschool Gifted Children." *G/C/T* 26:40-44 (January/February 1983).

Although the article is addressed to parents, teachers of gifted preschool children could also gain a great deal from reading this article. After a brief rationale for giving special attention to gifted preschoolers, the authors provide some excellent ideas for activities for children in each of four categories: the exceptionally bright, the creatively gifted, children advanced in reading, and children advanced in mathematics. Enough explanation is given that parents and teachers could generate more such activities on their own.

Sloan, Colleen, and Stedtnitz, Ulrike. "The Enrichment Triad Model for the Very Young Gifted." *Roeper Review* 6:204-6 (April 1984).

The authors explain quite clearly how and why the Enrichment Triad Model should be used with preschool and primary age gifted children. As an example, they describe a five-year-old boy's Type III project involving concern over the endangered status of the bald eagle.

Tittle, Bess M. "Why Montessori for the Gifted?" *G/C/T* 33:3-7 (May/ June 1984).

Tittle says that the Montessori method is particularly suited for the education of the gifted because it aims to teach things that will propel students to independence. An excellent rationale is presented, along with a chart that matches characteristics of the gifted with a particular phase or tenet of Montessori education.

Mathematics

Bartkovich, Kevin G., and George, William C. *Teaching the Gifted and Talented in the Mathematics Classroom.* Washington, D.C.: National Education Association, 1980. 48 pp.

Both authors draw on their experience with the Johns Hopkins University Study for Mathematically Precocious Youth in writing this clear, concise monograph. Identification, teaching strategies, evaluation, accelerative options, etc., are covered. Mathematics teachers and curriculum directors should read this report.

Bartkovich, Kevin G., and Mezynski, Karen. "Fast-Paced Precalculus Mathematics for Talented Junior High Students: Two Recent SMPY Programs." *Gifted Child Quarterly* 25:73-80 (Spring 1981).

The authors describe a summer program that used an instructional method of diagnostic testing followed by prescriptive instruction (DT—>PI). Using this approach, mathematically talented seventh graders were able to complete vast portions of a precalculus sequence given between forty and forty-eight hours of instruction (as compared to 270 to 280 fifty-minute classes spread over a year and a half to two years in the normative curriculum.

Chen, Alice W. "The 'Math Whiz' in Elementary School." *Momentum* 12:8-10 (February 1981).

Chen uses a brief case study of a mathematically precocious third grader to illustrate the need for special curriculum for youngsters gifted in mathematics.

"The Devil's Advocate: Sex Differences in Mathematical Reasoning Ability." *Journal for the Education of the Gifted* 4:169-76, 239-43 (Spring 1981).

This fascinating article is a conversation between the journal's editors and Drs. Julian Stanley and Camilla Benbow, both of Johns Hopkins University. After six annual talent searches, they have data from nearly 10,000 seventh and eighth graders on which to base the comments made in this article.

Fehr, Howard F. "The Secondary School Mathematics Improvement

Study: A Unified Mathematics Program." *Mathematics Teacher* 67:25–33 (January 1974).

The author describes the SSMCIS program, which is intended for the top 15 to 20 percent of secondary students.

Flagg, Elinor B. "Mathematics for Gifted Children: An Experimental Program." *Educational Leadership* 19:379–82 (March 1962).

The program's selection criteria, objectives, and topics covered are described in this article.

Fox, Lynn H. "Facilitating Educational Development of Mathematically Precocious Youth." *Journal of Special Education* 9:63–77 (Spring 1975).

The author presents several ways of providing for precocious youth—acceleration or enrichment of courses, grade skipping, early entrance to college, and taking college courses while still in secondary school. She provides brief case studies of seven precocious youth and how they should be provided for educationally.

_____. "Mathematically Able Girls: A Special Challenge." *Arithmetic Teacher* 28:22–23 (February 1981).

The author, an expert in the subject of gifted girls, explains how to encourage them by identifying them early, counseling parents and the girls themselves, individualizing instruction, and providing career education and role models for them.

Friesen, Charles D. "Problem Solving: Meeting the Needs of Mathematically Gifted Students." *School Science and Mathematics* 80:127–30 (February 1980).

Friesen recommends using the problems found in most mathematics journals to challenge gifted high school students. He provides a good rationale with examples.

George, William C., "Accelerating Mathematics Instruction." *Gifted Child Quarterly* 20:246–61 (Fall 1976).

George explains the concept of fast-paced mathematics courses presented at Johns Hopkins University. He then recounts the success that two school districts have had in implementing this highly accelerated program in their public schools. The curriculum is briefly covered.

George, William C., and Stanley, Julian C. "The Study of Mathematically Precocious Youth." *Gifted Child Quarterly* 23:518–25 (Fall 1979).

George provides a brief overview of the program and lists thirty of the publications that have resulted from the SMPY. This bibliography would be of value to mathematics curriculum planners.

Gough, John. "What Mathematics Should Be Taught to Gifted Children?" *Australian Mathematics Teacher* 36:7–10 (January 1981).

Gough recommends that gifted children be taught *real*

mathematics—not the moribund, static school mathematics currently being taught. This interesting article maintains that gifted
children need to be prepared to *use* the mathematics—in computers,
engineering, and other fields.

Greenes, Carole. "Identifying the Gifted Student in Mathematics."
Arithmetic Teacher 28:14–17 (February 1981).

This super article presents seven characteristics of children gifted
in mathematics, with illustrative examples for each of the seven.

Hersberger, James, and Wheatley, Grayson. "A Proposed Model for a
Gifted Elementary School Mathematics Program." *Gifted Child
Quarterly* 24:37–40 (Winter 1980).

The authors designed and implemented this model during the
1978–79 school year. They propose that classes for the gifted be more
individualized, that grades other than A, B, and C should be eliminated so that the gifted are not afraid of risk-taking in their problem
solving, that teachers be self-confident, and that calculators and microcomputers be utilized.

House, Peggy A. "One Small Step for the Mathematically Gifted."
School Science and Mathematics 81:195–99 (March 1981).

House describes the Minnesota Talented Youth Mathematics Project, which offers accelerated classes modeled after those of the Johns
Hopkins Study for Mathematically Precocious Youth.

House, Peggy, Gulliver, Markita, and Knoblauch, Susan F. "On Meeting the Needs of the Mathematically Talented: A Call to Action."
Mathematics Teacher 70:222–27 (March 1977).

The authors call on members of the National Council of Teachers of
Mathematics to assume leadership roles in bringing about needed
change in the way gifted students' needs are met. Their article claims
that the gifted are grossly underserved because of lack of resources,
inadequate teacher education, and poor public relations for their
cause. Suggestions for change are provided.

Keating, Daniel P. "The Study of Mathematically Precocious Youth."
Journal of Special Education 9:45–62 (Spring 1975).

The author provides a detailed description of the Johns Hopkins
University Study of Mathematically Precocious Youth. He presents
the SAT scores obtained by some of the early participants and such
concomitants of mathematics precocity as sibling position and vocational interest.

Keller, J. David. "Akron's Exploratory School Program: A Program for
Gifted and Talented in Mathematics and Science." *School Science and
Mathematics* 80:577–82 (November 1980).

The author, who is coordinator of the program he describes, provides an overview of Akron's Exploratory School Program for

fourth, fifth, and sixth graders. He explains the screening procedure and some of the "modules" that have been developed to incorporate various themes in science and mathematics. Other school districts may want to use the Akron model as a guide to developing their own program.

Kemeny, John G. "The Mathematically Talented Student." *National Association of Secondary School Principals Bulletin* 47:26–40 (April 1963).

This article is the address given by the author at the forty-seventh annual convention of the National Association of Secondary School Principals. Although presented over twenty-five years ago, many of his suggestions are still timely—mostly because they were not heeded in the early sixties. He recommends curriculum reform from the grade school through the graduate school in order to mobilize the vast amount of latent mathematical talent in the student population.

Klausmeier, Herbert J., and Laughlin, Leo T. "Behavior during Problem-Solving among Children of Low, Average, and High Intelligence." *Journal of Educational Psychology* 52:148–52 (June 1961).

The authors report on a study of high-, average-, and low-IQ children involved in mathematics problem-solving activities. They found that the high-IQ children noted and corrected mistakes independently, verified solutions, used logical approaches, and were more persistent and efficient in their problem solving.

Kulm, Gerald. "Geometry Enrichment for Mathematically Gifted Students." *Roeper Review* 6:150–51 (February 1984).

The author describes an intensive two-week summer course, held at a university, for fourteen mathematically gifted eighth graders identified during a mathematics talent search. Kulm believes that geometry content provides a context for strengthening the spatial reasoning and logical and reflective thinking of gifted students.

Lester, Frank K., Jr., and Schroeder, Thomas L. "Cognitive Characteristics of Mathematically Gifted Children." *Roeper Review* 5:26–28 (April/May 1983).

The authors discuss the research of Soviet psychologist V. A. Krutetskii. Over a twelve-year period, he studied a total of 192 children identified as mathematically gifted. A very helpful summary is presented in Table 1: Comparison of Selected Cognitive Characteristics of Mathematically Gifted and Non-gifted Students. Through their discussion of Krutetskii's work (and that of others) the authors conclude that more attention must be paid to cognitive characteristics that differentiate the gifted from the nongifted.

Mezynski, Karen, and Stanley, Julian C. "Advanced Placement Oriented Calculus for High School Students." *Journal of Research in Mathematics Education* 11:347–55 (November 1980).

The authors describe classes that used the BC (higher level) syllabus for AP calculus. Students did well on the AP exams.

Owens, James Patrick. "I Can Do That in My Head: Mental Mathematics in the Classroom." *G/C/T* 6:24–28 (January/February 1979).

The author presents formulas that are part of the "Mental Mathematics Secret Formula Kit," a system developed for and used in an enrichment program for gifted and talented students, grades five to eight. The formulas are clearly explained and have been used with great success with gifted and average students.

Parke, Beverly N. "Use of Self-Instructional Materials with Gifted Primary-Aged Students." *Gifted Child Quarterly* 27:29–34 (Winter 1984).

Parke briefly presents research results pro and con programmed learning. Then she discusses her study, which examined the effects of a self-instructional mathematics program on the mathematics achievement of high-achievement primary students. Her particular research question was whether or not these students could learn mathematics through a self-instructional process. Her results indicate it to be a viable approach for high-achieving students.

Payne, Joseph. "The Mathematics Curriculum for Talented Students." *Arithmetic Teacher* 28:18–21 (February 1981).

This good article summarizes what a mathematics curriculum for talented students should include—reflecting both the nature of mathematics and the nature of the able students.

Poole, M. A. "The M.A.T. Mathematics Problem Competitions." *Australian Mathematics Teacher* 28:11–12 (March 1972).

Poole presents several problems used in the Mathematics Problem Competition sponsored by the Mathematical Association of Tasmania. These problems would be great to give to gifted students.

Pratscher, Sandra K., and others. "Differentiating Instruction in Mathematics for Talented and Gifted Youngsters." *School Science and Mathematics* 82:365–72 (May/June 1982).

The authors stress the need for mathematically gifted students to participate in carefully planned and developed programs. They discuss four models for such a curriculum: (1) acceleration model, based on the SMPY, (2) breadth/depth model, (3) topics model, (4) enrichment model.

Rekdal, C. K. "Guiding the Gifted Female through Being Aware: The Math Connection." *G/C/T* 35:10–12 (November/December 1984).

Rekdal briefly reviews the literature on mathematics and women and draws conclusions that have implications for teachers and counselors of gifted females.

Shulte, Albert P. "Statistics and Probability for Gifted Middle School Students." *Roeper Review* 6:152–54 (February 1984).

The author, a recognized expert in the field of statistics, presents several topics and techniques that he has found appropriate for use with gifted students at the middle school level.

Sirr, Palma M. "A Proposed System for Differentiating Elementary Mathematics for Exceptionally Able Students." *Gifted Child Quarterly* 28:40–44 (Winter 1984).

Sirr reports on a pilot project that (1) surveyed teachers, parents, and students concerning their perceptions of needs in math; (2) looked at ITBS results to determine students at the 95th percentile and above; (3) involved tutoring a very able math student; (4) involved planning modifications in the existing mathematics curriculum.

Spector, David. "SOMA: A Unique Object for Mathematical Study." *Mathematics Teacher* 75:404–7 (May 1982).

The author describes a number of activities that he used with gifted elementary students during his two-year work on a Title IV project, "Interage Program for Critical Thinking." All the activities use the SOMA puzzle, which is a three-inch cube composed of seven different pieces.

Straker, Anita. "Mathematical Giftedness: A Short Course for Teachers and Children." *Mathematics in School* 11:4–5 (January 1982).

The author describes a program that involved both teachers and children gifted in mathematics in working and learning together.

Trafton, Paul. "Overview: Providing for Mathematically Able Students." *Arithmetic Teacher* 28:12–13 (February 1981).

This article introduces a special section in *Arithmetic Teacher* concerning gifted children.

Warman, Michele. "Fun with Logical Reasoning." *Arithmetic Teacher* 29:26–30 (May 1982).

The article presents a number of categories of logical reasoning problems. The author designed these when she was a high school mentor for a group of gifted elementary students.

Waters, Margaret M. "Strategies for Teaching Children Gifted in Elementary Mathematics." *Arithmetic Teacher* 27:14–17 (January 1980).

Waters says that, although little research has been done concerning elementary age children who are precocious in mathematical ability, there are implications to be drawn from research done with older students. Elementary teachers must plan systematic enrichment in mathematics. They must ensure that students who are exceptional in mathematics receive appropriate mathematics instruction and experiences after elementary school. Teachers must be sure to identify mathemetically precocious girls and make a special effort to encourage them.

Wavrik, John J. "Mathematics Education for the Gifted Elementary School Student." *Gifted Child Quarterly* 24:169–73 (Fall 1980).

Wavrik first makes a sharp contrast between standard mathematics instruction and nonstandard mathematics instruction, including the underlying philosophical bases and pedagogical consequences of the latter philosophy. Next, he makes quite clear how he thinks gifted students should be taught mathematics and describes a program, called The Math Course, which was offered to gifted students and their parents in order to orient them to learning mathematics on their own. All math teachers and math coordinators should read this article.

Weatherly, Myra S. "Why Probability?" *G/C/T* 35:6–9 (November/December 1984).

The author provides a strong rationale for using probability with gifted students and then explains ten activities designed to introduce the basic ideas of probability to gifted students in an experiential, informal, hands-on approach.

Wheatley, Grayson H. "A Mathematics Curriculum for the Gifted/Talented." *Gifted Child Quarterly* 27:77–80 (Spring 1983).

Wheatley discusses ten strands in elementary school around which to build a curriculum for gifted/talented students: problem solving, estimation and mental arithmetic, numeration, geometry and measurement, spatial visualization, probability and statistics, arithmetic and algebra concepts, facts and computations, applications, computer programming.

Science

Addison, Linda. "Activities: Stretching Their Minds." *Science and Children* 16:46–47 (March 1979).

The author discusses several characteristics of the gifted and how to build a science curriculum that capitalizes on those characteristics.

Anderson 1961. *See* Introduction

Awkerman, Gary. "Mess Management for Gifted Students." *Science and Children* 16:10–11 (March 1979).

The author describes Charleston's project OASIS (Opportunity for Advanced Students' Involvement in Systems), which tries to instruct gifted students (grades one through eight) in "mess management" (or collective problem solving). A mess is a set of interrelated problems.

Boyd, David E. "The Mad Scientist." *School Activities* 40:16–17 (November 1968).

Although the language used in the article is somewhat dated, it presents an idea that is still timely: engaging a bright child in science projects may help resolve some behavior problems.

Busse, Thomas V., and Mansfield, Richard S. "The Blooming of Creative Scientists: Early, Late and Otherwise." *Gifted Child Quarterly* 25:63–66 (Spring 1981).

The authors investigated fifteen of the most highly cited scientists (as determined by an earlier study) to find out at what age they first showed scientific talent, when they decided on a scientific career, the three experiences most important in the development of their scientific creativity, and when they became highly motivated to do scientific work. The implication cited by the authors is that "late bloomers" in science are not rare—and so graduate schools should not rule out a person just because he or she has only modest previous credentials. They should look instead at current motivation and creativity.

Campbell, James Reed. "The Phantom Class: A Viable Approach of Providing for Gifted and Talented High School Science Students." *Roeper Review* 7:228–31 (April 1985).

Campbell presents the results from a two-year study of what is done to motivate gifted and talented science students at fourteen metropolitan New York high schools. In each case, special research classes had been set up for the gifted/talented students, designed to promote independent research. He also found that the school principals, science teachers, and the students were key components to the success of the program.

Cooper, Carolyn R. "The English and Ecology Mix." *Clearing House* 47:423–26 (March 1973).

The author, an English teacher, describes the experiences of twenty gifted high school students and their teachers who embarked on a snake-hunting expedition in South Carolina. The students seemed really challenged and confronted by life for the first time.

Davis, Barbara S. "The Chesapeake Bay—a Classroom for Gifted Students." *G/C/T* 17:34–35 (March/April 1981).

Davis describes a course developed by the Virginia Beach Center for the Gifted and Talented—The Bay, Explore It. The course has as its goals increased awareness and greater understanding of the Chesapeake Bay.

Doyle, Charles, "An Energy Education Unit for Upper Elementary Grades." *NJEA Review* 54:26–27 (November 1980).

The author describes the products of a project designed to update the science curriculum and provide academically talented students with opportunities to utilize their creativity.

Edwards, Clifford H., and Fisher, Robert L. *Teaching Elementary School Science: A Competency-Based Approach.* New York: Praeger Publishers, 1977. 464 pp.

The authors use a competency-based approach for teachers learning to teach elementary school science. Some of the competencies covered include instructional objectives, assessment, planning, learning experiences, and contemporary programs in science.

Evans, Beth. "Hurricanes Come from Houston." *Science and Children* 16:54–55 (March 1979).

Evans says that if elementary school science is going to capture and stimulate gifted students' inquiring minds, then it must be related to events with which they can identify. A unit on hurricanes is the focus of her article.

Hood, C. Gregory. "Physical Science Cast in the Self-Paced Mode." *Science Teacher* 48:25–27 (December 1981).

The author reports on his success using a modified self-paced format to serve the learning needs of his students, including the very able. He explains how to set up three strands: the core strand for "average" students; the extended strand for very able students; and the modified strand for below-average students. He gives illustrative examples.

Kegley, Sandra, Boothby, Colet, Nelson, Cenie, and Stokes, Gen. "An Undersea Adventure in Oceanography." *G/C/T* 35:13–14 (November/December 1984).

Kegley describes a hands-on experience with oceanography that culminated an oceanography unit for gifted and talented fifth graders.

Knutsen, Lee. "Teaching Fifty Gifted Science Units in Two Easy Steps." *Science and Children* 16:51–53 (March 1979).

Knutsen has developed a way to get students to "design" science units. It seems that it works well with the gifted.

Kopelman, Milton, Galasso, Vincent G., and Strom, Pearl. "A Model Program for the Development of Creativity in Science." *Gifted Child Quarterly* 21:80–84 (Spring 1977).

The authors describe a program implemented at the Bronx High School of Science. It was founded on the notion that a planned educational program will significantly increase the creative productivity of students potentially creative in the sciences. An address for further information is included.

LaSalle, Donald P. "On Talcott Mountain." *Science and Children* 16:27–29 (March 1979).

The Talcott Mountain Science Center in Connecticut serves students of all ages and backgrounds. This article focuses on the programs designed for the gifted.

Lesser, Gerald S., David, Frederick B., and Nahemov, Lucille. "The Identification of Gifted Elementary School Children with Exceptional Scientific Talent." *Educational Psychological Measurement* 22:349–64 (Summer 1962).

The two forms of the Hunter Science Aptitude Test measure (1) the ability to recall scientific information, (2) the ability to assign meaning to observations, (3) the ability to apply scientific principles in making predictions, and (4) the ability to use the scientific method. Fairly high predictive validity coefficients were obtained.

Marshall, J. Stanley. "Science in the Elementary School." In *Curriculum Planning for the Gifted*, edited by Louis A. Fliegler. Englewood Cliffs, N.J.: Prentice-Hall, 1961.

Marshall discusses ways to identify students gifted in science and offers several "portraits" of such students. He also reports on the current state of science programs for the gifted.

Martin, Kathleen. "Science and the Gifted Adolescent." *Roeper Review* 2:25–26 (December 1979).

The author characterizes the adolescent as quite different from a child, and then applies these characteristics to an adolescent as a learner of science. Martin stresses that the science teacher is the key to whether or not the gifted adolescent learns. She states, "Science that has been truly experienced as knowledge is felt as a reverence for life and its place of being. Whoever it is that teaches science to the gifted adolescent must teach it in that spirit."

McCauley, Edith M. "The Story of a Vacant Lot." *Roeper Review* 7:11–12 (September 1984).

McCauley relates the experience of her fifth-grade class as they undertook a Type III activity that involved recording the history of a vacant lot. Their information was published as a book and was reviewed in the *Chicago Tribune:* "The book . . . is called *The Story of a Vacant Lot* and if you are looking for some good reading this summer, you ought to consider it. It is refreshingly void of sex and violence, but it speaks volumes about the cycles of life as most of us know it."

McCormick, Alan J. "Creativity—Funny Thing." *Science and Children* 16:48–50 (March 1979).

McCormick says that creativity and humor are more natural for the gifted than for others and should be encouraged. He provides several examples to demonstrate how.

McTighe, Jay. "The Summer Program at St. Mary's Center." *Science and Children* 16:24–26 (March 1979).

McTighe describes a summer program for gifted and talented students sponsored by the Maryland State Department of Education. The program serves 300 students who choose two of the following areas for intensive study: Artistic and Creative Expression, Problem Solving, Historical and Cultural Explorations, Environmental Studies.

Melzer, Peter. "The Real World of Physics Teaching: At the Bronx High School of Science." *Physics Teacher* 18:272–77 (April 1980).

It appears that Melzer's purpose was to dispel the "myth" that teaching gifted students in a special school is a bed of roses. He does not accomplish that purpose, but he does come across quite negatively toward the school and the system.

Nelson, Linda. "Science Succeeds in Montclair." *Science and Children* 17:38–39 (February 1980).

The author describes Montclair's program for students who are gifted and talented in one or more areas. Students interested in science not only study it as part of their core curriculum, but they may also choose it as an elective one or more times per day. The program extends from prekindergarten to eighth grade.

"North Carolina's School for Science, Math All-Stars." *Science* 210:411 (October 1980).

North Carolina's School of Science and Mathematics opened in September 1980. Nine hundred applicants were considered for the 150 places available. The school will eventually serve 900 students and is sure to be a model for the nation.

Noyes 1971. *See* Library

Parker, Jeanette P., and Kreamer, Jean T. "A Picture Is Worth a Thousand Words: Creative Science Teaching through Film." *G/C/T* 26:38–39 (January/February 1983).

Reviews several excellent films to use in science education. Suggestions for effective use are also included.

Pinelli, Thomas E. "Utilizing Community Resources to Encourage Student Scientific Creativity in All Grades." *Creative Child and Adult Quarterly* 2:156–63 (1977).

Pinelli explains ways to involve the community to further students' creativity in the sciences. He says it cannot be considered a panacea, but when used properly, with the guidance and cooperation of teachers, working within the curriculum, students can gain a great deal.

Pizzini, Edward L. "Improving Science Instruction for Gifted High School Students." *Roeper Review* 7:231–34 (April 1985).

Pizzini discusses the characteristics of people who became eminent scientists. He says that the present state of science education does little to encourage creative science exploration. He describes a Summer Research Participation Program at the University of Iowa where gifted science students work in laboratory situations, doing research, with a staff of scientists/mentors.

Pyryt, Michael. "Helping Scientifically Gifted Students." *Science and Children* 16:16–17 (March 1979).

Pyryt offers general suggestions to teachers.

Riner, Phillip S. "Establishing Scientific Methodology with Elementary Gifted Children through Field Biology." *G/C/T* 28:46–49 (May/June 1983).

Riner says that, while it is important for students to have basic factual knowledge of the scientific world, it is also important for them to understand how factual knowledge is established. His article presents a way for gifted elementary students to gain basic critical problem-solving skills that are embodied in scientific methodology. The article focuses on the skills of observation, problem finding and question asking, seeing relationships, note taking, sustaining interest and perseverance, and hypothesizing.

Ryder, Virginia P. "A Docent Program in Science for Gifted Elementary Pupils." *Exceptional Children* 38:629–31 (April 1972).

The author describes a program that trains elementary students to be docents at several California science museums. The program accommodates gifted and highly gifted students. All indications are that it is very successful.

Saunders, Walter, Turner, Darrel, West, James, and Moore, Gilbert. "Student Experiments Fly with the Shuttle." *Science Teacher* 46:25–26 (October 1979).

The authors explain how high school students in Utah are creating experiments to be carried aboard a space shuttle mission.

Schlichter, Carol. "A Tree Is Nice: Environmental Studies for the Young Gifted Child in the Regular Classroom." *Teaching Exceptional Children* 14:5–10 (September 1981).

The article provides numerous enrichment activities for gifted children mainstreamed into the regular classroom.

Strobert, Barbara, and Alvarez, Frank R. "The Convocation Model Project: A Creative Approach to Study of Science for Gifted Disadvantaged Students." *Elementary School Journal* 82:230–35 (January 1982).

A program funded by the federal office of gifted and talented and operated through the Union City, New Jersey, public school is the focus of this article. The authors describe convocations as "seminar programs that offer gifted students the opportunity to study scientific issues in depth and to do highly creative work by proposing solutions to real-life problems. Convocations are designed to reduce the gap between existing achievement and the real potential of gifted disadvantaged students through a variety of techniques." According to the article, the convocation model is quite successful and cost-effective.

Wiszowaty, Kenneth W. "A Special Science Program for Gifted Elementary School Children." *Gifted Child Quarterly* 5:121–26 (1961).

The author is a special science consultant at his school. He has no regular class but serves as a full-time consultant to students working on science projects. He describes the program and its successes.

Woolever, John D. "Pine View's Departmentalized Program." *Science and Children* 16:30–33 (March 1979).

This article describes the science program of a public school that serves only gifted students.

Youngs, Richard C. "The Science Gifted." *Roeper Review* 2:23–24 (December 1979).

The author says the outstanding characteristic of the science gifted is their curiosity. Youngs goes on to paint a complete picture of the science-gifted child.

Social Science

Ahlberg, Jean. "Futureguest: The Gifted Look at the Future." *Roeper Review* 4:25–26 (November 1981).

A special Youth Honors Program is described in this article. The program involved 120 students drawn from the top ninth and tenth graders in twelve high schools in Illinois. The overall goal was "to create and pilot a student future planning process." The three-month program was very successful.

Bleedorn, Bernice Bahr. "Way to Go and Ways to Get Going: Futures Study for the Gifted and Talented." *Roeper Review* 2:25–27 (May/June 1980).

The author notes the natural connection between futures studies and programs for the gifted, in terms of their ties to creativity and hemispheric research. She suggests several strategies to "get along" with futures studies.

Bunke, Clinton R. "The Humanities and the Gifted." *Roeper Review* 4:10–12 (November 1981).

The author says the *humanities* and the *gifted* need a new lease on on life—separately and in relation to each other—because (1) the humanities have diminished in importance by default, i.e., as interest in science and technology has proliferated; (2) in general, the gifted and their needs are misunderstood and rejected; (3) "the humanities and the gifted should be viewed as a badly needed and very special synergy toward the creation of a better future for all."

Carey, Jane, Czinner, Gertrude, and Kagan, Gloria. "Developing a Social Studies Unit for Gifted and Talented Children." *G/C/T* 16:33–36 (January/February 1981).

The authors are teachers at the Hunter College Elementary School (for gifted students). Their description of the unit they developed on ancient Egypt makes the reader wish to have been a child in the classroom. They describe the extensive planning and preparation they did (including enrolling in a class on Egyptian art and civilization at Columbia University). Vivid explanations of the children's participation in the study make it clear that the effort was worth the investment.

Casey, Marion. "History as Inquiry: Introducing Gifted Students to History." *Social Studies* 70:99–102 (May/June 1979).

Case advocates a double inquiry—that the inquiry method be used and that history itself be approached as inquiry. Historians ask unending questions and are constantly reassessing and reinterpreting their findings—and so too should gifted students involved in the inquiry of history. She provides a few examples of inquiry.

Connett, Jane. "An Experimental Approach to Humanities." *Roeper Review* 4:15–16 (November 1981).

Connett describes how Project DEEP (Diversified Educational Experiences Program) was used as the management system for a new humanities program started in Prince Edward County, Virginia. Classes in world civilization and American civilization were established, and the program was deemed successful.

Crabbe, Anne Borland, "Creating a Brighter Future: An Update on the Future Problem Solving Program." *Journal for the Education of the Gifted* 5:2–11 (Winter 1982).

Crabbe, who is director of the Future Problem Solving Program, focuses on the objectives of the program and how they are being achieved. The objectives are to help gifted children (1) develop richer images of the future; (2) become more creative in their thinking; (3) develop and increase their communication skills, both verbal and written; (4) develop and increase their teamwork skills; (5) integrate a problem-solving model into their lives; (6) develop and increase their research skills. Sources for more information, both people and materials, are listed.

Diers, Russell, and LoGuidice, James. "Archaeology: A Means of Challenging the Gifted Student." *G/C/T* 22: (March/April 1982).

The authors believe that archaeology is an excellent vehicle to use as an alternate program for gifted students because of the multidisciplinary nature of the field. The article includes a rationale for using archaeology with gifted students, the basic steps in an archaeological dig, and ten sample activities related to an archaeological dig. Some good resources are also listed for teachers or curriculum directors who are interested in exploring archaeology as a means to challenge their students.

Eggers, John R. "Editorial—Futuristics: A Step beyond Gifted and Talented." *Roeper Review* 2:2–3 (May/June 1980).

Eggers makes a case for integrating futuristics into the gifted/talented curriculum. He says that teachers of the gifted and talented need to be caring, sensitive human beings, proactive thinkers, and risk takers, and need to emphasize process as content.

Ellis, Arthur K. *Teaching and Learning Elementary Social Studies*. Boston: Allyn & Bacon, 1977. 374 pp.

The author's underlying theme is that social studies is people. His approach is very humanistic and integrative. This is a good methods book.

Flack, Jerry D., and Feldhusen, John F. "Future Studies in the Curricular Framework of the Purdue Three-Stage Model." *G/C/T* 27:2–9 (March/April 1983).

The authors say that the reasons for the increased interest in future studies for gifted students are: the time is right, teachers perceive the important role today's gifted students will play in the future, future studies provides rich opportunities for meeting the needs of gifted students. This article explains how to start a future studies program and how to design it based on the Purdue Three-Stage Enrichment Model. The article is very complete, including rationale, resources, and activities for all three stages.

Fletcher, Goeffrey H., and Wooddell, Gary D. "Milford Futurology Program: Effective Education for Gifted Students." *Roeper Review* 3:15–18 (September/October 1980).

The purpose of the program described in this article is to "assist gifted individuals to develop the skills, the perspective, and the characteristics necessary to deal effectively with change." The program's philosophy, modes of operation, and results are included.

Friedman, Joan Mann, and Master, Doris. "School and Museum: A Partnership for Learning." *Gifted Child Quarterly* 25:43–48 (Winter 1981).

The authors present a model that provides a legitimate justification for both cognitive and affective learning to take place in a museum setting. They describe, in quite a bit of detail, the broad considerations and the more minor concerns (such as scheduling) involved in implementing the type of program explained in the article. Any school within a reasonable proximity of a museum should consider the concept presented here.

Gregory, Robert J. "International Students: Resources for Exceptional Children." *Exceptional Children* 34:282–83 (December 1967).

The author makes a case for including international students on the list of resource persons to be invited to share with gifted students (and other exceptional students).

Hoomes, Eleanor Wolfe. "Future Problem Solving: Preparing Students for Today and Tomorrow." *G/C/T* 32:15–18 (March/April 1984).

The author gives the background of the Future Problem Solving Program and suggests resources for teachers who are new to it. One of the actual problems is included.

Jones, Helen E. "Developing Social Studies Units for the Gifted: A Conceptual Model." *G/C/T* 28:32–34 (May/June 1983).

The author believes that the typical social studies unit (for example, on transportation or the Civil War) is too narrow. The conceptual model she proposes is built around leadership styles. Her model includes ten steps, which she believes have three advantages over traditional models: (1) the model is built around a broad concept (leadership) that has universal implications; (2) there are an unlimited number of possibilities for exploration, all of which can lead to the unit goals; (3) the model is more likely to lead to generalizations that help students perceive the commonalities in behaviors and values within cultures. It would be worthwhile to use this model in a social studies teachers' inservice and have teachers develop these units for gifted students.

Joyce, Bruce R. *New Strategies for Social Education*. Chicago: Science Research Associates, 1972. 433 pp.

The author views social education as having an intellectual dimension, a social dimension, and a personal dimension. He brings a great deal of experience and research to the writing of this book.

Kolloff, Penny Britton. "The Center for Global Futures: Meeting the Needs of Gifted Students in a Laboratory School." *Roeper Review* 5:32–33 (February 1983).

The author, currently director of the Center for Global Futures, describes this innovative program which involves gifted students, fourth through twelfth grade, in future studies.

Lake, Thomas P. "The Arts and Humanities Come Alive for Gifted and Talented." *Exceptional Children* 41:261–64 (January 1975).

A group of artists, teachers, and national leaders met to explore the arts and humanities and their implications for gifted and talented youth. Some of their suggestions are contained in this article.

Letzter, Frederick Paul. "Meeting the Special Needs of the Gifted and

Creative Student in the World History Classroom." *Social Education* 46:195–99 (March 1982).

Letzter posits that history teachers must adapt their teaching approaches to meet the needs of gifted learners. He says teachers must be sensitive to their extraordinary curiosity (and not see it as a threat) and to their creativity. These teachers must develop strong communication skills and use high-level questioning strategies.

Lindsay, Bryan. "Cornerstone and Keystones: Humanities for the Gifted and Talented." *Roeper Review* 4:6–9 (November 1981).

Very eloquently, Lindsay makes a case for the humanities. Any school district in danger of losing its humanities department, or any school district attempting to build such a department, could use this article to undergird its argument for a humanities program for the gifted.

LoGuidice, James. "Philosophy: A Course of Study for Gifted Students in Grades 11 and 12." *G/C/T* 5:28–29, 57–61 (November/December 1978).

The author presents a course he designed for gifted students, its objectives, and general classroom procedures. An outline, including suggested readings and activities, is presented for each of five units: Orientation to Philosophy; Social, Political, and Legal Philosophy; Aesthetics; Ethics; and Overview of Modern Philosophy.

Muir, Sharon Pray. "Social Sciencing: Social Studies for Gifted Adolescents." *Clearing House* 53:323–27 (March 1980).

Muir defines *social sciencing* as a role-playing approach to social studies. Students must play roles limited to those of social scientists in the social studies disciplines. Muir discusses each of six disciplines and gives a social sciencing activity that could accompany the classroom study of each.

Neff, Herbert B. "Ways to Help Gifted Students Like Social Studies." *Gifted Child Quarterly* 11:108–11 (Summer 1967).

Neff determined ten reasons why social studies classes are so often disliked by gifted students. These reasons are listed along with suggestions for making social studies more interesting for the gifted. The article is worthwhile reading for social studies curriculum directors and/or department heads.

Perdue, Gervaise W. "Hip! Hip! Hooray!! HIP: A Humanities Interdisciplinary Program." *G/C/T* 11:37–39, 52–53 (January/February 1980).

The author, who is coordinator of the gifted program in the district where the Humanities Interdisciplinary Program is in place, tells about HIP, which serves ninth-grade gifted students. She describes how students were identified and selected for participation in the program and some of its benefits. Also, brief overviews of several units of study are included.

Ponder, Gerald, and Hirsh, Stephanie A. "Social Studies Education for the Gifted: Lessons from Other Pasts." *Roeper Review* 4:17–19 (November 1981).

The authors warn social studies teachers of the gifted not to become so immersed in gifted social studies curriculum that they forget the commonalities it shares with the broader field of social studies education.

Poole, F. Robert. "The New Evolution." *Roeper Review* 7:217–20 (April 1985).

Poole, an expert in futuristics, presents three sample lessons that he and two graduate assistants taught in a summer gifted institute. He also makes the point that "dabbling in" future studies is unwise—teachers need training and preparation so that they possess the necessary knowledge and conceptual framework involved in the futures instruction.

Roberts, Nancy M., and Haensly, Patricia A. "Holistic Synthesis in the Social Studies: A New Approach to Enrichment." *Roeper Review* 7:100–102 (November 1984).

The article presents a rationale for holistic synthesis, defined by the authors as not only involving "seeing events from a different view, thinking in terms of analogies, and making leaps of insight, but also perceiving and creating patterns and structures by extrapolating from a piece or part to the whole." The model is further explained, and then an example of how to implement it in the social studies classroom is presented. For teachers unfamiliar with the research on imagery and the right brain, more explanation would be needed so as to implement this in the classroom.

Robertson, Alan T. "A Step into the Past: What Was It Like Back When . . .?" *G/C/T* 19:22–25 (September/October 1981).

Students enrolled in the Williamsburg, Virginia, gifted and talented program were given the opportunity to work closely for sixteen weeks at colonial Williamsburg with master craftsmen. The Colonial Apprentice Project (CAP) is described, and an address is given for more information or to borrow the Type III products that were developed during the project.

Rose, Shirley E. "The Gifted Student and Social Studies Teaching." *Social Studies* 69:43–49 (March/April 1978).

Rose presents a "qualitatively differentiated" instructional model, Renzulli's Triad, as it can be used to build social studies curriculum for gifted and talented students.

Schroeder, Ella F., and Van Norden, Leslie. "An Integrative Curriculum for Gifted Junior High Students." *Roeper Review* 5:35–38 (April/May 1983).

The authors have used Clark's Integrative Education Model as the theoretical basis for reorganizing the curriculum for gifted junior high school students. The authors discuss how the curriculum at their junior high schools was modified using this model (specifically English and California history).

Schroeder, Fred E. H. "Trends for the Future in Humanities for the Gifted Student." *Roeper Review* 4:12–15 (November 1981).

After a general discussion of trends in the humanities, the author points out three corrective trends he perceives: historiography (the study of the study of history); engaging students in real historical research; interdisciplinary integrated humanities.

Schug, Mark C. "Using the Local Community to Improve Citizenship Education for the Gifted." *Roeper Review* 4:22–23 (November 1981).

Schug offers reasons why using the local community for citizenship education is important for gifted students. Ideas for establishing such a program are given, along with activities in the areas of citizenship, civics, history, and economics.

Seidman, Stanley, and Spain, Minta. "A Gifted Approach to the Development of a Social Studies Unit." *Roeper Review* 5:29–30 (April/May 1983).

The authors built an interdisciplinary learning program by expanding the uses of *National Geographic* materials. The students employed writing and research skills as they explored anthropology, sociology, and archaeology. Higher-level thinking skills were stressed.

Seif, Elliott. "Futures Education for the Gifted." *Roeper Review* 4:24–25 (November 1981).

Seif presents and explains five generalizations he has inferred from futurist literature. These generalizations can provide a framework for a futures curriculum.

Shaver, James P. "Helping Gifted Students to Analyze Public Issues: The Jurisprudential Approach." *Roeper Review* 7:4–7 (September 1984).

The jurisprudential approach to social studies is based on the assumption that all young people should be helped to comprehend and grapple reasonably with the issues continually confronting society. Shaver explains this approach and how it can be used with gifted students. He concludes that the approach offers an avenue to broaden and intensify gifted students' knowledge by capitalizing on their cognitive-moral development and their frequent interest in matters of morality.

Shermis, S. Samuel, and Clinkenbeard, Pamela R. "History Texts for the Gifted: A Look at the Past Century." *Roeper Review* 4:19–21 (November 1981).

The authors obtained history textbooks published within the last century, and approximately one per decade was selected for an analysis of its questions on the American Revolution. Even though social studies educators for the past one hundred years have espoused the necessity of asking higher-level questions in social studies, it appears that the textbooks have a heavy concentration of lower-level questions. This situation has improved only slightly since 1871. Recommendations for teachers of the gifted are included.

Silvernail, David L. "A Futuristic Curriculum Model for the Gifted Child." *Roeper Review* 2:16–18 (May/June 1980).

The author presents a rationale for and a description of a curriculum model that requires a futuristic perspective and provides for alternative programs, materials, and objectives. The curriculum should include a "basics" strand, a study-of-the-future strand (which includes a study of the past), a self-concept strand, and a valuing strand.

Subotnik, Rena F. "Emphasis on the Creative Dimension: Social Studies Curriculum Modifications for Gifted Intermediate and Secondary Students." *Roeper Review* 7:7–10 (September 1984).

Using "transportation" as the topic, the author demonstrates how teachers can use problem solving and future studies to modify the curriculum to better serve gifted students. This excellent article includes suggestions that all teachers could adapt.

Whaley, Charles E. "The Study of Global Futures and the Gifted." *Roeper Review* 2:28–29 (May/June 1980).

The author describes a conceptual framework model that he developed and implemented with gifted and talented students in fifth through twelfth grades in Michigan.

White, John R. "They Didn't Study It, They Did It: Archaeology Camp." *G/C/T* 35:2–4 (November/December 1984).

White discusses his experience working two summers with high school students on an archaeological dig. The program has been deemed a success.

Whitmore, Joanne Rand. "Social Studies: The Lifeblood of Education for the Gifted." *Social Education* 43:159–62 (February 1979).

Whitmore believes social studies are particularly well suited to the learning characteristics of gifted children. She explains why and then draws educational implications for social studies teachers (e.g., curriculum should be based on real world problems and should focus on the development of thinking and inquiry).

Willard, Diane E. "A 'Social' Social Studies Model for Gifted Students." *Teaching Exceptional Children* 17:18–22 (Fall 1984).

The author says that "democratic living in the public school classroom can serve as the superstructure for building social studies programs to develop the thinking and problem-solving abilities of academically talented students." In her article, Willard describes a full-year course of study for fifth-grade gifted students who participated in the one-day-per-week pullout program she taught.

Wooddell, Gary D., Fletcher, Goeffrey H., and Dixon, Thornton E. "Futures Study for the Adolescent Gifted: A Curriculum Evaluation." *Journal for the Education of the Gifted* 5:24–33 (Winter 1982).

This study documents the authors' efforts to begin to develop in a group of ninth grade students a certain set of abilities and qualities. These qualities were identified as a future perspective, self-actualization, and futuring competencies. The study was both a quasi research study and a rigorous and comprehensive curriculum evaluation. The authors believe the results suggest that a futures perspective may be an integral aspect of the makeup of gifted children.

Computers

Beasley, William A. "The Role of Microcomputers in the Education of the Gifted." *Roeper Review* 7:156–59 (February 1985).

Beasley says that educators must realize that the cognitive demands on students are different today, with the availability of computers, than they were ten years ago. He points out some key notions that teachers need to be aware of in order to help their students make full use of computers in their learning.

Datnow, Claire-Louise. "How to Join the Ranks of Today's Computer Literate Families." *G/C/T* 30:7–9 (November/December 1983).

Datnow recounts a few days in the life of a computer and "its" family. She makes clear the value of a home computer and explains how to get your family to a computer-literate stage.

————. "What to Say When They Say It's Baloney." *G/C/T* 36:29 (January/February 1985).

The author provides several arguments for gifted students learning how to program. She says, "Learning how to program a computer is similar to learning a foreign language or how to play a musical instrument. It is an exercise that takes time and effort but is well worth it."

Delclos, Victor R., Littlefield, Joan, and Bransford, John D. "Teaching Thinking through LOGO: The Importance of Method." *Roeper Review* 7:153–56 (February 1985).

The authors evaluate current methods of teaching LOGO and posit that they are the reasons for poor results indicating that LOGO is ineffective. They propose a carefully structured, mediational method.

Dirkes, M. Ann. "Problem-Solving: The Real Purpose for Computers in School." *G/C/T* 36:42–44 (January/February 1985).

Dirkes recommends numerous ways to improve students' problem-solving abilities through the use of computers.

Dover, Arlene. "Computers and the Gifted: Past, Present, and Future."
Gifted Child Quarterly 27:81–85 (Spring 1983).

Dover provides a strong, well-explained rationale for using computers in education for the gifted.

Ellis, Margaret, "Creating Computer Classrooms." *G/C/T* 30:12–14 (November/December 1983).

St. Paul's Episcopal School in Mobile, Alabama, earned money to buy computers for the school by offering computer classes to gifted students during summer camps and to other students and adults in the evening during the summer, fall, and spring. Anyone trying to set up a program might get some ideas from this article.

Fiday, David. "Programming from Second Grade On . . . and the Laraway LOGO Experience." *G/C/T* 30:16–19 (November/December 1983).

This is a two-part article. The first part is a rationale for teaching young children how to program. The second part explains the author's school's program for teaching young children the LOGO language. It has been a highly successful project and will be continued for the obvious reason that it works. One page is dedicated to names and addresses of recommended software packages.

Flank, Sandra. "Little Hands on the Computer." *G/C/T* 25:28–29 (November/December 1982).

The author says that often computers are used in ways inappropriate for gifted elementary school students (drill and practice). She recommends using them for word processing, mathematical "play," intuitive geometry, problem solving, and programming.

Hamlett, Carol L. "Microcomputer Activities for Gifted Elementary Children: Alternatives to Programming." *Teaching Exceptional Children* 16:253–57 (Summer 1984).

Suggestions are made on how teachers of elementary gifted students can provide valuable computer activities even when computer resources and expertise are limited.

Hampton, Carolyn. "Introduction to Computers." *G/C/T* 12:44–45 (March/April 1980).

The author describes a two-week minicourse presented to gifted and talented fourth through seventh graders at the National Space Technology Laboratories, Earth Resources Laboratory. Students learned about computers (BASIC and FORTRAN languages, flow charting, etc.), and they saw how a large computer is used at the laboratory to process satellite-acquired data.

Horn, Charles J., and Finn, David M. "Sources of Computing." *Focus on Exceptional Children* 16:1–16 (October 1983).

This article lists addresses for scores of hardware and software producers.

Jensen, Rita A., and Wedman, John. "The Computer's Role in Gifted Education." *G/C/T* 30:10–11 (November/December 1983).

The authors briefly discuss four topics related to incorporating computer technology into gifted education: computer literacy, computer-assisted instruction, computer programming, and problem solving. They conclude that "if computer technology is to have an impact on gifted education beyond developing future computer programmers and technicians, gifted education advocates, incorporating computer technology into their education efforts, must spotlight process learning and creative problem solving; they must allow and encourage students to become decision makers and active participants in the learning process. Only then will the programs be truly gifted and the computer instruction truly assisting the education of the more able."

Katz, Elinor Lipit. "Microcomputers: A Course of Study for Gifted Students." *Focus on Exceptional Children* 15:1–16 (February 1983).

Katz says the gifted seem to have a natural affinity for microcomputers. She presents a model for microcomputer education designed for gifted/talented students.

Kibler, Tom R., and Campbell, Patricia B. "Reading, Writing, and Computing: Skills of the Future." *Educational Technology* 19:44–46 (September 1976).

The authors make a strong case for the need for students to be just as competent in computing skills as they are in reading and writing skills.

Kirk, Laura. "For the Gifted Primary Student: Word Processing." *G/C/T* 30:20–21 (November/December 1983).

The author provides a glowing report of her TAG class's experience using the Bank Street Writer, a word-processing program designed for student use. For teachers and/or media coordinators considering a word-processing program, this article should be among those read.

Kulm, Gerald. "Team Spirit: A Computer Math Course for Parents and Gifted Children." *Teaching Exceptional Children* 16:168–71 (Spring 1984).

Kulm presents the idea of a college credit course designed for and implemented with gifted junior high and high school students and their parents. Results were positive.

Larsen, Sally Greenwood. "Kids and Computers: The Future Is Today." *Creative Computing* 5:58–60 (September 1979).

The author, who teaches BASIC programming to third- and fourth-grade gifted students, shares some of her materials, which have been highly successful.

Leimbach, Judy. "Spotlight on Computers: Students in Control." *School Library Journal* 28:37 (August 1982).

The author teaches gifted intermediate grade students, and she believes that gifted students should not just be running programs—they should be writing them. She explains how this came about at her school.

Lucito, Leonard J. "Join the Computer World." *G/C/T* 36:34–36 (January/ February 1985).

Lucito offers a "learn it yourself" article for teachers who have never used a microcomputer. He introduces a CAI (computer assisted instruction) package, too.

Mathews, F. Neil. "Parenting Update: Educational Implications of Microcomputers in the Home." *Journal for the Education of the Gifted* 6:294–300 (Summer 1983).

Mathews makes recommendations to parents regarding how to select hardware and software. He also believes in programming for young children and provides a rationale for using microcomputers in education. He says microcomputers provide opportunities for (1) continuous, active student participation; (2) prompt feedback and a basis for correcting errors; (3) individualized educational planning.

Pantiel, Mindy, and Petersen, Becky. *Kids, Teachers, and Computers: A Guide to Computers in the Elementary School.* Englewood Cliffs, N.J.: Prentice-Hall, 1984. 212 pp.

The authors have written an excellent text for teachers who are preparing to use computers in the classroom. It is very clearly written and easy to understand.

Roberts, Ruth E. "Curriculum Guide for Computer Literacy." *G/C/T* 36:37–41 (January/February 1985).

The author has developed a ten-area computer curriculum guide, which she includes in the article. The areas are performance, history, vocabulary, anatomy, capabilities, uses, algorithms, social, futuristics, and programming. For each, she states objectives, levels, suggested activities, sources, evaluation methods, and time frames. This is a very useful article!

Sisk, Dorothy. "Computers in the Classroom: An Invitation and a Challenge for the Gifted." *G/C/T* 1:18–21 (January/February 1978).

Sisk says that the gifted must become computer-literate—for all our sakes.

Steele, Kathleen J., Battista, Michael T., and Krockover, Gerald H. "The Effect of Microcomputer Assisted Instruction upon the Computer Literacy of High Ability Students." *Gifted Child Quarterly* 26:162–63 (Fall 1982).

The authors conducted a study involving computer assisted instruction (CAI). They provided evidence that assigning CAI mathematics drill and practice program on the microcomputer significantly improved the computer literacy of able fifth graders.

Tashner, John H. "Using Computers with Gifted Students." *Top of the News* 38:318–24 (Summer 1982).

Tashner provides a strong rationale for ensuring that the gifted become computer literate.

Tkach, John R. "Bytes for Brights: Four Spelling Games." *G/C/T* 34:43–44 (September/October 1984).

Four software packages designed for computer-assisted spelling instruction are reviewed.

————. "Computers: Everything You Ever Wanted to Know but Didn't Know How to Ask." *G/C/T* 36:31–33 (January/February 1985).

Tkach, who regularly reviews software for *G/C/T*, has written a very lucid explanation for novices about computers. He explains various terms that parents will need as they decide on a computer for their gifted children, and he makes recommendations concerning hardware and software.

Walkington, Pat, and Babcock, Eloise. "Educational Computing and the Gifted Child: A How-To Approach." *Teaching Exceptional Children* 16:266–69 (Summer 1984).

The authors discuss acceleration and computer-assisted instruction, problem solving with computers, and guidelines for computer planning with gifted students.

Wiebe, James H. "BASIC Programming for Gifted Elementary Students." *Arithmetic Teacher* 28:42–44 (March 1981).

The author's experience with a summer course in BASIC programming offered for gifted elementary students provided the content of this article. He makes ten valuable recommendations for anyone planning to teach a similar course. Also, a sampling of the assignments is included.

Career Education

Borman, Christopher, Nash, William, and Colson, Sharon. "Career Guidance for Gifted and Talented Students." *Vocational Guidance Quarterly* 27:72–76 (September 1978).

The authors describe the "Exemplary Career Education Model for Gifted and Talented Students," which was developed at Texas A&M University and implemented in the local school districts. All students who participated gave a favorable rating to the program, as did parents, teachers, and principals of these students.

Colson, Sharon. "The Evaluation of a Community-Based Career Education Program for Gifted and Talented Students as an Administrative Model for an Alternative Program." *Gifted Child Quarterly* 24:101–6 (Summer 1980).

The author investigated whether those students who had participated in a career education program had different perceptions regarding careers than did those students who had not participated in the program. Significant differences were found in the following ten areas:

1. Information regarding preparation for a career.
2. Identification of career field aptitudes.
3. Opportunities to interact with people in the student's field of interest.
4. Opportunities to pursue a special interest area.
5. Opportunities to get to know well someone engaged in the field of interest.
6. Information regarding career field entrance requirements.
7. Insights into personal needs, interests, and abilities.
8. Awareness of economic factors influencing career opportunities.
9. Insights into life-styles, personal characteristics, and responsibilities of individuals in the career field.
10. Information about job acquisition and retention methods.

Colson, Sharon, Godsey, Robert, Mayfield, Betty, Nash, William R., and Borman, Christopher. "Evaluating Career Education for Gifted and Talented Students." *Journal of Research and Development in Education* 12:51–62 (Spring 1979).

This article also deals with the Texas A&M Exemplary Career Education Model discussed by Borman et al. (see above). However, it provides more depth and particularly focuses on the evaluation of the model by teachers, parents, and student participants.

Delisle, James R. "The BIASED Model of Career Education and Guidance for Gifted Adolescents." *Journal for the Education of the Gifted* 8:95–106 (Fall 1984).

Delisle reviews current research regarding the status of career education for gifted adolescents, delineates specific guidance concerns of the gifted adolescent, and translates this available research into a model that promotes a true understanding of available career options. The BIASED model has the following purposes: (1) to provide Basic information; (2) to allow time for Introspection; (3) to provide opportunities for student to Adapt to particular occupations; (4) to encourage students to Select a career path; (5) to provide several career Directions for students who have yet to decide.

Digenakis, Paula, and Miller, Jo. "What's My Line? An In-Depth Experience with Professional Occupations." *G/C/T* 8:14–16, 18–19 (May/June 1979).

The authors present a very clear and well-designed unit on occupations for gifted students in grades three to five.

Dunham, Sister Gertrude, and Russo, Tony. "Career Education for the Disadvantaged Gifted: Some Thoughts for Educators." *Roeper Review* 5:26–28 (February 1983).

The authors point out that disadvantaged gifted students have unique needs when it comes to career education. They emphasize the need for informed guidance counselors who can help make the students aware of the career possibilities available—and who can help these students obtain the education and experience necessary to attain these careers.

Feldhusen, John F., and Kolloff, Margaret B. "An Approach to Career Education for the Gifted." *Roeper Review* 2:13–17 (December 1979).

The authors apply the Purdue Three Stage Model to career education.

Fox, Lynn H. "Career Education for Gifted Pre-Adolescents." *Gifted Child Quarterly* 20:262–73 (Fall 1976).

The author describes a career awareness program developed by the Intellectually Gifted Child Study Group at Johns Hopkins University. Four minicourses were offered to twenty-four students in fourth, fifth, or sixth grade. The courses—geometric drawing, statistics, probability, and computer science—were taught by college professors. Results were quite positive.

Haensly, Patricia A., and Roberts, Nancy M. "The Professional Productive Process and Its Implications for Gifted Studies." *Gifted Child Quarterly* 27:9–12 (Winter 1983).

The authors conducted a study of the work of professionals who have achieved local, state, and/or national eminence in a wide variety of fields in order to examine, in detail, the production and communication of projects and the selection and role of audiences. Their results are organized under the headings inspiration, preparation, products, task commitment, obstacles, and role of audience. They found that audience is an implicit part of creative production, and they recommend a diligent search for authentic and appropriate audiences for gifted students' products.

Herr, Edwin L. "Career Education for the Gifted and Talented: Some Observations." *Peabody Journal of Education* 53:98–103 (January 1976).

The author considers some concerns for the gifted and talented which planning for career education needs to reflect.

Hollinger, Constance L. "Multidimensional Determinants of Traditional and Nontraditional Career Aspirations for Mathematically Talented Female Adolescents." *Journal for the Education of the Gifted* 6:245–65 (Summer 1983).

Hollinger studied 123 mathematically talented women. Of the five career-relevant dimensions studied, self-perception of ability provided the greatest power to discriminate between various career aspirations. The author suggests implications for counselors working with gifted female adolescents.

Hoyt, Kenneth B. "Career Education for Gifted and Talented Persons." *Roeper Review* 1:9–11 (October 1978).

Hoyt says that career education skills include (1) basic academic skills, (2) good work habits, (3) personally meaningful work values, (4) understanding and appreciation of the private enterprise system, (5) self-understanding and understanding of education/work relationships, (6) career decision-making skills, (7) skills in productive use of leisure time, (8) job seeking/getting/holding skills, (9) skills in reducing stereotyping as a deterrent to full freedom of career choice, (10) skills in humanizing the workplace for oneself. Hoyt then offers six considerations concerning career education for gifted students.

Hoyt, Kenneth B., and Hebeler, Jean R. *Career Education for Gifted and Talented Students.* Salt Lake City, Utah: Olympus Publishing, 1974. 293 pp.

This book is the final result of a project funded by the U.S. Office of Education. The project plan called for identifying leaders in several areas of education, holding a conference, assigning written tasks to the experts attending the conference, holding a second conference, assembling the final papers for publication. This book is that publication. It contains background information and a strong rationale for career education for gifted and talented students. It also includes information on exemplary programs in gifted/talented career education, with implications for curriculum development. Even though the book is over ten years old, it provides an excellent starting point for gifted/talented curriculum designers.

Hyman, Mary B., and Brody, Linda. "Career Guidance for the Gifted." *G/C/T* 31:30–33 (January/February 1984).

Programs designed to facilitate prudent career choices for gifted students are held at Johns Hopkins University and Goucher College. The authors describe them, present their positive effects, and discuss the need for more such programs.

Lacy, Richard, and Beebe, David. "The Gifted—Displaced Persons in Business Education." *Journal of Business Education* 57:104–6 (December 1981).

The authors point out that often the gifted are discouraged from taking business classes, but that when they do, special considerations are necessary. For example, a teacher may accelerate, enrich, group homogeneously, exempt from some of the drill, or allow them to tutor.

Martin, Gay. "Finding the Right Slot." *G/C/T* 31:10–12 (January/February 1984).

Martin discusses the career education needs of gifted/talented students. She points out ways that students can gain experience and see a more realistic picture of what certain jobs entail so that a more prudent career choice is made.

Meeker, Mary. "Developing a Model for Career Guidance for the Gifted." *Roeper Review* 1:12 (October 1978).

Meeker expresses her concern that students with high IQ's are placed in special programs with little or no further differentiation. She suggests using the S.O.I. for the purpose of developing a model of career guidance based on abilities rather than grades or IQ scores.

Micklus, C. Samuel. "The Gifted/Talented Students in our Vocational Schools." *NJEA Review* 54:10–11 (February 1981).

Micklus believes gifted and talented students are neglected in vocational education. He offers ten suggestions for starting gifted/talented programs that will extend across the vocational education spectrum.

Moore, Barbara A. "Career Education for Disadvantaged, Gifted High School Students." *Gifted Child Quarterly* 22:332–37 (Fall 1978).

Moore discusses the Professional Career Exploration Program for Minority and/or Low Income, Gifted and Talented tenth grade students (PCEP). She justifies such an approach, explaining that gifted students need a different career education program than do other students. In 1978, two sites in Indiana were chosen to implement the PCEP. Students who participated were evaluated using two standardized measures. Although the results were not in when Moore wrote this article, the general consensus of participants and observers was that the program was beneficial.

————. "A Model Career Education Program for Gifted Disadvantaged Students." *Roeper Review* 2:20–22 (December 1979).

Moore describes the Professional Career Exploration Program for Minority and/or Low Income Gifted and Talented Students (PCEP). PCEP was implemented in several high schools with tenth graders. The selected students participated in classroom seminars focusing on program introduction, values and interest clarification, problem solving, and career information. These were followed up by community exploration experiences. The program was considered successful.

Nash, William R., Borman, Christopher, and Colson, Shawn. "Career Education for Gifted and Talented Students: A Senior High School Model." *Exceptional Children* 46:404–5 (February 1980).

This brief article reports on the career education program operated by the College Station Independent School District in conjunction with Texas A&M University. The model is comprised of three phases: guidance, mentorship, and internship. Response to the program has been very good.

OrRico, Michael J., and Feldhusen, John F. "Career Education for the Gifted, Creative, and Talented: Some Problems and Solutions:" G/C/T 10:37–40 (November/December 1979).

This article clearly delineates six problems in developing effective career education programs for gifted and talented youth—for example, difficulty narrowing down a career choice because of multipotentialities; rapidly changing higher-level occupations. Also described in the article is a simulation designed by the first author, entitled Operation DISCO (Designation of Inter-Space Community Occupations).

Owens, Thomas R. "Experience-Based Career Education: Summary and Implications of Research and Evaluation Findings." Child and Youth Services 4:77–91 (1982).

"The author summarizes the results of several evaluations of experience-based career education programs and concludes that they have a positive effect on career, cognitive, and affective outcomes." The special populations studied include gifted and talented youth.

Perrone, Phillip A., Male, Robert A., and Karshner, Warner W. "Career Development Needs of Talented Students: A Perspective for Counselors." School Counselor 27:16–23 (September 1979).

The authors have drawn on their experience in the University of Wisconsin—Madison Guidance Institute for Talented Students (GIFTS) to write this article. Seven brief case studies, plus the relevant career development concerns, are presented.

Rodenstein, Judith, Pfleger, L. R., and Colangelo, Nick. "Career Development of Gifted Women." Gifted Child Quarterly 21:340–58 (Fall 1977).

The authors' purposes in this article are (1) to report the unique development needs of gifted and talented students; (2) to emphasize the career development needs of gifted and talented females; and (3) to present to educators suggestions for meeting those needs.

Roeper, Annemarie. "The Young Gifted Girl: A Contemporary View." Roeper Review 1:6–8 (October 1978).

The author explores problems of gifted girls that result from the changing status of women.

Schlichter, Carol L. "The Multiple Talent Approach to the World of Work." Roeper Review 2:17–20 (December 1979).

The author's intent in this article is to illustrate how the thinking processes included in Taylor's Multiple Talent Approach to Teaching can be used by gifted children to explore the world of work. A brief overview of Taylor's model is presented, along with sample activities for four talents: Productive Thinking Talent, Forecasting Talent, Decision Making Talent, and Communication Talent.

Scobee, June, and Nash, William R. "A Survey of Highly Successful Space Scientists Concerning Education for Gifted and Talented Students." *Gifted Child Quarterly* 27:147–51 (Fall 1983).

The authors help operate a gifted program at Texas A&M, the Summer Space Science Program. They surveyed a group of highly successful space scientists to (1) identify educational practices experienced by the professionals that they considered helpful in preparing them for their chosen scientific profession; (2) elicit suggestions from them concerning educational experiences they would recommend for bright students who are interested in the field of space science as a future career; (3) identify factors they feel influenced their career choice and to which they attribute their success. The results are presented.

Taylor, Calvin W., Albo, Dominic, Holland, John, and Brandt, Gil. "Attributes of Excellence in Various Professions: Their Relevance to the Selection of Gifted/Talented Persons." *Gifted Child Quarterly* 29:29–34 (Winter 1985).

This article is based on a convention presentation for the National Association for Gifted Children. It presents research that shows the limited usefulness of school grades in predicting later career achievement. Support from those in the medical and sports profession is included.

Willings, David. "Issues in Career Choice for Gifted Students." *Teaching Exceptional Children* 15:226–33 (Summer 1983).

The article explores general problems associated with career choice and career development. It focuses specifically on the career problems of gifted and talented youth and offers suggestions for addressing these problems.

Wilson, Susan. "A New Decade: The Gifted and Career Choice." *Vocational Guidance Quarterly* 31:53–59 (September 1982).

The author conducted research with fifty-five high school students identified as gifted. The students completed a questionnaire concerning their career choices. Wilson recommends that career awareness programs for the gifted should stress jobs that allow for creativity, challenge, and personal satisfaction. She also points out that high school counselors must be highly supportive of gifted women's career goals, especially when these goals are nontraditional.

Young, Marilyn S., and McLamb, L. W. "Project CAPS: A Career Education Program for Secondary School Students." *G/C/T* 31:2–4 (January/February 1984).

CAPS (Career Awareness for Precocious Students) operates in the Virginia Beach Public Schools. Two components comprise this program: (1) the Professional Career Resource Center (designed to provide students with access to information on careers, colleges, scholarships, and values); (2) the Professional Apprenticeship Program (designed to match gifted high school students with community professionals).

The Arts

Aebischer, Delmar, and Sheridan, Wilma. "For John, Music Makes a Difference." *Music Educators Journal* 68:29 (April 1982).

The authors briefly recount the story of John, a boy with learning disabilities and concomitant emotional problems, who is also musically gifted.

Alexander, Robin A. "An Historical Perspective on the Gifted and Talented in Art." *Studies in Art Education* 22:38-48 (1981).

The author addresses three questions in her article: (1) Who are the gifted and talented in art? (2) What curriculum and programs should be provided for these youngsters? (3) How can these programs be adequately evaluated? Her review of the literature reflects "the vast wasteland of material about the gifted and talented in art available through conventional sources." Alexander provides an excellent bibliography.

Banschbach, Donald L. "Brainstorming in the Music Class." *G/C/T* 29:41-43 (September/October 1983).

The author, a teacher of general and instrumental music in the elementary school, explains the value of having students "brainstorm" with their instruments. He gives specific examples of what to say and how to manage the classroom.

Baskin, Barbara, and Harris, Karen. "Encouraging the Aesthetic Impulse in Young Gifted Children." *Roeper Review* 4:11-12 (February 1982).

The authors believe that young children can learn and enjoy much about certain aspects of art—how it functions, what it is about, how it can be created and described, and how personal and pleasurable the experience can be. They posit that, rather than being a passive activity, aesthetic development is an interactive activity, which is therefore appropriate for young students.

Buttermore, Phillip H. "Arts in Gifted Education." *Gifted Child Quarterly* 23:405-14 (Summer 1979).

The author discusses the components of an arts program for the gifted and for the artistically talented. The curriculum should include modeling and mentoring; the study of processes and systems for creativity and problem-solving; seeing art experientially as a communications system; integrating the arts into the life process, using arts as an alternative; chances to experience and participate in the arts; and developing and sharing ideas and material resources.

Carlisle, Barbara. "On a Scale of Ten, Where Are the Arts?" *Roeper Review* 2:21–24 (September 1979).

Carlisle's insightful and clearly written position paper on the state of education in the arts is must reading for anyone interested in gifted education in general and art education in particular. She supports the idea of arts education and makes four recommendations: (1) with the school principal, establish a procedure to follow when artistic talent is recognized; (2) establish a resource file of interested master artists and arts institutions; (3) get out of the way of the artistically gifted child; and (4) join forces among schools to establish a support system for students with interests in the arts.

Carroll, Karen Lee. "Alternative Programs in the Arts for Gifted and Talented Students." *Gifted Child Quarterly* 20:414–21 (Winter 1976).

Carroll explores ways in which schools for artistically talented students differ from other schools. These aspects are size of school, pupil-teacher ratio, time (for concentration), and dialogue (among peers, students and teachers, and students and artists).

Chetelat, Frank J. "Visual Arts Education for the Gifted Elementary Level Art Student." *Gifted Child Quarterly* 25:154–58 (Fall 1981).

Chetelat makes a strong case for a visual arts program for elementary school students. He discusses its necessary components and how to enhance it for gifted students.

Churchwell, Birdia. "The High School for Performing and Visual Arts—Where Arts and Academics Flourish." *Today's Education* 70:22–24 (February/March 1981).

Churchwell describes Houston's High School for the Performing and Visual Arts. The program is extremely successful.

Clark, Gilbert, and Zimmerman, Enid. "Toward a New Conception of Talent in the Visual Arts." *Roeper Review* 6:214–16 (April 1984).

The authors dispute several misconceptions regarding artistic talent. Then, they present their art education content model, which advocates designing arts curriculum that acknowledges beginning-level art students as naive in their understanding about art—and therefore needing instruction to move through a series of stages to a more sophisticated level.

Cohen, Elaine. "The Arts from the Inside Out: Developing a Performing Arts Curriculum." *G/C/T* 20:38–42 (November/December 1981).

The author said the impetus for developing her curriculum model for arts in education came when she realized that her students *reacted* to art (just as they reacted to television) rather than *interacting* with it. She then developed "The Arts from the Inside Out," designed as an interdisciplinary thematic model that touched all areas of the arts: mime, puppetry, drama, video, photography, filmmaking, sculpture, architecture, painting, creative writing, dance, music, and opera. Her article describes the project and some of its outcomes.

Cox, June, and Daniel, Neil. "Specialized School for High Ability Students." *G/C/T* 28:2–9 (May/June 1983).

This article is one of the series of articles that has resulted from the Richardson Study, a study funded by the Sid Richardson Foundation in Fort Worth, Texas. The study focused on three major questions: What programs for able learners exist and where are they located? Which are the most effective? Can recommendations be made to assist all types of schools in serving able learners? It reports on Cincinnati's Walnut Hills High School (college preparatory) and the School for Creative and Performing Arts, the Houston School for the Performing and Visual Arts, the Bronx High School of Science, the North Carolina School for Science and Mathematics, and the North Carolina School of the Arts. Recommendations for communities that want to start a specialized school are given.

Dorhout, Albert. "The Symposium for the Arts: An Activity for Students in the Visual and Performing Arts." *Roeper Review* 6:218–20 (April 1984).

Dorhout presents research on The Symposium for the Arts (a program that serves artistically gifted students). He found that the program significantly affects the attitudes of the participants: students were overwhelmingly positive toward the fact that they got to work with peers and with professional artists who shared their interests and that they could devote long periods to their work.

Dorn, Charles M. "The Advanced Placement Program in Studio Art." *Gifted Child Quarterly* 20:450–58 (Winter 1976).

The author, who serves as chief reader for the Advanced Placement Examination in Studio Arts, describes the AP exam in this field. He explains the rationale and method of rating the exams. Art teachers with students talented in studio art should be familiar with the information in this article.

Duffy, Rosaline. "Aesthetic Sensitivity and the Artistically Gifted." *Roeper Review* 2:24–27 (September 1979).

Duffy relates that children have various developmental stages in appreciating the aesthetic nature of things and that teaching can capitalize on these developmental periods.

_____. "An Analysis of Aesthetic Sensitivity and Creativity with Other Variables in Grades Four, Six, Eight, and Ten." *Journal of Educational Research* 73:26–30 (September/October 1979).

The author reports on her exploratory study, which used currently cited methods and nonverbal methods for assessing aesthetic sensitivity in children and youth.

Edmonston, Paul. "The Visually Creative Student." *School Arts* 80:6–11 (April 1981).

This interesting article iterates the characteristics of the visually creative and encourages teachers of such students to recognize and nurture this ability.

Essex, Martin. "A Public School Provides Unusual Opportunities for Musically Gifted." *Gifted Child Quarterly* 7:18–20 (Spring 1963).

Two programs are described. The first is a composers' contest for students in kindergarten through twelfth grade. Awards and scholarships are given. The second program is a summer creative-arts program that includes classes in art, music, drama, dancing, creative writing, and creative mathematics.

Gair, Sondra B. "Form and Function: Teaching Problem Learners through Art." *Teaching Exceptional Children* 9:30–32 (Winter 1977).

Gair describes a special program: Receptive-Expressive Learning through Art, a program which has been used effectively with problem learners, including gifted students who are developmentally lagging in one or more communication areas.

Gatty, Arthur. "The Pennsylvania Governor's School for the Arts." *Gifted Child Quarterly* 20:427–32 (Winter 1976).

Gatty describes the Governor's School for the Arts, which serves nearly 300 students (gifted in the arts) for five weeks in the summer. One unique aspect of the curriculum is the requirement that students become involved in an art field other than their own. This component nurtures "awareness of the aesthetic properties and problems faced by other artists and enhances the inter-relationship of students as people, and as artists."

Gibberd, Kathleen. "Virtuoso from Start to Finish." *Education Digest* 31:48–49 (February 1966).

The Yehudi Menuhin School for musically gifted children is briefly discussed. Twenty-seven children, ages eight to fifteen, live and learn at the school.

Gilbert, Janet P., and Beal, Mary R. "Music Experiences for the Gifted and Talented." *G/C/T* 24:50–51 (September/October 1982).

The authors provide a rationale for using Renzulli's Enrichment Triad Model in music. They also give an example of how to use the model (for investigating American folk music).

Gilmar, Sybil. "What If They're Interested in Art?" *G/C/T* 15:58–59 (November/December 1980).

Gilmar says that gifted children need to see the relationship of art to life, and they should therefore be exposed to fine art and given an opportunity to develop an appreciation of it. She tells about her class of gifted students and the experiences they had exploring and learning about the collection at the Philadelphia Museum of Art.

Gregory, Anne. "Applying the Purdue Three-Stage Model for Gifted Education to the Development of Art Education for G/C/T Students." *G/C/T* 25:23-26 (November/December 1982).

Gregory first gives a clear overview of the Purdue Three-Stage Model and then explains how to apply the model to the art education curriculum. The explanation is rather general, so people hoping to implement such a curriculum may want to do further reading.

Hartshorn, William E. "Musical Education of the Gifted." *Music Education Journal* 54:76-80 (February 1968).

This article is chapter six in the book *The Study of Music in Elementary School—A Conceptual Approach*. Most of the article lists activities appropriate for gifted students.

Hurwitz, Al. "ARTS: New Recognition for the Gifted in Art." *School Arts* 81:32-33 (September 1981).

Hurwitz briefly describes the Arts Recognition and Talent Search (ARTS) and tells the process by which artistically gifted students may enter the competition.

Isaacs, Ann F. "Musical Genius—It Is Both Inspiration and Perspiration." *Gifted Child Quarterly* 7:24-25 (Spring 1963a).

The author interviews a gifted young pianist who has been performing publicly since he was very young. The article would be good to read to a class of musically gifted youth.

————. "We Sat There in Our Beanies, or an Interview with an Archbishop Discussing an Exciting Musical Program for Gifted Boys." *Gifted Child Quarterly* 7:15-17 (Spring 1963b).

Isaacs tells about a special program for gifted boys (able to accomplish their academic work in half a day) who were also vocally gifted in music.

Johnson, Barbara. "What Can You Do for the Gifted on Monday Morning?" *Educational Leadership* 35:35-41 (October 1977).

The author discusses several very successful programs for gifted students.

Khatena, Joe. "The Nature of Imagery in the Visual and Performing Arts." *Gifted Child Quarterly* 23:735-47 (Winter 1979).

Khatena discusses various theories of imagery and how it can be encouraged in gifted youth.

Lally, Ann. "Encouraging Development of the Talented in the Fine Arts." *Education* 88:43-46 (September/October 1967).

Lally gives suggestions for ways to identify and nurture children talented in the fine arts.

Lowenfeld, Viktor, and Brittain, W. Lambert. *Creative and Mental Growth.* New York: Macmillan, 1970. 364 pp.

This book, in its fifth edition, is one of the classics in art education and should be read by any teachers planning to help their students experience art.

Maddy, Joseph E. "Musically Gifted Children Learn More in Less Time at the Interlochen Arts Academy and the National Music Camp." *Gifted Camp Quarterly* 7:21–22 (Spring 1963).

The author says that musically gifted children should have three educational provisions made for them: (1) close association with other young people of similar talent and ability; (2) exposure to competition with others of similar interest, so that they can evaluate their own abilities in comparison; and (3) opportunities to concentrate on their interests. He explains how the Interlochen Arts Academy makes these provisions.

Miller, Vera V. "Creativity and Intelligence in the Arts." *Education* 82:488–95 (April 1962).

Miller reports on research that led investigators to the conclusion that there is some correlation between intelligence and giftedness. However, not all bright children have talent, and the presence of such talent is not precluded by lesser intelligence. "Creativity is not necessarily associated with the highest intelligence, but artistic products of highest value are probably associated with unusual intellectual gifts."

Rogers, Karen B. "The Museum and the Gifted Child." *Roeper Review* 7:238–41 (April 1985).

Rogers introduces a variety of content, process, and product-questioning techniques useful for the visual analysis of objects of art to which children may be introduced. The ideas could be very useful for teachers taking students to museums and art shows, and to museum docents who direct tours for young people.

Schmidt, Lloyd. "Gifted Programs in Music: A Nuclear Model." *Roeper Review* 3:31–34 (February 1981).

The nuclear model holds that, in order to be effective, gifted programs must be precise: the identification procedures must be specific so that program activities may be relevant to the particular nature of individual talent. Schmidt explains this model in terms of programming for musically gifted students.

Simons, Gene M. "A Rationale for Early Training in Music." *Education* 99:259–64 (Spring 1979).

Simons says there are five sound reasons for beginning music training at a very young age: (1) under the proper conditions, children learn well during the earliest years of their lives; (2) children respond to music very early; (3) young children can and do acquire music skill and knowledge through environmental experiences and training; (4) early child-hood is the most critical period for learning music; (5) identification and training of musically gifted children must take place when they are very young. A discussion of each of these points comprises the article.

Stalker, Martha Zola. "Identification of the Gifted in Art." *Studies in Art Education* 22:49–56 (1981).

The author reports on her study of 103 college-level art students. The purpose of the study was "to develop a theoretical model for identify-ing gifted and talented in art that is congruent with emergent theories of art learning and would specify components that could be measured for individuals with relative objectivity." She found that executive draw-ing ability accounts for the largest amount of variance but that cognitive complexity and affective intensity also provide significant information for assessing the gifted and talented in art.

Stone, Samuel M. "NCSA: North Carolina's Venture into Professional Arts Training." *Gifted Child Quarterly* 20:422–26 (Winter 1976).

The author describes the educational program at the North Carolina School of the Arts. Students may attend the school for up to ten years (seventh grade through college), and may focus on one of many areas (e.g., dance, drama, music).

Szekely, George. "The Artist and the Child—a Model Program for the Ar-tistically Gifted." *Gifted Child Quarterly* 25:67–72 (Spring 1981).

This outstanding article relates the rationale behind and the need for setting up "Art Partnership Network" programs. These programs unite gifted art students with college-age artists who serve as teacher-/mentor/guide. This should be read.

_____. "Art Partnership Network: A Supportive Program for Artisti-cally Gifted Children" *Elementary School Journal* 83:59–66 (September 1982).

The author describes a program, developed at the University of Ken-tucky, that matches trained art students from the university with gifted elementary school children. "The primary objectives of the program are to help artistically talented children to: (1) identify with the world of art, artists and art making; (2) develop their artistic gifts and talents with continuity and guidance; (3) contend with a sense of isolation; (4) de-velop confidence in their creativity and a willingness to take risks to ex-pand; (5) develop the ability to work independently."

Thompson, Gail S., and Shapiro, Laura. "Inner Art: Guidance for High School Students Gifted in the Arts." *G/C/T* 10:18–20 (November/De-cember 1979).

The authors describe a voluntary program they developed out of con-cern for the special needs and problems of high school students who have been identified as artistically gifted and talented. They explain the structure of the program, give examples of activities in which the group participated, and discuss the implications of such a program.

Tirro, Frank. "Development of an Elementary Instrumental Music Program." *Music Education Journal* 51:56, 59 (September 1964).

The author recounts the effort of one school for the gifted to establish an instrumental music program.

Turnbull, William W. "National Arts Awards and Arts Recognition and Talent Search." *Art Education* 34:32–34 (January 1981).

Turnbull explains a new program of the Educational Testing Service that seeks to formally recognize individual accomplishments of young people.

Vautour, J. A. Camille. "Discovering and Motivating the Artistically Gifted Child." *Teaching Exceptional Children* 8:92–96 (Winter 1976).

From a group of children identified as learning disabled, four children were identified as artistically gifted. These children were taught through their artistic strength to improve their reading skills and their self-concepts.

Wilson, Brent, and Wilson, Marjorie. "Visual Narrative and the Artistically Gifted." *Gifted Child Quarterly* 20:432–47 (Winter 1976).

First, the authors point out that boredom gives rise to a great deal of creativity (in order to escape boredom). Next, they discuss visual narratives (stories told in pictures) as indicative of unique creative talent. Four case studies are included.

Wilson, M. Emett. "Encouraging the Musically Gifted." *Gifted Child Quarterly* 1:5 (July 1957).

Wilson suggests allowing gifted children to learn to play music by ear before having them attempt to learn to read music. He feels quite strongly regarding this, for he says, "Were it possible for a 'teacher' to compel the child, when learning to talk, to consider the position of his vocal chords, the tension of his lungs, the angle at which his tongue must be held, many children would hate to talk."

Wood, William R. "Musical Enrichment for the Gifted or Musically Talented Student." *Roeper Review* 7:242–46 (April 1985).

Wood discusses a six-step plan to meet gifted and/or musically talented students' musical learning needs: (1) evaluation, (2) musical environment, (3) exposure, (4) project selection, (5) finding resources, (6) guidance and supervision of the activity. Numerous ideas are given for steps four and five.

Worrel, J. W. "Problems of the Talented Child in Music." *Gifted Child Quarterly* 7:9–12 (Spring 1963).

The author bemoans the fact that so few schools offer music programs that really encourage students who are gifted in music. He makes recommendations for improving the situation. This article is apropos now because of the "basics" thrust, just as it was in the early 1960s.

Yeatts, Edward Hilary. "The Professional Artist: A Teacher for the Gifted." *Gifted Child Quarterly* 24:133–37 (Summer 1980).

The author cites research on a program held in his district that indicated that "he who can, does; and he who can, can also teach." An artist-in-residence program was implemented and was a great success.

Yunghans, Marion. "Why Art?" *G/C/T* 9:24–25 (September/October 1979).

Yunghans provides a good rationale for offering art instruction for gifted students. She encourages teachers to allow for creative expression through individualized instruction. A pictorial which illustrates "Why Art?" is in an article by that name in the January/February 1980 issue of *G/C/T*.

_____. "A Pull-Out Art Program for Gifted Elementary Students." *School Arts* 80:50–51 (April 1981).

The author, who has developed an art enrichment program for gifted third graders, urges teachers to encourage "production that leads to improved skill, more penetrating insight, and greater mastery of the media." A brief overview of the five units of her enrichment program is included.

CHAPTER 7

Education for Teachers
of the Gifted

In recent years, teacher education has come under increasing criticism—because of its apparent lack of relevance to real classroom situations and because it may have lower standards or provide higher grades than other disciplines within the university. Criticism has come from various sectors of the population—former teacher-education students (teachers), parents of public school students, personnel directors, and legislators, to name only a few. Probably the most valid complaint is the one made by former teacher education students, who claim that their training did not prepare them for the classroom situation in which they subsequently found themselves.

This chapter is not intended to suggest remedies for all the problems in teacher education; it is, however, intended to make recommendations for ways to better prepare teachers who will have gifted students as members of their heterogeneous classrooms and teachers whose sole responsibility will be gifted students. Because of the special population the latter will serve, specific learning outcomes should be expected from a teacher education program designed for them. In other words, an employer should be able to expect certain qualities and performance levels from someone trained to teach gifted learners. The teacher should be:

1. Intelligent.
2. Self-confident.
3. Enthusiastic.
4. Highly energetic.
5. Creative.
6. Strongly prepared in pedagogy—theory and practice.

7. Thoroughly familiar with characteristics of giftedness and how they affect learning.
8. Knowledge of, and practice in, curriculum design.
9. Familiarity with research regarding the gifted and its relevance to classroom practice.
10. Solid preparation in content areas to be taught.

In this chapter, we will attempt to answer the who, what, when, where, why, and how of an education that will produce a cadre of teachers who demonstrate the above qualities and performance levels.

WHO SHOULD TEACH THE GIFTED?

Webster's Deluxe Unabridged Dictionary (2nd ed.) defines a teacher as ''one who teaches or instructs; an instructor; a preceptor; a tutor; one whose occupation is to instruct others.'' Certain qualifications immediately come to mind as one characterizes a good teacher: intelligence, knowledge of subject matter, knowledge of pedagogy, an affinity for students, enthusiasm and zest for life. Admittedly, these characteristics are desirable for all teachers, but they are mandatory for teachers of the gifted. Davis (1954, 222) says, ''Raise the standards of a good teacher to the highest point of development, and you will have a gifted teacher for gifted pupils.''

One of the most fundamental characteristics for teachers of the gifted is intelligence. This is cited by researchers (Nelson & Cleland 1967), experts in the field (Bray 1979; Davis 1954), and gifted students (Bishop 1968; Dubner 1980; Milgram 1979). Above-average intelligence is an ingredient essential in teachers of the gifted for several reasons: (1) they must be able to converse with their able students on a level commensurate with the latter's ability; (2) they must be able to understand the research and writing being done about the gifted and be articulate enough to support their teaching with the current research; and (3) they must have enough intelligence to be self-confident about their own abilities. Insisting that teachers of the gifted possess superior intelligence does not have the additional stipulation that they be more intelligent than their students and, in fact, often this will not be the case.

One reason that teachers of the gifted do not have to be more intelligent than their students is that there is nothing wrong with saying ''I don't know'' when asked a question by a bright student. To be able to admit not knowing, however, requires a positive self-concept, which is another essential trait of a gifted teacher.

Teachers of the gifted must be self-assured. They must project the image, ''I am intelligent and am quite comfortable with my intelligence.'' This image will serve as a model for young gifted students, some of whom may not be comfortable with—let alone proud of—their academic ability. It is necessary for gifted students' teachers to have positive self-concepts that will allow them to praise students, to give them credit for new and better ideas, and not to feel threatened when their ideas are challenged by their students.

Good teachers of the gifted not only allow but encourage their students to challenge ideas in their search for knowledge. Successful teachers of the gifted are considered process- rather than product-oriented in their teaching (Barbe & Frierson 1962; Bray 1979). Their goal is for students to learn to learn—not just to learn facts, but rather to become lifelong learners, as they themselves are. Such teachers epitomize intellectual excitement, and this affects those students fortunate enough to be in their classes.

Modeling joy in learning is another essential characteristic of teachers for the gifted. This joy may be exemplified through avidly pursued avocations, courses taken to satisfy an interest or curiosity, books and magazines that address a particular passionate interest, traveling to broaden horizons, or new words that have been discovered and learned. All the above should be enthusiastically shared with students as they embark on a quest for their own joy in learning.

The enthusiasm displayed by a good teacher is indicative of several other desirable characteristics. Enthusiasm cannot be feigned for very long—and real enthusiasm in teaching stems from a basic joy in life, in students, in teaching, and in learning. Gifted students want to be excited about learning, and their teacher can demonstrate and foster that excitement.

A gifted teacher's enthusiasm should result in imaginative, risk-taking behavior in the classroom. The mastering of skills and procedures is not as important as mastering the excitement of learning. If dressing up as a character in a book entices children to read, if memorizing scary poetry to recite in front of a videorecorder provides the impetus for gifted children to do the same, if letting snakes slither around one's neck demonstrates a key biology concept—a teacher of the gifted will take part. If an experience will help the students learn or grow or experience, then the successful teacher of the gifted will partake without concern for the fact that it is scary, or looks silly, or appears undignified. Learning is the primary concern.

It requires creativity to ensure that learning is taking place. The teacher must not only possess the elements of creativity (fluency, flexibility, originality, and elaboration) but must continually nurture them and employ them in lesson planning. Because they are constantly changing and growing and encouraging those around them to do the same, effectual teachers of the gifted do not get stuck in ruts. For the gifted, this is an extremely healthy atmosphere in which to learn.

Just providing a nurturing atmosphere is not enough to ensure that learning will take place. A good teacher of the gifted knows that the gifted need instruction just as much as other students do. Experience and training have convinced the effective teacher of this fact. Therefore, the teacher uses the best teaching methods and is willing to search for other, even more successful ones. Personal and professional perspectives are broadened by taking classes and attending conferences.

The classes or conferences that the outstanding teacher of the gifted attend may be related to various subfields of education (gifted, curriculum, administration) or they may be related to specific content fields (reading, mathematics, social studies, science, art). It should go without saying that teachers of the gifted need to be highly competent in their content field and preferably in some related fields as well. Broad content field knowledge is desirable not only for teachers in high school but in elementary schools as well. There is much controversy over the training of teachers; some believe that teachers should first receive a degree in a content field and then complete a year of course work to be certified as a teacher. While we are not going to argue for or against this position, we do think that teachers of the gifted need a firm content-area background undergirding their preparation in pedagogy.

In addition to intelligence, solid preparation in appropriate content areas, knowledge of pedagogy, creativity, enthusiasm, and joy for life and learning, teachers of the gifted should possess other characteristics:

1. Because of the incredible demands of teaching gifted students, good health is a necessity.
2. Because of its value in teaching and relating to gifted students, a sense of humor is desirable.
3. Because of gifted students' sense of right and wrong, their teachers need to be democratic and to be both fair and firm with them.
4. Because one of the most readily identifiable characteristics of gifted students is sensitivity, their teachers need to have a well-developed understanding of children and giftedness.
5. The importance of the final characteristics cannot be underestimated. Teachers for the gifted must have a sincere desire to work

with the gifted. They must have a predilection for gifted students and a zeal for the gifted-education movement. Teachers may possess all the previously mentioned characteristics, but unless they *want* to teach the gifted, the relationship should not be forced.

The role of the teacher of the gifted is incredibly demanding, and therefore, special care must be taken in selecting the people to serve in this role. Wilson (1961, 183) says that nurturing the gifted

> is not unlike the constant care and culture of choice breeds and crops practiced in animal husbandry and agriculture. . . . for his good seed, the farmer prepares his best soil with care and cultivates and nourishes the crop with almost daily attention, knowing full well that the choice seed will respond miraculously to loving care. Teacher education programs also must prepare new teachers to nourish the choice seed.

Gifted students are the choice seed and they need and deserve teachers who know how to nourish them.

TRAINING OF TEACHERS

Virtually all teachers—preschool, elementary, middle school, high school—will have gifted children in their classrooms. Because of this, all teachers need some exposure to, and training in, the education of the gifted. Such work will, of course, be much less extensive than that recommended for teachers who will primarily teach gifted students. Because of its greater extensiveness, the latter-mentioned training will be discussed first.

Teachers of the gifted should be experienced classroom teachers. Training should be at the graduate level, enrolling people who have already taught for two or more years and are returning to school for master's degrees or for graduate certification in gifted education (Karnes & Parker 1983).

Standards for this education have been recommended jointly by The Association for the Gifted (TAG) and the National Association for Gifted Children (NAGC) (see Seeley, Jenkins, & Hultgren 1981 for a more extensive explanation).

> *Standard I: Admission and Selection Criteria:* The institution should publish specific criteria for admission to programs at each degree level. These criteria should include cognitive and affective evidence obtained from multiple sources and should be congruent with state program philosophy and goals.
> *Standard II: Curriculum and Competency Areas:* Training pro-

grams should establish a coherent, comprehensive and discernible curriculum that addresses the major areas of gifted education as well as related studies. The curriculum should address theory, practice, and research in each of these areas.

Standard III: Degree Programs: Degree programs with a major emphasis in gifted education should be offered only at the graduate level and should be differentiated from each other appropriate to level (i.e., master's specialist, doctoral).

Standard IV: Faculty for Graduate Programs: Faculty members with major teaching responsibilities in graduate programs should hold the doctorate with advanced study in gifted child education, or have competence in the field as demonstrated by significant research, writing or leadership in gifted education. Faculty members who conduct the advanced programs should be engaged in scholarly activity that supports their specialization in the field, and have experience which relates directly to gifted/talented child education.

Standard V: Administrative Structure: Staffing: The faculty for advanced programs should include at least one full-time doctoral person who holds an appropriate degree or has demonstrated competence, and at least three persons who hold the doctorate in fields which directly support the degree programs.

Standard VI: Administrative Structure: Evaluation: The program's mission and course offerings should be reviewed regularly. The results of this evaluation should be used in program modification and improvement efforts. Systematic opportunities should be provided for student and faculty input into program administration, review and planning.

Standard VII: Resources and Facilities: Institutions that offer graduate programs in gifted education should assure adequate human and material resources and facilities to implement their prescribed course of study. (Seeley, Jenkins, & Hultgren 1981, 165–68)

It is imperative that training for teachers of the gifted include internship and/or practicum experiences (Cassidy & Vukelich 1978; Feldhusen 1977; Jenkins & Stewart 1979). These experiences may be part of a semester-long or summer program, and they must be supervised by people who have demonstrated successful teaching with gifted students. The supervisors do not necessarily have to be full-time university faculty but could be master teachers from public or private schools hired specifically to supervise gifted teachers in training.

Prior to the practicum experience, courses reflecting the major areas of gifted education should be required: identification and characteristics; curriculum models; teaching strategies; cognitive and affective development; program development, implementation, maintenance, and evaluation. Courses in related areas, such as learning theory, psychology, and administration, could round out the curriculum for a teacher preparing to teach gifted students.

At present, the vast majority of gifted students are served within the regular classroom and not by teachers who have had the extensive education recommended above. What provisions can be made so that the gifted in the regular classrooms are more adequately served? The two most viable solutions involved preservice and in-service education.

Preservice teacher training must be expanded to include *at least one entire course* on the gifted (Seeley 1979; Whitmore 1983). This course would include learning, social, emotional, and behavioral characteristics of the gifted; teaching strategies appropriate for the gifted; and classroom-management techniques. It must be taught by a person who has actually been trained in gifted education, has taught gifted students, and preferably has conducted research concerning the gifted. In addition, the methods courses must be modified to include components that address the learning needs of the gifted.

In order for methods courses to be appropriately altered, in-service training should be conducted for the college faculty who teach these courses. The most expedient way to introduce college personnel to gifted education is to bring in nationally known experts to do a series of weekend workshops and other training events. Participants would be more able to modify courses and amenable to doing so after receiving such training. For example, the elementary and secondary reading methods courses should provide a rationale for and ways to more effectively meet the differential reading needs of the gifted; math methods courses should provide specific means for differentiating and/or accelerating the math curriculum for gifted students; social studies courses should emphasize the need for integrating the various component subjects of social studies when teaching the gifted. College instructors could have their students modify existing lesson plans and curriculum so that it more appropriately addresses gifted students' needs. Student teaching supervisors could expect that their students who had taken such modified courses could plan lessons individualized to meet the learning needs of both average and gifted students within a regular classroom.

After participating in a program such as the one briefly described above, first-year teachers who enter their classrooms and find that they have students ranging from far below level to far above level (in both performance and potential) will not throw up their hands and "teach to the middle" assuming that the "bright kids will get it on their own."

Instead, they will be prepared to recognize and plan for the various abilities of their students.

On the other hand, for teachers who completed their traditional training years ago, it is necessary to plan extensive in-service programs to essentially "retrain" them to successfully serve those gifted students in their classrooms. Requiring teachers to attend a few happenstance staff-development presentations on the education of the gifted in *not* enough. Instead, an intensive, well-planned in-service must be prepared with very specific goals and objectives along with ways to assess whether those goals are being met. Such a program could very easily take several months to plan and a year to implement (Marks 1980; Weslander 1983). But if the proper time and care is given to such a program, the results will be well worth the effort.

Almost all teachers who teach more than a year or two will have gifted students (identified or not) in their charge. It is therefore imperative that all teachers have a working knowledge of the characteristics and needs of the gifted. Those teachers who deal primarily with highly able students must have a well-developed knowledge base from which to practice. Changes in preservice, in-service, and graduate training for teachers are mandatory.

AVAILABILITY OF PROGRAMS

Nearly all universities with departments or colleges of education provide one or two courses in gifted education. In far too many cases, the courses are taught by people who have had no advanced coursework in the field, have had limited experience successfully teaching the gifted, and have done little or no reading and research in the area of gifted education. Such instructors may do more to promote stereotypes than they do to foster positive attitudes or to develop appropriate educational provisions for the gifted. However, a number of colleges and universities in most states are developing or continuing effective, successful programs for preparing teachers of the gifted. Interested persons are directed to the annotated bibliography at the end of this section for specific references.

NEED FOR TRAINING

Teaching is a skill, and like other skills (such as tennis or writing), it is partly natural ability and partly training. Natural ability without training usually results in someone who is good but not great at a craft.

Training without natural ability results in technically correct performance that lacks "heart" or vibrancy. The same is true for teaching—natural ability must be coupled with training in order to bring the "performance" from good to great. And *great* teachers are needed for the gifted.

Part of being a great teacher is matching instruction to a student's learning needs. Teachers must be taught to identify the gifted and to tailor learning experiences for them. When the students are highly gifted, adjusting the curriculum is not just desirable—it is mandatory. Gifted students are as different from average students as average students are from students who comprise the lower levels of exceptionality. It is ludicrous to expect a person with no specialized training to teach students who are mentally retarded, learning disabled, or developmentally handicapped. Likewise, expecting teachers to adequately serve gifted students without specialized training is absurd.

Teachers who are not primarily employed to teach the gifted are also in grave need of education on the gifted. Probably the number one hindrance to the proliferation of gifted education is attitudinal (Fox 1968). Stereotyped views of gifted students are often held by teachers (Jackson, Famiglietti, & Robinson 1981; Salvia, Clark, & Ysseldyke 1973; Smidchens & Sellin 1976), school administrators (Wiener & O'Shea 1963), school support staff such as counselors and librarians (Wiener 1968), parents of gifted and nongifted students, and community members (Mills & Berry 1979). The majority of these stereotypes actually impede progress toward adequate special education for the gifted. In numerous studies, it has been found that both education concerning the gifted and direct experience with them significantly affect attitudes toward highly able children (Bruch 1967; Buttery 1978; Jacobs 1972; Nicely, Small, & Furman 1980; Weiss & Gallagher 1980; but see also Deiulio 1984). As with virtually all misconceptions, education serves to remove the blinders that are the root of the prejudice.

As in-service training educates teachers in the area of giftedness, the tension that often exists between "regular" classroom teachers and gifted classroom teachers will diminish or disappear. As teachers come to understand the differentiated learning needs of their gifted students, resentment about special programs also lessens. There will then exist the much greater likelihood that school personnel can work together to ensure the most beneficial educational program for their gifted students (and their other students, as well).

Gifted students are necessarily the victims of the attitudes and education of the teachers and other personnel employed to serve them. It is therefore incumbent upon those persons committed to appropriate education for the gifted to ensure that school personnel are adequately trained for the task.

ENSURING ADEQUATE TRAINING

Both experts and the lay people interested in gifted education bear an almost compulsory obligation to work toward satisfactory education for teachers in order to ensure commensurate education for gifted students. Neither competent teacher education nor suitable education for the gifted will come about unless a great deal of hard work is accomplished and pressure is brought to bear on school districts, teacher preparation programs, and legislators.

School districts can lead the way in the effort to upgrade the preparation of teachers for students who comprise special populations (such as the gifted). As special programs for serving the gifted are implemented, and as the requirements inherent in the task of educating gifted students both within and beyond the regular classroom are recognized, school districts should require a specified course of study for their teachers. For example, a master's degree in gifted education or at least fifteen hours of graduate work in gifted education might be required of full-time teachers of the gifted, and at least one undergraduate course in gifted education and further in-service preparation might be asked of teachers of heterogeneous classrooms. When school districts let it be known that they expect and indeed require teachers to possess certain minimum competencies concerning the education of the gifted, colleges of education will have to respond or their graduates will be unable to find employment—which is not a legacy coveted by teacher-preparation institutions.

The colleges and universities that claim to prepare teachers must be held responsible for doing just that. It is reasonable to expect students who graduate from a four- or five-year program to be qualified to tackle the myriad of challenges that a classroom of young people presents. As has been iterated throughout this chapter, teachers must be educated concerning the characteristics of the gifted and then in how to assess their particular strengths in order to design an apposite course of study for them. School districts, being the primary consumers of the products of teacher-training institutions, are the most natural forces for initiating changes in the curriculum offered to preservice teachers.

School district personnel and college of education faculty should work concurrently in setting up suitable programs. During the transition period, there could actually be a symbiotic relationship between a university and a school district. Experienced classroom teachers, with advanced course work and research in teaching the gifted, could help educate university faculty through lectures, recommended readings, classroom observation, and supervised practice teaching. These specially trained faculty would later teach courses on the gifted for preservice and/or in-service teacher training.

Not all colleges of education will respond to school districts' expectations that undergraduate and graduate programs will be in place to prepare teachers of the gifted in either homogeneous or heterogeneous classrooms. It is therefore necessary for states to require certification in the area of gifted education for teachers whose primary responsibility is to the gifted, and to require modifications in certification to include at least one course in the psychology and education of the gifted for all teachers, regardless of their specialty or level. (See Karnes & Parker 1983 for a certification model for teachers of the gifted.)

At this time, only thirteen states require certification for the gifted. It is urgent that advocates of gifted education lobby state boards of education and state legislators to pass certification requirements for teachers of the gifted. Most of these lawmakers will first require some education concerning the gifted to help establish a basis in their minds for mandating such certification.

To get certification mandated in all fifty states is a monumental, but achievable, task. Those knowledgeable in the field of gifted education must be peremptory in their quest for increased standards for teachers. To be lackadaisical about this mission is to ensure continued inadequate preparation for teachers—and continued inadequate education for gifted students. Neither of these situations is tolerable.

SELECTED BIBLIOGRAPHY

Teacher Education

Abroms, Kippy. "Gifted and Learning Disabled." *G/C/T* 2:26–28 (March/April 1978).
   Abroms discusses gifted students who are learning disabled, using the framework of Guilford's Structure of Intellect model.
Adkins, Darlene, and Harty, Harold. "Longitudinal View of Teacher-Leaders' Reactions toward Gifted Education." *Roeper Review* 7:36–40 (September 1984).
   The authors conducted a study in which twelve in-service teacher-leaders were chosen to be trained and to serve as change agents in

their schools. Pretests, posttests, and delayed posttests indicate that, as the teachers felt more competent in gifted education, their attitudes toward the gifted and gifted education became more positive and supportive.

Akers, Diane. "Teacher Behaviors that Enhance Creativity." *G/C/T* 16:47 (January/February 1981).

Akers suggests six ways that teachers can enhance the quantity, complexity, and creativity of student ideas expressed in the classroom: eliminate judgmental responses; probe; attribute (give students credit for their ideas); model; reflect and/or rephrase; be silent to give students time to think, reflect, or expand on an idea.

Anderson, Bev. "Project Headstop." *G/C/T* 10:21 (November/December 1979).

Anderson's tongue-in-cheek article about how to "identify and decelerate overprivileged students" would be perfect for sending to school board members or administrators who oppose gifted education.

Anderson, Robert H. "Viewpoint: Teachers of Gifted Children." *Roeper Review* 7:137-39 (February 1985).

Anderson recommends that gifted students be served by a "team" of teachers who are in charge of a large group of children—spanning several grades and a wide range of abilities. He believes that teachers of the gifted need to possess integrity, authenticity, flexibility, deep commitment to their work life, and a zest for living.

Barbe, Walter B., and Frierson, Edward C. "Teaching the Gifted: A New Frame of Reference." *Education* 82:465-67 (April 1962).

The authors posit that teachers of the gifted cannot be satisfied with just teaching more, or more rapidly, but instead must teach differently—they must be process oriented rather than product oriented. This idea is further explained in the article.

Berghoff, Beth K., and Berghoff, Paul J. "Communication Techniques for Gifted/Talented Support Teachers." *Journal for the Education of the Gifted* 3:105-7 (1979).

Several excellent suggestions are offered to teachers and consultants who serve in a support role in education of the gifted and talented. The authors point out that if the teacher being "helped" feels threatened or accused, then the help and suggestions go unheeded.

Bishop, W. E. "Successful Teachers of the Gifted." *Exceptional Children* 34:317-25 (1968).

The author reports on an extensive study designed to determine what personal and social traits and behaviors, what professional attitudes and educational viewpoints, and what classroom behaviors and perceptions characterize teachers chosen by gifted high school students as their best teacher. The results indicate that these teachers tend to be mature and experienced, mentally superior, high achievers, student centered, organized, imaginative in their teaching, and supportive of special education for the gifted. Other results are also given.

Bray, James L. "Characteristics of G/C/T Teachers." *G/C/T* 6:50 (January/February 1979).

Bray explains the characteristics he looks for when hiring teachers for gifted students—intelligence, educational risk taking, interest in theories more than facts, divergent thinking, concern with process more than product, ability to cross academic disciplines.

Bruch, Catherine B. "Persistence of Changes of Attitudes toward Gifted Children." *Gifted Child Quarterly* 7:172–77 (Autumn 1967).

Bruch's research indicates that a summer workshop for teachers had long-lasting positive effects on the participants' attitudes toward the gifted (e.g., on special programs for the gifted, appreciation of the gifted, recognition of the special role of the teacher in the education of the gifted).

————. "Current Degree Programs in Gifted Education." *Gifted Child Quarterly* 21:141–54 (Summer 1977).

State by state, colleges and universities that offer either courses, certificates, or degrees in gifted education are listed. Contact people and addresses given for most programs.

Buttery, Thomas J. "Pre-Service Teachers' Attitudes regarding Gifted Children." *College Student Journal* 12:288–89 (Fall 1978).

Using a previously constructed instrument (Jacobs 1972, see annotation) for measuring attitudes towards the gifted, this author assessed the attitudes of preservice teachers just completing a course on exceptional children (which included a module on gifted children). Although their responses were more favorable than those of the in-service teachers previously tested, they fell far short of the responses of a selected group of private-school teachers of the gifted.

Cassidy, Jack, and Vukelich, Carol. "Providing for the Young Academically Talented: A Pilot Program for Teachers and Children." *Journal for the Education of the Gifted* 1:70–76 (February 1978).

A three-week pilot program was designed and implemented for the purpose of providing academically talented preschoolers with learning experiences that would enhance their communication skills. A secondary purpose of the program was to provide preschool and kindergarten teachers with strategies and materials for developing these communication skills in their precocious students. The program is described.

Coletta, Anthony J. "Reflective Didactic Styles for Teachers of the

Young, Gifted, Poor Children." *Gifted Child Quarterly* 19:230–40 (Fall 1975).

Coletta describes how three models (Flanders' Interaction, Gordon's, and Bloom's) can be combined to effectively provide teachers with a framework for being retrained to improve their style of interaction with children.

Copenhaver, R. W., Byrd, David M., McIntyre, D. John, and Norris, William R. "Cooperative Research: Answering Questions for Teachers of the Gifted." *Roeper Review* 6:85–86 (November 1983).

The authors make a good case for collaborative research involving university professors and classroom teachers. They discuss major obstacles and ways of removing them.

Corn, Anne L., and Bishop, Virginia E. "Educating Teachers of the Gifted Handicapped: A Survey of Teacher Education Programs." *Journal for the Education of the Gifted* 7:137–45 (1984).

Two hundred colleges and universities were surveyed to gather specific information regarding the extent to which the education of gifted handicapped children is approached in teacher-education programs and to determine whether teacher educators feel the need to further develop programs and standards for those preparing to work with gifted handicapped children. The survey results are included and their implications discussed.

Cummings, Alysa. "A Day in the Life of a Gifted Teacher." *G/C/T* 24:44–45 (September/October 1982).

Cummings takes a humorous (but realistic) look at a gifted classroom teacher's day.

_____. "Gifted/Creative/Talented Teacher Survival Simulation Test." *G/C/T* 29:17–18 (September/October 1983).

Cummings presents six situations, with multiple choices for handling each situation.

Curry, James, and Sato, Irving S. "Training on the Right Track." *Gifted Child Quarterly* 21:200–04 (Summer 1977).

The authors describe the type of training offered by the National/State Leadership Training Institute for Gifted and Talented (N/S-LTI-G/T). Their principles are that training should (1) meet various levels of expertise; (2) serve individuals in different roles; (3) strive to meet specific needs of participants; (4) be problem and product oriented; (5) be team-centered; (6) be both practical and philosophical; (7) bring change; (8) demonstrate replicable models; (9) be planned, coordinated, and purposeful; (10) be reinforced and extended through appropriate materials; and (11) strive toward excellence.

Davis, Nelda. "Teachers for the Gifted." *Journal of Teacher Education* 5:221–24 (September 1954).

Davis offers general information regarding who should teach the gifted and the sort of preparation they should have.

Deiulio, Judith M. "Attitudes of School Counselors and Psychologists toward Gifted Children." *Journal for the Education of the Gifted* 7:164–69 (1984).

From the results of the Wiener Attitude Scale and a brief questionnaire, the attitudes of school counselors and school psychologists toward the gifted were determined. It was found that the counselors and psychologists from districts with gifted and talented programs held significantly more negative attitudes than did those from districts without such programs.

Dettmer, Peggy. "Improving Teacher Attitudes toward Characteristics of the Creatively Gifted." *Gifted Child Quarterly* 25:11–16 (Winter 1981).

The author reports on a study conducted to help teachers recognize and accept creative personality types—especially types different from their own personality types.

————. "Preventing Burnout in Teachers of the Gifted." *G/C/T* 21:37–41 (January/February 1982).

Dettmer posits that burnout among teachers of the gifted is potentially quite high. She justifies her stance and provides excellent suggestions for protective activities before, during, and after teaching the gifted.

Downing, Gloria, and Todd, Anita. "LRP = IN(5PS/3ST) = SD/GTP: A Formula for Staff Development for Programming for Gifted and Talented Students." *Journal for the Education of the Gifted* 3:52–60 (1979).

The authors present a "change-agentry" model for staff development. The model is well explained and could be used in developing a school district's in-service program.

Dubner, Frances S. "Thirteen Ways of Looking at a Gifted Teacher." *Journal for the Education of the Gifted* 3:143–46 (1980).

Dubner sent a questionnaire to 850 students who had been students in the IMPACT program (a secondary-school gifted program in Georgia). Three hundred fifty-one returned the questionnaires, on which they had been asked to answer the question, What do you feel the functions of the IMPACT teacher should be? In order of importance (from most to least), their responses were: guide, facilitator, liberator, supervisor/administrator, psychologist, friend, creator/originator, generalist, evaluator, instructor, scholar, wit/enthusiast, counselor.

Feldhusen, John. "Meeting the Needs of Gifted Children and Teachers in a University Course." *Gifted Child Quarterly* 21:195–200 (Summer 1977).

The author describes the Purdue University course "Gifted, Creative and Talented Children," which is open to both graduate and undergraduate students. It is taught during the long semesters and the summer. Part of the course involves a practicum and actually working with gifted children. The goals and objectives are listed. (See also: Feldhusen, John. "Practicum Activities for Students and Gifted Children in a University Course." *Gifted Child Quarterly* 17:124–29 [Summer 1973].)

Fox, Gudelia A. "The Gifted: How Are They Viewed?" *Gifted Child Quarterly* 12:23–33 (Spring 1968).

Fox explores the factors that have led to an anti-intellectual stance by most of our culture. She discusses numerous studies that have tried to determine attitudes toward the gifted. Some of the studies cited could have their methods questioned.

Frasier, Mary M. "The Third Dimension." *Gifted Child Quarterly* 21:207–13 (Summer 1977).

Frasier proposes that the third dimension in teacher training should be to enable teachers of the gifted to serve as change agents. In her article, she discusses the rationale behind such a dimension.

Frasier, Mary M., and Carland, Joann. "A Study to Identify Key Factors That Affect the Establishment of a Positive Relationship between Teachers of the Gifted and Regular Classroom Teachers." *Journal for the Education of the Gifted* 3:225–27 (1980).

The authors report on Phase I of a two-part study designed to assess the nature of the relationship between teachers of the gifted and regular classroom teachers. Strong administrative support, clear communication regarding goals and objectives for the gifted program, and care in scheduling were among the factors perceived as influencing the relationship.

Gallagher, James J., Greenman, Margaret, Karnes, Merle, and King, Alvin. "Individual Classroom Adjustments for Gifted Children in Elementary Schools." *Exceptional Children* 26:409–22, 432 (1960).

Fifty-four highly gifted children (IQ 150+, grades two to five) were investigated through the case study method. Each child had curricular adjustments planned on the basis of test results, observations, and interviews. An extensive explanation of the results of this study is included. Positive outcomes occurred but were limited by three factors: (1) deficiencies in teacher knowledge (e.g., a teacher limited in mathematical expertise cannot adequately stimulate a child gifted in mathematics); (2) limited availability of such auxiliary personnel as reading specialists and psychologists; (3) the school's inability to deal with problems outside its realm—for example, in the student's home.

Gear, Gayle, "Teachers of the Gifted: A Student's Perspective." *Roeper Review* 1:18–20 (March 1979).

Gear says the four outstanding teachers she had all shared five characteristics: (1) intelligence, (2) strong academic backgrounds along with pride and enthusiasm for their subjects, (3) the ability to serve as excellent role models, (4) empathy, (5) commitment to creativity.

Gowan, John Curtis. "The View from Myopia." *Gifted Child Quarterly* 21:154–60 (Summer 1977).

Gowan makes several recommendations concerning training teachers in gifted education. His remarks center on (1) integrated experience, (2) cognitive models, (3) affirmative growth and cognitive development of staff and trainees, (4) guidance, (5) paraprofessional support, and (6) comments.

Gowan, John C., Morrison, Charlotte, Groth, Norma Jean, Pastgerfnak, Marian, and Drake, Marian. "New Aspects in Guiding the Gifted in Demonstration Classes." *Gifted Child Quarterly* 13:103–12 (Summer 1969).

The authors discuss some of the unexpected results of having one counselor for each class of twenty-five students participating in a special summer workshop for gifted students in California. Several brief discussions of individual cases along with the rationale for and the positive outcomes of such a counselor-student ratio are also included.

Graves, Myrna, and Thompson, Jack. "An In-Service Program with Teachers of Gifted Children." *Gifted Child Quarterly* 5:91–92 (1961).

Graves and Thompson report on an in-service program for six people. Its objectives were to help teachers (1) better understand the gifted child, (2) provide appropriate curriculum experience for the gifted child, and (3) generalize their learning to all children.

Haberman, Martin, and Raths, James D. "High, Average, Low: And What Makes Teachers Think So." *Elementary School Journal* 68:241–45 (February 1968).

The authors conducted a study to determine whether there is a relationship between the range of achievement in a group and the teacher's perception as to which children need remedial help or enrichment. They found that no matter what the range, teachers perceive of a high, middle, and low group. It appears that the pupil's standing in the class has a greater influence on the teacher's perception than the child's actual achievement.

Hall, Eleanor G. "The Learning Center Approach to Teacher Training." *Roeper Review* 6:30–32 (September 1983).

The author advocates using a learning center approach to train teachers. She explains how to construct a portable learning center and provides the content and objectives for one such center.

Hershey, Myrliss. "Telephone Instruction: An Alternative Delivery System for Teacher In-Service." *Gifted Child Quarterly* 21:213–18 (Summer 1977).

The author reports on a study that assessed the cognitive outcomes of a course presented in two different ways: (1) via telenetwork: (2) via face-to-face instruction. The telenetwork course participants had a higher mean score on the post test than did the face-to-face group. Rationale for using telenetworking is provided.

_____. "Toward a Theory of Teacher Education for Gifted and Talented." *Roeper Review* 1:12–14 (March 1979).

Hershey supports the idea of screening teachers for the gifted. She also discusses the theory of "andragogy"—the science of helping mature students learn.

Hershey, Myrliss, and Hall, Holton. "Summer Programs for the Gifted: Keys to Future Teacher Training." *Journal for the Education of the Gifted* 1:38–43 (February 1978).

The authors describe how Kansas State University offered summer practica at six public schools in Kansas in order to help personnel meet criteria for certification as teachers of the gifted. The responsibilities of the various participants are listed (e.g., university facilitator, lead teachers, practicum teachers).

Hord, Shirley. "The Concerns of Teachers of Gifted Youth: Using Concerns to Improve Staff Development." *Roeper Review* 5:32–34 (November 1982).

The author, a researcher, introduces the "Concerns-Based Adoption Model" which can be used to assess teachers' concerns. This information can then be used to tailor in-service training to meet teachers' needs more specifically.

House, Peggy A. "Through the Eyes of Their Teachers: Stereotypes of Gifted Pupils." *Journal for the Education of the Gifted* 2:220–24 (Summer 1979).

House studied twenty-four participants in the Minnesota Gifted Education Master's Program by assessing their attitudes toward the gifted. She used an adaptation of the Adjective Checklist. She found that the involvement in the program helped participants develop a clearer perception of gifted students, but that some stereotypes and biases remained.

Isaacs, Ann F. "A Survey of Suggested Preparation for Teachers of the Gifted." *Gifted Child Quarterly* 10: 72–77 (Summer 1966).

After a discussion about teachers of the gifted, Isaacs reports results of a survey about gifted-teacher education, sent to 250 people in the nation. The top-rated course offerings for teachers of the gifted are basic courses in the psychology and education of the gifted, methods and materials for teaching the gifted, and learning problems of the gifted (including underachievement).

Jackson, Nancy Ewald, Famiglietti, Joseph, and Robinson, Halbert B. "Kindergarten and First Grade Teachers' Attitudes toward Early Entrants, Intellectually Advanced Students, and Average Students." *Journal for the Education of the Gifted* 4:132–42 (Winter 1981).

The authors report on results of a questionnaire completed by seventy-two kindergarten and first-grade teachers—median age forty years, median teaching experience eleven or twelve years. On the questionnaire, the teachers were asked to rank children, whose profiles were given, according to how well each would adapt to the teacher's classroom. The results confirm previously found biases against early entrants. The profiles given to the teachers are included so that the study can be replicated.

Jacobs, Jon C. "Teacher Attitudes toward Gifted Children." *Gifted Child Quarterly* 16:23–26 (Spring 1972).

The author developed a measure to assess the attitudes of teachers toward the gifted. He found that private-school teachers had very high positive attitudes, while regular first-grade classroom teachers had very low positive attitudes toward the gifted. The instrument he designed is included in the article.

Jenkins, Reva C. W., and Stewart, Emily D. "And into the Fire—a Guide to G/C/T Internship Experiences for Preprofessionals." *Journal for the Education of the Gifted* 3:1–6 (1979).

The authors have developed an Internship Guide, which is described in the article. They say that the major benefits of an internship program for students in graduate teacher training are (1) the opportunity to integrate academic, theoretical aspects of a graduate training program in applied pragmatic settings which require action as well as reflection; and (2) to build individual confidence by reinforcing self-perception as an effective leader.

Jenkins-Friedman, Reva. "Self-Directed Learning for Educators of Gifted and Talented Students: Teachers Need It, Too." *Journal for the Education of the Gifted* 5:104–19 (1982).

In two of her own courses on teaching the gifted, the author piloted a model of self-directed learning (SDL) in an effort to get teachers of the gifted more familiar with the notion of SDL. She hoped that as they became more familiar with the technique they would employ it in their classrooms. This excellent article includes a rationale for the model along with course descriptions and lists of related activities.

Jones, Reginald L. "The Hierarchical Structure of Attitudes toward the Exceptional." *Exceptional Children* 40:430–35 (March 1974).

The author used a hierarchical factor analysis to investigate 264 college students' attitudes toward exceptional persons. A general factor that cut across categories of disability and interpersonal situations was found. A separate factor of attitudes toward the gifted emerged.

Jones, Vern. "Current Trends in Classroom Management: Implications for Gifted Students." *Roeper Review* 6:26–30 (September 1983).

Jones, an expert in the area of classroom management, reviews the current literature on managing student behavior. He believes that many of the practices learned during teacher training are inappropriate for use with gifted children. In the article, he justifies this stance and recommends alternatives for teacher training. The bibliography is extensive.

Karnes, Frances A., and Collins, Emily. "Teacher Certification in Gifted Education: A National Survey." *Gifted Child Quarterly* 21:204–7 (Summer 1977).

The authors say that teacher-training programs do not appear to be keeping pace with the growing interest in giftedness. This article summarizes the results of a survey undertaken to assess course offerings for certificates in the teaching of the gifted.

_____. "Teacher Certification in the Education of the Gifted: An Update." *Journal for the Education of the Gifted* 4:123–31 (Winter 1981).

According to a 1979 survey of state consultants for gifted education, ten states have certification requirements for teachers of the gifted. Their requirements, along with the year the certification was put into effect (all in the 1970s), are summarized in a table. Other information obtained through the survey is also included in the article.

Karnes, Frances A., and Parker, Jeanette P. "Teacher Certification in Gifted Education: The State of the Art and Considerations for the Future." *Roeper Review* 6:18–19 (September 1983).

Karnes and Parker have compiled a list of the thirteen states that currently require certification for teachers of the gifted. They offer brief descriptions of each state's certification requirements and then offer two models of certification: one for teachers of the gifted and one for teachers of the fine and performing arts.

Levy, Phyllis Saltzman. "The Story of Marie, David, Richard, Jane,

and John: Teaching Gifted Children in the Regular Classroom."
Teaching Exceptional Children 13:136–42 (Summer 1981).

Levy has written a wonderful article that clearly indicates that she cares about the gifted students in her regular class and works hard to make accommodations for their special abilities. She paints insightful verbal pictures of each of the five students on whom she focuses and makes lucid, realistic recommendations for regular classroom teachers who have gifted students in their classrooms.

Lewis, Judith Forman. "Bulldozers or Chairs? Gifted Students Describe Their Ideal Teacher." *G/C/T* 23:16–19 (May/June 1982).

Lewis describes the process gifted students went through to arrive at a checklist of desirable characteristics for teachers of the gifted. The checklist is actually used by gifted students in the district to evaluate their teachers.

Lindsay, Margaret. *Training Teachers of the Gifted.* New York: Teachers College Press, 1980. 60 pp.

This is one book from the Perspectives on Gifted/Talented Education series. It includes chapters on current trends in education for teachers of the gifted, kinds of teachers needed, and how to develop this kind of teacher. A competency-based program is suggested.

Love, Harold D. *Educating Exceptional Children in Regular Classrooms.* Springfield, Ill.: Charles C. Thomas, 1972. 235 pp.

The author provides a concise account of gifted students—their needs and characteristics. He advocates educating the gifted within the regular classroom. Chapter 3 is "The Gifted Child in the Regular Classroom."

Malone, Charlotte, E. "Implementing a Differential School Program for the Gifted." *Gifted Child Quarterly* 19:316–27 (Winter 1975).

Malone says that in-service education can be divided into three main components: districtwide, on-site, and individualized. Various methods of providing these types are discussed (e.g., videotapes, consultants, conferences, seminars).

Marks, Diana. "Inservice for Teachers of Academically Talented Students." *G/C/T* 11:41–44 (January/February 1980).

The author has written a very simply and clearly explained overview of how to design an effective in-service program for teachers of the gifted. Her district received a Title IV grant to train teachers of the gifted, and she explains how it was done.

Mattson, Bruce D. "Hey Teacher! You Don't Have to Do It All!" *G/C/T* 17:18–19 (March/April 1981).

Mattson urges teachers to share the responsibility for selected gifted students with "alter teachers"—volunteers from the community who serve as mentors. He points out seven benefits for those students who have such mentors.

McHardy, Roberta J. "Masters and Ph.D. Programs in Gifted Education." *G/C/T* 20:17–20 (November/December 1981).

McHardy has made a map showing the states that have colleges and universities offering degrees in education of the gifted. Names and addresses of contact people at the universities are included on a separate page.

Mertens, Sally. "Is There a Place for Teacher Education in Gifted Education?" *Roeper Review* 6:13–17 (September 1983).

The author presents an admittedly somewhat exaggerated graduate program in gifted education. She then evaluates the state of gifted education as currently reflected in the literature.

Meyers, Edie. "A Study of Concerns of Classroom Teachers Regarding a Resource Room Program for the Gifted." *Roeper Review* 7:32–36 (September 1984).

The author addresses the significant problem of regular classroom teachers' attitudes toward the gifted and their pull-out programs. She summarizes the findings and recommendations from her study under five categories: (1) ownership through involvement, (2) communication, (3) criteria for selection, (4) scheduling and fragmentation, and (5) impact on student performance.

Milgram, Roberta M. "Perceptions of Teacher Behavior in Gifted and Nongifted Children." *Journal of Educational Psychology* 71:125–28 (February 1979).

Four hundred fifty-nine Israeli children in grades four through six were divided into four intelligence levels (average, high average, superior, and very superior) and asked to rate the importance of intelligence, creativity, and personal-social characteristics in teachers' classroom behavior. Regardless of age, sex, or intelligence, students chose intelligence as the most important factor in their teachers.

Miller, Maurice. "Recommendations for G/T Teacher Preparation and Graduate Programs." *Roeper Review* 5:24–26 (February 1983).

Miller makes general recommendations based on recent research and scholarly publications.

Mills, Barbara Nash, and Berry, Gordon L. "Perceptions of Decision Making Groups toward Programs for the Mentally Gifted." *Educational Research Quarterly* 4:66–76 (Summer 1979).

The authors report on their study which investigated attitudinal differences toward gifted children and their school programs among teachers, school administrators, parents of gifted children, community leaders, gifted children, and the lay public. Their results indicate that there are attitudinal differences among the aforementioned decision-making groups: teachers and parents of the gifted are more favorable than the others. Implications for the education of the gifted are included.

Mitchell, Patricia Bruce, and Erickson, Donald K. "The Education of Gifted and Talented Children: A Status Report." *Exceptional Children* 45:12–16 (September 1978).

The authors report on a national survey conducted by the Council for Exceptional Children. One of the five categories was "preparation of personnel." They found: (1) forty-five states reported having at least one institution of higher education that offers one or more courses specifically concerning education of gifted/talented; (2) 177 institutions of higher education in the United States offer one or more courses on education of gifted/talented; (3) forty-two states reported sponsoring in-service training in the area of gifted/talented education during 1976–77.

Musgrove, Walter J., and Estroff, Elsie H. "Scale to Measure Attitudes of Intellectually Gifted toward an Enrichment Program." *Exceptional Children* 43:375–77 (March 1977).

The authors describe how they constructed the GAS (Gifted Attitude Scale). The final scale is included and could be adapted for use with other programs.

Nelson, Joan B., and Cleland, Donald L. "The Role of the Teacher of the Gifted." *Education* 88:47–51 (September/October 1967).

The authors stress the importance of the teacher in the education of the gifted. They discuss traits possessed by effective teachers of the gifted.

Newland, T. Ernest. "Some Observations on Essential Qualifications of Teachers of the Mentally Superior." *Exceptional Children* 29:111–14 (November 1962).

Newland says the essential qualifications for teachers of the gifted include emotional security, intellectual curiosity, intellectual agility, moderate to high energy level, appropriate basic intellectual potential, two to three years of highly effective teaching experience, functional comprehension of the nature of the conceptualization process, subject matter competency, sensitivity to dynamic and developmental aspects of children, understanding of twentieth-century education, functional grasp of elementary concepts of educational and psychological measurement, knowledge of research regarding the gifted, and functional commitment primarily to the ends of education, rather than the means.

Nicely, Robert F., Jr., Small, John D., and Furman, Robert L. "Teachers' Attitudes toward Gifted Children and Programs—Implications for Instructional Leadership." *Education* 101:12–15 (Fall 1980).

The authors developed and administered a survey to teachers at all levels up to twelfth grade. The survey results indicated that the more teachers know about the gifted, the more likely they are to be positively disposed toward them.

Noland, Ronald G., English, Dewey W., and von Eschenbach, John F. "Effect of Laboratory Experiences on Undergraduates' Perception of the Ideal Pupil." *Roeper Review* 7:27–30 (September 1984).

The authors report on their study, which attempted to reveal additional insights concerning the effect of laboratory experiences on prospective elementary teachers' perceptions of the productive and creative pupil. The instrument they used was the Ideal Pupil Checklist developed by E. Paul Torrance. From their findings, they made four recommendations: (1) college methods courses should focus on creativity and its enhancement; (2) in-service training is necessary for elementary teachers if they are to endorse and encourage creative behavior among their students; (3) closer supervision of the various on- and off-campus laboratory experiences is necessary to ensure that preservice teachers get consistent emphasis on creativity; (4) educators must confer and agree to support creative behavior if students are to be equipped for the future.

Parker, Jeanette P., and Karnes, Frances A. "Graduate Degree Programs in the Education of the Gifted." *Journal for the Education of the Gifted* 7:205–17 (1984).

The authors have compiled a list of 101 institutions in thirty-eight states and the District of Columbia that offer programs culminating in one or more graduate degrees in education of the gifted. The institution, contact person, address, degree(s), and major(s) are listed.

Plowman, Paul D. "Training Teachers." *Roeper Review* 1:14–17 (March 1979).

Plowman discusses an in-service program in California.

Powell, Jack V. "Mainstreaming Eight Types of Exceptionalities." *Education* 99:55–58 (Fall 1978).

One of the eight types of exceptionalities discussed is giftedness. The author recommends a challenging, stimulating physical setting; flexible instructional activities; multimedia materials; teaching strategies that include peer teaching, independent study, and exploration; and flexibility and encouragement in dealing with the gifted's socioemotional needs.

Renzulli, Joseph S. "Instructional Management Systems: A Model for Organizing and Developing In-Service Training Workshops." *Gifted Child Quarterly* 21:186–95 (Summer 1977).

The model presented in this article grew out of a concern about the questionable effectiveness and limited impact of short-term workshops for teachers attempting to acquire new skills. The objectives of the Instructional Management System approach are (1) to compress a large amount of highly relevant information into a relatively short training period; (2) to provide a "structure" or "scaffolding" of knowledge for the topic being presented; and (3) to provide a series of "packaged" workshops. An excellent overview of the model and its use is presented.

_____. "Are Teachers of the Gifted Specialists? A Landmark Decision on Employment Practices in Special Education for the Gifted." *Gifted Child Quarterly* 29:24–28 (Winter 1985).

Renzulli reports on a case involving a teacher of the gifted who was retained during a reduction in force (RIF) while a regular classroom teacher (with more seniority) was dismissed. Implications for schools and teachers are also presented.

Renzulli, Joseph S., and Gable, Robert K. "A Factorial Study of the Attitudes of Gifted Students toward Independent Study." *Gifted Child Quarterly* 20:1–99+ (Spring 1976).

The development of a twenty-seven-item scale designed to measure gifted students' attitudes toward independent study is explained. The five dimensions that were factored out of the scale are (1) influence of independent study on motivation and career; (2) freedom to pursue personal interests; (3) effect of independent study on study habits and thinking processes; (4) degree to which independent study helps to fulfill personal objectives; (5) degree of challenge and opportunity for self-expression. The instrument is appended to the article.

Robards, Shirley N. "Teacher Education: Reality and Challenge." *Roeper Review* 6:6–7 (September 1983).

Robards presents ten challenges that exist for teacher education today. It is apparent that she feels adamant on the subject of doing something to improve teacher education or, as she says, "to leave it better than we found it."

Rogers, Brenda G. "Metacognition: Implications for Training Teachers of the Gifted." *Roeper Review* 6:20–21 (September 1983).

The author recommends that teachers preparing to teach the gifted learn about their own learning through metacognitive activities. She believes this will facilitate their learning, which will later help them in their teaching.

Rosenfeld, Sylvia. "Consultation in a Teacher Center: A Network Model." *Journal of School Psychology* 18:74–78 (Spring 1980).

Rosenfeld discusses how a network of representatives from a special school for the gifted, several community school districts, private schools, three universities, and the New York State Education Department came together to form a consortium, which developed a Teacher Center for Teachers of the Gifted and Talented. This successful teacher center was formed on a network model, which is explained in the article.

Roth, Edith Brill. "Two-Way TV Trains Teachers." *American Education* 16:20–28 (November 1980).

This article is about Project GETT UP (Gifted Education via Telecommunications: Teacher Upgrade), which operates in Virginia. The project involves two-way interactive telecommunications between in-service teachers and experts in gifted education. The project is a success, and many hope for its expansion.

Rubenzer, Ronald L., and Twaite, James A. "Attitudes of 1,200 Educators toward the Education of the Gifted and Talented: Implications for Teacher Preparation." *Journal for the Education of the Gifted* 2: 202–13 (Summer 1979).

The authors report on their study, which had three major purposes: (1) to describe what teachers perceive to be the needs and characteristics of the gifted and talented with respect to identification, programming, and teacher preparation; (2) to determine what teacher characteristics are related to significant differences and expressed attitudes toward the gifted and talented; and (3) to provide recommendations to directors of in-service and university training programs for developing gifted and talented in-services and courses. They used a modified Likert attitude survey with ten forced choice and three free-answer items, along with a brief questionnaire.

Salvia, John, Clark, Gary M., and Ysseldyke, James E. "Teacher Retention of Stereotypes of Exceptionality." *Exceptional Children* 39:651–52 (May 1973).

Preservice teachers rated students labeled *gifted* more positively than those labeled *normal*, who were in turn rated more positively than those rated as *retarded*.

Schnur, James O. "Teachers for the Gifted—Past, Present, and Future." *Roeper Review* 2:5–7 (May/June 1980).

Schnur posits that teachers of the gifted need to have a philosophy that reflects the historical and philosophical antecedents of gifted education. He lists numerous characteristics that other authors have believed necessary for teachers of gifted students. Lastly, he calls for programs to train master teachers to deal with the academically able.

Seeley, Kenneth R. "Competence for Teachers of Gifted and Talented Children." *Journal for the Education of the Gifted:* 3:7–13 (1979).

The author surveyed thirty colleges and universities in the United States for their comments on state certification and other issues in gifted education. He summarized the findings as follows: (1) teachers who teach primarily gifted students should hold a master's degree in gifted education; (2) state certification and endorsement standards should be mandatory (with a phase-in program until sufficient qualified teachers are available); (3) all teachers in training should learn about teaching the gifted; (4) one to two years' prior experience should be required of a teacher assigned to a gifted group; (5) teachers of the gifted should have strong content-field preparation.

Seeley, Ken, Jenkins, Reva, and Hultgren, Holly. "Professional Standards for Training Programs in Gifted Education." *Journal for the Education of the Gifted* 4:165–68 (Spring 1981).

The standards listed and explained in this article were proposed by the TAG (The Association for the Gifted) Teacher Education Task Force and the Professional Training Committee of the NAGC (National Association for Gifted Children). The standards were recommended for adoption by TAG, NAGC, and the Council of State Directors of Programs for the Gifted.

Short, Debra Deahn. "From the Other Side of the Desk." *G/C/T* 37:19–21 (March/April 1985).

A gifted child who grew up to be a teacher shares how it feels to be gifted and in a regular classroom. The presentation is cogent.

Sisk, Dorothy. "Teaching the Gifted and Talented Teacher: A Training Model." *Gifted Child Quarterly* 19:81–88 (Spring 1975).

Sisk presents the model used at the University of Florida for training students who plan to teach the gifted. All the courses offered are listed along with the premises upon which the program is built.

Smidchens, Uldis, and Sellin, Donald. "Attitudes toward Mentally Gifted Learners." *Gifted Child Quarterly* 20:109–13 (Spring 1976).

The authors surveyed 116 graduate students regarding their attitudes toward gifted children. Their results support the need for special training for teachers of gifted learners in addition to special consultative services.

Smith, James E., Jr., and Schindler, W. Jean. "Certification Requirements of General Educators Concerning Exceptional Pupils." *Exceptional Children* 46:394–96 (February 1980).

Includes the results of a survey of the fifty states concerning whether or not preservice regular teachers had to meet any requirements in their coursework relative to the needs of exceptional learners. Only fifteen states did require such coursework.

Taylor, Calvin W. "Be Talent Developers as Well as Knowledge Dispensers." *Today's Education* 57:67–69 (December 1968).

Taylor discusses his multiple-talent approach to identifying gifted students.

_____. "Multiple Talent Teaching." *Today's Education* 63:71–74 (March 1974).

Taylor says teachers can "become miners of talent" in their classrooms. He describes one school district in Utah where his multiple-talent model is used with success.

Taylor, Vicki L. "Are You a Gifted Principal? Check List." *G/C/T* 31:16–18 (January/February 1984).

The checklist comprises eighteen items with explanations. It would be very useful for in-service training of administrators.

Torrance, E. Paul, and Kaufmann, Felice. "Teacher Education for Career Education of the Gifted and Talented." *Gifted Child Quarterly* 21:176–85 (Summer 1977).

The authors discuss the need for teacher training in the area of career education for gifted and talented students. They offer goals that can be set forth for such a program along with ways to reach those goals.

Vassar, William G., and Renzulli, Joseph S. "Course Offerings on the Psychology and Education of the Gifted." *Gifted Child Quarterly* 13:37–44 (Spring 1969).

The article is comprised of a chart that summarizes the results of the NAGC survey to determine college courses in the area of gifted education.

Vukelich, Carol, Kliman, Deborah S., and Meyers, Judith. "A Summer Institute for Teachers and Administrators of Young Gifted Children." *Journal for the Education of the Gifted* 2:242–47 (Summer 1979).

When gifted education became a low priority in the state of Delaware, advocates of gifted education determined that gifted students' needs would be met only by regular classroom teachers. So, a program to train teachers of young children was designed. Its description and estimates of its potential impact are presented.

Walker, Joseph. "Gifted Teacher, Know Thyself." *Gifted Child Quarterly* 17:288–92 (Winter 1973).

The author has developed a programmed instrument to introduce teachers of the gifted to the idea of self-assessment using the Flanders Verbal Interaction System. His research indicates that the programmed instrument is useful for this purpose.

Waskin, Yvonne. "Filling the Gap." *Roeper Review* 1:9–11 (March 1979).

Waskin calls for immediate steps to be taken to educate in-service teachers in regards to teaching the gifted.

Weiss, Patricia, and Gallagher, James J. "The Effects of Personal Experience on Attitudes toward Gifted Education." *Journal for the Education of the Gifted* 3:194–206 (1980).

Weiss and Gallagher conducted a study to compare the attitudes toward gifted education held by adults who had direct experience in a program for gifted children with those who had no such experience. They constructed the Gifted Education Questionnaire, which consisted of twenty-four Likert-type items. Responses were received from 586 university faculty, and the results are presented in tabular form. The two notions that garnered the most "Strongly Agree" responses were: (1) gifted children have a right to special education provided by the schools; (2) society needs its top students educated to their potential.

Weslander, Darrell: "Results of an Inservice Program." *G/C/T* 30:51–53 (November/December 1983).

Weslander reports on the Des Moines Independent Community School District's long-term in-service program for teachers of gifted/talented. The evaluation, which was rather involved, indicated that the year-long, ongoing program was successful in that it (1) increased teachers' knowledge about teaching the talented and gifted; (2) increased the number of Type III activities on the part of students.

Whitmore, Joanne R. "Changes in Teacher Education: The Key to Survival for Gifted Education." *Roeper Review* 6:8–13 (September 1983).

Whitmore makes an impassioned plea for gifted education to be infused into training programs for all preservice teachers. Her article is organized around a five-part call to action.

Wiener, Jean L. "Attitudes of Psychologists and Psychometrists toward Gifted Children and Programs for the Gifted." *Exceptional Children* 34:354 (January 1968).

The author found that the females in her sample were more inclined to favor the gifted than were the males. Also, she found that those who had worked with the gifted and/or those with more experience in their fields favored the gifted more than those who had not worked with the gifted or who had less experience.

Wiener, Jean L., and O'Shea, Harriet E. "Attitudes of University Faculty, Administrators, Teachers, Supervisors, and University Students toward the Gifted." *Exceptional Children* 30:163–65 (December 1963).

The attitudes of 109 university faculty, 127 administrators, 38 supervisors, 947 teachers, and 450 university students were assessed. The supervisors were most favorable toward the gifted, while the students were least favorable.

Willings, David. "Portrait of an Outdated Teacher." *Roeper Review* 6:32–34 (September 1983).

Willings paints a picture of Miss D., his teacher in England—from whom he first obtained an education. Fun and pertinent reading.

Wilson, Frank T. "Teacher Education and the Gifted." *Journal of Teacher Education* 6:263–67 (December 1955).

Wilson offers "justification for urging more suitable education for able children and the special preparation of teachers to provide it."

_____. "Motivation of the Gifted and Teacher Education." *Journal of Teacher Education* 12:179–84 (June 1961).

It is noted that the following ways have been found by teachers to be helpful in motivating and fostering the development of gifted and creative children: (1) Find out the nature and degree of unusual abilities. (2) Foster parental and school acceptance of the special abilities as worthy. (3) Generously provide materials and use them suitably. Learn cooperatively and share satisfaction. (5) Provide guidance by parents and teachers. The author also calls for improved preservice teacher education designed to acquaint future teachers with the nature and nurture of gifted children.

Witters, Lee A. "The Needs of Rural Teachers in Gifted Education." *Journal of the Education of the Gifted* 3:79–82 (1979).

The author's survey revealed a tremendous need for instructional services in the following areas of gifted education: (1) knowledge of the needs and problems of the gifted/talented; (2) use of formal/informal identification instruments; (3) preparation of curriculum materials and activities; (4) evaluation of teaching skills and pupil achievement in the cognitive and affective domains; (5) teaching the gifted underachiever.

Wyatt, Flora. "Responsibility for Gifted Learners—A Plea for the Encouragement of Classroom Teacher Support." *Gifted Child Quarterly* 26:140–43 (Summer 1982).

Wyatt attempted to identify what specialists believe supportive teachers do for the gifted learner which in turn causes these teachers to be viewed as "supportive" of the gifted. She used open-ended questions on her questionnaire. The article provides two tables of results along with her explanation of the results.

Zabel, Mary Kay, Dettmer, Peggy A., and Zabel, Robert H. "Factors of Emotional Exhaustion, Depersonalization, and Sense of Accomplishment among Teachers of the Gifted." *Gifted Child Quarterly* 28:65–69 (Spring 1984).

In their study of 601 special-education teachers in Kansas, the authors found that teachers of the gifted appear to be at higher risk for emotional exhaustion than teachers in all other exceptionalities except emotional disturbance and hearing impairment.

CHAPTER 8

Parenting Gifted Children

Being a parent is not easy, but neither is being a child. Being a gifted child's parent is neither easier nor harder than being any other child's parent. Although it is neither easier nor harder, it is different—but in a manageable kind of way. The one word that characterizes the differences is *intensity*. The parent of a gifted child can expect a fervency in the relationship and in the responsibility that may not be required in the relationship with a nongifted offspring.

Such fervency results from the intensity of the child and the effort that may have to be expended to ensure quality education for her. The child's intensity has the capacity to generate moments or months of sheer agony for the parent, who empathizes, as only a parent can, with the child's frustration, rejection, or defeat. Frustration often results from inadequate teachers or curriculum or from inability to do something attempted. Rejection is experienced if age-mates taunt and tease the gifted child out of envy or misunderstanding. Any defeat is exquisitely painful because of the gifted child's tendency toward perfectionism, which renders anything less than number one unacceptable—worthless. The gifted child's intensity, however, also has the potential for producing moments or months of triumph as she delights in discovery, motivates others to move, or is recognized for an artistic endeavor. Raising a gifted child can have poignant lows, but it has incredible highs, too—ones that result from the differences in the gifted child, and the experiences that parenting a gifted child elicit (Coleman 1982).

When do the differences in parenting begin? They are felt almost as soon as the child is born. Different demands are made on the parent whether or not the child has been identified as gifted, but a parent may recognize the differences more after identification. Early signs of giftedness may include one or more of the following: early use of an extensive vocabulary; early reading; math proficiency (adding and subtracting without ever being shown); asking rather abstract questions—and both wanting and expecting an answer; unusual organizing and leadership ability; or precocious propensity in dance, music, or art.

If a child's giftedness is not identified while he is still a preschooler, it will probably be picked up if he enters a school system where there is an organized program for identification. The child's parents may be notified that their child is exceptional when it becomes apparent that he learns very rapidly and/or already possesses broad knowledge on a variety of subjects that most youngsters do not.

Or parents may not be aware of their child's giftedness until a school suspension requires a psychological workup. The testing reveals that the child has an IQ of 155; because the schooling that he has received has been totally inappropriate, chronic misbehavior and underachievement have emerged.

Any of these scenarios and a thousand others could give parents the news that they have been blessed with a gifted offspring. Obviously, some of the scenarios are more desirable than others.

For gifted children and their parents, early discovery of giftedness is the most desirable. The family then has time to learn about the child's special abilities and to make the necessary adjustments for living and schooling. There are likenesses and differences in rearing gifted and average children. The purpose of this chapter is to introduce some of those likenesses and, particularly, some of the differences.

Parents, whether raising a first or fifth child, often have doubts about their capabilities. Whereas in most tasks, the results are immediately apparent, in the task of parenting, the results may not be manifested for ten, twenty, or thirty years. So, few indicators are available by which parents can measure themselves. Other bricks in the wall of doubt are mortared by the differing recommendations from "experts" on how to be successful in the parenting task. Experts such as grandparents, neighbors, ministers, teachers, child psychologists, and authors barrage parents with advice. Who can the parents believe? They usually have to delve within themselves, examining their own values and upbringing before going ahead with their task.

But what happens when a couple (or a single parent) discovers that their child is gifted? Does the parenting task change, or is it only the perception of it that changes?

Whether rearing a handicapped child, an "average" child, a gifted child, or a gifted/handicapped child, the parenting task is essentially the same: to provide the background, nurturance, and guidance necessary to enable the child to grow and develop into an adult capable of being a contributing member of society. This includes having a positive sense of self, having respect for others, and being productive and/or satisfied in a vocation or avocation.

Even though the goals are virtually the same, if their child is gifted, parents are often flooded with additional doubts regarding their abilities to parent. Why does the task perception change?

It changes, in part, due to the notion that somehow, children and young adults who are gifted are disparate beings—demanding a whole different set of parenting skills. Fortunately, this is not so, and consequently, a significant concept for parents to keep in mind is that gifted children are children and gifted adolescents are adolescents.

Therefore, if parents have doubts about their skills as parents, the doubts should be no more pronounced if their child is gifted. Whatever distinct demands result from the child's giftedness, they can all be met by "average" parents provided they are familiar with the characteristics and needs of their gifted child. This chapter will be organized according to some of those needs.

Need for Information

One of the first worries parents have upon hearing that their child is gifted is the possible disparity between their own intelligence and that of their gifted child. ("What if I'm not smart enough to converse with my own child? Is she going to talk over my head? Will I appear stupid?") Parents should let this concern evaporate. The primary job of parents is to provide affection and approval for their children. This, above all else, is what children seek from their parents. Gifted children do not expect their parents to be fountains of knowledge, nor should parents feel inadequate if they are not.

Instead, since one of the needs of gifted children is for ready availability of information (to slake their unquenchable thirst for knowledge), parents should assume the role of facilitator, not necessarily direct provider of information. A facilitator helps smooth the way by removing impediments or difficulties. For parents of gifted children, limited access to information is one obstacle that must be removed.

Parents should become well acquainted with the reference librarians at the public or university library nearby, and they should model the role of "seekers" for information. They should be observed ferreting out knowledge—from reference books, phone books, newspapers, magazines, and other people, either as direct sources or to *find* the proper places to look for the needed information.

Parents, teachers, and mentors of gifted young people are often probed for information far beyond the adults' limits. So, a sentence that gifted children should be familiar with is, "I don't know the answer to that question, but let's find out." They perceive the honesty and willingness to help in that statement and lose no respect for the person(s) making it. On the other hand, as a cover-up for lack of knowledge, adults may give false information or a brush-off ("Don't bother me with all those questions. I don't have time for them!"). Such responses reduce their stature in the eyes of gifted young people.

Special Direction and Attention

Another concern parents might experience is, "I can't afford private lessons, expensive camps, sophisticated equipment, and countless sets of books. Financially, how can I provide for my gifted child?" Gifted children do need direction and attention in their specific areas of giftedness, which may mean some form of training, tutoring, or guidance. Private lessons for children who are particularly interested or adept in certain artistic areas are great, but there are numerous other options if these will not fit into the family budget. Community centers, synagogues, churches, schools, and gifted advocacy groups often make lessons available at a reasonable cost. Scholarships may also be obtainable, especially for children who exhibit talent or promise in a particular area. Parents should not be reticent about asking whether scholarships are available and, if so, what the procedures are for obtaining one. The role of facilitator extends to removing lack of financing as an obstruction to learning.

In many parts of the country, camps and other special programs are offered. (See the annual March/April issue of *G/C/T* for a partial listing.) Many of these programs provide financial assistance through scholarships or sliding fee scales. Another avenue parents could pursue is their place of work. For example, if a child who excels in mathematics has a parent working at an engineering or computer-design firm, the company may see fit to encourage the child and pay the tuition to a special camp. Parents should constantly remind themselves, the *worst* the company can say is no.

The number-one place to encourage children's curiosity and love of learning is at the library. Not only are libraries full of information (that leads to more information that leads to more information . . .) and people who know how to find that information—but libraries are free!

Nurturing a love of books and the information contained in them is the best tool parents can provide for gifted children, whether the child is gifted in mathematics, science, dance, or leadership. Reading with children should be started almost at birth, and toddlers should have regular trips to the library. Some library visits should involve the parent (facilitator) and the gifted child exclusively—to work on a project or to explore a special area of interest. Other trips should involve the whole family. Gifted children need some time devoted specifically to them, but one task of their family is to help them live within a group and to experience the benefits of being part of a group.

Living in Society

In providing for gifted children within a family, all else should not be sacrificed for them. That would put undue pressure on the gifted ("Everybody's sacrificing for me, I sure better perform") and set an unhealthy precedent, since the whole world is not going to sacrifice for them later on. In addition, sacrificing for the gifted makes for bad feelings among other family members. If they never get to do anything special or must always do without so that the gifted child can do special things and not have to do without, resentment toward that child could easily result.

It is unhealthy for everyone involved when a family's world revolves around one child, gifted or otherwise (Fine 1977). If the gifted child is the only child, parents should not make that child the hub of the family. Doing so is not conducive to accomplishing the task of providing the background, nurturance, and guidance necessary to enable the child to grow and develop into an adult capable of contributing to society. If there are other children in the family, the parents must constantly work toward nurturing and guiding them all. Each child must feel special—not better, not worse, not superior, not inferior to the others in the family. This situation is not accomplished without effort, but making each child feel unique in the family and worthy in his or her own right is vital to personal development and self-concept.

Comparisons must be avoided. For example, if the youngest son in a family is academically gifted, and his older brother is less able, comparing the two does not encourage the older to try harder but in fact is potentially harmful. Likewise, comparing the academically gifted youngster to his artistically gifted sister in order to motivate him to be more creative in his art is fruitless. Such comparisons motivate no one and often do just the opposite. If parents hold up one sibling as the one to be emulated, it only makes the others feel put down. And if the other children feel they can never be as good as the "model," they will not only not try to compete but may give up in that area altogether.

Instead of making comparisons between siblings, parents should focus on the qualities and abilities of each child and build those up (Peterson 1977). Demonstrate that differentness is valued. Encouragement and acceptance should be meted out to all family members—but also, a measure of expectance.

Expectations and Encouragement

Gifted children need to know they are valued and accepted for who they are, not just for what they can do (Fine 1977; Sebring 1983). The environment in which they grow up should be encouraging and accepting, so that they know their family is there to support them and back them up, whether in failure or success. This is important for gifted children because often they are extremely critical of themselves and their own efforts. They need a place where someone can temper their self-criticism with acceptance and love.

The love in the home needs to be an "anyhow" kind of love ("You did well and I love you anyhow" or "You messed up and I love you anyhow"), not a "because" kind of love ("I love you because you got all A's" or "I love you because you are going to be a famous scientist"). These statements do not have to be verbalized for the children to get the message they carry. Since gifted students have a tendency to be perfectionists and to make unreasonable demands upon themselves, parents need to balance support with supportive criticism (Fine 1977).

This "anyhow" kind of love does not give the children a license for "anything goes." Parents need to have expectations of their gifted children and adolescents—and these expectations need to be voiced—for example, "You've done some good research for your report, but it doesn't seem that you have been as careful writing it up as you usually are. Is there some way I can help?" The last statement is the key; it demonstrates that, although there are high expectations, the parents are willing to become involved in helping their child meet those expectations. In order to have and voice the appropriate expectations (which vary depending upon the child's giftedness), parents must have information regarding their child's talents.

How can parents obtain this information? Although parental intuition is valuable, when possible, additional avenues should be explored for information. First, children and youth who have been identified as (or are suspected of being) gifted should be tested and observed by professionals knowledgeable in the area of giftedness. Parents should discuss the results with the psychologists, counselors, or other professionals who administered the tests and/or conducted the observations. Second, teachers and others who work closely with the gifted children should be asked to share with the parents their perceptions of where the children's talents lie. Third, parents should ask their children. Gifted children are aware of many of their strengths and weaknesses, and because they are often quite verbal, they may be able to express their assessment succinctly, articulately, and with powerful insight.

For much of the information that parents would like, going straight to the source is often the most expedient. It is definitely the best way to discover the direction of these children's interests and hopes. This knowledge may help prevent gifted children's parents from living vicariously through them. For example, a mother who was unable to matriculate and work toward an advanced degree in mathematical theory may see her daughter's math ability leading her toward a Ph.D. in that field. When asked, the daughter, although realizing her giftedness in math, voices an interest in a related field, astrophysics. Prudent parents will heed their children's interest and will not force them, directly or indirectly, to live out their parents' dreams.

Independence

Gifted children and youth should be allowed to live their own lives to a reasonable degree, just as other children and youth should. As with all children, a sufficient amount of guidance must be provided, but in order for able learners to become fully contributing members of society, they must be able to develop independently—out from under the protectiveness that may be elicited by their talents. Often, gifted youngsters are quite independent, from a very early age on, and some parents have trouble dealing with this facet of their child's personality; they do not feel needed. They are, in fact, desperately needed by their able child(ren), but it may not be shown in the same ways as it is by their other children.

Some gifted children assert their independence from the time they are very young. They enjoy being alone and working alone. This should not be discouraged. Gifted children, especially highly creative ones, need *time* and time alone. This allows ideas to form and incubate until they can come into fruition.

Gifted children also need a space that is theirs. It does not have to be a whole room, but it does need to be an area where they can work privately on a project and which affords a place to store their materials, books, or whatever, with no fear that either they or their work will be disturbed.

To some parents, allowing privacy may conjure up visions of gifted children's rooms as total wrecks. Some would conjecture that allowing private, undisturbed space would encourage these children to have messy rooms, messy desks, messy closets—in other words, total disorganization. This is not the end that most parents would desire for their children.

Instead, since gifted children live within a family and within society, part of the parenting task includes helping these gifted children become functioning members of society, with the family being a microcosm of that society. By designing a specific space as a private area for the gifted child, parents are saying, ''I respect you and your need for privacy. I respect the work you do and your need to have it undisturbed.'' By demonstration, this indicates to gifted children that they, in turn, need to respect others and their need for privacy.

A second lesson that can be taught through this private space is organization. The minds of the gifted are often racing—reflecting on new knowledge, planning upcoming projects, and generating ideas. If some organization is not imposed, they may lose valuable time and energy searching for items or redoing work that has been lost. Some gifted children are fastidious concerning neatness and organization. If anything, these children will have to be urged to ''loosen up a bit.'' But for others, neatness and organization are less than top priority. Parents who wait until these children are in high school or college to help them become organized are probably pursuing a lost cause. Providing instruction and guidance from the time they are very young will have much more positive results (for suggestions, see Hunt 1983).

Parents can capitalize on young gifted children's love of categorizing things. They should have a label maker and an assortment of boxes of varying sizes or cabinets with lots of little drawers in them. Parents should obtain all kinds of containers in which the children can place things: cans with lids, plastic bags that lock (Ziplock), envelopes of many sizes, jars, etc. As the children begin to write or collect sheets of paper with information on them, they should have notebooks and folders. A drawer in their desk, a file cabinet, or a file box should then be designated as the place to store these folders and notebooks. If these sorts of tools are provided, gifted children will be much more likely to organize their materials. They may not like picking up their materials every evening (or whenever) but should learn to do it as a matter of self-discipline. Their reward will be ease in finding whatever they are looking for the next time they need it.

Self-Discipline

If parents teach their gifted children self-discipline, many of the problems cited by parents of other able children will be diminished or eliminated. One of the most obvious examples is the dilemma of gifted underachievers. These are the highly able youngsters who work far below their ability. The problem generally begins in elementary school, magnifies throughout middle school and high school, and may lead to wasted time in college, no college, or a career beneath the potential of the gifted person.

As discussed in the section on the underachieving gifted, some children acquire this habit in elementary school when their giftedness is not recognized or provided for. If gifted students discover that they can "get by" with very little effort, and that no more is expected or required of them by either their teachers or their parents, then those without self-discipline and the inner motivation to achieve will settle for less than that of which they are capable. This is a tragic loss not only for individual gifted children but also for their society.

Self-discipline and inner strength serve gifted individuals in arenas other than the classroom. As able children and youth mature, they confront situations that may result in tragedy if self-discipline and inner strength are lacking. For example, cults actively recruit gifted youth—and know the means to woo these individuals into their groups. A strong sense of self is required to withstand the enticement of such undesirable associations.

To ensure that gifted children mature into adults willing and able to use their talents to accomplish great artistic works, to discover long-sought cures for diseases, to write and speak with the power to move people, or to lead communities in positive causes, a strong inner self must be developed and nurtured. The home is the starting place for this process and should be the checkpoint of it throughout the gifted person's life.

Guidance

There will be struggles between gifted children and adults. The children's abilities are often at the root of these struggles, and it is up to the parents to guide them in the most positive direction. For example, gifted children tend to be strong willed and highly verbal. If parents are not watchful, gifted children can control their families. Hackney (1981) posits that a gifted child can become almost like a "third parent" in the family system. Their quick minds and talent with words enable them to manipulate situations to their liking. Parents have to establish their place in the family structure, not by being authoritarian, but through demonstration, understanding, and leadership. Verbal arguments should be avoided because they usually result in power struggles that have no real winner. Instead, parents should use alternative means (verbal and otherwise) to portray their message. Reasoning with gifted children is very effective if it is done prudently. Trying to reason with gifted children who are angered or in some way out of sorts is futile. But talking calmly with them works well as a preventative measure or after a problem. Their intellect makes connections and sees relationships in a way that helps them perceive the reasons behind situations and decisions—even those that affect them.

Need for Advocates

Many assume that life is easy for the gifted—especially life at school. Unfortunately, this is an extremely harmful misconception. Being bright does not guarantee that school will be easy. The gifted are not equally adept in all subjects—and school is much more than just academics anyway.

Gifted students can run into several problems in school—academic and otherwise. When a child is identified as gifted, some people automatically form a prejudice that is often grounded in misunderstanding and jealousy. Some teachers feel threatened by highly able students, and they may resort to ridicule or some other punishment as a means of lashing out ("Oh my, our gifted student, Marie, actually has a question about her social studies").

Problems may also arise if a student is highly capable in one area, such as mathematics, but is not as able in another, such as foreign language. Since it is assumed that high ability in one area is indicative of high ability in all areas, a teacher can be less than understanding with a student who is gifted but not performing in one area.

Gifted students who have not been identified as gifted, or those who have been but have not had special educational provisions made for them, may have problems in school because their intellectual needs are not being met. The result can be misbehavior, underachievement, and a tragic waste of potential (see Chapter 4). For this and previously stated reasons, gifted students need advocates.

An advocate is one who defends, espouses, and pleads the case of another—in this case, the gifted student. The gifted need someone to defend their right to an appropriate education. Because of the societal bias against exceptionally bright people and the fear that educating them will result in some sort of elite cadre, many ignore the fact that democracy is best served by educating everyone so that they can achieve their potential. So, when budget belts are being tightened and schools want to cut programs for the gifted, advocates must be there to ensure that the programs remain.

One function of parent advocates is to provide a broad base of support for gifted programs. Because teachers and administrators who support differentiated education for able learners are in the minority of their profession, parental support groups are desperately needed to inform the uninformed and unsupportive members of the community. The involvement of parents in the education of their gifted child can be a significant positive force'' (Dettman & Colangelo 1980, 158). Likewise, noninvolvement of the parents of gifted children can be a significantly negative force.

Advocates espouse the cause of gifted education. They participate and become involved in that which will further the cause. This may be in a broad fashion, such as lobbying members of Congress regarding funding, or it may be in a narrow fashion, such as working to gain early admission into college science courses for a specific gifted youth. Both types of involvement are crucial for able students (Gogel & McCumsey 1983).

Weiss and Gallagher (1983) report that in the last two decades, parents have joined together as advocates for their gifted children. Sometimes gifted youngsters need adult advocates to plead their cases for them. This may be because the adults have the tools with which to plead, or because the listeners cannot or will not hear the gifted youth pleading their own cases. For whatever reason, the gifted must have advocates, and usually the parents fill that role.

> In education as in other political spheres, virtue is not necessarily rewarded. The most logical and appropriate actions in education will not necessarily be the ones that are taken. Instead, all sorts of special pleading by special interest groups in the community can be expected to intervene. It is in the direct interest of the parents of gifted children that they become an active part of this educational political scene if they expect a fair share of the educational resources to be provided for those youngsters whose intellectual and creative superiority mark them as future major contributors to our society. (Weiss & Gallagher 1983, 6)

The role is not an easy one, but the investment will reap the rewards deserved by the gifted—and needed by the society.

What do parents of gifted students need? It has already been established that parenting gifted children makes some demands different from those of parenting nongifted children. One of the demands, but also one of the necessities of being the parent of a gifted student, is being involved in some sort of parent group (e.g., Buisman 1979; Clayman 1979; Harris & Bauer 1983; Ness 1979; Riggs 1982).

Parents do not need to be islands—left out in the vast ocean to survive the barrage of wind, waves, and unexpected changes in the weather. It is much better to be a part of an archipelago which, although it will not stop the wind, waves, and unexpected weather, will buffer some of the shocks. For parents trying to justify joining a group comprised of other parents of gifted youngsters, three broad personal reasons are evident: for moral support, to exchange ideas, and to do things together.

Rearing a gifted child undoubtedly raises questions in parents' minds: Am I smart enough? Am I providing the correct type of home environment to nurture this child? Are my other children suffering? How do I discipline this child? If we have other children, will they be gifted, too? How do I deal with the teacher who only sees my child as an errand runner? Will my child grow up thinking I'm dumb? How do I make sure her intellect is used constructively in this world? How do I win an argument with my child?

These questions and a hundred more descend on parents' minds when they learn that one or more of their children is gifted. Through participation in a parent group, they will discover that they are not the only ones questioning themselves and their parenting skills.

Besides this discovery, there are answers to be found to many of the questions being asked. Parent groups that provide a time for "rapping" will serve their members in this way. Probably at least one of the other parents has gone through similar problems and has discovered a solution through experience or through hindsight. Even if informal rap sessions are not a part of the group's activities, contacts are made that can be followed up by a phone call or a personal meeting. Just knowing that there is a person to call can provide respite to a parent in the throes of parenting a gifted child.

The parent of an academically able child may have to make choices that are unpopular with grandparents, neighbors, or good friends—even if they are in the best interests of the child. To move the child from one school to another, accelerate the student, or attend school board meetings to speak for gifted education may meet with disapproval. It is very, very hard to pursue alternatives for one's gifted child and then to stand up for them if the voices against the alternatives are loud and clear and close. Moral support from within the assemblage of gifted children's parents can make all the difference. The empathy, support, and advice offered by other parents will become vital to the family of a gifted child.

Finally, if a gifted youth has, for example, just been selected to participate in the Johns Hopkins Study for Mathematically Precocious Youth, parents need someone with whom to share this wonderful news. Some people will have no idea what the SMPY is, and others will simply not be interested or will perceive it as bragging (whereas if the child has made the football team, it would not be bragging!). But other parents of precocious children, having made the commitment to join a group of parents like themselves, having taken the time to be informed about giftedness, and having an appreciation of the struggles and rewards of having a gifted child, will know what the SMPY is, or will want to know, and will share in the triumph with that child and those parents. This type of support is essential, as any parent who has had to do without it will attest.

Along with moral support, parent groups provide a forum for the exchange of ideas. Knowing that others share the same concerns is important, but being able to get some answers is even more important. One such scenario could be that a number of parents are experiencing problems disciplining their gifted adolescents. If no one has a viable solution, the group may decide to invite an expert in the field to discuss the problems. That way, parents not only get their own questions answered but gain from hearing the answers to other parents' questions. Such an opportunity would not be available to the parents operating as islands.

Sharing ideas is helpful, and so are sharing time and activities with other parents of academically capable children and youth. The group can help "dream up" ideas of places to go or things to do, and having several families participate may make the outing or activity more enjoyable and educational for the gifted children, their siblings, and their parents. If group rates are available, the arrangement may also be financially advantageous.

Depending on the neighborhood, the size of the community, and/or the school gifted children attend, finding friends and companions may or may not be a problem. If families join together in some activities, the children gain an opportunity for new friendships (Gensley 1972). Obviously, nothing guarantees that two gifted youngsters will become fast friends, but it is worth a try.

Including others in plans is a mind set that gifted children's parents should cultivate. If the family has planned an outing to the planetarium at a nearby community college, the parents can call up those other parents who have mentioned their daughter's interest in things celestial. If one's academically talented children have requested that their father teach them how to arrange flowers, offering a mini class to five or six other gifted children could be considered.

Including others involves some effort, but it offers rewards, too—both for one's children and for oneself. A possible reward that some parents might not admit they yearn for is rest—respite from their gifted offspring. By offering a minicourse for youngsters, or by taking other people's children on an outing, those gifted children's parents are either allowed some time with their other children or are afforded some time alone. Most parents need a reprieve from the constant barrage of questions and needs of gifted children. Parents should not be afraid to admit that need, especially to the parents of other gifted children.

All the above reasons are valid ones for forming or joining a group for the parents of gifted children and youth. The need is perennial; it is one that will remain as long as there are gifted children and as long as there are parents. Belonging to such a group will offer many personal rewards and will provide numerous opportunities to help one's gifted child(ren).

Producing, living with, and nurturing a gifted child will furnish a parent with trials and tribulations—but with joys and jubilations, too (Moore 1982, 10). The latter set of memories will remain long after the former has faded.

We would like to close this chapter with ''A Bill of Rights for Parents of Gifted Children'' (Riggs 1982, 10). It should be read and reread and circulated.

1. Parents have the right to a free public education for their gifted children.
2. The right to an education that enables them to learn all they are able to learn.
3. The right to educators' awareness that gifted children learn earlier, better, faster and often differently from most other children.
4. The right to be accepted and respected as parents of children with legitimate and special learning needs.
5. The right to be involved in the planning for the education of their gifted children.
6. The right to information in the child's file, and the right to explanations if that information is in unfamiliar terms.
7. The right to freedom of expression as they voice the joys and problems of raising gifted children.
8. The right to become change agents in the legislature and schools when gifted children are not adequately served.

9. The right to an environment of acceptance and pride in what gifted children can accomplish for themselves first but also for the quality of all our lives.[1]

SELECTED BIBLIOGRAPHY

Parents Who Nurture; Nurturance for Parents

Abelman, Robert. "Television and the Gifted Child." *Roeper Review* 7:115–18 (November 1984).

The author, who is a member of the National Council for Children and Television, reports on an exploratory and descriptive analysis of the relationship between gifted children and television in the home and in the classroom.

Albert, Robert S. "Observations and Suggestions Regarding Giftedness, Familial Influence, and the Achievement of Eminence." *Gifted Child Quarterly* 22:201–11 (Summer 1978).

Albert raises six questions, then answers them by synthesizing a great deal of research regarding eminent adults and the forces in their childhoods that may have propelled them to achieve. He believes the Study for Mathematically Precocious Youth is the most important piece of research on giftedness since Hollingworth's study of children with 180+ IQ's. He believes the longitudinal study will yield results that indicate which patterns of interests, family, and other factors produce eminent adults.

————. "Exceptionally Gifted Boys and Their Parents." *Gifted Child Quarterly* 24:174–79 (Fall 1980).

Albert investigated twenty-six mathematically precocious boys and twenty-six intellectually gifted boys (IQ 150+). The article discusses the findings. Albert concluded that "cognitive giftedness and creative giftedness are very much related to one another and may be manifestations of the same complex, multi-faceted abilities."

Anthony, Margaret. "Parents of Gifted and Talented Children: True/False Test." *G/C/T* 16:21–23 (January/February 1981).

Along with the twenty-question true-false test are explanations of

---

1. "A Bill of Rights" in "Parents of Gifted and Talented Children: Unite!" by Gina G. Riggs from *G/C/T* 21: 9–10 (January/February 1982). Copyright © 1984 by *G/C/T* Inc. Reprinted by permission of *G/C/T* Inc.

the correct answers. The test is designed for parents of gifted children to assess their knowledge about giftedness.

Anthony, Sylvia. "Suggestions to "Turn On" Bright Children at Home." *G/C/T* 25:22 (November/December 1982).

Anthony offers twenty-five suggestions for parents—some specific, some general.

Ballering, Laurie D., and Koch, Alberta. "Family Relations When a Child Is Gifted." *Gifted Child Quarterly* 28:140–43 (Summer 1984).

The authors report on research that compared perceived relationships with all other family members from the perspectives of the gifted and nongifted siblings in the family. They found that giftedness does affect perceived familial relationships.

Buisman, Jackie. "Organizing a Parent Support Group for Talented and Gifted." *G/C/T* 6:38–42+ (January/February 1979).

This is a basic, how-to article.

Clayman, Deborah P. "Parents as Advocates for Gifted Children." *Social Education* 43:158, 160 (February 1979).

In this brief article, the mother of a gifted child tells how a support group grew out of a class she taught called Understanding the Gifted Child. The group became politically active and started enrichment programs for gifted youngsters.

Colangelo, Nicholas, and Dettmann, David F. "A Review of Research on Parents and Families of Gifted Children." *Exceptional Children* 50:20–27 (September 1983).

Following their review, the authors make six observations: (1) more research is needed regarding the parent–gifted child interaction; (2) parents can play important roles in identification and educational development; (3) parents' confusion regarding their gifted youngsters results from insufficient knowledge of giftedness and creativity; (4) parents are confused about their role at school; (5) characteristics of achievement and creativity appear to be related to parental characteristics and home environment; and (6) educators are not always aware of the different challenges posed by gifted children and have therefore not provided adequate direction to parents.

Coleman, Dona. "Parenting the Gifted: Is This a Job for Superparent?" *G/C/T* 22:47–50 (March/April 1982).

Coleman says "the challenges of parenting a gifted child are similar to those of parenting a child of average intelligence. The added stresses appear to be in acceptance of a creative child's unique value system, coping with school discipline problems arising from boredom, and letting the child decide on and map his own future."

Dettman, David F., and Colangelo, Nicholas. "A Functional Model for

Counseling Parents of Gifted Students." *Gifted Child Quarterly* 24:158-61 (Fall 1980).

The authors discuss three approaches counselors can use when working with parents of the gifted: Parent-Centered, School-Centered, or Partnership.

Feldhusen, John F., and Kroll, Mark D. "Parent Perceptions of Gifted Children's Educational Needs." *Roeper Review* 7:249-52 (April 1985).

The authors surveyed parents to determine how well they believed their gifted children's needs were being met and whether or not they favored full-time, self-contained classes. The results indicate that parents do not perceive that their present school systems are meeting their high-ability children's needs. Also, there is substantial agreement among these parents that their children would be better served by a full-time school for the gifted.

Fine, Marvin J. "Facilitating Parent-Child Relationships for Creativity." *Gifted Child Quarterly* 21:487-500 (Winter 1977).

This excellent article presents lucid ideas for parents on nurturing their gifted child(ren).

French, Joseph L., and Murphy, James P. "Parenting of Gifted Children: A Two-Edged Sword." *Roeper Review* 5:36-37 (February 1983).

The authors describe issues that lead to the joys and pains of parenting gifted children. The book would be very helpful for parents or for teachers and counselors working with parents.

Gensley, Juliana. "The Gifted Isolate, or Where Are the Peers?" *Gifted Child Quarterly* 16:246-47 (Fall 1972).

Gensley urges parents to aid their gifted child in finding a peer group and offers a few suggestions for how to do it.

Ginsberg, G., and Harrison, C. H. *How to Help Your Gifted Child.* New York: Simon & Schuster, 1977. 197 pp.

This is an outstanding "how to" book for parents of gifted children. Without using any jargon, the authors give tips for living with a gifted child—and recognizing that you have one! They also give very specific directions for setting up a parent organization and enrichment courses for gifted youngsters.

Gogel, Ella Mae, and McCumsey, Janet. "What Parents Are Saying." *G/C/T* 26:52-54 (January/February 1983).

This article presents partial results from a questionnaire mailed out all over the United States, funded by a Title IV Gifted and Talented grant. Parents are convinced that unless they continue to be persistent, gifted education will be in jeopardy. The article would encourage parents who feel that they are alone in their frustration.

Groth, Norma J. "Mothers of Gifted." *Gifted Child Quarterly* 19:217-22 (Fall 1975).

Groth discusses the results of a questionnaire mailed to 600 parents of gifted children. Of those returned, 240 were answered by mothers. Results indicate that the mothers had above-average educations, felt younger than their chronological age, and had smaller-than-average families.

Hackney, Harold. "The Gifted Child, the Family, and the School." *Gifted Child Quarterly* 25:51–54 (Spring 1981).

Hackney discusses the outcome of a project for gifted children and their parents at Purdue University (1980). While children were involved in enrichment activities, parents met to discuss common issues and to receive advice, assurance, and suggestions. Five issues were common: family roles were altered, parental feelings were affected, special adaptations were necessary in the family, the neighborhood presented issues, and so did the school.

Harris, Ruth L., and Bauer, Harold. "A Program for Parents of Gifted Preschoolers." *Roeper Review* 5:18–19 (May 1983).

The article describes the PAL (Potentially Able Learners) Program used in Rockford, Illinois. It involves both parents and youngsters.

Hayes, Donald G. "A Rating Scale for Parents: Motivation and Discipline." *G/C/T* 29:14 (September/October 1983).

Parents could use this simple, one-page scale to clarify their strengths and weaknesses in disciplining and motivating their gifted children.

Hayes, Donald G., and Levitt, Michael. "Stress: An Inventory for Parents." *G/C/T* 24:8–12 (September/October 1982).

Hayes helps parents realize the stress that their gifted youngsters are under. Includes a checklist parents could use to recognize signs of stress, possible causes, and possible responses to help their children deal with the stress.

Hunt, Nancy. "Creative Parenting." Parts 1, 2. *G/C/T* 22:28–29 (March/April 1982); 28:30–31 (May/June 1983).

The author, parent and teacher of gifted children, provides several suggestions for discipline, using "The Subtle Approach" or "Backdoor Psychology." She recommends that parents be consistent and firm and that they evaluate the methods they are currently using—especially if they are not working. Part 2 is a wonderful article that provides *specific* suggestions for helping gifted children pick up their rooms, remember things, and do their homework. It should be shared at a parents' meeting.

Jenkins-Friedman, Reva, and Fine, Marvin J. "A Useful Framework for Parent-Teacher Contacts." *Roeper Review* 6:155–58 (February 1984).

The authors explore some components of TA (transactional analysis) as they pertain to increasing teachers' awareness and skills in the context of working with the parents of gifted children. Their suggestions could be useful for teacher in-service training regarding parent-teacher conferences.

Karnes, Frances A., and Karnes, M. Ray. "Parents and Schools: Educating Gifted and Talented Children." *Elementary School Journal* 82:236–48 (January 1982).

The article discusses characteristics of young gifted children and points out that parents may need to take steps to have their gifted child identified prior to first grade. Authors suggest provisions that parents can make for their gifted children. Two appendices list references for parents and the names and addresses of state coordinators for the gifted.

Karnes, Merle B., Shwedel, Alan, and Steinberg, Deborah. "Styles of Parenting among Parents of Young Gifted Children." *Roeper Review* 6:232–35 (April 1984).

The authors designed their study to investigate three basic questions: (1) What are the attitudes, values, and behaviors of parents as they relate to their young gifted child? (2) Are there meaningful differences in attitudes, values and behaviors between parents of young gifted children and parents of young nongifted children? (3) What can professionals do to help parents be more effective in rearing their gifted child? Thirty-nine parents were interviewed. More similarities than differences were found, but parents of the gifted spent more time with their children in reading and academically related activities.

Kaufman, Felice A., and Sexton, David. "Some Implications for Home-School Linkages." *Roeper Review* 6:49–51 (September 1983).

The authors report the results of a survey of parents of gifted children. The purpose of the survey was to gain insight into the perceptions of parents and to identify possible areas for linkages between home and school. Areas were identified and recommendations made.

Malone, Charlotte E. "Education for Parents of the Gifted." *Gifted Child Quarterly* 19:233–25 (Fall 1975).

Malone discusses a class that she taught for parents of gifted children. She relays concerns and beliefs expressed by the parents about their children and urges more parent education.

Marion, Robert L. "Communicating with Parents of Culturally Diverse Exceptional Children." *Exceptional Children* 46:616–23 (May 1980).

Marion discusses the problems schools may encounter in communicating with culturally diverse parents regarding their exceptional child—either mentally retarded or gifted. He suggests using language the parents can understand, working to overcome negative feelings the parents may have about the program, and *listening*. He says that only well-informed parents can be intelligent consumers of information.

Mathews, F. Neil. "Influencing Parents' Attitudes toward Gifted Education." *Exceptional Children* 48:140–42 (October 1981).

The author did a study of parental attitudes toward the gifted in a small community in Massachusetts. He found that parents who attended an educational meeting were much more positive toward gifted education than those who did not. Mathews recommends programs about the gifted for all parents, not just those with gifted children.

Montemayor, Raymond. "Changes in Parent and Peer Relationships between Childhood and Adolescence: A Research Agenda for Gifted Adolescents." *Journal for the Education of the Gifted* 8:9–23 (Fall 1984).

Montemayor reviews the theoretical writing and empirical research on changes in parental relations during late childhood and early adolescence. He focuses on "average" adolescents since little has been done in this area concerning gifted/talented adolescents. The final section does address gifted/talented youth, and some questions are posed that should spark research in this area.

Moore, Nancy Delano. "The Joys and Challenges in Raising a Gifted Child." *G/C/T* 25:8–11 (November/December 1982).

This article describes the author's family's search for appropriate schooling for their highly gifted daughter. They found acceleration to be the best for her along with much outside involvement. The family had many struggles along the way, but their reward has been seeing their daughter happy and excelling.

Morrow, William R., and Wilson, Robert C. "Family Relations of Bright High-Achieving and Underachieving High School Boys." *Child Development* 32:501–10 (September 1961).

This study compared forty-eight high-achieving bright boys with forty-eight underachieving bright boys (ninth and tenth graders). It found that bright high achievers' parents engaged in more sharing of activities, ideas, and confidences; were more approving, trusting, and encouraging with respect to achievement (but without pressuring); were less restrictive and severe; and had their standards better accepted by their children. Results also indicated that family morale promotes academic achievement among bright high school boys by fostering a positive attitude regarding school, teachers, and intellectual activities.

Ness, Beverly J. "Establishing Programs for Parents of the Gifted Child." *G/C/T* 6:14–16 (January/February 1979).

The article lists eleven steps for establishing a course for parents and then describes a ten-week model course that has been taught to parents of gifted children.

Nolte, Jean, and Dinklocker, Christina. "Paraphernalia for Parents." *G/C/T* 17:44 (March/April 1981).

This article presents a succinct "plan of attack" for promoting positive school-community relations regarding gifted education.

O'Neill, Kathleen Kenney. "Parent Involvement: A Key to the Education of Gifted Children." *Gifted Child Quarterly* 22:235–42 (Summer 1978).

A teacher who had nine gifted children in her heterogeneous first-grade classroom tells how she involved the parents in enriching their gifted children's education. She provides examples of the homework the children were to do with their parents.

Ostrom, Gladys. "The Self-Concept of Gifted Children Grows through Freedom of Choice, Freedom of Movement, and Freedom to Do What Is Right." *Gifted Child Quarterly* 17:285–87 (Winter 1974).

Ostrom suggests that the self-concepts of gifted children are delicate because they are closely tied to the attitudes they have about themselves as they learn. Gifted children must be guided with both intelligence and understanding.

Page, Beverly A. "A Parent's Guide to Understanding the Behavior of Gifted Children." *Roeper Review* 5:39–42 (May 1983).

This well-written article is focused around quotes from *On Being Gifted,* a book by gifted adolescents. It would be good reading for all parents of gifted children.

Parrot, Margot Nicholas. "A Parent Speaks Up for Acceleration." *G/C/T* 12:12–13 (March/April 1980).

This testimonial would be appreciated by parents considering acceleration as an alternative for their gifted child.

Perry, Anne M., and Shoop, Jon. "A Good Beginning for Parent Involvement." *G/C/T* 16:8–10 (January/February 1981).

The authors describe one school district's use of Reflections for Living, a values-clarification curriculum for parents. Address and cost for program are included.

Peterson, Diane Cyzmoure. "The Heterogeneously Gifted Family." *Gifted Child Quarterly* 21:396–98 (Fall 1977).

Peterson provides good, commonsense suggestions to parents about keeping their family balanced when one child is gifted. Highlighting positive attributes of each member is the key.

Riggs, Gina Ginsberg. "Parents of Gifted and Talented Children: UNITE!" *G/C/T* 21:9–10 (January/February 1982).

This article is a call to action and includes a Bill of Rights that all parents of gifted children should post on their refrigerators.

————. "Parent Power: Wanted for Organization." *Gifted Child Quarterly* 28:111–14 (Summer 1984).

Riggs makes recommendations for parent groups based on the twenty-six-year-old Gifted Child Society of New Jersey. Any organizing group should take these suggestions and lessons into consideration.

Roberts, Donna J., Carter, Kyle R., and Mosley, Daniel. "A Comparison of the Perceptions of Gifted Children and Their Parents." *G/C/T* 24:46–49 (September/October 1982).

This article reports on the results of questionnaires filled out by 466 gifted children and 457 of their parents. The questionnaires included items on identification procedures, academic interests, family characteristics, and interpersonal relations.

Schatz, Eleanor M. "Determinants of Guidance within the Home." *G/C/T* 27:59–60 (March/April 1983).

Based on a study guide used with videotapes on gifted education, this article gives parents of gifted children suggestions in four categories: materials, modeling, space, and time.

Sebring, Albert D. "Parental Factors in the Social and Emotional Adjustment of the Gifted." *Roeper Review* 6:97–99 (November 1983).

Sebring's article posits that if parents are aware of the behaviors of gifted children, they may be able to adjust their own behavior to alleviate some possible problems and better meet their children's needs. He advocates six precepts for parents to remember: value child's individuality, show approval and acceptance, watch for perfectionist tendencies, allow the child to be a child, provide decision-making opportunities, and become informed about the child's giftedness.

Siegelbaum, Laura, and Rotner, Susan. "Ideas and Activities for Parents of Preschool Gifted Children." *G/C/T* 26:40–44 (January/February 1983).

This article provides marvelous suggestions for activities that will encourage preschool children's giftedness in the areas of exceptional intelligence, creativity, giftedness in reading, and giftedness in mathematics.

Sisk, Dorothy A. "What If Your Child Is Gifted?" *American Education* 13:23–26 (October 1977).

This excellent article presents several vignettes illustrating characteristics of gifted children. The author suggests steps parents can take to ensure appropriate education for their gifted children.

Wiess, Patricia, and Gallagher, James. "Parental Educational Preferences for Gifted Children." *G/C/T* 30:2–6 (November/December 1983).

The article discusses the results of a survey done through organizations and magazines about the gifted to determine what parents believe to be most important for their gifted child's education.

Wilcox, Carol Harting. "A Mother's Lament (and Suggestions)." *G/C/T* 17:52–53 (March/April 1981).

The author suggests that school boards cast their nets broadly to search for scholars—who are not necessarily credentialed teachers—to teach the gifted. She broadly outlines a history curriculum for junior and senior high school students.

Conclusion

THE FUTURE OF EDUCATION FOR THE GIFTED

After reviewing, reading, and annotating the hundreds of articles, books, and materials we researched for this book, we have seen one message emerge above all others—gifted students cannot "make it" on their own. They cannot teach themselves, identify themselves, counsel themselves, serve as advocates for themselves, or obtain favorable legislation for themselves. This book recognizes that local control of our public education has not favored the gifted. They comprise a group of children requiring special education but, unlike other children in need of special education, they receive little compassion.

The gifted must have knowledgeable support from many sectors of society who will pave the way for them to achieve up to the levels of which they are capable. It is incumbent upon those who believe in education, those who believe in educating the ablest, and those who believe that the future of the world depends on the intellectual abilities of the gifted to ensure that these students are given the educational opportunities which will allow them to become tomorrow's leaders, creators, and decision makers. This brief chapter will reflect on some of the issues facing gifted education in the years ahead.

As was discussed in the chapter on the history of gifted education, the political and economic climate of the country has always determined the degree of attention paid to exceptionally bright students. In the mid-eighties, we have a somewhat paradoxical situation. On the one hand, there are loud public outcries for excellence in education; on

434

the other hand, there are calls for budget cuts, especially in areas that directly affect funding to public schools and special programs. The message that must be carried over and over to legislators and others who determine public policy is that *excellence in education must include education for the excellent.* The additional message is that while there is a cost to be paid for such education, it is only a fraction of what it would cost our nation to let these excellent minds lie fallow. Elected public officials such as federal and state senators and representatives, school board members, city council members, and mayors listen to their constituency and usually follow its mandates. So, prolocutors of increased attention and funding for the gifted must make their voices heard in order to have the desired effect.

Advocates must work toward informing and organizing others who can then go out and further inform and organize. The biggest hindrance to gifted education is lack of knowledge on the part of the public—including parents, teachers, students, school administrators, legislators, and business people. When people understand the needs and goals of gifted education, they are much less likely to be antagonistic and much more likely to become proponents of the movement.

If there is one type of institution in America that stands to have more influence than any other on the future of the gifted-child movement, it is the teacher-training institutions and colleges of education. From within these schools come the rank and file of future teachers. The knowledge and attitudes instilled while teachers are in preservice or in-service training will shape their behavior and thought in the classroom. Therefore, gifted advocacy groups must find and invite faculty and administration from colleges of education to become affiliated with the groups—and to hear the groups' philosophy. The professors can then effect change in their own classes and also in the whole college, in terms of the information disseminated and the types of courses offered. Possibly, these professors can serve as the catalysts for special programs that recognize excellence and encourage able students to become teachers. They may also institute special programs during the summer or school year, to meet the learning needs of gifted and talented children and youth.

Special projects that are already well under way (e.g., Johns Hopkins University Study for Mathematically Precocious Youth, and the Gifted Students Institute Pyramid Project, Fort Worth, Texas) must continue in their efforts to aid public and private schools that serve some of the same sorts of students.

Funding could be sought from businesses and agencies that will directly benefit from the increased ability of the students who have participated in these unique ventures. This funding could be earmarked for public outreach programs that would affect the schools and the community by providing services that might otherwise be unavailable—for example, training for teachers and parents of able students; presentation of results from the special program to civic clubs. A multiple purpose can be served here: (1) information about extraordinary ability is disseminated thereby dispelling stereotypes; and (2) goodwill is established between the university or sponsoring agency and the public.

Getting businesses involved financially is only one necessity of the future. Getting men and women from business, the arts, the sciences, and the professions to commit themselves to students of extraordinary ability and potential is an even more pressing need. These adults are needed to serve in a multitude of roles that cannot be filled from within the school systems—they are needed as role models, tutors, mentors, advocates, counselors, and career advisors. Educating able students includes getting them on the right track and keeping them there for life. The biographies and autobiographies of virtually all successful people credit their success to someone who took a special interest in them as they were developing.

In addition to the advising function that community members can serve, gifted children and youth must have increased access to counselors who have been specially trained for working with the able. It is too much to expect one guidance counselor to adequately serve an entire elementary school—let alone two or three schools, as is often the case. And with the many chores thrust upon guidance counselors in high school, their ranks must be swelled so that they can provide counseling and career/college advising to a reasonable number of students. Their sensitivity and training must be enhanced in order that the able students in their charge can be beneficially served.

One of the areas in which counselors must take a more active role is preventing underachievement among the gifted. Especially important is coordination of efforts of teachers, parents, school administrators, and community volunteers. Advocates for able students must not permit the gifted to perform far below their potential. Just as certain states (e.g., Texas) have passed laws that compel local school districts to search for alternatives for students who behave unacceptably rather than giving up and expelling them, we need mandates that schools cannot ''give up on'' students of high intellectual and/or creative ability. Talent is a resource the nation cannot afford to squander.

In the future, more effort must be expended to locate talent. Identification procedures must become more broadbased and a concerted ef-

fort must be made to pick out the gifted and talented from among minority and handicapped populations. Efforts at more adequate
identification of minority students must involve members of that culture in order to properly determine what is valued by the culture and
how it is manifested in its members.

Research concerning identification and programming must be continued. This research is needed not only to further our knowledge
about the gifted but also as evidence of the imperative need for differentiated education for the gifted.

In order to maintain the gains in knowledge and education of the
gifted—and in order to make further strides—it is vital that experts and
lay people in the field form a coalition. If we do not, we can be quite
certain that interest will decline, and the cycle will run through its
downswing. But if we do band together, then at some future time the
phrase "gifted child movement" will no longer need to be used, because education for the ablest will be an accepted and expected part of
our educational system. May that day come soon.

APPENDIX 1

State Involvement

The information in this appendix was obtained by sending a request to all state departments of education asking them to supply specific information regarding legislation for the gifted and that they provide copies of any guidelines, curriculum guides, etc. The request was honored by all states. Data on state funding and numbers of children served by each state were obtained from *Communique*, a publication of NAGC.

The data in the tables are generally self-explanatory. In two categories, however, it is necessary to use numbers to identify the appropriate information. In the category of definition, it is obvious that Sydney P. Marland's 1972 report to Congress has had an impact on the selection of criteria used to define those students labeled gifted. Marland's definition included six criteria which are listed below. Most states use some or all of these criteria. A seventh criterion has been added to reflect an additional category named by several states.

1. General intellectual ability.
2. Specific academic aptitude.
3. Creative or productive thinking.
4. Leadership ability.
5. Visual and performing arts.
6. Psychomotor ability.
7. Gifted and talented.

The second category in which numbers will be used to represent the needed information is types of programs. The following list represents the specific programs named by states that are in effect in those states.

1. Acceleration.
2. Advanced placement.
3. Honors.
4. Pullout.
5. IEP.
6. Mentorships/internships.
7. Special programs.
8. Enrichment (independent projects, field trips, seminars, etc.).
9. Cluster grouping.
10. Resource centers.
11. Self-contained classrooms.

Table 1. State Educational Programs for Talented and Gifted Children

State	1984 # G/T Children Served	State Funds Spent on G/T	Year of Latest Legislation
Alabama	14,000	N/A	1973
Alaska	3,450	N/A	1982
Arizona	19,080	N/A	1982
Arkansas	12,000	$310,000	1979
California	200,000	$17.8 million	1983
Colorado	9,900	—	1973
Connecticut	18,000	$12 million	1983
Delaware	3,516	$915,000	1979
Florida	41,000	$30 million	1980
Georgia	43,937	$15.3 million	1979
Hawaii	7,588	$107,491	1982
Idaho	2,286	N/A	1983
Illinois	N/A	$7.7 million	1980
Indiana	30,000	$2 million	1981
Iowa	5,950	—	1981
Kansas	10,137	$3.8 million	1983
Kentucky	25,000	$5.1 million	1980
Louisiana	13,162	N/A	1980

State	1984 # G/T Children Served	State Funds Spent on G/T	Year of Latest Legislation
Maine	N/A	$2 million	1982
Maryland	44,779	$7.1 million	1975
Massachusetts	30,000	$125,000	1978
Michigan	N/A	$830,000	1974
Minnesota	74,139	N/A	1982
Mississippi	12,450	$8 million	1974
Missouri	11,686	$3.7 million	1973
Montana	3,433	$200,000	1979
Nebraska	20,860	N/A	1979
Nevada	4,646	$1.1 million	1979
New Hampshire	N/A	$91,000	—
New Jersey	N/A	$100,000	1982
New Mexico	5,200	N/A	1982
New York	106,590	$4.3 million	1982
North Carolina	60,506	$20.5 million	—
North Dakota	1,269	$192,058	1973
Ohio	20,000	$5.4 million	1975
Oklahoma	29,521	$2.5 million	—
Oregon	N/A	$345,000	1979
Pennsylvania	60,000	$30 million	1978
Rhode Island	N/A	$422,500	1982
South Carolina	19,706	$1.6 million	1982
South Dakota	2,223	$485,136	1981
Tennessee	7,325	$2.9 million	—
Texas	N/A	$4.5 million	1979
Utah	N/A	$500,348	1975
Vermont	N/A	$10,000	—
Virginia	60,000	$4.2 million	1982
Washington	5,600	N/A	1979

State	1984 # G/T Children Served	State Funds Spent on G/T	Year of Latest Legislation
West Virginia	7,998	N/A	1979
Wisconsin	N/A	N/A	—
Wyoming	1,171	N/A	—
District of Columbia	4,000	N/A	—

Table 2. State Agencies Responsible for Education of the Gifted

State	Agency Responsible	Definition	Type of Program
Alabama	Excep. Ch.	1	1,2,3,4,6,10
Alaska	Excep. Ch.	1,3	5
Arizona	Special Ed.	2	1,2,3,7
Arkansas	Special Ed.	7	1,6,7
California	G/T	1,2,3,4,5	1,4,6,8,9
Colorado	G/T	1,2,3,4,5,6	1,2,6,7,8,9,10
Connecticut	G/T	1,3	3,7,8,10
Delaware	G/T	1,2,3,4,5,6	1,6,7,8,9
Florida	Excep. Ch.	1	5,6,7,8,9,10
Georgia	Excep. Ch.	1	1,2,3,7,8,9,10,11
Hawaii	G/T	1,3,4,5,6	1,5,8,9
Idaho	Excep. Ch.	1,2,3,4,5	5,6,8,9,10
Illinois	G/T	1,3,5	1,4,8,10,11
Indiana	G/T	1,2,3,4,5	1,8
Iowa	G/T	1,2,3,4,5	1,7,9
Kansas	Special Ed.	1,2,3	1,2,7,8
Kentucky	G/T	1,2,3,4,5	7,8
Louisiana	Special Ed.	1,5	1,3,6,7,9
Maine	Special Ed.	1,2,3,5	1,4,6,7,8,9

State	Agency Responsible	Definition	Type of Program
Maryland	G/T	1,2,3,4,5	6,7,8,9
Massachusetts	Curric. & I.	1,2,3,4,5,6	6,7,8
Michigan	G/T	1,2,3,4,5	1,2,6,7,8
Minnesota	G/T	7	3,6,7,8,9,10,11
Mississippi	Excep. Ch.	1,2,3,4,5	2,7,11
Missouri	G/T	1,5	7,8,10
Montana	Special Ed.	7	1,4,7,8,9
Nebraska	G/T	1,2,3,4,5,6	none listed
Nevada	Special Ed.	1	7
New Hampshire	Special Ed.	1,2,3,4,5	none listed
New Jersey	Special Ed.	1,2,3,4,5,6	1,6,7,10,11
New Mexico	Special Ed.	1,2,3	none listed
New York	G/T	1,2,5	1,4,6,7,9
North Carolina	Excep. Ch.	none	11
North Dakota	Excep. Ch.	7	1,6,7,8,10
Ohio	Special Ed.	1,2,3,4,5,6	1,6,7,8,9
Oklahoma	—	1,2,3,4,5	1,6,8
Oregon	G/T	1,2,3,4,5	1,6,7,8
Pennsylvania	Special Ed.	1	1,2,3,5,7,8,11
Rhode Island	G/T	1,2,3,5	1,7,8,10
South Carolina	G/T	1,2,3,4,5	2,6,7,8,9,10,11
South Dakota	Special Ed.	1	1,4,5,6,7,8,9,10,11
Tennessee	Special Ed.	1	1,3,7,8,9
Texas	G/T	1,2,3,4,5,6	1,6,8,9
Utah	—	1,2,3,4,5,6	local option
Vermont	none	none	none
Virginia	Special Ed.	1,2,3,4,5	1,2,4,6,7,8,9
Washington	Special Ed.	1,3	1,2,9
West Virginia	Excep. Ch.	1	9,10
Wisconsin	none	none	none
Wyoming	G/T	1,2,3,4,5	1,8,9

Table 3. State Certification Requirements, Guidelines, Curricular and Other
Publications in Gifted Education

State	Cert.	State Guidelines	Curric. Guide	Other Publications
Alabama	No	No	No	None
Alaska	No	Yes	No	Resources for Gifted
Arizona	No	Yes	Yes	None
Arkansas	No	Yes	No	Reports on programs
California	Yes	Yes	Yes	15 on curriculum
Colorado	No	Yes	No	None
Connecticut	Yes	Yes	Yes	11 on curriculum
Delaware	No	Yes	No	Identification guide
Florida	Yes	Yes	No	Resource manual
Georgia	Yes	Yes	Yes	None
Hawaii	No	Yes	Yes	None
Idaho	No	Yes	No	None
Illinois	No	Yes	No	None
Indiana	No	Yes	Yes	4 on curriculum
Iowa	No	Yes	No	None
Kansas	Yes	Yes	No	None
Kentucky	No	Yes	No	Program descriptions
Louisiana	Yes	Yes	Yes	None
Maine	No	Yes	No	Identification guides
Maryland	No	Yes	No	None
Massachusetts	No	Yes	No	None
Michigan	No	No	No	None
Minnesota	No	No	No	None
Mississippi	No	Yes	Yes	None
Missouri	No	Yes	No	None
Montana	No	Yes	No	List of programs
Nebraska	No	Yes	Yes	10 on curriculum
Nevada	No	Yes	No	None
New Hampshire	No	No	No	Parenting/teaching

State	Cert.	State Guidelines	Curric. Guide	Other Publications
New Jersey	No	Yes	No	None
New Mexico	Yes	Yes	No	None
New York	No	Yes	No	Parenting/ident.
North Carolina	Yes	No	Yes	Ident./Gov. Sch.
North Dakota	Yes	Yes	No	None
Ohio	No	Yes	No	None
Oklahoma	No	Yes	No	None
Oregon	No	Yes	No	None
Pennsylvania	Yes	Yes	No	None
Rhode Island	No	Yes	No	None
South Carolina	No	Yes	No	Creative arts
South Dakota	No	Yes	No	Handouts
Tennessee	Yes	Yes	No	None
Texas	No	Yes	No	None
Utah	No	Yes	No	None
Vermont	No	No	No	Fostering creativity
Virginia	No	Yes	No	Suggested resources
Washington	No	Yes	No	None
West Virginia	No	Yes	No	Parenting
Wisconsin	No	No	No	Identification
Wyoming	No	No	No	Identification

Evaluations of Curriculum Materials

The materials that are listed here are those that we have evaluated and believe are worth purchasing with the stipulations we give. These materials are grouped by publishing company. No prices are given, as they are subject to frequent change.

CURRICULUM ASSOCIATES

Title: *Capitalization and Punctuation: Intermediate,* 1981.
Author: Arnold F. Checchi.
Description: 128-page consumable workbook is intended to be used by each student independently. Teachers are to give pretests that indicate which sections a student needs to do.
Skills: Capitalization and punctuation.
Use: Would be useful in a heterogeneous classroom, so that students who already knew something would not have to endure the reteaching of it.
Level: Gifted grades three to five.
Evaluation: Good if used in moderation.

Title: *Following Directions: Advanced,* 1979.
Authors: Rikki Kessler and Joyce Friedland.
Description: The consumable workbook contains thirty-four lessons which require students to read carefully and follow directions.
Skills: Following directions.
Use: Selectively with intermediate gifted students.

Level: Grades three to five.
Evaluation: Best use would be to make each page into a transparency and do some activities together as a class.

Title: *Lessons in Paragraphing,* 1976.
Authors: Jean N. Alley and Elaine B. Dohan.
Description: Intended to be consumable, this workbook has eighty-four pages and an answer section. It begins fairly simply, asking students to find the main idea of paragraphs and concludes by having students recognize the type of paragraph and offer support for citing that type.
Skills: Paragraphing.
Use: Gifted language arts classes.
Level: Gifted grades four to six.
Evaluation: Good as a supplement if the teacher is also expecting a great deal of student writing.

Title: *Lessons for Vocabulary Power—Level II,* 1981.
Author: Robert G. Forest.
Description: A nonconsumable softcover book which contains twenty lessons. Each lesson introduces students to a collection of words that share a common theme. Each lesson has six pages which include definitions, activities with synonyms, antonyms, prefixes, origins and word usage. At the end of each of the three main sections there is a post-test.
Skills: Vocabulary development.
Use: Language arts/English classes.
Level: Gifted grades six through ten.
Evaluation: Excellent.

Title: *Reading, Writing and Rating Stories,* 1982.
Author: Carol Sager.
Description: The softcover book has 149 pages. Answers to all exercises go on separate paper which the students are instructed to organize and keep in a work folder. The book is divided into four sections, each of which emphasizes a different quality of good writing: vocabulary, elaboration, organization, structure. Each section has ten to fifteen lessons.
Skills: Recognizing good and poor elements in a story, which will then allow students to assess and improve their own writing.
Use: Language arts.
Level: Gifted grades three to five.

Evaluation: Excellent lessons which provide guidance in evaluating effective writing techniques and then require students to apply those techniques.

Title: *Thirty Lessons in Outlining,* 1971.
Authors: Elizabeth A. Ross and Thomas E. Culliton, Jr.
Description: Very systematically, the workbook leads students from grouping lists of words through constructing a full outline from a text. The workbook, which is not intended to be consumable, provides an answer key.
Skills: Categorizing and outlining.
Use: Language arts/English.
Level: Gifted grades six to nine.
Evaluation: Good if used wisely and with other materials.

D.O.K. Publishers

Title: *Classroom Ideas for Encouraging Thinking and Feeling,* 1970.
Author: Frank Williams.
Description: A softcover book that includes 387 ideas for developing thinking and feeling. The activities are organized around Williams's eighteen strategies and encompass the curriculum areas of language arts, science, social studies, math, and art.
Skills: Thinking and feeling.
Use: Language arts, science, social studies, math, art.
Level: Activities 1-137 primary, activities 138-250 middle grades, activities 251-387 upper grades.
Evaluation: Particularly useful for a teacher who wants to implement Williams's strategies.

Title: *Discovering Archaeology,* 1981.
Authors: Gloria McCarthy and Molly Marso.
Description: A softbound, fifty-two-page book of classroom-proven activities, with a separate student activity book. Intended to develop independent thinking and an understanding regarding how we learn about past cultures.
Skills: Independent thinking.
Use: Social studies.
Level: Gifted grades three to eight.
Evaluation: A coherent and sequential plan for making archaeology understandable. Well worth the modest price.

Title: *Thinking Skills that Last,* 1982.
Author: Arlis Swartzendruber.
Description: This ninety-six-page softcover book is intended to pro-
             vide activities that are product oriented, that use
             higher-order thinking skills, and that are long-term in
             nature. Activities are organized in five areas of gifted-
             ness: academic, arts, creativity, intelligence, and lead-
             ership.
Skills: Thinking.
Use: In the general curriculum to apply aspects of Bloom's
             Taxonomy and Renzulli's Enrichment Triad.
Level: Gifted grades four to twelve.
Evaluation: A provocative stimulus for creative research.

Good Apple

Title: *Connecting Rainbows,* 1982.
Author: Bob Stanish.
Description: This eighty-four-page softcover book is a combination
             of activity pages (intended for duplication) and teacher
             direction sheets on how to conduct the group activities.
Skills: Self-esteem, values, empathy, cooperation, creativity.
Use: Small groups.
Level: Grades three through twelve.
Evaluation: A good resource book for teachers, counselors, and
             group leaders.

Title: *Creativity for Kids: Through Word Play,* 1983.
Author: Bob Stanish.
Description: This sixty-page softcover book is part of a series of four
             "Creativity for Kids" books, the others being *Through
             Word Analysis, Through Vocabulary Development,* and
             Through Writing. The book has twenty-six activities that
             use the four elements of creativity: fluency, flexibility,
             elaboration, and originality.
Skills: Creative thinking and word awareness.
Use: Language arts.
Level: Gifted grades two to four.
Evaluation: Excellent.

Title: *Fact, Fantasy and Folklore: Expanding Language Arts
             and Critical Thinking Skills,* 1977.
Authors: Greta B. Lipsom and Baxter Morrison.
Description: This softbound book contains eleven lessons, each of
             which is based on a familiar folktale (e.g., Hansel and

Gretel). Each lesson includes a synopsis of the story and a number of activities designed to enable a student to answer a question about the story.

Skills: Critical and creative thinking.
Use: Language arts, English, social studies.
Level: Gifted grades five to twelve.
Evaluation: Outstanding!

Title: *Hippogriff Feathers: Encounters with Creative Thinking* 1981.
Author: Bob Stanish.
Description: The softcover book of 101 pages is filled with "directions" on how to be creative. It contains seven chapters, each of which deals with a particular methodology for developing creativity and sharpening problem-solving skills. Each chapter provides an introduction to the method, along with activities and suggestions for application.
Skills: Creative thinking.
Use: Olympics of the Mind, Future Problem Solving Bowl, etc.
Level: Gifted grades one through twelve.
Evaluation: Super!

Title: *Mighty Myth: A Modern Interpretation of Greek Myths for the Classroom,* 1982.
Authors: Greta B. Lipsom and Sidney M. Bolkosky.
Description: This softcover book contains 144 pages. Each of the twelve chapters is based on a Greek myth that has been condensed so it can be read aloud. Each chapter also lists insights for the teachers, reflective questions, follow-up activities and a role-playing situation set in modern America.
Skills: Reading, writing, thinking, role play.
Use: Language arts, English, world history.
Level: Gifted grades five through twelve.
Evaluation: Well done.

Title: *Secrets and Surprises,* 1977.
Authors: Joe Wayman and Lorraine Plum.
Description: This softcover book is filled with eighty pages of activities involving moving, imagining, writing, thinking, and listening. Each group of activities centers around a theme (e.g., cats, monsters, ice cream).
Skills: All language arts, movement, self-concept.

Use: General curriculum.
Level: Kindergarten through fifth grade.
Evaluation: Very good, but teachers in some school districts may have trouble justifying some of the activities if learning is seen as working quietly at your seat.

Title: *Sprouts: Projects for Creative Growth in Children*, 1981.
Authors: Harriet H. Green and Sue G. Martin.
Description: The softcover book contains eighty-four games designed to enhance children's sensory awareness. Many of the activities use stories, poetry, and music as integral parts of the game.
Skills: Reading, writing, listening, oral language, thinking.
Use: General curriculum.
Level: Kindergarten through sixth grade.
Evaluation: Well-conceived games that should be used selectively.

Title: *Treasure Hunts*, 1983.
Authors: Harriet H. Green and Sue G. Martin.
Description: This softbound 140-page book contains activities based on ten classic stories (e.g., *Alice in Wonderland, Treasure Island*). The goals of the activities vary from reinforcing the plot to helping the students see the stories from different points of view. Each activity is set forth with stated objectives, materials, and the procedures clearly explained.
Skills: Critical and creative reading, writing, thinking.
Use: Language arts, English.
Level: Gifted grades four through eight.
Evaluation: Would be worth having so that one or two of the stories could be done each year.

Title: *The Unconventional Invention Book: Classroom Activities for Activating Student Inventiveness*, 1981.
Author: Bob Stanish.
Description: The book is softbound with black-and-white illustrations. Many of the pages are intended to be duplicated. The rest are for teacher use in helping students develop inventive thinking abilities.
Skills: Creative thinking and writing.
Use: General curriculum.
Level: Grades three through twelve.
Evaluation: Excellent, but one could overdose.

Jamestown Publishers

Title: *Skimming and Scanning,* Middle 1982, Advanced 1978.
Author: Edward B. Fry.
Description: The book is a 145-page softcover workbook to be used with teacher direction and extension. It can be used in any content area.
Skills: Skimming and scanning.
Use: General curriculum.
Level: Middle, grades five through eight; Advanced, grades nine through twelve.
Evaluation: The selections are of high interest, and the exercises will be useful if employed selectively.

Kathy Kolbe Concepts

Title: *Enigmas,* 1983.
Author: Kathy Kolbe.
Description: This softbound book of 102 pages is divided into eleven chapters, each of which is one of the great mysteries (e.g., Stonehenge, black holes). In each chapter, a brief background of the enigma is provided, and then several pages of activities follow. The activities challenge students to investigate, ask questions, develop hypotheses, etc.
Skills: Thinking, writing, reading.
Use: In learning centers or for individual projects.
Level: Gifted grades four through eight.
Evaluation: Well written and well conceived. Gifted children will find these enigmas very intriguing.

Title: *Risk-Taking,* 1982.
Authors: Kathy Kolbe, Don Tate, and Patricia Tate.
Description: This 101-page book is replete with activities which encourage students to be risk takers. Although the pages are designed to be photocopied, many would be appropriate to use as a discussion guide.
Skills: Creative thinking, risk taking.
Use: General curriculum.
Level: Gifted grades four through eight.
Evaluation: Excellent for learning and application.

Mafex Associates

Title: *A Gifted Program That Works*, 1982.
Authors: Trudy Emmerling, Ceil Frey, and Sybil Gilmar.
Description: This 163-page softcover book was written by three teachers of the gifted. The lesson plans and activities have been field-tested with gifted students and have undergone extensive evaluation through in-service workshops. The underlying concept of the book rests on Renzulli's Enrichment Triad model. The book is comprised of a rationale for the program, seven major units of study, and a useful appendix.
Skills: Writing, thinking, creating, research.
Use: General curriculum.
Level: Grades two through ten.
Evaluation: Excellent and based on sound theory.

Title: *TNT: Talented and Thinking*, 1982.
Author: Franny F. McAleer.
Description: The program is comprised of fifteen study guides and a teacher's handbook. The study guides are intended for student use and are consumable. Each guide has approximately forty pages with information about the topic, questions that require both convergent and divergent thinking, and activities that allow for creativity. A sampling of titles: Foreign Culture Craze, Science Fiction Findings, The Hall of Famers, Creative Poetry.
Skills: Thinking, writing, speaking, planning.
Use: Language arts.
Level: Grades two through six.
Evaluation: Most of the study guides are worth using.

Midwest Publication Company

Title: *Building Thinking Skills*, 1984.
Authors: Howard Black and Sandra Black.
Description: The four softcover books average 275 pages and are meant to be consumable, but that is not necessary. The skills increase in difficulty.
Skills: Figural similarities, figural sequences, figural classification, figural analogies, verbal similarities and differences, verbal classification, verbal analogies.
Use: As a supplement to general curriculum.
Level: Grades four through eight.

Evaluation: Fine, if used when needed and not as a workbook to be completed by all.

Title: *Critical Thinking,* Books 1 and 2, 1976, 1980.
Author: Anita Harnadek.
Description: These are softcover, nonconsumable workbooks to be used for class discussion. Book 1 is 178 pages and Book 2 is 247 pages. The critical thinking skills of logic, propaganda, advertising, and examining arguments are among the skills developed in increasing sophistication.
Skills: Critical thinking.
Use: Class discussion, debate, etc.
Level: Gifted grades four through twelve.
Evaluation: Excellent, if used as a stimulus for discussion.

Opportunities for Learning

Title: *Energy Activity Pack,* 1977.
Authors: Linda Schwartz and Sue Aleksich.
Description: The "activity pack" is in booklet form, but the pages are printed on heavy paper and are perforated, so the activities could be placed in a card file.
Skills: Research, creative writing, math, art, vocabulary.
Use: Science, learning center.
Level: Gifted grades one through three.
Evaluation: Most of the activities are good but should be encouraged and guided by the teacher rather than used as busy work.

Title: *Space Travel Activity Pack,* 1977. The information is the same as for the *Energy Activity Pack,* described above.

Title: *Word Ways: Activities for Following Directions,* Books A and B, 1984.
Author: Linda Jensine Falk.
Description: Both softcover books have forty-eight pages, which include teacher directions, eighty student activities and answer keys. There are two activities on each page, which could easily be cut apart, glued to five-by-eight-inch cards, and laminated.
Skills: Following directions, seeing analogous relationships.
Use: General curriculum, small group or class.

Level: Book A, gifted grades two and three; Book B, gifted grades four and five.
Evaluation: Worth having as a filler.

Resources for the Gifted

Title: *Character Building—Concept to Curtain,* 1982.
Author: Kathy Kolbe.
Description: The kit contains a 111-page book, seventy five-by-eight-inch activity cards, and a collection of small props. The book is designed to enable students to "become" other characters—for both acting and writing purposes. The students will learn how to observe others, write dialogue, convey a character, design a plot, etc. The process could take between a semester and a year.
Skills: Thinking, writing, expressing, speaking.
Use: Language arts, English, drama.
Level: Gifted grades five through twelve.
Evaluation: Definitely recommended.

Title: *How-To Who Done It,* 1982.
Author: Sheila Whalen.
Description: This 117-page paperback book is designed to teach students how to write mysteries. It is divided into five types: classic British, Gothic, locked room, codes, and psychological. Each section explains the unique characteristics of that type of mystery, gives an example, and then leads the student to create a mystery.
Skills: Writing, thinking.
Use: Language arts, English.
Level: Gifted grades five through twelve.
Evaluation: Excellent! It is written so that students who use this experience success.

Title: *Lessons 'n Logic,* 1983.
Author: Roger Hufford.
Description: The 104-page softbound book combines logic theory with practice in doing logic problems. Several different types of problems are presented, with accompanying explanations of how to "see" to solve the problem.
Skills: Logical and creative thinking.
Use: General curriculum.
Level: Gifted grades four through twelve.
Evaluation: Excellent!

Title: *Mind's Eye: A Game of Visual Perception,* 1980.
Description: The game packet includes two pads of playing patterns and six plastic master grids. The object of the game is to place the plastic grids over the playing patterns so that three of one person's marks show, along with one of the other person's.
Skills: Visual perception.
Use: General curriculum.
Level: Any age.
Evaluation: Buy it!

Title: *Puzzler Pack: Library Lingo,* 1983.
Author: Kathy Kolbe.
Description: Contained in a cigar box, this 100-card activity pack encourages children to find out about the library.
Skills: Library usage.
Use: Language arts, social studies.
Level: Gifted grades two to six.
Evaluation: Many good ideas, but some of the cards seem unnecessary.

Title: *TV: A Tool to Turn on Thinking,* 1982.
Author: Eleanor Villapando.
Description: The book claims that its "format eliminates the need for teacher or parent preparation time. Everything is student-directed and ready to go." The claim is valid. The softcover 112-page book is divided into seven sections, each of which uses a different segment of TV as its focus: sitcoms, news, advertisements, changing the channel, cartoons, game shows, and sports.
Skills: Critical and creative thinking, writing, watching.
Use: Language arts, social studies.
Level: Gifted grades three to six.
Evaluation: Outstanding! Many products claim to use TV to teach skills—but this actually does.

Sunburst Communications

Title: *Creative Problem Solving: Be an Inventor,* 1983.
Authors: James A. McAlpine, Betty Weincek, Marion E. Finkbinder, Susan Jeweler.
Description: This kit contains a sixty-seven-page teacher's guide, sixty-four five-by-eight-inch activity cards with both

sides used, and thirty reproducible sheets to teach students about creative problem solving.

Skills: Creative problem solving.

Use: General curriculum, class, or learning center.

Level: Gifted grades three through nine.

Evaluation: Outstanding. Well designed and founded on principles for differentiating curriculum for the gifted.

Title: *Have I Got a Problem for You! Math for Math Lovers,* 1982.

Description: A kit for use at a learning center. The kit contains five sections: combinations, permutations and probability; logic and deduction; general topology; notorious numbers; and early algebra. Each section has five to ten activity cards, eight by eleven inches, printed front and back. The front of each card has a mathematical problem and the back provides a strategy for solving the problem (but not the solution). A teacher's guide and twenty-six extending activity sheets are also included.

Skills: Problem solving.

Use: Math.

Level: Gifted grades four through eight.

Evaluation: The material is designed to challenge able students and to stimulate their thinking—both divergently and convergently. It lives up to its objectives.

Title: *I Want to Know More about Good Books I,* 1980.

Author: Terry Kingsland.

Description: This self-contained reading kit contains two copies each of seven outstanding books (e.g., *A Wrinkle in Time*), an outstanding teacher's guide, and two identical packets of activity cards to accompany the books.

Skills: Critical and creative thinking and writing.

Use: Language arts, reading.

Level: Gifted grades four through six.

Evaluation: Exemplary materials for gifted students.

Synergetics

Title: *Grokking into the Future,* 1981.

Authors: Edith Doherty and Louise C. Evans.

Description: This nearly 300-page softback book is filled with an enrichment curriculum for gifted elementary and middle school students. The authors have worked extensively with the gifted and are steeped in the writing and research in the area of differentiated curriculum. All this has enabled them to produce a fine collection of units about the future.

Skills: Problem solving, critical thinking.
Use: Future Problem Solving Bowl, general curriculum.
Level: Gifted grades four through eight.
Evaluation: Buy it.

Title: *Primary Independent Study*, 1983.
Authors: Edith Doherty and Louise C. Evans.
Description: This 60+ page book explains the authors' PIS program, which they have designed and successfully implemented. The accompanying booklet is for students to use as they participate in the program.
Evaluation: Valuable as an in-service training tool.

Title: *Self-Starter Kit for Independent Study: A Practical Guide to the Independent Study Process for the Gifted Student*, 1980.
Authors: Edith Doherty and Louise C. Evans.
Description: The authors have put together a book that solves many of the problems that teachers of the gifted have when their students do independent study projects.
Use: For teachers of the gifted.
Evaluation: Useful.

Think Ink Publications

Title: *Options and Observations*, 1980.
Authors: Dee Johnson and Kathy Kolbe.
Description: This sixty-four-page softcover book is intended to develop students' abilities to observe and perceive the world around them. The pages are meant to be duplicated.
Skills: Creative thinking.
Use: Science, language arts, social studies.
Level: Gifted grades three through seven.
Evaluation: Very good. Activities are sound and attractively presented.

Ventura County, California, Schools

Title: *Inservice Training Manual: Activities for Developing Curriculum for the Gifted/Talented,* 1979.
Author: Sandra N. Kaplan.
Description: This manual is designed to enable a school district to train its teachers and administrators to provide a differentiated curriculum for the gifted. It is set up in a step-by-step way that could be used as is or as a supplement to ongoing in-service training.

Title: *A Guidebook for Evaluating Programs for the Gifted and Talented,* 1975.
Author: Joseph Renzulli.
Description: The book is divided into two sections. The first is comprised of four chapters that deal with evaluation—who needs it, models of evaluation design, and selection of an evaluator. The second section contains several useful bibliographies and numerous evaluation instruments. The book is well worth having.

Index

Prepared by Kristina Masiulis

459

M. Jean Greenlaw is Regents Professor at the University of North Texas, where she teaches seminars on developmental reading, materials and trends in reading, and gifted education. She has been involved in reading education for more than 20 years. Greenlaw holds a PhD from Michigan State University and has written numerous books and articles on topics in education and reading.

Margaret E. McIntosh is a Graduate Fellow in the Meadows Foundation Excellence in Teaching Program at the University of North Texas, where she teaches courses on methods of teaching reading and language arts and reading in the content areas. She has worked as a teacher in both mainstream and gifted education classes and has published research articles and teaching ideas in many journals and magazines.